XERXES

XERXES

A PERSIAN LIFE

RICHARD STONEMAN

YALE UNIVERSITY PRESS
NEW HAVEN AND LONDON

For information about this and other Yale University Press publications, please contact:
U.S. Office: sales.press@yale.edu   www.yalebooks.com
Europe Office: sales@yaleup.co.uk   www.yalebooks.co.uk

Typeset in Sabon by IDSUK (DataConnection) Ltd
Printed in the United Kingdom by Gomer Press Ltd, Llandysul

Library of Congress Cataloging-in-Publication Data

Stoneman, Richard.
   Xerxes: a Persian life/Richard Stoneman.
      pages cm
   Includes bibliographical references and index.
   ISBN 978-0-300-18007-7 (cl: alk. paper)
1. Xerxes I, King of Persia, 519 B.C.–465 B.C. or 464 B.C. 2. Iran—Kings and rulers—Biography. 3. Iran—History—To 640. I. Title.
   DS283.S76 2015
   937'.705092—dc23
   [B]
                                                                          2015017637

A catalogue record for this book is available from the British Library.

10 9 8 7 6 5 4 3 2 1

Frontispiece: Seal of Xerxes from Dascyleion. After Kaptan 2002.

Contents

List of Illustrations vi
Preface viii

Introduction 1
1 Accession 17
2 The Persian Empire 35
3 The Image of a King 69
4 The Religion of Xerxes 88
5 Invasion (I): The Cornerstone of Greek Freedom 109
6 Invasion (II): The Wooden Walls 139
7 Persepolis 160
8 Family Romances 181
9 Assassination 195
Conclusion 210

Appendix 1 Xerxes in Opera and Drama 219
Appendix 2 The Birth of Persian Kings 223
Appendix 3 The Chronology of Xerxes' Advance through Greece 226
Abbreviations 229
Notes 230
Bibliography 258
Index 268

Illustrations

between pages 84–85

1 Frontispiece to Colley Cibber, *Xerxes*, London 1736.
2 The Treasury Relief, currently in the Tehran Museum.
3 Detail from the Treasury Relief: the petitioner, perhaps the *hazarapatiš*, or another court dignitary.
4 Pasargadae: view from Tell-i-Takht.
5 The Zendan-i-Suleiman (Prison of Solomon) at Pasargadae
6 The Qa'aba of Zoroaster at Naqsh-i-Rustam, near Persepolis.
7 Relief from the Tripylon at Persepolis: lion attacking bull.
8 A gold armlet from the Oxus Treasure, currently in the British Museum.
9 Gold rhyton (pouring vessel), currently in the Tehran Museum.
10 Hunting relief from Celaenae, currently in the Çanakkale Museum.
11 Relief of musician and warriors from the 'Polyxena tomb', currently in the Çanakkale Museum.
12 Taşkule, the 'stone tower', Foça, Turkey.
13 The trilingual inscription from the Letoön (Sanctuary of Leto) near Xanthos, Turkey.
14 Coins of the Persian Empire. (a) Gold siglos of Darius the Great © BibleLandPictures.com/Alamy. (b) Silver coin of Shapur I. (c) Coin of Mazaeus.
15 Tiled floor in the palace of Darius I at Susa.
16 The Tomb of Cyrus at Pasargadae.
17 Hunting relief from Taq-e-Bostan near Kermanshah.
18 A Magus, or Zoroastrian priest.
19 Relief from the tomb of Darius I at Naqsh-e-Rustam: the king before a fire-altar.
20 Cypress tree at Abarkuh.
21 Xerxes' 'daeva-inscription', currently in the Oriental Institute, University of Chicago.
22 A winged disk from a pilaster at Persepolis.

between pages 180–81

23 H. Fletcher, an engraving of Babylon, 1690.
24 The Hellespont: view from the south.
25 Thermopylae: the Leonidas monument.
26 Thermopylae: general view
27 The Persian army, engraving from Samuel Pitiscus' edition of
    Q. Curtius Rufus, *Historia Alexandri Magni*, Utrecht 1683.
28 The present-day ruins of Sardis.
29 A map of the island and straits of Salamis.
30 The battlefield of Plataea: view to the north.
31 The approach to Persepolis.
32 Gateway of All Lands.
33 Ganj-nameh on the outskirts of Hamadan, Iran.
34 Reliefs from the Apadana at Persepolis.
35 Detail of a Bactrian with an urn.
36 View of Persepolis from Kuh-i-Rahmat.
37 The king and attendants depicted on a door jamb of the
    Palace of Xerxes.
38 A rendering of the Gateway of All Lands, engraving by Johan
    van den Avele from Samuel Pitiscus' edition of Q. Curtius Rufus,
    Historia Alexandri Magni, Utrecht 1683.
39 Cornelius De Bruyn, engraving from *Travels in the Levant*, 1698.
40 Charles Chipiez, Darius' 'original plan' for Persepolis.
41 Mirza Hassan Akasbashi, photograph of Persepolis before
    excavation 1859.
42 Photograph of the Apadana after excavation, 1933.
43 Claeissens, Anthuenis, Esther before King Ahasuerus with
    Haman being sent to the Gallows beyond, 1577. Private
    Collection / Photo © Bonhams, London, UK / Bridgeman Images.
44 Erich Schmidt, Xerxes I tomb at Naqsh-e-Rustam.

Maps

		page
1	The Persian Empire	37
2	The Road to Thermopylae 1	119
3	The Road to Thermopylae 2	120
4	The Hellespont	131

Tables

1	The Family of Xerxes	x
2	The Legendary Genealogy of the Persian Kings	12
3	Tabari's Version of the Genealogy of the Persian Kings	13
4	The Families of Spitama and Cyrus	97

Preface

This is the first attempt at a serious biography of Xerxes, or any Achaemenid king, since, I believe, Plutarch's *Life of Artaxerxes*, written in the second century AD. It grew out of my interest in the figure of Alexander III of Macedon, who overthrew the Achaemenid Persian Empire and demonised the memory of Xerxes to throw into relief his own virtues. The expression 'biography' in such a case has to be taken with a pinch of salt. But I have tried to make this book more than just a packaged history of the period. A writer in the twenty-first century has some advantages over Plutarch, both in the obvious academic resources available and in the more sophisticated under-standing of personality that has emerged in the modern world. In addition, I have been inspired by the attempt of Pierre Briant in his book *Darius dans l'ombre d'Alexandre* (2003) to gain access to a Persian view of the reign of the king in question through medieval Persian writings. The problems and possible rewards of such an approach are outlined in the Introduction.

Writing a biography leads one into a great many specialist fields; in this case, they include art history, economic history, Biblical Studies and the history of warfare. Of particular importance here is Achaemenid Studies, a discipline effectively founded by the late Heleen Sancisi-Weerdenburg in the 1980s, and practised by a growing number of scholars highly trained in the variety of ancient languages spoken throughout the Achaemenid Empire: besides the usual classical languages and Old Persian, these include Elamite, Akkadian, Egyptian and Aramaic. Often what can be deduced from the clay tablets and other documents in these languages is at odds with what we are told by the familiar classical authors, creating a temptation to reject

Herodotus and the rest as of little or no value. This is throwing the baby out with the bathwater, for without Herodotus and Ctesias, Plutarch and Justin, there would have been little motive to study Achaemenid history in the first place. A balance has to be kept.

I have been fortunate to be able to make use of the resources of the University of Exeter, which has welcomed me as an associate since my move to the area in 2007. I studied Persian language with Leonard Lewisohn and Ali Mossadegh, two excellent and gifted teachers who opened a window onto a new world of literature unfamiliar to most classicists. In October 2014 I travelled to Iran with a small group organised by Lynette Mitchell of the University of Exeter through the travel company Travel the Unknown. This enabled me to revisit the sites of Persepolis, Naqsh-e-Rostam and Naqsh-e-Rajab for the first time since 1977, and to visit most of the other major Achaemenid and Sassanid sites for the first time (including Susa, Pasargadae, Firuzabad, Bishapur). Conversations on site enriched my understanding (and I hope that of the others) of what we saw; portions of this book were also read by Lynette Mitchell and Diana Darke. Richard Seaford was as always an endlessly stimulating companion.

I have benefited from the learning of four readers for Yale University Press, two of whom worked extremely hard in providing detailed comments and a useful bibliography.

I am grateful as always to my editor (and friend) Heather McCallum for her support throughout the writing of this book, and her incisive and constructive comments on an earlier draft. The copy-editor, Richard Mason, helped me to think harder about clarity of expression at many points.

It is customary for writers on classical subjects to include an apology or a caveat about inconsistency in the transliteration of Greek words and names. I try to use the familiar Latinate forms of Greek proper names (Thucydides not Thoukydides, Aeschylus not Aischylos), but to transliterate Greek words and less familiar names according to the Greek spelling (*skytale*, Artemision). To this trap for the unwary I can add another, about the transliteration of Persian. I attempt to follow consistently the usage of *Encyclopaedia Iranica* where available (Ferdowsi, Mir Khwand, Esfandiyar), but many of the texts quoted will use an Arabised form (Firdausi, Mirkhond, Asfandiyar or Esfandiyadh). I hope readers will brace themselves for some minor confusions. Emma Bridges, *Imagining Xerxes* (Bloomsbury 2014) appeared after this book was already in the hands of the publishers, and I have been unable to take account of it.

Richard Stoneman

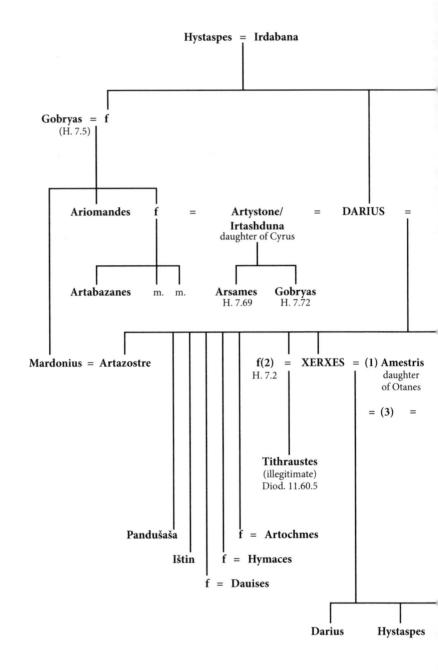

Table 1 The Family of Xerxes

This genealogy shows full brothers and sisters of Xerxes (i.e. sons and daughters of Darius).
For some half-brothers and cousins of Xerxes, see the list of the High Command of the
invasion of Greece on pp. 122–23. On Xerxes' children, see Brosius 1996, 73.
On Darius' wives, see Brosius 1996, 50–52.

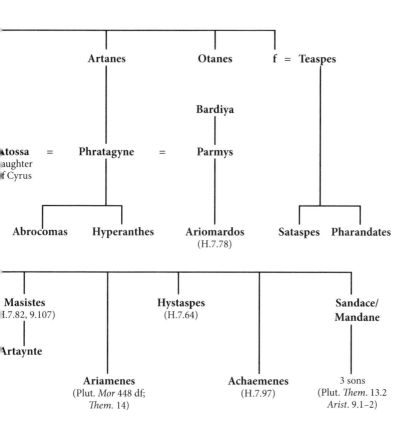

Artanes   Otanes   f = Teaspes

Bardiya

Atossa = Phratagyne = Parmys
daughter
of Cyrus

Abrocomas   Hyperanthes   Ariomardos   Sataspes   Pharandates
(H.7.78)

Masistes   Hystaspes   Sandace/
(H.7.82, 9.107)   (H.7.64)   Mandane

Artaynte

Ariamenes   Achaemenes   3 sons
(Plut. *Mor* 448 df;   (H.7.97)   (Plut. *Them.* 13.2
Them. 14)   *Arist.* 9.1–2)

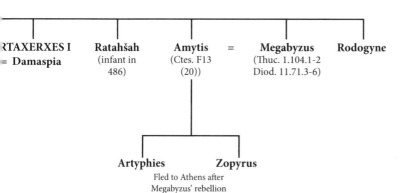

ARTAXERXES I   Ratahšah   Amytis   =   Megabyzus   Rodogyne
= Damaspia   (infant in   (Ctes. F13   (Thuc. 1.104.1-2
486)   (20))   Diod. 11.71.3-6)

Artyphies   Zopyrus
Fled to Athens after
Megabyzus' rebellion

Introduction

Xerxes, who was laden with all the gifts and prizes of fortune, was not
contented with his cavalry, his mass of infantry, the multitude of his ships or
the infinite weight of his gold, but offered a prize for the man who could invent
a new pleasure; yet even with this he was not satisfied; in fact, desire will never
reach an end.
Cicero, *Tusculan Disputations* V. 7.20

X was King Xerxes
Who, more than all Turks, is
Renowned for his fashion
Of fury and passion
X
Angry old Xerxes!
Edward Lear

Xerxes (Khshayarsha, ca. 518–465 BC), who ruled the Persian Empire from
486 to 465 BC, has largely had a bad press from history, and even worse from
the moralists. He is remembered mainly as the king who failed to conquer
Greece, the villain of a heroic story of resistance. The memory is a partial
one, and Xerxes should equally be recognised for his achievements: he
reigned for twenty years, crushed several provincial revolts, bequeathed to his
heirs an empire whose boundaries were to remain stable for almost 150 years,
and brought to a conclusion (apart from minor later additions) one of the
greatest building projects of antiquity, the imperial city of Persepolis. Because

our surviving early sources are Greek, primarily Aeschylus' play *The Persians* and Herodotus' *Histories*, written by denizens of the little country that defeated the great empire, the view we have inherited is of Xerxes as a failure. And his failure was clearly the result not only of moral inadequacies in the king himself but of structural ones in the empire he ruled. As long ago as 1867 Henry Rawlinson saw Xerxes as the epitome of idleness, self-indulgence and corruption: 'the character of Xerxes sank below that of any of his pre-decessors'.[1] David Stronach in a passing remark refers to 'Xerxes, a man of less penetrating intellect'[2] (than his father), as if we had access to his IQ tests. But the characterisation repeats itself. Montaigne[3] did not mince his words when he reprised Cicero's anecdote: 'Xerxes was an idiot to offer a reward to anyone who could invent some new pleasure for him when he was already surrounded by every pleasure known to man.'

The judgement is an easy one to make on the basis of this anecdote – Xerxes as spoilt child – and it is of a piece with Greek Stoic thinking in general (Aristotle's pupil Clearchus made the same remark about Darius III).[4] Cicero's extension of the moral coincides with one leitmotif of the legendary tradition about Alexander the Great. In the story of Alexander's journey to Paradise, the learned Jew explains that 'the eye of man, as long as it has access to the light of life, is constantly agitated with the heat of desire'.[5] Often in Greek presentations and discussions influenced by Greek sources (as virtually all of them are) Xerxes and Alexander appear as kinds of weather vanes; the one constantly counterpoises the other. Xerxes is the exemplar of the vices that are opposed to the virtues of Alexander.[6] In fact, much of Xerxes' bad press is due to Alexander's propaganda: it was the conqueror who made him a villain, while Herodotus' depiction is a much more nuanced portrait of a tragic figure.[7] Alexander made play with his crossing of the Hellespont and his visit to Ilion, where Xerxes had also sacri-ficed to the gods, and the Macedonian king boasted of having restored Esagila in Babylon, which he falsely claimed had been destroyed by Xerxes. At Persepolis, Alexander burnt only the buildings that had been erected by Xerxes.[8] His bridge of boats on the River Indus outclassed Xerxes' bridge over the Hellespont. (It was not, like Xerxes', washed away before it could be used.) In subsequent tradition, Xerxes and Alexander are mirror images of one another; but Alexander learns his lesson, and abandons desire, where Xerxes does not. Perhaps Alexander can afford to, since his has always counted as a story of worldly success cut short, whereas Xerxes' career is seen as one of failure (in his attack on Greece), despite a reign continuing for a further fifteen years after the defeats of Salamis and Plataea. This equipoise will confront us constantly as we set about constructing a picture of the Persian king in his own right.

The dominant view that comes out of Herodotus, the Greek historian of the Persian Wars, is of Xerxes as a commander who does not know his own mind, consistently takes the wrong advice, and wrongly thinks the gods are on his side when the Greeks know their gods are on theirs; he is then destroyed by that moral failing most characteristic of the Greek tragic hero, his own arrogance (hubris), which sets the gods against him.[9] He is not an ogre, but he consistently makes the wrong choice.[10]

The picture presented by Herodotus can be substantiated from many passages in his work, as well as being the leitmotif of the presentation of Xerxes onstage in Aeschylus' *The Persians*, dressed in rags and wailing piteously as he drags himself and the remains of his army back from Salamis to his mother in Persepolis.[11] Even the ghost of his father Darius asserts that his mind is diseased (line 750) and 'my son Xerxes is a young man who thinks young thoughts and does not remember my injunction' (lines 782–83). (Xerxes was probably in his thirties when he undertook his expedition; but at H. 7.13 he confesses to immature powers of judgement.) Later writers in antiquity took a similar view. Ctesias' surviving remarks on Xerxes are too brief to offer an interpretation, but Plato (*Laws* 695ce) saw Xerxes as the degenerate son of a great father, ruined by a 'womanish' education. Lysias in his *Funeral Speech*, composed at the end of the fifth century, stated 'Xerxes King of Asia came to despise Greece. He was cheated of his hope, humiliated by events, oppressed by disaster, and angry at those responsible.'[12]

The picture hardens in medieval and modern writers. John Lydgate[13] wrote:

> This was cheeff conceit off his fantasies,
> To haue al erthe under subieccioun.
> Thouhte his power rauhte aboue the skies,
> Off surquedie & fals presumpcioun.

Sir Walter Ralegh, in his *History of the World*, summed up the received view: 'as ill able to govern himself in peace as to guide his army in war . . . such is generally the effect of luxury when it is joined with absolute power'.[14] Early in the twentieth century the great Dutch novelist Louis Couperus wrote a novel about Xerxes entitled simply *Arrogance: The Conquests of Xerxes*.[15] 'His eyes, roaming about, were replete with the vision of an unexampled might. Asia was his. Europe would be his. His was the earth, and the skies were his to be. His would be the winds, obedient to his sceptre. His would be the grain, and its ears would bow to him in their fullness. Those Greeks, that wretched little people yonder, he would trample in the dust. An immeasurable emotion swelled within him and caused him to smile silently.'[16]

Strangely, this is a view of royal behaviour that also pervades Ferdowsi's *Shahnameh*, the Iranian 'national epic'. Kings become successful, and this leads to arrogance and then to a fall. One thinks of Kai Kavus' flying machine, built to challenge God himself, or his suicidal attack on the demons dwelling in Mazanderan.[17] The king must be a model of rectitude, but if he lies, God abandons him. Persian, unlike Greek, does not seem to have a word for *hybris*, but the concept is there. 'If the son brings shame on his father's name, then call him a stranger, not a son. If he slights his father's example, he deserves to suffer at the hands of fate.'[18]

Xenophon in the fourth century, in his fictional biography of Cyrus the Great (8.8.6ff), repeated the story of the moral decline of the Persians as a whole: they have forgotten the gods and are unjust to their fellow men, which is a far stronger censure than merely losing a war. Not just the king but the whole society was decadent and the empire moribund. The inadequacy of the Persian Empire became a kind of historians' tic; everyone who wrote about the empire regarded it as a moribund institution (even though it was less than 250 years old when it fell to Alexander), and its kings as degenerate and incompetent rulers and commanders. Its people were essentially unwarlike because of the enervating climate, as the author of the fourth-century Hippocratic tract *Airs Waters Places* (12–16) declared: 'The small varieties of climate to which the Asiatics are subject, extremes of both heat and cold being avoided, account for their mental flabbiness and cowardice.' The opinion was echoed by Xenophon in *History of Greece* (7.13.8). Only in recent years has this view of Persia been effectively overturned by the industry of Pierre Briant, who has argued with force and at length a case that was already adumbrated by George Grote in the nineteenth century.[19]

There are other elements too in the traditional picture of Xerxes, few of them favourable. Besides being arrogant and self-indulgent, he is also weepy, cruel and prone to rage. At the crossing of the Hellespont he sheds tears to think how few of that glorious array will be alive at the end of the campaign.[20] One cannot imagine Alexander falling prey to such self-doubt, even though he, like Xerxes, was in the first instance carrying on the unfinished business of his father.

Xerxes' anger, too, is shown not only in the famous anecdote of his whipping the Hellespont, but in a passage in Plutarch's essay, 'On the control of anger' (*Mor.* 455e). This tells how the king wrote a threatening letter to Mount Athos before starting work on cutting a canal through it: 'Noble Athos, whose summit reaches heaven, do not put in the way of my deeds great stones difficult to work. Else I shall hew you down and cast you into the sea.'[21] 'Madness fires his mind, the waves he lashes, and enchains the wind.'[22] Rage possesses the operatic Xerxes at the end of Handel's *Serse* (III.xi), when he discovers he has been fooled by both the women in his life: 'Crolli il mondo, e "l sole s'eclissi a quest" ira, che spira il mio seno.'

The stories of hideous torture are so numerous and often introduced so casually by Herodotus as to constitute a key part of the Herodotean portrait.[23] They seem to militate against any view of the king's humanity. Xerxes comes across as a man with deformed values whose weeping is for his own shame.

These stories form an important strand of the character depicted in Colley Cibber's forgotten play *Xerxes*, which ran to a single performance in 1699, and met with 'entire damnation':[24] a wardrobe sale soon afterwards advertised 'the imperial robes of Xerxes, worn only once'.[25] Cibber (1671–1757) was an important figure in the theatre of the period, though his talent was more for comedy.[26] Arrogance is a dominant characteristic of this king, who actually holds a triumph following his retreat from Greece and follows it up with a Masque of Luxury (II. 25). The search for new pleasures pops up in Act V, soon followed by a street demonstration in which

> Three dead virgins, whom you had lately ravish'd,
> In spiteful pomp were carried through the streets,
> To turn the people's hearts against you.

The play ends with Xerxes' death in a duel with Artabanus, and in general it seems to have been received as a kind of morality tale for kings.

Even more bizarre, a famous story in Herodotus tells how Xerxes 'fell in love with' a beautiful plane tree not far from Sardis and adorned it with jewels and precious gifts.[27] The story caught the imagination of the poet Nicola Minato in the seventeenth century, and became the opening number of an opera about Xerxes set by several composers including Francesco Cavalli (*Xerse* 1655),[28] before achieving immortality in Handel's *Serse*, whose 'Ombra mai fu' has become one of his most famous arias. (A production by English Touring Opera in 2011 relocated the action to a First World War aircraft base, where the beautiful plane tree became simply an adorable 'plane.) The action of Handel's opera otherwise has nothing to do with history, revolving around a complex love-triangle with some wholly fictional female characters in addition to the historical Amestris.[29] But the affection of the king for a beautiful tree is consistent with a love of gardens that has always characterised Persian culture (see Chapter 3). The impulse to create a beautiful setting out of nature is an important part of the Persian king's mastery of his environment.[30] An ancient Greek might see this as a sign of decadence; a garden for a Greek is a place where you grow onions.[31]

BIOGRAPHIES OF ANCIENT SUBJECTS

Writing a biography of an ancient subject is an exercise of a very special kind. The writer does not have access to original documents, except of the most limited nature, and all his information has already been filtered through other writers. Furthermore, ancient writers were not, as a rule, interested in constructing biographies in the modern sense – certainly not on the scale of some modern tomes. Ancient historians did recognise the importance of individual character in historical events, but preferred, like Herodotus, to let it emerge through accounts of the events and actions themselves. They also regarded character traits as being fixed, and subjects for moral praise or censure, rather than supposing that character is formed through the decisions that press on a subject as he goes through life. Herodotus does, however, present alternative interpretations of people's actions, side by side, and he allows us to choose what to believe. He recognises that sources are a problem.[32]

Works that seem to contradict this rule are, like Xenophon's *Education of Cyrus*, largely fictional, or, like his *Memoirs of Socrates*, a collection of anecdotes offering something like a character sketch. His *Agesilaus* is more like a Life but still describes itself as an *epainos*, an encomium. All these were written in the early fourth century BC. A little later, Satyrus wrote a *Life of Euripides*, of which we know very little except that it took the form of a dialogue. Most Hellenistic biography is lost, and the writer who was perhaps the founder of the genre, Antigonus of Carystus, was also a writer of wonder-tales and paradoxography. Writing about individuals was a literary activity akin to that of the novelist, not a scientific exercise. Ulrich von Wilamowitz-Moellendorff characterised Antigonus' work as follows:[33]

> The tone is throughout subjective, the narrator speaks not with that dispassionate tedium that the philistines have always taken for objectivity, because it is forbidden them to wax enthusiastic about any subject, but from personal understanding and personal sensibility.

Even in antiquity the art of biography came close to fiction, although Arnaldo Momigliano, in the classic account of the subject, insisted 'Nobody nowadays is likely to doubt that biography is some kind of history.'[34] He went on to define biography as 'an account of the life of a man from birth to death'.

There are a few statements by ancient writers that take us further. Polybius, when he began to describe the career of Philopoemen, reflected on this matter:

> It is strangely inconsistent in historians to record in elaborate detail the founding of cities, stating when and how and by whom they were established, and even the circumstances and difficulties which accompanied the transaction, and yet to pass over in complete silence the characteristics and aims of the men by whom the whole thing was done, though these are in fact the points of greatest value. For as one feels more roused to emulation and imitation by men that have life, than by buildings that have none, it is natural that the history of the former should have a greater educational value.[35]

Polybius goes on to emphasise that history differs from encomium, a tension alluded to by Cicero when he invites his friend Lucceius to write a biography of him (since autobiography, he thinks, requires too much modesty to make a realistic account!).[36] A biography of an individual, for Cicero, has to include elements of eulogy. (In his case, of course, no admixture of blame would be necessary.)

Plutarch went furthest in developing a theory of biography, in a famous passage from the beginning of his *Life of Alexander*:

> I am not writing history but biography, and the most outstanding exploits do not always have the property of revealing the goodness or badness of the agent; often, in fact, a casual action, the odd phrase, or a jest reveals character better than battles involving the loss of thousands upon thousands of lives, huge troop movements, and whole cities besieged.[37]

Plutarch, it is clear, saw a moral purpose in writing biography. This is a far cry from understanding character for its own sake; as for Polybius, an educational aim lies behind his work. Key moments are selected for judgement, and there is no sense of 'development' of a character. A modern biographer, as Tomas Hägg says, must enter into the mind of his subject.[38] But in this we are hampered by the lack of any kind of introspection or reflexivity in most ancient writings, Augustine and (perhaps) Cicero being the most notable exceptions. Certainly there is no hint of individual personality in Xerxes' recorded writings, even the inscription (XPh) in which he expresses a kind of creed: 'The man who has respect for that law which Ahura Mazda has established, and worships Ahura Mazda and Arta reverently, he both becomes happy when living and becomes blessed when dead.' Did Xerxes think he had had a happy life?

It may have been the extreme lack of personal documents that made the writing by Greeks of biographies of Persian subjects so rare. The only real example is Plutarch's biography of the Persian King Artaxerxes II. Judith Mossman,[39] in a sensitive analysis of this *Life*, suggests that the Persian ruler provided a less satisfactory object on which to exercise the characteristic faculty of moral judgement; beginning with some signs of virtue, he is not just corrupted by prosperity – a trite judgement – but the personality actually disappears inside the office. Artaxerxes' role as king means that he can only be a king and tyrant; his personality is beside the point.

When Plutarch collected anecdotes for his *Sayings of Kings and Commanders* he could find only four relating to Xerxes – not enough to build up a philosophical picture of a man of action in his time. They convey an impression of caprice, of a king who could do or decree whatever he wanted, even something as absurd as ordering the Babylonians to cease from bearing arms and instead to devote themselves to song and dance, affairs with prostitutes and wearing long robes. Cornelius Nepos, having run through the most notable Greek statesmen and commanders, passed over the Persian kings in a brief paragraph, and Xerxes in a sentence (31.3): 'Xerxes is most notable for the fact that he led the largest army in human memory to war against Greece by land and sea.' True, but in no way a description of a 'life'.

That is why the art of the novelist may in some ways be the better way in to the understanding of an ancient individual. Some might say that Herodotus is more of a novelist than a historian: a current school of thought would reject him in favour of Persian sources every time.[40] But every history is an interpretation.[41] That is why I have given some rein to Gore Vidal's carefully researched novel, *Creation* (1981), in this book. Vidal was proud of this work, though the critical response was hostile and it is not the easiest of reads. Through the narrator, Cyrus Spitama, a friend of Xerxes and his ambassador to the courts of India, China and Greece, Vidal creates a detailed and nuanced historical portrait of the king. His novel remains true to the facts in as far as we know them, makes many intelligent interventions in controversial matters of historical interpretation, and produces a rounded portrait of Xerxes as a human being. At times one is almost overwhelmed by the amassed circumstantial detail. He writes not as a scholar but as a connoisseur of human behaviour especially in the political arena. He does not swallow Herodotus whole but reads him as Herodotus would have wanted, with an eye to possibilities. The novelist can pretend to what the historian can never have, access to others' minds. Vidal's interpretation deserves to be given place alongside that of conventional historians, even though in the end I am not persuaded by his portrait of a Xerxes who succumbed to ennui and, after the Greek campaign, just 'couldn't be bothered'.[42] But I can see why he thinks it.

Similar serious consideration is, however, by no means due to the two other novelists I have from time to time quoted in these pages: Louis Couperus' *Arrogance* (1930) and F. Marion Crawford's *Zoroaster* (1885). The first is largely a rehash of the Herodotean narrative, with the leitmotif indicated by the title; no attempt at revaluation here. Crawford's novel is lurid and melo-dramatic, often absurd, with no sense of a researched attempt to understand the world he is writing about; but he occasionally has a good idea.

A very particular angle on Xerxes' personality is offered by seventeenth- and eighteenth-century drama and opera. Colley Cibber's play and Handel's *Serse* have already been mentioned, and Metastasio's libretto for *Temistocle* will feature in Appendix 1. The operas mostly focus on romantic entangle-ments and the magnanimity of the tyrant who turns to virtue, but they offer no real interpretative possibilities.[43] More may be gained from the biblical Book of Esther, which also casts Xerxes as a lover, but to rather different purpose. The erotic is an aspect that scarcely features in the Greek accounts. In the Greek writers, the dominant woman in Xerxes' life is his mother Atossa (another pre-echo of Alexander who was moulded by his forceful mother Olympias). The assassination of Xerxes is made by Herodotus the result of impermissible erotic desires, but they are of a kind that Greeks often attributed to Persians, and which echoed, as we shall see, through the stories of the Persian court that Ctesias gathered in his long residence there at the end of the fifth century.

In the Book of Esther, Xerxes' susceptibility becomes a virtuous trait, for his love for Esther results in magnanimous treatment of the whole Jewish population within the empire. We shall look more carefully at this story in Chapter 8, but there is little doubt that, fictional though it is, the King Ahasuerus of the Book of Esther stands for the historical Xerxes. The story in Esther is so different in character from anything in the Greeks (even Ctesias) that it brings home to us how dependent we are and always have been on the Greek authors for the picture we hold of Xerxes.

What have we learnt of Xerxes so far? He is an incompetent commander in war, and in private he is weepy, angry, cruel, arrogant, hedonistic, never satisfied. In the Book of Esther he is a drunkard, ill-advised and excessively pliable.[44] Not an attractive mixture, to be sure, but for Vidal it is one that should make sense to an age that has lived through existentialism. Xerxes' vice, for Vidal, is ennui. Aelian (*VH* 14.2) tells us that the Persian king never went anywhere without a piece of wood, to while away the tedious hours by whittling. Ennui is the downside of freedom. Xerxes has everything, is free to do whatever he wants. He is condemned to be free and descends into a nihilistic listlessness. Nothing matters, he has seen it all before, life has no value (least of all that of others).

Furthermore, Xerxes knows he cannot live up to the greatness of his father, Darius. This is a regular theme of Persian writing about their kings: in the *Shahnameh* the father's values are constantly reasserted to the discomfiture of the son.[45] The same thing happens, for that matter, in Turgenev's *Fathers and Sons*, and the failure of the free-thinker Bazarov is blamed on his *hybris*.[46] The Persian psyche turns the Oedipus complex upside down: 'the Iranian collective fantasy is anchored in an anxiety of disobedience that wishes for an absolute obedience. The sons, while desiring to rebel, know unconsciously that if they do so they might get killed, and so in a way they settle for the fear of castration.'[47]

Could this be the key to Xerxes' historical fate? He never grew out of the shadow of his father, and in the end he *couldn't be bothered*? Such evidence as we can muster from non-Greek sources should enable us to temper this negative picture, and show that in at least some respects his achievement was as great as his father's – even if he never quite realised it.

XERXES THE BUILDER

First of all there is archaeology. There is no doubt that Xerxes was a great builder. Both before and after the Greek campaign, he was busy with the completion of the palatial complex at Persepolis begun by Darius, and many of the buildings can be without doubt attributed to his reign and patronage. Alexander was careful to select for complete destruction only those edifices at Persepolis that had been built by Xerxes.[48] In Babylon too he was a builder. On some of those buildings there are inscriptions;[49] not only is the king depicted in splendour (even Herodotus [7.187] acknowledges the Persian king's magnificence – a virtuous trait at last), but his words are put up for all to see. They announce his devotion to Truth, Goodness and Justice, his religious toleration, as well as his devotion to the Mazdaean religion of the Achaemenids. Sadly, his preserved words are few (Darius has many more),[50] and can be as easily dismissed as the platitudes of politicians. There are no diaries: probably the Persian kings could not even read and write, they had staff to do that for them. We should love to know more about the chronicles mentioned in Esther 6.1 and Ctesias.[51] Somehow a tradition became current that the Greek campaign was a victory, and the second-century AD rhetor Dio Chrysostom[52] tells us that he heard this as common knowledge in Persia. Anything the Persians might have written down may well have been destroyed in the aftermath of Alexander's conquest, but if oral tradition carried on stories of the Achaemenid kings, they seldom surface in our Greek sources.

Increased study of archaeological and epigraphic data, including the cuneiform tablets from Persepolis and Babylon (see Chapters 2 and 4 for important revisions of traditional views), has highlighted inconsistencies between the Greek and Near Eastern records of the Persian Empire, sometimes to the Greeks' disadvantage; but they do not help much with the personality of the king.

PERSIAN VERSIONS

I have already suggested that there may be a Persian 'national character', expressed in certain reactions and tics, that can be helpful in constructing a portrait of Xerxes; in this I derive some support from the book of Gohar Homayounpour (2012), which provides a psychoanalytic portrait of the Persian soul. Persian poets have a particular outlook on life, which has become almost too familiar to Western readers through its brilliant mediation by Edward Fitzgerald in his recreation of the world of Omar Khayyam. Where the Greek outlook on life is tragic, in the sense that disaster may always be waiting around the corner, and no man may be called happy until he is dead, the Persian is a 'culture of mourning', in which the short-lived blossoming of the rose is a symbol of the shortness of life that will never come again and must be enjoyed while we can. Greeks were puzzled by this 'oriental' view, which they saw epitomised in the statue in 'Babylon'[53] of the Assyrian king Sardanapalus, 'snapping his fingers', 'for, apart from enjoyment, nothing else is worth as much as that'.[54] But this melancholy is not just an excuse for hedonism. It is an essentially conservative trait that doubts the ultimate value of all achievement. This view of life pervades even the stories of the great deeds of the kings and heroes of Ferdowsi's *Shahnameh*.

It has always seemed surprising that there is almost no reflection of Achaemenid history in the Persian writings of later ages. When Ferdowsi came to write his *Shahnameh (Book of Kings)* in the tenth century

Table 2 The Legendary Genealogy of the Persian Kings

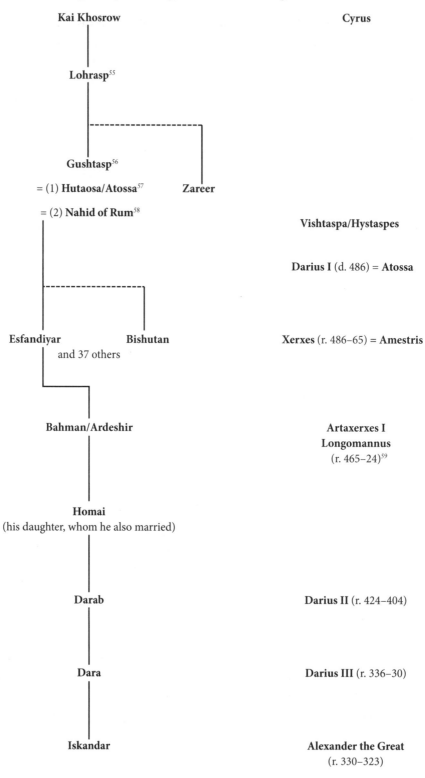

Kai Khosrow

Lohrasp[55]

Gushtasp[56]

= (1) Hutaosa/Atossa[57]   Zareer

= (2) Nahid of Rum[58]

Esfandiyar   Bishutan
and 37 others

Bahman/Ardeshir

Homai
(his daughter, whom he also married)

Darab

Dara

Iskandar

Cyrus

Vishtaspa/Hystaspes

Darius I (d. 486) = Atossa

Xerxes (r. 486–65) = Amestris

Artaxerxes I
Longomannus
(r. 465–24)[59]

Darius II (r. 424–404)

Darius III (r. 336–30)

Alexander the Great
(r. 330–323)

AD – basing it in large part on the lost Parthian *Khoday-nameh (Book of Lords)* – the place of the Achaemenid kings, between the purely legendary figures of the distant past and the arrival of Alexander the Great in Persia in 334 BC,[60] is taken by the legendary Kayanids. Kai Khosrow, the founder, is succeeded by Lohrasp, whose son is Gushtasp, whose name is the same as the Greek form Hystaspes, the father of Darius. In the nineteenth century it was assumed that the legendary and the historical genealogies could be matched up, as follows.

One of the best reasons for thinking that this legendary genealogy preserves some kind of historical memory is the name of Gushtasp (Hystaspes, also Vishtaspa), in whose reign, according to Ferdowsi, the prophet Zoroaster appeared and created a new Achaemenid religion. We will examine this tradition more closely in Chapters 1 and 4. The tenth-century Arab historian Tabari[61] has a variant of this genealogy, which attempts to reconcile different historical data:

Table 3 Tabari's Version of the Genealogy of the Persian Kings

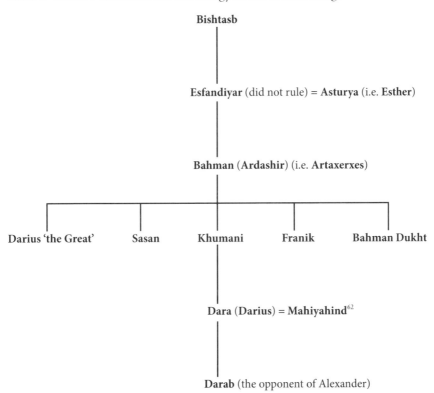

Bishtasb

Esfandiyar (did not rule) = **Asturya** (i.e. **Esther**)

Bahman (**Ardashir**) (i.e. **Artaxerxes**)

Darius 'the Great'   **Sasan**   **Khumani**   **Franik**   **Bahman Dukht**

Dara (**Darius**) = **Mahiyahind**[62]

Darab (the opponent of Alexander)

In this account, Esfandiyar did not rule and Bahman succeeded Bishtasb. Bahman's daughter-wife Khumani (i.e. Homai in Persian) is said to have reigned for thirty years and to have built Istakhr (i.e. Persepolis).

The adventures of Esfandiyar (Isfendiyadh in Arabic) are recounted at length in both the *Shahnameh* (completed in 1010) and the *History of the Kings of Persia* by al-Tha'alibi (961/2–1037/8).[63] The latter's source was not Ferdowsi, but besides Persian texts he made use of Tabari and Ibn Khordadbeh. Imprisoned by his father Gushtasp as a suspected traitor, Esfandiyar is released to lead a campaign against the Turks, who are destroying the Persians' fire-temples. He captures the Turkish commander Kourksar, who is renowned for his cunning, trickery and bravery, and compels him to reveal to Esfandiyar the way to the City of Brass. This is a perilous journey of Seven Stages (Haft Khan); Esfandiyar defeats in turn a demon, a lion, an elephant and a dragon. He garrottes a witch with a chain impervious to her magic. He then has to deal with the *simurgh* (*anqa* in Arabic), a gigantic bird that can carry off elephants. He leads his army through a region of freezing cold and snow, which is dispelled by the power of prayer. This is followed by a desert, after which the City of Brass comes into view. Esfandiyar goes in disguise to the court of its ruler Arjasp, conquers his army and seizes the treasure of Afrasiab. He returns in triumph to his father, only to be set the further, impossible, task of capturing the invincible hero Rostam. His mother Katayoun begs him not to go, but he sets off nonetheless and is killed by Rostam who has the assistance of the simurgh.

This story of adventure, despite its catastrophic end, seems in several ways to be a calque on that of the victorious Alexander of the *Romance*: the propensity for disguises, the fight with a dragon, the visit to the City of Brass, are all known from Arabic versions of the Alexander story. Although neither of these authors mentions it, Qazvini has a story that it was Esfandiyar who built the wall against Gog and Magog that is normally attributed to Alexander.[64] (It could not, in fact, be in Ferdowsi since he makes this a deed of Alexander.) As in the Greek tradition, Xerxes/Esfandiyar has been modelled to be an inversion of the greater king who is to come. He fails in his earthly mission, whereas Alexander succeeds and his only failure is that he does not achieve immortality.

But can Esfandiyar really be the Xerxes of history? What seems to have happened is that during not only Alexander's brief reign but also the two centuries of the Seleucid Empire that succeeded him in most of Asia, many of the traditions of the rulers of Fars were forgotten – or perhaps suppressed by the Macedonian elite. When the Persian Empire was refounded by the

Parthians in 247 BC, displacing the Seleucids from the Iranian lands, the new rulers, originating from East Iran, and with a capital north of the Oxus at Hecatompylus in present-day Turkmenistan, brought their own stories and legends with them. These largely focused around tales of the northern marches of Persia and struggles with the Turanians (early Turks) such as Afrasiab, the opponent of Kai Khosrow. However, some names of the Achaemenid kings attached themselves in the confused way of oral legend to the exploits of the East Iranian heroes. The fact that the Parthian kings, too, hardly figure in the *Shahnameh* is to be explained by a further suppression of Parthian tradition by the Sassanian rulers who succeeded them.[65]

Our task is to determine whether any memory of what the Persian kings actually did also penetrates Ferdowsi and other medieval writers. Can we tell a story about Xerxes that uses the exploits of Esfandiyar? His name is probably a corrupt form of Sphendadates, which anchors him, at least precariously, in the Achaemenid story, since Sphendadates (meaning something like 'Law of Generosity') is the name of the false Magus disposed of by Darius in the account of Ctesias: Persian accounts call him Gaumata.[66]

Our results will, like our deployment of Gore Vidal's novel, be more suggestive than historical. Pierre Briant attempted something similar in his recreation of Darius III, *Darius dans l'ombre d'Alexandre*, in which he employed the traditions of the *Shahnameh* to recover something of a Persian viewpoint on that later and much more tragic Persian king. He had the advantage that Darius III is recognisable as a character in the *Shahnameh* and elsewhere, whereas the congruence of Esfandiyar and Xerxes is fleeting at best. However, Briant's principle can with some modifications be applied to the earlier king.

The aim of this book is to recreate something of what it was to be the ruler of the largest empire the world had yet seen, in the fifth century BC – and also to investigate how the dominant picture of Xerxes, which the modern world has inherited, came into being. The conflict with 'plucky little Greece' has come to be a defining image of European civilisation against the oriental 'Other'. When President Reagan coined the phrase 'the evil empire' to describe the world beyond the Iron Curtain, it was an echo of that immemorial conflict of east and west, a conflict that defined itself even more sharply as America's enemy became again a power based in the same geographical location as the ancient Persian Empire. Fortunately there are signs (2015) that the polarisation is becoming less intense. It will be to the good of us all to get beyond this dichotomy, to slip behind the curtain and see what it was really like to live – and to be a king – in Persia. More Greeks lived under Persian rule at the beginning of the fifth century BC than in Greece itself. How did they accommodate themselves to imperial rule? Herodotus, Aeschylus and Ferdowsi are among the greatest writers in the world, but that does not mean the picture they paint of Persia is unvarnished truth.

CHAPTER ONE

Accession

Saith Xerxes the King: Other sons of Darius there were, (but) – thus unto
Ahuramazda was the desire – Darius my father made me the greatest after
himself. When my father Darius went away from the throne, by the will of
Ahuramazda I became king on my father's throne.

XPf 27–33

Your majesty, you're like the radiant sun
Bestowing light and life on everyone:
May greed and anger never touch your reign
And may your enemies live wracked with pain.
Monarch with whom no monarch can compete,
All other kings are dust beneath your feet.

**Ferdowsi, *Shahnameh* (tr. D. Davis), 328: Rostam greets the new king
Kai Khosrow**

DARIUS THE USURPER; XERXES THE HEIR

December is mild at Persepolis, though a little rain may fall to settle
the scudding dust-devils of the plain of Marvdasht, and if heavy may make
the land marshy.[1] The nights are cold, and clouds often obscure
the brilliant panorama of the stars; but the fogs that cloak the Zagros
Mountains in winter do not affect this more low-lying region. Temperatures
rarely fall below freezing, and snow is unusual. Nevertheless, the roses of
Shiraz are improved by a period of winter cold. No roses grow now at

Persepolis, where stunted pine, plane, poplar and tamarisk dominate the landscape, but in antiquity the plain was irrigated by the waters of the River Pulvar as it leaves its rocky gorge, and gardens blossomed below the platform on which the palace is built. In the nineteenth century, and probably for thousands of years before that, storks paced the riverbanks and gazelles scurried across the plain.[2] At night hyenas could be heard in the hills, and in the day the hoopoe, the sacred bird of King Solomon, could sometimes be seen calling 'hoop-hoop' from a high perch.

It was to Persepolis, the autumn residence of the Persian kings,[3] that Darius I (the Great) returned at the conclusion of his campaign against the Scythians. He made the usual sacrifices that marked the end of a successful campaign, and began his preparations for an attack on Greece, which he had been meditating ever since the defeat at Marathon in 490. Now Egypt, too, rose in revolt against Persia and made the matter more urgent. As soon as spring arrived to make the march feasible, the Persian army would set out. But before the preparations could advance very far, Darius fell ill, and 'after an illness of thirty days he passed away. He had lived for seventy-two years and reigned for thirty-one.'[4] It was the beginning of December 486 BC.[5]

As the king who spread the Persian Empire to its fullest extent and created many of its defining institutions, Darius can never have been out of Xerxes' mind. He was a model to emulate, but as Xerxes prepared for his accession he must have looked back at the difficulties his father had encountered on coming to the throne, and hoped that he would not have to face the problems associated with what was widely seen as a usurpation. The story of Darius' rise to power introduces many of the characteristic themes and tensions of Persian history, for its actors as well as for those who wrote – and write – about it.

Darius had become king of the Persian Empire by unorthodox means. As with so many of the key events of Achaemenid history, the sources are contradictory and probably reflect deliberate obfuscation by the participants. In his own words in his great inscription at Bisutun Darius states that he had to put down nine kings in order to secure his accession to the throne:[6] Gaumata the Magus or Bardiya, whom the Greeks called Smerdis, as well as the kings of Elam, Babylon, Media, Sagartia, Margiana and Armenia, and two pretenders in Persia, one of whom also called himself Smerdis. First came the affair of Gaumata the Magus, starting on 11 March 522; and the series of further revolts preoccupied the king until at least July 521.[7] Gaumata 'seized the kingship' from Cambyses, passing himself off as Cambyses' brother Bardiya (in Greek, Smerdis or Mardos):[8]

There was no man, neither a Persian nor a Mede, nor anyone of our family, who could take away the kingship from that Gaumata the magus. The people were very much afraid of him, thinking that he would kill many people who had known Bardiya previously. . . . [On 29 September 522] I, with a few men, killed Gaumata the Magus. . . . The kingdom which had been taken away from our family, I re-established it, I put it back in its place. In accordance with what had been previously, I made the cult-centres, which Gaumata the Magus destroyed. I restored to the people, the pastures and herds, the household slaves and the houses/domains, which Gaumata the Magus took away from them.[9]

Darius' tale is one of a usurper who caused social and religious upheaval: the text could be interpreted as implying a redistribution of land and property as a populist move to please his supporters. This interpretation is supported by the Roman historian Justin (second century AD),[10] who writes that this usurper 'Cometes' killed 'Mergis' and substituted his own brother 'Oropastes' as king. (This character does not occur in Darius' account, but is in that of the Greek historians, as will be seen in the next paragraph.) 'Then, in order to curry favour with the people, the magi lifted military and tribute obligations for three years, in order to consolidate, through indulgence and largesse, a kingship obtained by fraud.'

Herodotus tells a much more richly elaborated tale:[11] Cambyses had a brother, Smerdis, and one night in a dream he saw Smerdis sitting on his throne as a usurper. So he decided to eliminate Smerdis, and sent an emissary, Prexaspes, to get rid of him, which he did either by taking him hunting or by drowning him in the sea. But now a magus, Patizeithes, decided to seize the kingship. His own brother, who by chance was also called Smerdis, looked extremely like the murdered Smerdis, and so Patizeithes put him forward as the legitimate successor.[12] When Cambyses returned to Susa[13] and found that his brother was apparently still alive, he summoned Prexaspes to account for himself; but Prexaspes cottoned on to what had happened. When he explained it to Cambyses, the latter understood the truth of his dream. Shortly after he wounded himself in a riding accident: he drove his own sword through his thigh as he was leaping onto his horse. Knowing that he was about to die, he summoned his Persian courtiers and urged them, 'in particular those of you here who are Achaemenids: do not allow power to pass back to the Medes!'

But when Cambyses died, leaving no heir, the magus, the false Smerdis (Bardiya) ruled for seven months and was much beloved by his subjects for his kindness, notably for remitting all tribute and military service for three years. But in the eighth month the magus was unmasked by a noble called Otanes, whose daughter Phaidymie had been one of the wives of Cambyses, all of whom had been taken over by Smerdis. It emerged that she had never seen her husband, and neither had any of the other wives, including Atossa. Clearly Persian kings preferred to make love in the dark. Otanes advised his daughter to feel for her husband's ears when he was asleep: if he had ears, he would be Cambyses' brother, but if not he would be the impostor Smerdis who was known to have had his ears cut off by Cyrus at some time in the past. When Otanes' daughter came to bed, she slipped her hands into the thick flowing curls of his carefully dressed hair . . . Sure enough – no ears!

Otanes now got five other Persians on his side, and then a sixth, Darius, whose father Hystaspes was governor of Parthia. (Herodotus says Persia, but Darius' own information is surely right.) The group of seven concocted a plan. Gobryas expressed the view of all of them: 'My friends, when will there be a better time to take back power, or if we fail, to die? Seeing that we are Persians being ruled by a Mede, a magus – and he has not even got ears!'

The names of these seven are given by Herodotus as Otanes, Aspathines, Gobryas, Megabyxus, Intaphernes, Hydarnes and Darius. Six of these names correspond to Darius' own list: Vindafarna, Hutana, Gaubaruva, Vidarna, Bagabukhsha and Ardumanish.[14] Only Ardumanish is clearly a different name from Aspathines.[15]

Quickly the seven made their way to the palace, were admitted without demur by the guards, overpowered the eunuchs in the inner court and entered the men's quarters where the two magi were in discussion. There was a fierce fight and then Darius and Gobryas entered the innermost sanctum; in the dark Darius was lucky enough to strike the magus and not his ally Gobryas. They displayed the heads of the two magi on poles, and a bloodbath followed in which the Persians struck down any of the magi they came across. In later times, according to Herodotus, a regular festival was celebrated called 'The Murder of the Magi' to commemorate this moment when Persian royal power was reasserted against the Median clan.

Darius himself describes the conspiracy when he appears as a ghost in Aeschylus' *Persians*, written some decades before the *Histories*. He lists the successive kings but names as his predecessor simply Mardos (i.e. Bardiya, Smerdis), 'a disgrace to his country and to his ancestral throne'.[16] There is no mention of Gaumata.

Ctesias, writing a century later than Herodotus and claiming to 'correct Herodotus' errors', gives a rather different version. In this Cambyses' brother is killed long before Cambyses' death but before the Egyptian campaign.

The names of the protagonists also differ. Cambyses' brother is called Tanyoxarces:[17] this brother punished a magus, Sphendadates,[18] for some crime with a flogging, and the magus then started making accusations against Tanyoxarces to Cambyses. Eventually Sphendadates convinced Cambyses of the justice of his complaints, and persuaded Cambyses to have his brother Tanyoxarces put to death. But because Sphendadates closely resembled Tanyoxarces, he suggested that he take his place and the brother be executed on the pretence that he was the unpopular magus. The motive was apparently to avoid upsetting Amytis, the mother of Cambyses and Tanyoxarces. When she discovered how she had been tricked, Amytis demanded Sphendadates be handed over to her for punishment; when Cambyses refused, she drank bull's blood and died. Later, when Cambyses died after accidentally inflicting a mortal wound on himself while carving wood, the magus was able to succeed him as king.

The names of the conspirators also differ in Ctesias. The only one that corresponds to the list in Darius or Herodotus, apart from Darius himself, is Idernes (i.e. Hydarnes). The others are Onophas, Norondobates, Mardonius, Barisses and Ataphernes (who might be Intaphernes). However, as Amélie Kuhrt points out,[19] Mardonius was the son of Gobryas and Onophas the son of Otanes, so Ctesias might be abbreviating a list of names that included the conspirators' sons.

Did Gaumata Exist?

Clearly variant versions of the whole story were circulating in the fifth and fourth centuries BC. The variants are so great that some scholars have preferred to regard the whole story as fiction. Gore Vidal's Xerxes expresses it succinctly: 'There was no Magian. There was only the Great King [sc. Mardos] and Darius killed him.'[20] That is the train of events implied by Aeschylus, and it is the explanation favoured by Kuhrt.[21] Gaumata did not exist and the whole story is made up to conceal the fact that Darius' claim to the throne was tenuous in the extreme: he was a descendant of Teispes, the father of Cyrus, but no closer than that to the royal line. Later legend put Darius' father back in to direct descent from Cyrus (Kai Khosrow) of course: the sequence runs Kai Khosrow – Lohrasp – Gushtasp (see Introduction).

If Darius did simply murder Mardos/Smerdis/Bardiya, the legitimate king, Vidal has a nice explanation for the role of Atossa (the mother of Xerxes) in the whole affair.[22] Atossa, having been married to Mardos, who was also her brother, knows that Darius has killed him – and also Cambyses.

Darius protests that he had indeed killed her husband, yet Mardos was not her brother but the impostor Gaumata. Atossa replies: 'You are the usurper, Darius, son of Hystaspes; and one word from me to the clans, and all of Persia will go into rebellion.' Atossa has Darius in the palm of her hand, forces him to marry her and to make her son Xerxes his designated successor.

The plot is neat, but can Gaumata be so easily explained away? He is, after all, the subject of a 'portrait', prostrate under Darius' foot, on the cliff face at Bisutun. The information about his social revolution also seems circumstantial, if hardly extensive. Accepting Gaumata's existence need not entail accepting the folk tale about the magus' close resemblance to the murdered Bardiya, and the ears. Few will have seen the king in full view, and a cynic might remark that Persian kings, with their long carefully dressed locks, magnificent beards and heavy make-up, all look remarkably alike anyway.

A complex but attractive theory elaborated by Abolala Soudavar represents the conflict between Darius and Gaumata as one between two rival clans with hereditary priestly roles: the magi, represented by Gaumata (and his brother) and the *parsas*, represented by Darius. The expression in DNa para 2, 'I Darius . . . son of Vishtaspa the Achemenid, a *parsa*, son of *parsa*, an Aryan', is usually translated as 'a Persian'; Soudavar argues persuasively that the word actually has a religious designation, since it is also used to caption images of Darius and Xerxes facing a fire altar on their tomb facades.[23] Herodotus says of the Persian tribes 'of these the Pasargadai are the most noble, of whom also the Achaimenidai are a clan'.[24] Darius has a hereditary role as a parsa, who seems to be a keeper of the sacred fire.

If this is accepted, many things fall into place. The magi represent a rival clan claiming the right to kingship; their representative Gaumata overturns religious establishments which Darius has to set right; and Darius is a true son of his father Hystaspes, who is known traditionally as the patron of Zoroaster, the introducer of the form of religion that characterised the Achaemenid kings from Darius onwards but not, apparently, Cyrus (see further, Chapter 4). Clan rivalry, social revolution and religious schism are all part of the mix in Darius' rise to power. Vidal has a place for Hystaspes in the drama too:

'Did Hystaspes know?' I asked.
'Oh yes. He knew. He was horrified. He hoped that by devoting himself to Zoroaster he could expiate the crime of Darius. But that's not possible, is it?'[25]

The seven conspirators now drew lots to decide which of them should be king – by a horse-oracle, according to Ctesias[26] – and the lot fell upon Darius.[27] Darius, the son of Hystaspes, thus became king of the Persian Empire. Like Cambyses, but unlike his successors, he had numerous wives, including the daughter of Gobryas, the daughter of Bardiya, and two sisters, Artystone and Atossa, both daughters of Cyrus; he also married his own niece Phratagyne, who bore him two sons. No brothers are named in the sources, but Darius had at least four sisters: one of them married Otanes and became the mother of Amestris, Xerxes' wife; a third married Teaspes; and a fourth married Gobryas[28] and became the mother of the general Mardonius.

Xerxes Becomes King

Xerxes' accession, in the end, was a much more straightforward affair than his father's, and rival claims were weak. Xerxes was the son of Atossa and was the first of Darius' sons to be born while he was on the throne of Persia. When Darius died, according to Herodotus, a dispute arose as to who was to be his successor. The eldest son was Artobarzanes (Herodotus) or Ariaramnes (Justin), but Xerxes argued that this brother had been born when Darius was still a private citizen, and not yet king, and therefore had a lesser claim to the throne. (Artobarzanes, if that was his name, must therefore have been close to forty years old.) Furthermore, Xerxes' mother, Atossa, was the daughter of Cyrus, while Darius' first wife was also not of royal blood. As Darius had at least three other wives, including another daughter of Cyrus, Artystone, there must have been a considerable number of potential claimants to the throne. Justin and Herodotus have different accounts of how the dispute was resolved. For both of them there are only two brothers who come into question. According to Justin, they went to Darius' brother Artaphernes and asked him to adjudicate, and he gave the preference to Xerxes. 'The princes maintained a completely fraternal attitude throughout the dispute; neither did the victor display haughtiness nor the vanquished resentment. Even during their quarrel, they sent each other presents and invited each other to feasts, where trust just as much as conviviality reigned.'[29] Herodotus has a different story: according to him, the reigning king must appoint his successor before he goes on campaign, so the matter had all been sorted out before Darius' death. He makes the arbiter the exiled king Demaratus of Sparta, who had recently arrived in Susa and advised Xerxes to push his case with his father. 'However,' Herodotus concludes, 'I think that even without this advice, Xerxes would have become king: for Atossa was all-powerful.'[30]

For Vidal it was Atossa who had pushed Darius into his position of supreme power, and 'from the first moment that Xerxes knew the true story of his father's rise, he foresaw with perfect clarity his own bloody end. This foreknowledge explains who he was, and what he did.'[31] The shadow of the father hung over the son in an extreme degree.

Justin's source for his version is uncertain, though we should beware of supposing that Herodotus, because he lived closer in time to the events, gave a more reliable account. No doubt this is what Demaratus told Herodotus, and maybe he exaggerated his part in the affair. But we do not know whether what he says is true, that the king had to appoint his successor before leaving on campaign. (We are never told, for example, that Darius III had designated a successor before he advanced against Alexander's army.) The fact that Herodotus locates the discussion at Susa also gives pause for thought. The Persian king was peripatetic and, according to the Greek author Athenaeus, he spent the winters in Susa (which is sweltering in summer), the summers in Ecbatana (which is cooler because of its higher elevation), the autumn in Persepolis, and 'the rest of the year' (which has to mean spring) in Babylon.[32] If these events really took place in Susa, then that must have been nearly a year before the king's death. But Greek writers generally regard Susa as the centre of the Persian kingdom, and no writer before Alexander ever mentions Persepolis.[33] We should not rule out the possibility that events took place in Persepolis even if our sources locate them elsewhere.

The story cannot be true as it stands in any case, since the relief of Darius at Persepolis (according to most interpretations) clearly shows Xerxes behind him in the position of crown prince.[34] Any dispute there may have been must have taken place, and been satisfactorily resolved, some years before. Plutarch[35] has a story that Ariamenes (presumably the same as Justin's Ariaramnes), the brother of Xerxes son of Darius, was on his way down from the Bactrian country to contest Xerxes' right to the kingdom. Xerxes accordingly sent him gifts, bidding those who offered them to say, 'With these gifts your brother Xerxes now honours you; and if he be proclaimed king, you shall be the highest at the court.' When Xerxes was designated as the king, Ariamenes at once paid homage to him, and placed the crown upon his brother's head, and Xerxes gave him a rank second only to himself.

Although the paragraph might most naturally be read as describing a continuous sequence, there is no difficulty in assuming that the dispute and the gift-giving took place years before Darius' death. However, in *On Brotherly*

Love Plutarch explicitly says that Ariamenes came down ('from the country of the Medes' this time), after Darius' death and when Xerxes was already 'acting' king.[36] But as Plutarch goes on to suggest that the decision as to who would be king depended on a vote of the Persians, the detail of the story is hardly to be taken at face value. These democratic Persians then elect Artabanus as 'judge' to decree who would be king. For all his hostility to Xerxes, Herodotus has no hesitation in describing him as the best candidate for the throne by far.[37]

In both Plutarchan accounts, Ariamenes is given a position second only to that of Xerxes himself. But he is never mentioned again except as dying at Salamis,[38] and he is not among the brothers named by Herodotus, who does not mention any of the brothers dying in the battle; nor is he in the litany of names of those who died at Salamis that Xerxes utters in Aeschylus' *Persians*. It would be a shame, but it is certainly possible that the man never existed.

It seems at least that the Persian king was expected to choose his successor; mere primogeniture was not enough. In Xenophon's *Education of Cyrus*, the dying Cyrus chooses his heir while he is lying on his deathbed. Here, too, the choice is presented as taking place at the last minute, so to speak; but it is clearly a choice. Was Xerxes the best candidate? We have only Darius' action in preferring him to go by. As far as we can tell, no succession myth circulated of the type that gave support to many other Persian kings, from Cyrus the Great to the Sassanian Ardashir.[39]

The succession myth is so pervasive that it is rather remarkable to find no trace of it in relation to Xerxes, except perhaps in the legend of Gushtasp's mistrust of his son Esfandiyar (in the *Shahnameh* and elsewhere), in which he is imprisoned (like Ahiqar) but re-emerges to succeed his father. These legends no doubt circulated orally, but they leave no mark in the official inscriptions of the Achaemenid kings. Nor would one expect them to. For all we know, Xerxes was a cherished child, doted on by his mother Atossa, and succeeding without conflict or controversy to the position of crown prince, as Cyrus does in Xenophon's account.

In his own statement of his accession Xerxes says nothing of all this. 'King Xerxes proclaims: Darius had other sons also; but thus was the desire of Ahuramazda: Darius, my father, made me the greatest after himself. When my father Darius went to his allotted place, by the favour of Ahuramazda I became king in my father's place.'[40] Xerxes was clearly the designated successor before his father's death, perhaps many years before, and for all we know the succession went smoothly. For Pierre Briant, the involvement of Atossa is a fantasy of Herodotus: though her prestige at court was high, she 'had no right to interfere'.[41] That may be true, but a formidable lady in middle age does not always need a legal justification in order to get her way in the family and in other affairs. Her reputation must have been considerable since she clearly made an impression on the Greek writers; not only does she have a role to play here in Herodotus, but she dominates the stage for the second half of Aeschylus' *Persians*, when she welcomes her conquered and bedraggled son back to his capital, which may be Susa or Persepolis.[42]

The designated heir to the throne was probably born about 518/19, soon after Darius' accession in 522, and was therefore about thirty-two on his accession. His birth will have been celebrated with a big party, as Plato describes: 'When the heir of the kingdom is born, all the subjects of the king feast; and the day of his birth is ever afterwards kept as a holiday and time of sacrifice by all Asia.'[43] But for the next years the biographer here faces a common gap in the record, the childhood and upbringing of a man before he became famous. Xenophon in his book about Cyrus filled the gap by describing the traditional upbringing of a Persian noble, and we shall do the same.

EDUCATION

Xerxes' upbringing undoubtedly followed the pattern outlined by Xenophon for Persian nobles. Herodotus summarises the main features of a noble Persian's education in a single sentence: he learns 'to shoot, to ride, and to tell the truth'.[44] Darius himself alludes to such a training: 'I am trained in my hands and in my feet; as a horseman, I am a good horseman; as a bowman, I am a good bowman, both on foot and on horseback; as a spearman, I am a good spearman, both on foot and on horseback'.[45] Note that there is no mention of learning to read! Xenophon developed this thumbnail description in considerable detail in his account of Persian education in *The Education of Cyrus*.[46] It is difficult to tell how far Xenophon's account provides genuine information, and how far it is an idealised presentation of what Xenophon thought Greek states ought to be like. Much of it has seemed too close to Spartan practice to be convincing, while the fact that Plato[47] uses some of Xenophon's ideas as taking-off points for the ideal state envisaged in the *Laws* might suggest that we are looking here at a discussion between two philosophers about ideal education. However, at least some of Xenophon's information is circumstantial enough, and corroborated by Herodotus, to be convincing. Strabo adds some details that are clearly not taken from either Xenophon or Herodotus and thus betoken an independent source.[48]

To begin with, Xenophon asserts that the aim of the Persian laws is to make the citizens not just well-behaved, but *incapable* of wickedness. For a start, nobles (one must assume he is talking about the nobility, not the hoi polloi) must not sully their hands with buying and selling in any form. The commercial market is kept well away from the main square of the city, known as Freedom Square, where the citizens gather – boys, youths, men and elders each in their own quarter. The young men sleep there too to guard the public buildings, while the boys, presumably, receive instruction in their own corner of the square after presenting themselves there at daybreak. Most of their education is of a moral nature: they learn justice, generosity and gratitude, self-restraint, obedience to authority, and continence in physical wants. Their food is bread and nasturtium leaves. (The nasturtiums recur in Strabo, and indeed peppery greens are much consumed in Persia even now: they are called *tareh* – a kind of chives.) One pictures something like the *meidan* in Isfahan, where today turbaned mullahs teach their charges to memorise the Qur'an. Most of the people, Strabo says, wear a double tunic that reaches to the middle of the shin, and a piece of linen cloth around the head. So the appearance of the square in ancient Susa did not differ greatly from that of Isfahan over the last five hundred years or so.

Strabo adds some detail to Xenophon: after waking the boys before dawn with the sound of brazen instruments (*psophoi chalkou* – gongs or trumpets?), the teachers 'interweave their teachings with the mythical element, thus reducing that element to a useful purpose, and rehearse both with song and without song the deeds both of the gods and of the noblest men'.[49] Xerxes, then, grew up reciting the deeds of the heroes, the adventures of the young Cyrus and so on, as part of his training in ethics.

Plato was much more caustic about Persian education: 'The king spent his entire life on campaign, and handed over his children to the women to bring up.' Xerxes' education reverted to the 'royal pampering' that had ruined Cambyses: 'So Xerxes, being a product of the same type of education, naturally had a career that closely reproduced the pattern of Cambyses' misfortunes'.[50] There is a much more positive view of Persian education in *Alcibiades* I, which may not be by Plato at all.[51] Persian princes are brought up by eunuchs, not by nurses. At age seven, they receive lessons in riding and hunting; at age fourteen, they are put in the care of *paidagogoi*, teachers, who are drawn from the nobility and are four in number: they teach the lads to be wise, just, prudent and brave. They teach them the fundamentals of Zoroastrian religion, as well as to tell the truth, to exercise self-restraint in pleasures, and to be brave. Fear, for a Persian, is the equivalent of slavery.

Reverence for Ahura Mazda is central, and that is reflected in Xerxes' own proclamations about his devotion to the god (see Chapter 4).

After studying at school until the age of sixteen or seventeen, the young men then enter on their 'national service' for ten years. At any one time half of them are in the city, practising archery and javelin (not too close to the school corner, one hopes) and competing for prizes, while the other half are out hunting, a sport of which Xenophon was passionately fond and which he regarded as an excellent military training:

> The reason of this public sanction of the chase is not far to seek: the king leads just as he does in war, hunting in person at the head of the field, and making his men follow, because it is felt that the exercise itself is the best possible training for the needs of war. It accustoms a man to early rising; it hardens him to endure heat and cold; it teaches him to march and to run at the top of his speed; he must perforce learn to let fly arrow and javelin the moment the quarry is across his path; and, above all, the edge of his spirit must needs be sharpened by encountering any of the mightier beasts: he must deal his stroke when the creature closes, and stand on guard when it makes its rush: indeed, it would be hard to find a case in war that has not its parallel in the chase.[52]

The youths learn also to go without food throughout the day, and to enjoy their bread and nasturtiums when it is over, though sometimes they are allowed a share of the game they have caught as well.

For the next twenty-five years or so the men are on call as soldiers, after which they graduate to the status of elders and king's counsellors.

This picture of elite education is reinforced by Xenophon's account of the Younger Cyrus, whom he knew well, in his *Anabasis*. In a kind of obituary for the young prince he recounts his virtues: 'all the children of Persian nobles are brought up at the Court, and there a child can pick up many lessons in good behaviour while having no chance of seeing or hearing anything bad'.[53] They learn to obey and to command. Cyrus excelled in archery, javelin-throwing and hunting. As a grown man and a commander, he knew the value of gift-giving as well as how to show proper gratitude for others' gifts (which he generally shared with others). His severity to evil-doers was equally admired by Xenophon: 'his punishments were exceptionally severe, and along the more frequented roads one often saw people who had been blinded or had had their hands or feet cut off. The result was that in Cyrus' provinces anyone, whether Greek or native, who was doing no harm could travel without fear wherever he liked and could take with him whatever he wanted.'[54]

The younger Cyrus is also praised for his support of horticulture: 'when he saw that a man was a capable administrator, acting on just principles, improving the land under his control and making it bring in a profit, he never took his post away from him, but always gave him additional responsibility'.[55] The virtue of land improvement was valued among satraps (see Chapter 3).

This then is the kind of upbringing that Xerxes received. His experience may not have been all that different from that of later Persian kings. In the seventeenth century, the young Shah Abbas was educated alongside house-hold 'slaves' who would later be his military and administrative leaders. His education was entrusted to a sheikh from Mashad, 'and would have included instruction in the Koran, the Sharia and the principal teachings of Shi'ism, as well as the study of some of the masterpieces of Persian poetry, in particular the national epic, the *Shahnameh* of Ferdowsi. Book learning, however, seems to have had little appeal to Abbas at this time, and he is said often to have skipped his studies in order to go hunting. . . . By the time he became king at the age of seventeen he could do little more than read and write.'[56]

Xerxes may never have learned to read or write: certainly there was no written literature for him to study and all his stories would have been oral. But the general tenor of the regime seems strangely similar. One thinks too of Alexander III of Macedon being brought up with noble companions (though not 'slaves') who later become his chief commanders; their teacher Aristotle was the best that money could buy in Philip's kingdom. Alexander, however, was a great reader and perhaps even an author (of the satyr play, *Agen*).

Perhaps Xerxes' obedience also extended to marrying the girl he was told to, like the docile Artaxerxes II in Plutarch's *Life of Artaxerxes*.[57] So Vidal at any rate supposes: Atossa chose Amestris, the daughter of Otanes, not just because of her money, but 'because Amestris is like Atossa . . . she is polit-ical'.[58] We do not know when Xerxes married Amestris, who was to be his only wife until the unfortunate affair that precipitated his assassination, some forty years after his accession. In Handel's opera, set at the beginning of the Greek campaign, his devotion to Amestris is under threat from his passion for Romilda for most of the plot, though he sees the light at the end; while in Metastasio's libretto for *Temistocle* (set by several composers), which takes place in the aftermath of the Greek expedition, he betrays his wife, here called Roxane, by falling for her maid, who turns out to be Themistocles' daughter, before seeing the error of his ways. Neither of these plots reflects anything we know about the Persian court at this time.

We also know nothing about the education that Amestris, a first cousin, may have received. Probably little more was on offer to girls than in a strict Muslim state today. None of our sources breathes a word about the education of women, though they attained a political and an economic status that compared favourably with that of contemporary Greek women. Herodotus may have exaggerated the role of Atossa in Xerxes' succession, but both she and Amestris showed themselves to be formidable players later in his career (see Chapter 8).

<h2 style="text-align:center">INVESTITURE</h2>

Xerxes' investiture as king was a major event in the life of the court. The sacred fires were all extinguished on the death of the king his father, to be rekindled at the investiture of the new one. We have no idea how long an interval elapsed between these events, but there seems to be no reason to suppose it was a long one. A period of mourning intervened, and the dead king, perhaps embalmed in some way or maybe excarnated in the later Zoroastrian fashion by birds and his bones placed in an ossuary, was carried to the place of interment on 'a richly draped bier' or a 'sumptuously ornamented chariot'.[59] The tombs of the Achaemenid kings are empty now, so we can never know in what form their bodies were preserved before being laid to rest.

Pierre Briant states without comment that the coronation took place at Pasargadae,[60] which is the location suggested by our only account of a Persian coronation, that in Plutarch's life of Artaxerxes II:

> It was not long after the death of Darius II that the new king went to Pasargadae, to have the ceremony of his inauguration consummated by the Persian priests. Here there is a sanctuary dedicated to a warlike goddess, whom one might liken to Athena, into which when the royal person to be initiated has passed, he must strip himself of his own robe, and put on that which Cyrus the Elder wore before he was king; then he must eat a cake of figs, chew some turpentine-wood, and drink a cup of sour milk.[61]

The burial of Darius at Persepolis was no doubt followed by a period of mourning, after which the court would process the 25 miles north-east to Pasargadae, where Cyrus the Founder had his tomb. Pasargadae is at the northern edge of Fars. The road climbs, following the course of the River Pulvar, whose remaining waters are now drawn off to irrigate the peach trees, vines, beets and cabbages that adorn the valley, along with modern additions like maize and sunflowers. The *dasht-e-morghab* ('plain of water-birds') where Pasargadae stands is arid and has neither birds nor water; but in antiquity it was green. The palace of Cyrus stood in a well-watered park. In 1888 E. G. Browne was able to observe the migrations of tribal peoples through this region:

> On the road, which wound through beautiful grassy valleys bedecked with sweet spring flowers, we met many more, all bound for the highland pastures which we were leaving behind us, and a pretty sight it was to see them pass; stalwart, hardy-looking men with dark, weather-beaten faces; lithe, graceful boys clothed in skins; and tall, active women with resolute faces, not devoid of a comeliness which no veil concealed.

Wild hyacinths lined the paths and the sward was dotted with the vivid deep pink of Judas trees. Perhaps the investiture was timed to coincide with the New Year ceremony which, from time immemorial, has taken place in Persia on the spring equinox.

The ceremony described by Plutarch is intriguing, and the eating of 'turpentine-wood' sounds simply bizarre. The Greek is *terminthos*, and terebinth is indeed the commonest Greek form (with lentisk) of that family of plants. But Greek terebinth is *pistacia terebinthus*. Recall now that Iran (along with the plain of Gaziantep) lays claim to the best pistachios in the world, and that they grow beside the River Choaspes,[62] from which alone the king could drink the water,[63] and it seems more than a little likely that what the king actually did was to eat some figs and pistachios, and wash them down with a beaker of *ayran*, or *dugh*, the refreshing and healthful liquid yogurt popular in both Iran and Turkey.[64]

The goddess in whose sanctuary the investiture took place must certainly be Anahita, an Iranian deity who had taken over many of the traits and much of the iconography of the Babylonian Ishtar. If Anahita really did preside over the inauguration of the new king, this might provide some explanation of why the wife of Gushtasp in Zoroastrian tradition is said to be a Rumi (Byzantine Greek) called Nahid. It is notable that the mother of Darab in the *Shahnameh* is also called Nahid:[65] the new king Iskandar is not only of royal blood but the son of a goddess. Artaxerxes I seems to have had a particular fondness for Anahita, whom he celebrates also in his inscriptions, and whose temple he set up in Babylon.[66] He also instituted her worship in Elymais and at Ecbatana. It is, however, far from certain that this rite was current at the time of Xerxes' investiture, and one is further given pause by the knowledge that the religion of both Darius and Xerxes seems to be exclusively Mazdaean, with little role for any of the other Iranian gods; their successors were more accommodating (see Chapter 4). But no alternative suggestions are available for Xerxes' coronation, and the tradition is worth following through.

Various suggestions have been made for the location of Anahita's shrine at Pasargadae. Two plinths at the western end of the 'sacred enclosure' have been proposed as altars to Ahura Mazda and Anahita, but if this is so the absence of the third member of the triad, Mithra, is surprising.[67] Carsten Binder states without arguing the case that the building known as Zendan-e-Suleiman ('Prison of Solomon') was the investiture palace and thus also the shrine of Anahita.[68] David Stronach suggests that it might have been a repository for the king's regalia, which is not incompatible with the temple theory.[69] There seems at any rate to be no better candidate available. If it was the investiture building, it should have had the eternal fire of the Zoroastrians burning inside it; but Mary Boyce pointed out that such a fire would have been impossible to maintain except by carrying quantities of fuel up the high staircase every day.[70] If there was a flame, it was more likely a temporary one brought for the occasion.

The Zendan is a tall building comparable to the 'tower-temples' of Urartu. It has a better-preserved twin at Persepolis, the 'Qa'aba of Zoroaster', whose original function is likewise a mystery. Only one wall of the Zendan still stands, in which there are the remains of a door at a high level. A long staircase ascends from the ground to this door. One may picture the new king, accompanied by his courtiers and priests, ascending this staircase and disappearing from view into the chamber at the top. Here he receives the blessing of the goddess Anahita, patron of both wisdom and warfare, like Athena. He dons the robe of Cyrus the Founder, which has been stored here since Cyrus' death and burial nearby. He appears at the top of the steps, resplendent in the regalia of royalty and surrounded by the *farr* (the Persian royal glory) that glimmers at the shoulders of Persian kings – the glow from the flame burning within the chamber would accentuate this effect – to receive the acclaim of the crowds waiting below.

It would not surprise us to learn that the ceremony was followed by a feast. If the coronation coincided with *Now Ruz*, the Persian New Year festival, and perhaps also qualified as the king's 'official birthday', there were multiple reasons for feasting. Herodotus says that the king's birthday was always celebrated with a banquet.[71] Wine and musical instruments had been introduced by the legendary Jamshid. Tabari's *Commentary on the Qur'an*[72] lists the instruments which ought to be abjured, along with wine, in the name of Islam: they include the harp (*barbat*), long-necked guitar (*tanbur*), lute (*chang*), as well as accompanied singing. This gives a good guide to what was played in pre-Islamic Iran, and indeed all these are still part of the traditional repertory of Iranian music.

We know something about Persian feasts because a Greek author, Polyaenus, preserves an account of the dinner that was served to Alexander after his conquest of Persepolis, in accordance with a menu that was permanently inscribed on a bronze pillar along with other rules of dining and etiquette established by Cyrus. To begin with, the supplies required one thousand *artabae* of wheat flour. An *artaba* is a Persian measure equivalent to an Attic *medimnus*, conventionally translated as a bushel, or (for Herodotus) one bushel and three *choinikes*, a *choinix* being an Attic dry measure equivalent to half a gallon. If half a gallon might weigh about four pounds, or four loaves of bread of a modern size, we are looking at upwards of ten thousand loaves of bread for the king's dinner, which suggests quite a lot of guests. The remaining quantities are similarly vast: as much barley bread as wheat, ten *artabae* of salad, one-third of an *artaba* of mustard seed, a whole *artaba* of cumin. Things become easier to envisage with the livestock: 400 sheep as well as 300 lambs, 100 oxen, 30 horses, 400 geese, 300 turtles, 600 assorted small birds, 100 goslings, 30 deer. New calculations come into play with the drinks. Polyaenus writes 'Of milk, ten *maris*es (a *maris* contains ten Attic *choas*).' One *chous* is probably a gallon, so we are looking at 100 gallons of milk, the same of yoghurt (or *dugh*), 50 gallons of sweet wine, 100 gallons of sesame oil, 30 gallons of almond oil. There were 500 *marises* – which is 5,000 gallons – of wine, half palm wine and half made from grapes. Then he continues, 'of fluid honey a hundred square *palathae*, containing the weight of about ten *minae*'. (An Attic *mina* is 431 grams, an Aeginetan half as much again: on the assumption that Polyaenus was using Attic measures, that is 431 kilos of honey.) No wonder that, according to the story, Alexander ordered the menu pillar to be immediately destroyed, commenting that 'it was no advantage to a king to live in so luxurious a manner, for cowardice and dastardly were the certain consequences of luxury and dissipation'.[73] The Greek as usual managed to draw a moral from the contrast of oriental opulence and Greek hardiness and austerity; but one has to remember that ostentatious displays of wealth, in the Persian Empire as later among the Ptolemies (not to mention the Trobriand islanders with their potlatch ceremonies), were a way of establishing status and creating awe among the subjects.[74] When the Portuguese envoy Antonio De Gouvea visited Persia in the seventeenth century, the banquet he attended at the court of Allahvirdi Khan reminded him of the grandeur of the ancient Persian kings.[75]

The luxury described is sharply at odds with the austerity of diet that Xenophon attributes to the Persians, as distinct from the defeated Medes. Whether Xerxes indulged himself on this scale or not, his duties would not allow him to devote his next years to what medieval Persians called *razm o bazm* – 'fighting and feasting'. ('Fighting' here connotes not only warfare but hunting and sport.) His ennui is what later generations remembered – his search for 'a new pleasure' – but it is unlikely that he found one. The *razm* (in the sense of warfare) kept him too busy for the *bazm*.

THE INVENTOR OF CHESS?

A persistent legend, however, has made Xerxes the inventor of the game of chess.[76] Was this the 'new pleasure' he craved? The story seems to begin with the medieval writer Jacobus de Cessolis, whose *Liber de moribus hominum et officiis nobilium* (ca. 1300) was a best-seller over two centuries.[77] William Caxton's English version, *The Game and Playe of the Chesse*, was printed in 1475 and again in 1483. According to Jacobus, chess was invented by one Xerxes, who however was not our Xerxes but the tutor of the son of King Nebuchadnezzar of Babylon. This was taken up by Arthur Saul in his *The Famous Game of Chesseplay* (1614) where he wrote that the game 'hath been practised now 2227 years'. This would take us to 614 BC, a date which might fit Nebuchadnezzar (who acceded in 605 BC) but scarcely his son, and certainly not the Persian Xerxes. Perhaps Saul was confused by the slightly more plausible alternative legend that chess was introduced to the Western world by Indian ambassadors to the later Persian Sassanian king, Chosrow Anushirvan (Chosrow of the Immortal Soul).[78] The Indians challenged the king to work out the rules of the game by examining the board and the pieces; but it was Chosrow's vizier, Bozorjmehr, who by the application of thought and reasoning discovered the method of play, and then proceeded to confound the Indians by inventing, in turn, the game of backgammon and challenging them to work *that* one out.[79]

Certainly chess was popular by the end of the Sassanian period. It is referred to in the *Shatrang-namah* (*Book of Chess*) of the seventh century AD, as well as making an earlier appearance among the achievements of the boy king Ardashir (the founder of the Sassanian dynasty, AD 224–240) in the *Karnamag-e-Ardashir*, along with ball-play, horsemanship and hunting.[80] So, though Ardashir may have been an adept of the chessboard, sadly we cannot envisage the young Xerxes whiling away the hours with black and white artificial armies. A greater military challenge was in store for him.

CHAPTER TWO

The Persian Empire

Saith Xerxes the king: By the favour of Ahuramazda these are the countries of which I was king outside Persia; I ruled them; they bore me tribute. The law that was mine, that held them (firm/stable): Media, Elam, Arachosia, Armenia, Drangiana, Parthia, Aria, Bactria, Sogdiana, Chorasmia, Babylonia, Assyria, Sattagydia, Sardis, Egypt, Ionians, those who dwell by the sea and those who dwell across the sea, the Maka people, Arabia, Gandara, Indus, Cappadocia, Dahae, Scythians who drink haoma, Pointed-Cap Scythians, Skudra, the Akaufaka people,[1] Libyans, Carians, Nubians.
                 XPh 13–28 (Kuhrt I. 304–05)

THE EXTENT OF THE EMPIRE

The ceremonies and celebrations of accession completed, Xerxes set about the business of governing his empire. The Persian Empire had been founded by Cyrus the Great, who in 559 BC became king of Persis (equivalent to the modern Fars province in Iran). After the death of Nebuchadnezzar of Babylon in 562, and a series of short-lived kings, Nabonidus ascended the Babylonian throne in 556 and entered into an alliance with Cyrus for a campaign against Media. Cyrus captured the Median capital, Ecbatana, in 550 and incorporated it within his now enlarged kingdom, transferring its wealth to Persis. (The Greeks, however, continued to use the name 'Medes' for his enlarged kingdom of Persia.) After Media fell, King Croesus of Lydia saw an opportunity, or made a pre-emptive strike, and launched an attack on

Cyrus; but Cyrus repelled him and sacked the Lydian capital of Sardis in 547. At the same time he obtained control over the Greek population of western Asia Minor, who had arrived during the Bronze Age and settled in Miletus and elsewhere. In 539 Cyrus turned on Babylon and added that too to his empire, as well as Syria. He also extended his power into central Asia as far as the River Jaxartes (Syr Darya).

It was Cyrus who created the system of satrapies, provinces and regions ruled by a governor or satrap for the Great King. His was not the first empire in the Near East by a long way: there had been empires in Mesopotamia since the third millennium, and both the conquered Assyria and the region of Elam had considerable influence on Achaemenid style. But the empire of Cyrus became the most extensive of them all. As he says in the Book of Chronicles, 'all the kingdoms of the earth . . . were given me'.[2] We know little of the means by which the empire grew, though Cyrus met his death in 530 while campaigning against the Massagetae, a Scythian tribe in central Asia, who were threatening the Jaxartes frontier from the vast steppes that lie to the north of that green river. Cyrus' outposts on this frontier were refurbished by Alexander, who later made this the natural limit of his conquests when he founded Alexandria-the-Furthest (Khojend).

Cyrus' son Cambyses added Egypt to the empire; it was under his successor, Xerxes' father Darius I (the Great), that the empire reached its largest extent, incorporating (for how long a period is uncertain) Sind and Punjab, as well as Thrace and the northern parts of mainland Greece, including Macedon from about 512. A text found in four copies, two inscribed on gold tablets and two on silver ones, from the *apadana* (audience hall) at Persepolis, proclaims:

> Darius, the great king, king of kings, king of countries, an Achaemenid. King Darius proclaims: this is the kingdom which I hold, from the Saca who are beyond Sogdiana, from there as far as Kush, from the Indus as far as Sardis, which Ahura Mazda, the greatest of the gods, bestowed on me.[3]

Darius' accession in 522 represented a turning point in the history of the empire.[4] Herodotus represents the king and nobles, after their successful coup against the false Bardiya, engaging in a discussion of the most suitable form of government, including candidates as improbable as Greek-style radical democracy. The scene has generally been dismissed as fiction, but it is not unlikely that some debate took place as to how the empire should be ruled from here on. Not least, the introduction of writing in the form

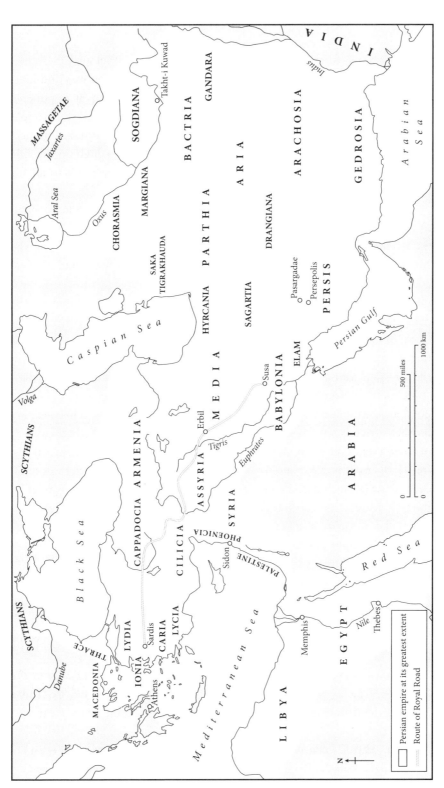

Map 1 The Persian Empire

of inscriptions, in the wedge-based cuneiform script developed in Sumer, denotes a change in public relations. Most of the population was undoubtedly illiterate, relying on a scribal class for administration: it is possible (as noted earlier) that even the kings could not read, though Ashurbanipal in Assyria, in the seventh century, had prided himself on his ability.[5] Writing, however few could actually read it, or even see it high on the cliff at Bisutun, represented a 'loud-hailer' (in Sancisi-Weerdenburg's term) for the regime.

In the Bisutun inscription Darius[6] laid claim to an empire that extended to India and to central Asia beyond the Oxus, into modern Uzbekistan as far as the Saca lands, westward to Ethiopia and to the shores of the Mediterranean (Sardis is 50 miles from the Mediterranean, and Darius' control certainly reached the sea). All told, twenty-three territories (*dahyu*, plural *daheyawa*) came under his dominion[7] – the same number as the delegations depicted on the apadana reliefs at Persepolis. But other inscriptions, of both Darius and Xerxes, have different numbers of territories, and further names are provided by the Persepolis tablets.[8] Cyrus the Younger in the fourth century BC told his Greek supporters 'my father's kingdom stretches to the south where men cannot live because of the heat, and to the north they cannot do so because of the cold; and all that lies in between my brother's friends hold as satraps'.[9] According to the Book of Esther,[10] a work of fiction set in the reign of Xerxes, the Great King controlled 127 provinces, from India to Ethiopia. Herodotus has a more realistic list of twenty satrapies, each of which includes several regions.[11] The Alexander historians refer to thirty-four different 'satrapies'; but these variable numbers of 'lands' seem to fall under a small number of 'mega-satrapies', with capitals at Sardis, Babylon, Memphis, Ecbatana, Pasargadae, Bactra and Arachoti, which were all administered by royal princes.

The kings also sent out explorers to survey lands that were not yet theirs: Darius sent Scylax to India and Xerxes sent Sataspes to Africa.[12] The latter, like Sir Walter Ralegh, was given a last chance to escape a sentence of death by a great discovery; but when Sataspes came back, Xerxes did not believe his account of what he had seen, and had him impaled anyway.

An ancient Persian text, the *Videvdad* or *Vendidad* (*The Law against the Demons*),[13] has a rather different list of sixteen lands created by Ahura Mazda. Identification is sometimes problematic but a number are clear:

> Ahura Mazda spake unto Spitama Zarathustra, saying: I have made every
> land dear to its dwellers, even though it had no charms whatever in it: had

I not made every land dear to its dwellers, even though it had no charms whatever in it, then the whole living world would have invaded the Airyana Vaejo [i.e. Eranvezh, the ancestral land of the Iranians in central Asia].

The god goes on to divide Eranvezh 'by the good river Daitya' (later, the Araxes) into the following provinces: Sogdia, Merv, Balkh, Nisaya, Haraiva (Areia or Hari-Rud), 'Vaekereta' (Kabul), Urva (said to be Tus), Hyrcania (Gorgan), Harahvaiti (Arachosia), Hetumant (Helmand), Ragha (Rayy), Kakhra (unidentified), Varena (possibly the Elburz), the Seven Rivers (Punjab, though *punj/panj* means 'five'), and the 'land by the floods of the Rangha, where the headless people live'.[14] The last is clearly mythical and is situated somewhere by the encircling river that the Greeks called Ocean. This Persian tradition must be the origin of the report by Darius' emissary Scylax of Caryanda about these monstrous folk, who reappear also in Ctesias' account of the men 'whose heads do grow beneath their shoulders'.

Each of the provinces is also characterised by a physical disadvantage or moral flaw, created by the evil spirit 'Angra-Mainyu, who is all death': these include the river-serpents in Eramezh, cattle-flies in Sogdia, unbelief in Nisaya, mosquitoes in Areia, pride in Urva, burial of the dead in Arachosia (as opposed to exposure), witchcraft in Helmand, burning of the dead in Kakhra and cold winters in Ragha.

The *Vendidad* is subject to the problem common to all Zoroastrian literature, that the MSS date from no earlier than the ninth century AD, and the works were almost certainly not written down until the later Sassanian period (sixth century AD).[15] But these religious texts were faithfully preserved, in their highly archaic dialect, from earliest times, by continual oral recitation. It is thus reasonable to suppose that the book contains information that would have been acceptable in the fifth century BC. It is notable that the lands listed in the *Vendidad* are all in eastern Iran – Media and Khorasan. Persis/Fars is not mentioned (though Darmesteter hazards that Urva might be Isfahan). Cyrus was the first to incorporate Persis within the empire; to traditional Iranians, not least the Magi whose tribal centre was Media, Achaemenid Persis was never really part of their world. The advance to Persis is alluded to in the *Vendidad*, when Yima, 'the good shepherd' (another name for the culture hero Jamshid),

Stepped forward, southwards, to meet the sun . . . And Yima made the earth grow larger by one third than it was before, and there came flocks and herds of men, at his will and wish, as many as he wished.[16]

He went on to lay out a *vara*, with streets and houses, rivers, birds, trees, seeds, sheep and oxen – in short 'a paradise'.

Darius presents a new vision of the Persian Empire in his palace at Persepolis, not just Iranian but multi-national. The magnificent relief of the tribute bearers at Persepolis depicts the inhabitants of all parts of the empire in their distinctive garb, bearing their particular gifts of tribute, from Bactrian camels to honeycombs. On the northern royal tomb at Persepolis there are again tribute bearers, here helpfully labelled in three languages, and including (there are some gaps) one each of the following: Persians, Medes, Elamites, Parthians, Areians, Bactrians, Sogdians, Chorasmians . . . Drangianians, Arachosians, Sattagydians, Gandarans, Indians and the *homa*-drinking Saca. These then are the Iranian-speaking peoples, the Saca being specified as those who share the sacred custom of drinking *homa*. The bottom row has one each of: Pointed Hat Saca, Babylonians, Assyrians, Arabs, Egyptians, Armenians, Cappadocians, Sardians, Ionians, Scythians across the sea, Thracians, *petasos*-wearing Ionians, Libyans and Nubians. On the base are men of Maka (possibly Makran) and Caria.

The much more extensive display of racial types on the staircase to the apadana unfortunately lacks captions, but the same attention to clothing that specifies the pointed hats of the Scythians and the wide floppy hats of some of the Ionians enables us to identify many of the tributary peoples. Curiously, there seem to be no Jews, even though the Jewish people had been returned from their captivity in Babylon by Cyrus: but Paul Kriwaczek has suggested that one group, usually identified as Lydians, may be Jews wearing the distinctive long locks of hair around their ears.

Not all the groups can be identified with certainty, but among the more secure are: the pointed-hat Scythians, bringing a horse, gold bracelets, rolls of cloth and trousers; Bactrians with vessels and a two-humped camel; Egyptians bringing a bull; Armenians with a horse and a vase; Cilicians, carrying vessels, tanned skins, clothing and two rams;[17] Elamites with bows, daggers, a lioness and two lion cubs; Scythians from the region of Samarkand, bringing a dagger, bracelets, axes and a horse; Phoenicians with gold, flower vases, vessels, armlets and a two-horse chariot; Indians with unidentifiable offerings suspended from the shoulders in baskets, plus a donkey and axes; Arabs with cloth and a dromedary; people of Punt with a mountain goat and a chariot; Ethiopians bringing a giraffe; Babylonians wearing tall pointed fez-like hats with long tassels and bringing folded textiles and a bull; Ionians bearing the puzzling spherical objects that have been interpreted as balls of wool, but which to my mind recall the legend in the *Alexander Romance* that

Alexander put a stop to the paying by the Greeks of a tribute of golden eggs to Persia: the writer of this story had seen the reliefs and been as puzzled as we are before deciding that the round objects must be eggs.[18]

No fewer than four delegations carry golden armlets of the kind recovered in the 1870s in the Oxus Treasure; such adornments were evidently particularly prized at the Persian court.

What did it mean for the king to claim the overlordship of all these peoples, both Iranian and non-Iranian? Can we really imagine that delegations arrived with all these gifts, giraffes, bulls and camels, trekking for thousands of miles across desert and plain to fill a zoo of which there is no trace? Surely the giraffes did not simply meet a swift end in the hunting parks, like those that in later centuries were brought to Rome to die for the pleasure of the Roman people. It is better to interpret the reliefs as symbolic, representing the distinctive products of every region and symbolising the variety and extent of the Persian dominion. One thinks of those eighteenth-century paintings that depict the four continents, each with its presiding goddess surrounded by every animal and bird characteristic of that continent in a picturesque but impossible assemblage.[19]

According to Herodotus:

> During the reigns of Cyrus and Cambyses there was no such thing as a fixed amount of tribute, but the various peoples brought donations. Because he established the tribute system and other related systems too, the Persians describe Darius as a retailer (since he put a price on everything).[20]

According to this account, Darius' reliefs are a record of a system of tribute that he himself had just made obsolete, and converted it into a cash contribution. But Herodotus' claim is not tenable. Recent study of the archives in Babylon by Michael Jursa makes clear that tribute continued to be collected in much the same way both before and after the accession of Darius, and in monetary form; where Darius did make a difference was in an increased demand for corvée labour for military purposes.[21] The accusation that Darius was greedy for cash, rather than settling for giraffes and honeycombs, may be an implied criticism of the increasing rapacity of the Athenian Empire in the second half of the fifth century, when Herodotus was writing.

It was the first time in history that such a wide area had come under the rule of a central power; the Assyrian Empire had been on a small scale by comparison, and the example of China was unknown to the peoples of western

Asia. A remarkable feature of the Persian Empire is its toleration – within limits.[22] Although cruelty was used as a political instrument,[23] there was no wholesale repression of subject peoples in the way of, say, the Roman Empire or the Soviet bloc. Although the style of Achaemenid art has much in common with that of the predecessor empire of Assyria, it is notable that it never depicts battles or scenes of cruel punishment. Peaceful scenes of tribute-bearing stand side by side with representations of the king wrestling with the demons of Evil; though there are bound prisoners on the Bisutun relief, and one trampled enemy, there are no rows of impaled bodies as in Ashurbanipal's reliefs, or even clashing warriors as in the wall paintings of Egypt.[24] Sassanian art develops this trend even further, concentrating on scenes of hunting, rarely battle – though the portrayal of the humiliation of the Roman emperor Valerian by Shapur I is an exception.

Revolts there were, but they were few, though Warwick Ball perhaps underplays their significance. The lack of information about any such revolt in Bactria or India may be simply the result of lack of sources; certainly the Indian provinces had fallen away by the time of Alexander's arrival in 326 BC. Darius had to deal with revolts in Babylon, Scythia and Ionia; the Greeks were a thorn in Xerxes' flesh for all his reign. Egypt revolted in 350 and 343 and required invasion. But Alexander's invasion was seen by Darius III to begin with as simply another small local revolt, easy to put down. Persia's central power base was a vast enough region to withstand such shocks on the fringes. That is why in the end the failure of Xerxes' Greek campaign, though it meant so much to the Greeks, may have been of little importance to Persia. Expansion ceased but the long reign of Xerxes' successor, Artaxerxes I, was a time of consolidation. Like America in Iraq, Persia lost the war but increased its influence.

Even if the tribute reliefs, with their processions bringing everything from camels to kudus and balls of wool to honeycombs, can hardly depict a historical reality, they nonetheless evoke an empire where people might travel vast distances to deliver their goods. In Persepolis they might mingle with fellow subjects from the far ends of the earth. The Persian Royal Road from Sardis to Susa was famous for its good communications: according to Herodotus, who must have had access to documentary information, the distance of 13,500 *stades*, or 450 *parasangs*, about 2,400 kilometres or 1,490 miles, was broken by no fewer than 111 staging-posts, and could be covered in ninety days.[25] By comparison, the riders for the American Pony Express, which operated from 1860 to 1861, could cover the distance from St Joseph, Missouri, to Sacramento, California – a distance of approximately

1,900 miles – in ten days. They relied on 184 stations as close as ten miles apart where they could change horses; besides their mail bag they carried nothing but a Bible, a water-pouch and two guns. Persian postmen must have proceeded much more slowly, largely on foot if they only made an average of 16 miles a day. As well as the royal road, many other routes ran through the empire, linking the centre with the outlying provinces, and they were both passable and safe.

It was an empire without cities, except in the Greek west, though Bactria bore the puzzling sobriquet of 'Land of a Thousand Cities'. Armenia had only villages, as Xenophon makes clear in the *Anabasis*, and the same was true of Cissia (Elam) according to Philostratus.[26] The population consisted largely of *autourgoi*, small farmers, as Aelian tells us.[27] Aelian also says that both Persians and Indians are 'brave and free, but idle in commerce'.[28] There were no market towns of the kind that developed in the west.[29] Predominantly the lands of the Great King consisted of great estates. In Sassanian and medieval Iran, it was the lords of these estates, the *dehqans* (by a strange mutation, in modern Persian the word means 'peasant'), who controlled their lands and even the cities.[30] In ancient Persia, all wealth and all authority derived from and returned to the king; the estate owners were no more than intermediaries in this process of tribute-collection. The surplus became a hoard.

THE ECONOMY

Like other Near Eastern empires, the Persian Empire had a highly centralised economy, resembling the palace economies of Minoan Crete as well as Mesopotamia. Wealth came in to the king and was distributed according to need or the king's pleasure. Although it presented itself as functioning on the basis of *baji*, gifts in kind,[31] the king's income consisted, besides tribute, of taxes and tolls.

Strabo writes:

Polycritus [he surely means Polyclitus of Larissa, the Alexander historian, *FGrH* 128 F 3] says that in Susa [does he mean Persepolis?] each one of the kings built for himself on the acropolis a separate habitation, treasure-houses, and storage places for what tributes they exacted, as memorials of his administration; and that they exacted silver from the people on the sea-board, and from the people in the interior such things as each country produced, so that they also received dyes, drugs, hair, or wool, or something else of the kind, and likewise cattle; and that the king who organised the separate tributes was Darius called the Long-armed [the epithet is usually attached to Artaxerxes I: does he mean Darius I?].[32]

But as 'Aristotle' describes,[33] in a more sophisticated account, satrapal income is of six kinds: from land, from local products, from trade, from dues, from herds, and 'other' (including poll tax and craftsman tax). What went to the satraps went in due course to the king, so what 'Aristotle' says applies also to the royal treasury.

On the reliefs, all this variety of income is symbolised by the second category, local products. Much of the exchange must indeed have been in kind. Pay, too, as we learn from the Persepolis Fortification Tablets, consisted mainly of generous supplies of 'rations' – mainly grain, wine and sheep.[34] Yet the Persian treasuries at Sardis, Susa and Persepolis were stuffed full with gold and silver; at Persepolis there was so much when Alexander removed it that he had to commission 1,000 camels to carry it away. Silver was also used to pay workers, and there were conversion rates for commuting payments of, say, sheep into coin.[35] It is indeed difficult to see how a worker could make use of pay of 'one sheep per day'[36] or 30 quarts of flour per month, let alone 'one-ninth of a sheep per month';[37] such quantities would have to be 'banked' and drawn on in small amounts. There was a sophisticated system of letters of credit available to those who travelled on the empire's business, and perhaps this extended also to the hoi polloi: the value of all their sheep would be supported by the gold in the treasury. Tribute, too, may have been credited to local accounts of the king and looked after by the satrap:[38] so Alexander got his first injection of wealth from capturing the treasury at Sardis.

The wealth of the empire consisted of bullion, often poured in molten form into large clay jars, but also coined. Most of it never circulated, any more than the gold in Fort Knox circulates. Although Greece and Ionia coined money, most parts of the empire did not. Herodotus (3.96) refers to tribute in coin, and Strabo (11.13.8) distinguished between *argyrikon telos*, monetary tribute, and payments in kind.[39] Where coinage was not in use, e.g. in Judaea and Babylonia, tribute was collected by the satraps in weighed metal, and some complained of having to mortgage their land or sell their children as slaves to raise the necessary specie.[40] So the treasury at Persepolis was full to bursting with precious metals and coin. However, at Dascyleion, the treasury bullae are evidence of a storehouse full of agricultural products as well as silver and raw materials.[41]

Because there was no extensive circulation of cash, historians have often accused the Persian Empire of 'economic stagnation'. In a proper capitalist system, it was supposed, all that wealth should be reinvested and used for the creation of more wealth. The 'Asiatic mode of production' (as Marxists call it) allowed no investment, no growth; all wealth was sucked to the centre, and limited amounts were disbursed in rations in a centralised economy. The accusation is surely misguided, driven by the propaganda that began with Alexander's historians who regarded the Persian Empire as 'ripe for overthrow'. (It should, however, have been more to the honour of Alexander if the Persians had been formidable opponents, and not what Sir Walter Ralegh wonderfully described as the subjects of 'a May-game king [who came] into the field, encumbered with a most unnecessary train of strumpets . . . and for the most part so effeminate and so rich in gold and in garments, as the same could not but have encouraged the nakedest nation of the world against them'.)[42]

If coinage was in limited circulation, still it had its uses, both for paying mercenaries and for purposes of trade. The exceptional purity of Persian gold *darics* was famous,[43] but they functioned more as ingots in practical sizes than as actual coinage.[44] (The monthly pay of a mercenary soldier was one gold daric in 401 BC.)[45] Why did the Persians mint them? Lydians and after them Greeks (especially the state of Corinth and Aegina) had been setting the example by using coinage for trade since at least the middle of the sixth century. As Richard Seaford remarks, 'even if we knew that coinage had been introduced for a specific use, say paying Greek mercenaries, it is difficult to see how payment with small pieces of precious metal (as opposed to, say, food) would be generally acceptable unless those pieces also had fairly general exchange-value in a wide area'.[46] Strabo comments on the limited availability of coined money:[47] gold and silver objects were regarded as better for gift-giving. In the fifth century, and in the heartland, barter was just as common; Xenophon also refers to riverine populations who brought to Babylon millstones to exchange for food.[48] (The shop's cash register must have been enormous.) However, the absence of trade in the Persian Empire may be exaggerated by Herodotus out of a characteristic Greek prejudice against it: for example, he tells us that there were no marketplaces in the Persian Empire, which is certainly untrue.[49] By 400 the use of coin was much more common, at least in the west, since the survivors of the Ten Thousand, whom Xenophon led back to the sea after their participation in the failed revolt of Cyrus the Younger against Artaxerxes II, were able to buy supplies in markets that had been opened up by Tissaphernes.[50]

Where did the gold come from? Herodotus told a story that it was dug up by giant ants in Bactria, near a place called Caspatyrus,[51] which may have been

Peshawar. Caspatyrus was where Scylax of Caryanda started his voyage in which he observed the headless men, so this tall story may originate with him. (One of these Greek writers perhaps confused the word for a marmot [in modern Persian, *mūsh-e-khormā*] with the Greek word for ant, *myrmex*.) Gold is by its nature hard to tie down to particular seams, but the mineral wealth of central Asia seems the most obvious source; once Cyrus had crossed the Oxus, he had access to the mines of Tajikistan, and his agents could pan for gold in the River Zarafshan that runs by Samarkand. The Greeks called it the Polytimetus ('very valuable' river), while alluvial gold is also found in the upper reaches of the Oxus itself.[52] Silver too is mined in central Asia. Lydia, which was said by the Greeks to have been the first region to mint coinage (though in fact the Greeks did it first), because of the gold-bearing River Pactolus which runs through Sardis, actually produced mainly electrum coinage, as did the neighbouring island of Lesbos. Pure gold and silver came later, though no doubt the legendary wealth of Sardis ('as rich as Croesus') was a bonus for Cyrus when he defeated the Lydian king in his ill-advised attack on Persia.

An Imperial Style?

Many empires impose their style throughout their dominions. The British Empire is a classic example. Railways stations look much the same from St Pancras to Calcutta, and the villas of Simla might be in the Home Counties. Robert Byron waxes eloquent on the shock of 'Hindu Gothic'.[53] One of the most inclusive of empires was the Roman Empire, with its grant of universal citizenship (from AD 121), the creation of colonies and the spread of modified Roman architectural styles from end to end of the empire. Ancient Egypt, too, imposed its architectural style on neighbouring Nubia. The Moghul Empire was held together by its Persianate culture and common language, though a Moghul miniature is not hard to distinguish from a medieval Persian one, and the flamboyance of the Moghul emperors in dress and court had no parallel in Isfahan or Bukhara. American imperialism is expressed in the universality of Coca-Cola and Nike trainers, even in the countries that hate America most, such as Iran.

The Persian Empire, by contrast, did not export the style of Persepolis beyond the borders of Persis.[54] In this it more resembles the Ottoman Empire: an empire held together by religion (though its European dominions were mostly Christian), it naturally had mosques and madrassahs in every town, but the style of Edirne is unlike that of Cairo, and its languages were multifarious. Constantinople was the eye of the Ottoman Empire but in magnificence Damascus or Cairo would hardly yield to it. Persepolis, magnificent though it is, was not a model or cynosure for all the inhabitants of the Persian Empire; indeed, the Greeks had hardly heard of it and never mention it before the expedition of Alexander, regarding Susa as the centre of the Great King's power.

Nevertheless, there is a sense in which the existence of the Persian Empire was the enabling condition of cultural, including architectural and even literary, development in the furthest parts of the empire. Josef Wiesehöfer proposes, plausibly, that elites across the empire welcomed the stability that universal rule brought with it[55] (though a fringe ruler like Polycrates might have disagreed with this assessment when he hung on his cross). The statement is a bold one, and there is extremely little evidence for the reception of Persian rule in the more easterly satrapies such as Bactria. But both Greeks and Jews, the most profuse in literature of the peoples of the empire, defined themselves in important ways by their relationship to the Persian Empire.[56] Even in the early centuries AD, the Greek novelists were still using the ancient Persian Empire as the stage-set for the endless Mediterranean wanderings of their heroes and heroines. The first best-seller in history, the *Tale of Ahiqar*, set in Babylon before Cyrus' conquest, achieved its circulation in the fifth century AD through the greater ease of communication encouraged by the Persian Empire in the fifth century BC. It describes the fall and rehabilitation of the wise minister Ahiqar, who even advises the Pharaoh, and builds him a flying machine, but ends by boring his nephew so comprehensively with his sage advice that the nephew explodes.[57] One of the earliest pieces of papyrus evidence is an Aramaic papyrus from Elephantine in Egypt. The use of Aramaic – not Persian – as the lingua franca of the empire facilitated the spread of stories like this, as well as official communication. What is in question is facilitation, not domination.

Persians did not commonly settle, apart from the major satraps, in other parts of the empire, though there is more evidence for wandering Persians now than there was when A. D. Momigliano wrote his classic study.[58] Even the satraps' palaces are surprisingly hard to track down archaeologically. The best of our evidence, as for much of this chapter's topics, comes from Asia Minor and the Greek borderlands. The satrapal palace at Sardis was more or less a replica, on a smaller scale, of the Great King's court in Parsa, as descriptions by Xenophon and Plutarch make clear.[59] The palace at Dascyleion, described by Xenophon,[60] has been identified, and there is evidence of that at Celaenae, described below in the section on gardens.[61] Xenophon[62] also refers to the palace of Asidases in the Caicus valley. Arrian[63] refers to a garden and orchard complex at Mesambria, which is probably Bushire on the Persian Gulf. Some 200 stades further on was Taoce on the River Granis, and 200 stades inland from there was a Persian royal residence.[64] Taoce is no doubt Tauka of the Treasury Tablets,[65] where there were hundreds of *kurtaš*, or foreign labourers, summoned from Thrace, Lycia and Cappadocia, as well as free peasants and landowners. One of the tablets, for example, states:

> 18 *marriš* of wine, procured by Huçaya, were received by Bagabadush, the 'travelling companion'. He gave it to 547 Egyptian workers. They were on their way to Tauka. He carried a sealed document for Bagapana [the satrap of Elam]. 21st year.[66]

The presence of the Persian-named Megabyxus (*bagabakhsha*, 'freed by God') as a eunuch priest of Artemis at Ephesus is also suggestive of Persian presence in the far west of the empire; but it is hard to multiply examples.

Evidence of Achaemenid cultural or political influence in the western empire is generally slight.[67] One area that seems to have something in common with the homeland is Lycia, always in equipoise between Persian and Athenian hegemony.[68] The rock-cut tombs recall those of Naqsh-e-Rostam, while the house tombs also have something in common with that of Cyrus at Pasargadae, and one fourth-century sarcophagus at Xanthos is carved with a near-replica of the lion-attacking-bull motif from Persepolis. The Payava sarcophagus from Xanthos, now in the British Museum, bears a relief of an audience scene in the Persian style. On the Nereid Monument from Xanthos, also in the British Museum, bearers bring offerings of Persian-style trousers with built-in feet. Furthermore, the bilingual inscribed pillar at Xanthos tells of a local dignitary named Harpagus; not the Persian general of the fifth century, for the pillar is a century later, but surely a descendant, or at least a Lycian with a Median name.[69] The coins, too, of the dynast Kuprlli bear Iranian motifs.[70] Persians were settling in Lycia, which displays a fascinating merging of Greek and oriental styles. Greeks perceived Lycia as somewhat exotic and associated it particularly with stories of legendary prophets who could foretell the future. Since Herodotus prided the Greeks on their superior ability to interpret oracles, it would be ironic if the technique of foretelling the future actually originated in Persia (though probably Babylon is as important an influence).

A few tombs also display Achaemenid styles in the western provinces, indicating settlement by Persians or at least Persian stylistic dominance. One of the most striking is that known as Taşkule outside Foça (ancient Phocaea): a unique monolithic structure with a tomb chamber hollowed out of the solid rock, it carries some typically Achaemenid mouldings and may include the remains of a fire pit. Probably dating from the years 540–480, it seems likely to have been the tomb of a satrap or other local dignitary.[71]

There is a relief from the site of Dascyleion, now in the Istanbul Museum, which is thoroughly Achaemenid in style; while in the Çanakkale Museum there is a carved sarcophagus from Celaenae (Altıkılaç) depicting a Persian hunter, which would not be out of place in central Persia.[72] This dates from the fourth century BC, while the earlier, sixth-century 'Polyxena' sarcophagus in the same museum (found at Kızöldün in 1994) is in an archaic Greek style that has prompted some observers to comparisons with the work of Eric Gill. If it is possible to base a trend on two examples, one might see an increasing dominance of Persian style in this region after the end of the wars of the fifth century, which left Persia holding the balance of power between the warring Greek states. The powerful satraps Pharnabazus and Tissaphernes perhaps made a more permanent mark on the region than their sixth-century predecessors: Xerxes' war was not without results for the eastern fringe of his empire, and Persian style may have been quite noticeable in the age of Xenophon.

Other tombs displaying Achaemenid elements include the Karaburun and Kizilbel tombs near Elmalı, decorated with paintings in a strikingly Persian style,[73] and the pyramid tomb.[74] One wonders what the painting of Darius' bridge on the Bosphorus, dedicated by the architect Mandrocles in his home island of Samos,[75] looked like. While many tomb types seem to reflect a local (Dusinberre calls it 'autonomous') tradition, like the tumuli of Lydia, small finds such as cups and jewellery are generally more Achaemenid in style.[76]

Further east, the Achaemenid mark is more pronounced. Achaemenid reliefs have been found at Çatbaşı köyü near Senköy, not far from Antakya: there are several seated or standing figures of gods, and four of them show the 'king' worshipping a winged solar disc. The reliefs are carved on standing stones in a grove of karst pinnacles like miniature fairy chimneys; though they are on private farmland, which the workmen take a break from their pruning to show you, it is easy to see why this numinous spot would have been felt as a suitable place for devotion.

Still earlier, and further east, the capital of the Luwian king of Purundu (seventh–sixth century) at Meydancıkkale in Cilicia was taken over in the Persian period as a fort and administrative centre: the fortifications were rebuilt, the gate was reinforced by walls, and the city's name inscribed in Aramaic at the entrance. From Cilicia to Lydia, inscriptions make clear that the region is under Persian rule. Often bilingual in local languages, the common factor is the Aramaic version.[77]

In the west, without doubt, the Greek style is paramount. The emergence of Greek temple architecture is commonly taken as beginning with the creation of the monumental temple of Hera on Samos. The earliest structures belong to the eighth and the seventh centuries BC, but in about 570 BC the architect Rhoecus was engaged to erect a much larger structure, this time in full-blown Ionic style. The temple may date from the period after the rise to power of Polycrates as tyrant, about 535 BC. Polycrates used his powerful fleet to try to play off the Egyptian pharaoh Amasis aginst Darius I of Persia, but eventually the Persian satrap lured the tyrant into his clutches, and Polycrates was crucified. This temple was the first of the great Ionic temples of the Greek world. Samos was of course outside the Persian Empire at this period – though not beyond its sphere of influence – and the temple's construction cannot be attributed to Persian encouragement. This temple was quickly followed by the construction of the first classical temple of Artemis at Ephesus, a few miles away on the Asian mainland. Like Rhoecus and Theodorus, Artemis' architects, Chersiphron and Metagenes, were Greeks, from Cnossos in Crete. Building was begun in 560, in the reign of the Lydian king Croesus, but was interrupted by the Persian conquest. Pliny tells us that it was 120 years in the building, which would imply a completion in 440, when Persian rule was stable and created the conditions for conspicuous expenditure.

Through such magnificent structures Greek craftsmen acquired a reputation for their artistic skills in stone-working. Greeks are found among the craftsmen and the supervisors at Persepolis. One of the Fortification Tablets (number 1771) is even written in Greek.[78] An architect, Mandrocles, as well as a Phocaean sculptor, Telephanes, are known to have worked at Persepolis.[79] Some of these stone-workers may have been imported especially, but others may have been resident for some time following deportations in the 490s.[80] Their presence raises the question of possible Greek influence on the architecture of Xerxes' buildings, about which there is controversy (see Chapter 5).

In Judaea Cyrus' conquest of Babylon occasioned the return of the Jews from exile and the rebuilding of the Temple in Jerusalem, which however did not begin in earnest until about 520. Apart from this, no architectural work can be identified from the period in Judaea.

THE PEOPLES OF THE EMPIRE: GREEKS

When King Xerxes was entertained by the father of Democritus, he
left instructors there, from whom, while still a boy, he learned theology
and astronomy.

Diogenes Laertius 9.34

Two literate peoples have left us the most extensive records of what it was
like to live in the Persian Empire: Greeks and Jews. It may seem paradoxical
to speak of Achaemenid literature. Surely there is nothing beyond the few
inscribed utterances of the Great Kings? Yet when we consider what literature was written in the area covered by the Persian Empire, we come to realise
that many of the early Greek authors, including Herodotus, are Xerxian
authors. It is from their writings, and those of the Jews, that we learn most
of what we know about Persia, and both Greeks and Jews defined themselves, in a certain sense, in relation to Persia.[81] It was the Persian Empire,
the *pax Persica*, that facilitated the spread of stories and ideas.[82] Aramaic, as
the lingua franca of administration, also became an important medium of
communication and for the circulation of stories like the *Tale of Ahiqar*.
Few of antiquity's other best-sellers can be traced back as early as the fifth
century, but the cultural orbit defined by the Persian Empire became the
field of circulation of, for example, *Kalila wa Dimna*, and even the Greek
Life of Aesop, to say nothing of the *Alexander Romance* that focuses on the
destruction and reinvention of the empire.

Xerxes himself knew some Greek authors. The oracles of Onomacritus
were recited to him by their author in person,[83] presumably through an interpreter. And his familiarity with Homer is evident from his actions at Troy
and the Hellespont (see Chapter 5).[84] There was even a 'Persian version' of
the Trojan War story, elements of which are preserved in Ctesias.[85] In this,
Memnon led the Assyrians (not the Ethiopians) as allies to Troy. The Persians,
as successors to the Assyrian Empire, saw themselves as successors of Troy
as well. Greeks felt the same. After the Persian War, Simonides too saw the
conflict in terms of Greeks versus Trojans.

Of literature as such in Persian we can say little. Herodotus has usually
been thought to have made use of documents from Persian archives, for
example for his satrapy list, the description of the road system and the catalogue of the troops of Xerxes, but more recent scholarship is more sceptical.[86] Whether such documents existed or not, they were not the sum of
Persian writings. The Book of Esther tells us that when the king could not

sleep, he asked to be read to from the βασιλικαὶ δίφθεραι,[87] the books or ledgers of the kings: the Persian translation of the Greek phrase would be *Shahnameh*.[88] Lucian too refers to 'the annals of the Persians and Assyrians'.[89] Dinon of Colophon[90] recorded that the Persians had epic poems, including one about Cyrus, and the later writer Aelian went so far as to state that there was a Persian translation of Homer, though he may be confusing this with the equally startling statement by Dio Chrysostom that the Indians had translated Homer.[91] Alexander certainly heard songs and tales recited at the Persian court, notably that of Zariadres.[92]

The existence of Persian royal archives in Babylon is also indicated by the First Book of Esdras,[93] and indeed some fragments have survived. On Xerxes' annals are also mentioned in the Book of Esther, and in several passages of Herodotus. During the campaign Xerxes has his scribes make notes on the composition of his army, and to take note of any commander who does noteworthy service in battle, so that they can be added to 'the list of the king's benefactors'.[94] The Book of Malachi took it as natural that a 'book of remembrance' should be composed to record the names of 'them that feared the Lord'.[95] Most of the stories in Ctesias must come from such writings, or else from oral telling.[96] We should not doubt that stories circulated freely across national and linguistic boundaries.[97] Arthur Christensen's theory that Herodotus, Ctesias and Xenophon all made use of a written Persian epic, is, however, to be discounted.[98] A. D. Momigliano suggested that the 'autobiographical' writings of Ezra and Nehemiah were modelled on the inscribed pronouncements of Persian (and Egyptian) kings, but the stylistic distance seems too great for this to be convincing. However, Greeks may have learnt from the Persians how to make use of archives.

Several of the best of the early Greek writers lived through the Persian conquest of 546 and moved outside the confines of the empire to continue their work among like-minded Greeks. They include the poet Anacreon (563–478), who left Teos in 545 for what seemed like a haven at the court of the Greek tyrant Polycrates (himself later the subject of a Persian best-seller, *Vamiq o 'Adhra*).[99] Polycrates' Samos seemed like a cultural oasis on the fringe of the empire, giving birth also to Pythagoras, who however soon left for life in the Greek west. Polycrates himself fell foul of the local satrap and ended his days on a cross, 'washed by the moon and anointed by the Sun'. Such events contributed to the growth of Greeks' instinctive hostility to Persia, which was so vividly expressed in writers like Aeschylus and Aristophanes, and later Isocrates and the Alexander historians; it is notable, however, that Herodotus himself does not demonise the Persians.

Another writer who left his home town as Persia marched in was Xenophanes of Colophon (570–475), the poet and philosopher, who spent the next sixty-seven years wandering from city to city. One of Xenophanes' most notable contributions to thought was his relativism in matters of religion; not only did he realise that Greeks had gods who looked like themselves, Thracians had gods with red hair, and that donkeys, if they had gods, would make them look like donkeys; he also developed a form of monotheism that insists on the non-anthropomorphic form of god, which seems likely to have some connection to the tenets of Mazdaean religion and the preaching of Zoroaster (see Chapter 4).

Other writers who stayed put in their home towns after the Persian conquest include Herodotus' uncle Panyassis of Halicarnassus; though he wrote his epic poem in Greek on a Greek subject, the life of Heracles, his name is Carian not Greek. Xanthus of Lydia wrote a history of Lydia, used by Herodotus, which went up to the fall of the kingdom to Cyrus in 547/6. Greeks of the sixth century looked on Lydia as a byword for luxury and gracious living, and the arrival of the warlike Persians must have been a shock. Xanthus' book seems to have contained a good many colourful stories, for example about the resurrection of a dead dragon,[100] some topographical and geographical information, and a good deal of mythology, including that of Troy. It may have contained a 'Croesus Romance', which provided the structure of Herodotus' narrative of the fall of Sardis. Xanthus also wrote about the Magi, 'who have sexual intercourse with their mothers', thus initiating one strand of Greek horrified perception of the otherness of the Persians. He is said to have mentioned the Sicilian philosopher and wizard Empedocles in his work, who was born in 492 (so Xanthus must have lived at least until about 460);[101] perhaps Xanthus cited him in the course of a discussion of the Magi, some of whose doctrines seem to have had an impact on the Sicilian thinker.[102] Empedocles, for example, like Zoroaster, claimed to remember an earlier existence as a bush. The connection may have come from a magus who turned up at the court of Gela claiming to have circumnavigated Libya.[103]

Another Greek writer, of whose works scraps are preserved, entered the employ of Darius I. Scylax of Caryanda was engaged by the king to explore and report on the Indus region:[104] his account included tales about Sciapods, one-eyed men and people who cover themselves with their enormous ears when they sleep. The same improbable races appear also in the *Videvdad*,[105] which presumably draws on the same sources as Scylax employed. Scylax also wrote a biography of the Carian tyrant Heraclides of Mylasa.

Miletus had become a centre of philosophical speculation as early as the beginning of the sixth century, with the careers of Thales (b. ca. 625) and Anaximander (ca. 610–545). Both show some signs of awareness of eastern ideas:[106] Thales, who predicted an eclipse, must have known something of Babylonian astronomy, while Anaximander's theory of cosmic balance[107] seems to echo Mazdaean ideas of the strife between good and evil, a kind of see-saw of Ahura Mazda and Ahriman. His concentric circles of earth–stars–moon–sun are in the same order as in the texts of the Avesta, and differ from the Babylonian picture that puts the stars furthest out. Empedocles' teaching on the cycles of love and strife seems likewise to be indebted to such ideas, with which he perhaps became familiar through his acquaintance with Xanthus of Lydia.

Anaximander's follower Anaximenes was probably born about 550 and was a mature man when Xerxes came to the throne. Hecataeus the geographer took sides in the Ionian Revolt of 500 (he was against it) and was therefore perhaps born around 540.

Philosophical activity continued in the reign of Xerxes. One of the most notable representatives is Heraclitus of Ephesus, whose doctrines have been thought to contain strong elements of Zoroastrianism. Fire, for example, is the ruling principle of the universe, and the importance of *dike*, justice, recalls that of Arta/Aša in Persian thought. The 'One Wise' has a resemblance to the 'Mindful Lord' Ahura Mazda. The ideas of cosmic war and resurrection also find their parallels in Persian thought. When Heraclitus writes that 'corpses are more worthless than dung', he is not, to be sure, saying something a magus could agree with, but the idea might recall the practice of exposure of the dead.[108]

A definite link with Xerxes is established in the case of the philosopher Anaxagoras of Clazomenae, who arrived in Athens in the entourage of the king in 480, and stayed to bring cosmological speculation to the mainland Greeks.[109] Xerxes is also said to have been put up, with his entourage, by a distinguished gentleman of Abdera, who became the father of the philosopher Democritus; unfortunately Democritus must have been born too late to remember the visit of the Great King.

The giant of Xerxian literature is, of course, Herodotus (ca. 500–420), without whom none of the present book could have been written or, indeed, thought of. A native of Halicarnassus, and a Greek, he nonetheless had non-Greek relatives, as the case of Panyassis proves. He left Halicarnassus when young, to write his book in Athens, but his Carian background gave him his themes and many of his attitudes; it may account for the prominence of the

Carian queen Artemisia in his account of Xerxes' invasion of Greece. Ion of Chios (ca. 480–422) was born on the fringe of the empire but moved to Athens as a teenager. After the Persian defeats the epicentre of Greek letters moved to the rising imperial power of Athens. Besides numerous tragedies and satyr plays, songs, and a history of Chios, Ion wrote memoirs in which he described his meetings with great Greek writers. What a treasure they would be if we had them! He seems to signal the end of the Achaemenid moment in Greek letters, though Xenophon, for example, would have had little to write about were it not for the continuing vitality of Persian rule beyond the Aegean.

The dominance of Greek is notable. Extensive written histories were, it seems, not written in Persian – or in any of the other languages of the empire, from those of Sind and Bactria to Ethiopia. Xanthus chose Greek, not Lydian. There is no Lycian or Carian literature, though there are inscriptions from the fourth century in two or three languages, including the trilingual (Greek, Carian and Aramaic) from the Letoön (in the Fethiye Museum)[110] and the bilingual pillar (Greek, Lycian) still standing at Xanthos. Lycians surely had their stories, that of Bellerophon being the most securely located in the area. Egypt is a special case since works of literary art had been produced there for thousands of years before Cambyses' conquest. Although Persian rule was the catalyst, it was the Greek language that enabled literature to emerge and circulate. We are told that Xerxes' magus Osthanes wrote a book about Zoroastrianism,[111] but it is not clear what language it was written in. In other languages, parts of the Book of Isaiah belong to this period, and the Phoenician writer Sanchuniathon may have been active at any time between about 700 and 500 BC. For discussion of the later Hebrew books that describe the Persian Empire, see the next section.

The explanation Aristotle offered for the rise of philosophical speculation in Miletus was the emergence of a class that had sufficient leisure to think instead of simply scrabbling for a living. It seems not unreasonable to attribute this increased prosperity at least in part to a *pax Persica* following the establishment of Persian rule. Communications improved with the creation of the road system, and centralised management of production may have benefited others besides the satraps and tax-collectors.

THE JEWS UNDER PERSIAN RULE

Jewish writings pose a different set of problems when one tries to use them to evoke fifth-century Persia. Jewish writing, devoted to explicating the relations of Yahweh with his people, works on different principles from the critical historical method invented by the Greeks, of which we are the heirs. The Jewish material sheds a more oblique light, but nonetheless some elements of narrative, as well as atmosphere, can be derived from the books of the Hebrew Bible. When a royal court is described in these books, the Achaemenid court is the model.[112] The book that seems most obviously to describe the reign of Xerxes is the Book of Esther, which was probably written about the year 400 or later.[113] Its textual history is complex. There is also an early version of the plot, set at Darius' court and with different characters, in the Qumran text.[114] The book itself is not represented at Qumran. The first surviving Hebrew version of Esther is quite short, while the Greek version in the Septuagint contains 70 per cent more material, and may be a translation of an earlier Hebrew (or Semitic) original.[115] It was revised again, at an undetermined date, in the 'Additions' to Esther, represented by four manuscripts.

In this book, King Ahasuerus rejects his wife Vashti for refusing to appear before his guests and show off her beauty. (Her refusal echoes the story in Herodotus where Persians demand a sight of Greek women; when the latter are brought in, they are men in disguise, who promptly kill the lustful Persians.) He seeks out a replacement: like the king in the *Arabian Nights*, he tries out a girl a night until, after four years, his choice falls on the beautiful Jewess Esther, daughter of Mordecai, and he decides to make her permanent. The position is quite close to the procedure of the Ottoman Sultans:

> The Grand Turk has a palace of women at quite a distance from his own. There he keeps a great number of young Christian slave girls. . . . From these the Grand Turk chooses whoever pleases him the most, and keeps her separate for two months, and amuses himself with her as he pleases; if she becomes pregnant, he takes her as his consort, otherwise he marries her to one of his men.[116]

Esther then foils a plot by the wicked Haman to organise a pogrom against the Jews, and the story culminates in the punishment of Haman and his sons, and the vindication of Mordecai, who is raised to high office, as it is 'written in the book of the chronicles of the kings of Media and Persia. For Mordecai the Jew was next unto king Ahasuerus, and great among the Jews, and accepted of the multitude of his brethren, seeking the wealth of his people, and speaking peace to all his seed'.[117]

Ahasuerus is a Hebrew rendering of the Persian Khshayarsha, who is Xerxes. However, the Septuagint, in translating the name into Greek, makes it instead Artaxerxes, thus introducing a fine confusion that is perpetuated by Josephus in *Antiquities of the Jews* (11.184), when he places the story of Esther in the reign of Artaxerxes I. Josephus further confuses things by setting the career of Ezra, which took place under Artaxerxes, in the reign of his predecessor Xerxes.[118] The Arab historians, however, made the correct identification and present Esther as the wife of Xerxes/Esfandiyar.[119]

The story is set in Susa, where the Persian palace courtyard was paved with red, blue, black and white marble; tall marble pillars were linked by festoons of curtains in white, green and blue, swagged with cords of purple linen. The guests reclined on couches of gold and silver, overlooking the garden that struggled on in the sweltering plain (over 40 degrees in summer) watered by the River Choaspes. The multicoloured marbles sound dazzling and are not contradicted by the evidence of archaeology; the bright hangings as they drifted in the breeze must have provided some relief from the 'hot and scorching' atmosphere of Susa, where, as Strabo records, 'when the sun is hottest, at noon, the lizards and the snakes could not cross the streets in the city quickly enough to prevent their being burnt to death in the middle of the streets'.[120] This enervating climate provided the background for the story of love, subterfuge and revenge that is the Book of Esther. That the story itself is fiction is plain for many reasons, not least the echoes of the Joseph story in Genesis.[121]

The Jewish evidence for the Persian Empire is even more difficult to use than the Greek, but as Momigliano pointed out,[122] both Greeks and Jews tended to define themselves in relation to Persia.[123] Jerusalem had been sacked in 586 and its people (or the elite) deported to Babylon. Weeping by the waters of Babylon, the Hebrew people remembered Sion;[124] their sorrows are reflected in the second part of Isaiah[125] and the prophecies of Jeremiah. When Cyrus conquered Babylon he decreed that the Jews might return to their homeland.[126] The Return proceeded gradually from 539, spurred on by the prophecies of Ezekiel. Several books of the Hebrew Bible were written under the Persian Empire, mostly in the early period from Cyrus I to Darius I. After the Return in 539 the kingdom of Judah became a theocracy – the word was coined by Josephus in the second century AD[127] – first under the enigmatic Sheshbazzar, 'prince of Judah',[128] who took responsibility for the return of the treasure to Jerusalem. The Book of Ezra 2 lists the names of all those who returned with Zerubbabel, implying that they all arrived immediately after Cyrus' decree. It is more probable that they came a little later, around 520. Zerubbabel, a grandson of the exiled king Jehoiachin, was appointed as governor by the Persian king, and seems to have had quasi-royal authority, though the Book of Zechariah gives greater importance to

Joshua.[129] The restoration of the Temple was begun at this time, and Haggai and Zechariah, writing around 520, challenge the initial disappointment of the returned exiles and look forward to its completion, which probably took place in 515 BC. By this time Zerubbabel has disappeared from the scene, since he is not mentioned at the Temple's dedication. In the Book of Malachi the Temple has been rebuilt, but it, as well as the walls of Jerusalem, seems to have been in a poor state again in 445 BC when Nehemiah arrived in Jerusalem, 'in the 20th year of Artaxerxes' (i.e. Artaxerxes I). It has some-times been supposed that the Temple and walls had been damaged in a revolt against Xerxes in 484 BC, concomitant with the revolt of Babylon (or perhaps in 448 BC when the satrap Megabyzos revolted). On this scenario, Zerubbabel the Persian governor was displaying Messianic pretensions, and trying to break away from the Persian Empire. It seems perhaps unlikely that the Children of Israel would be so ungrateful as to contemplate revolt so soon after the generosity shown to them by the Return,[130] but then again, perhaps that is precisely the moment you might expect it: given an inch, they try to take a mile. The evidence, however, is far from compelling.

The next biblical books to reflect Persian rule show a period of relative stability. The Book of Isaiah, Chapter 3 (i.e. chapters 56–66) describes a time when the Temple is rebuilt but life is hard. Ezra and Nehemiah are the most informative about Persian rule, but despite Josephus' incorrect placing of their careers under Xerxes, it is certain that they belong to that of his successor. Ezra probably arrived in Jerusalem in 458 BC, Year 7 of Artaxerxes I (though a variant view puts this in Year 7 of Artaxerxes II, 398 BC), while Nehemiah was active from 445 BC, Year 20 of Artaxerxes I. With Ezra came a further group of Jews returning from Babylon. Ezra was neither a governor nor a High Priest, but seems to have had the function of establishing the Torah among the people ('to teach in Israel statutes and judgments');[131] L. L. Grabbe compares Ezra's mission with that of Udjahorresnet in Egypt,[132] who re-established the 'House of Life' under Cambyses, and codified the laws under Darius. His mission is part of a general move to allow each part of the empire to use its own laws and customs.

Nehemiah's mission, in 445/4 BC, was to rebuild the walls of Jerusalem; he had heard, at home in Susa, of the poor state of Jerusalem's defences, and requested permission from the Persian king (Artaxerxes I) to undertake their restoration. This was twelve years after a revolt in Egypt had been put down by Megabyzus, the satrap of Trans-Euphrates: in making terms with the rebels, he had promised the leaders their lives, but the king's mother Amestris, true to form, demanded their execution.

Megabyzus was so incensed at this undermining of his authority that he raised a revolt himself in 449. Later, however, he was reconciled to the king. Was this the context in which the walls of Jerusalem had been damaged? If so, it was remarkably generous of the king to allow their repair. It seems more likely that what Nehemiah was dealing with was general disrepair dating back to the period of the Exile.

There was no doubt some tension in Judah between the existing population and the returning exiles from Babylon, which would have put great pressure on the land. Tenants who had taken over the land they farmed when their landlords were exiled were now dispossessed. The economy of the region was agrarian and the demands of creating a sufficient surplus to pay the Persian tribute must have been considerable. Nehemiah describes a society of day-labourers, smallholders and tenant farmers, and poverty so extreme that some were forced to mortgage their children into slavery,[133] a problem analogous to that facing Solon in sixth-century Athens. Questions also arose about marriages outside the ethnic group, and these issues are reflected in the Book of Malachi, from the mid-fifth century BC. 'Judah hath dealt treacherously,' he rants, 'and an abomination is committed in Israel and in Jerusalem; for Judah hath profaned the holiness of the Lord which he loved, and hath married the daughter of a strange god.'[134] This controversy is reflected in the Book of Esther, set in the reign of Xerxes, though written about 400 BC.

THE BOOK OF JUDITH

Another Jewish book that reflects the early Persian period is the Book of Judith.[135] This book poses a notorious historical puzzle: it describes how Nebuchadnezzar, king of Assyria, went to war against Arphaxad, king of Media. After five years Nebuchadnezzar successfully stormed the capital Ecbatana. The next year, he sent his general, Holofernes, to demand earth and water from the rebellious nations of the west. Marching in three days with an enormous army from Nineveh to Cilicia, a distance of 300 miles, he crosses Put (Punt, Yemen) and Lud (Lydia) to reach Damascus and the coastal cities. The High Priest Joachim orders the Israelites to prepare for war. A widow named Judith from Bethulia, a small city south of Esdraelon, devises a plan. She first captivates and then decapitates the enemy general Holofernes. Great rejoicing follows and Judith lives to old age with great honours.

The problems are several. There is no Assyrian king named Nebuchadnezzar; it is impossible to march from Nineveh to Cilicia in three days; Yemen is not on the way to the Mediterranean; the Median king Arphaxad is unidentifiable; and so on. Nonetheless the story looks as if it ought to be broadly historical, describing events several centuries earlier than the date of its composition, about 135–105 BC. It contains numerous authentic details about the Persian Empire, such as the demand for earth and water as tokens of submission, the threat to destroy the gods of the enemy, the custom of prostration before Holofernes, and the appearance of a eunuch named Bagoas at a great feast.[136] Turban, sword and satrap are all mentioned.[137] Judith's kosher diet is emphasised.[138] The tale also contains fleeting reminiscences of the Alexander story, particularly as told in the *Romance* – notably the beauty of the enemy general (like Darius in the *Romance*) and Judith's exulting at taking over the general's tent (cf. Alexander after the Battle of Issus).[139] The bizarre geography and chronology also recall the narrative style of the *Alexander Romance*, written perhaps a hundred years earlier.

Various attempts have been made to save Judith as a historical record, by making the characters ciphers for actors from some other historical period, from Sennacherib's menacing of Jerusalem,[140] or a rising against Artaxerxes III,[141] or the Maccabees, to the time of Rome's Mithridatic Wars or even the Roman Empire under Trajan.[142] A more penetrating argument is that of Claus Schedl, who draws attention to the appearance in Darius' Bisutun inscription (DB 49) of an Armenian prince named Araka who seized power in Tubal (north of Armenia) under the name of Nebuchadnezzar.[143] His revolt failed and Darius had him and his followers impaled in Babylon. If this is the Nebuchadnezzar of the Book of Judith, some other details click into place. The emphasis on neighbouring Media becomes natural. Holofernes is a Median name. Arphaxad is not a name but a title, Arta-kšatra, 'leader of the knights'; if there was such a leader of a revolt in Media at this time, Darius does not mention it in his inscription because it was Nebuchadnezzar who actually put it down. (Arphaxad might, however, be a title for the rebel Bardiya.) Schedl further argues that Assyria can often mean Syria, and thus that the reference to Nebuchadnezzar being king of Assyria actually identifies the region controlled by Holofernes as the Trans-Euphrates region, including Judaea. It may in this way be possible to recover a little bit of Persian history from the fiction that is the Book of Judith.

THE IMPERIAL STAFF

Xerxes at his court was surrounded by many staff for both his comfort and his safety, and for affairs of state. The guards were paramount among them: the

Immortals and the Bodyguards: the former were so called because if ever one of them fell in battle he was immediately replaced, so that the complement remained always 1,000. The army commanders dwelt close to the king: Diodorus says that their residences surrounded the royal palace at Persepolis.[144] Just as Shah Abbas' chief ministers were the Chief Steward and the Grand Marshal,[145] so Xerxes turned first to his vizier, though Briant[146] suggests there may have been several viziers, or at least a succession, and to his generals.

The king also needed his advisers. Many of these were nobles and princes, and at least in Darius' case there was a Council of Seven – the 'seven princes which saw the king's face'.[147] Many other servants and officials also came in sevens, not least the seven conspirators (including Darius) against Smerdis (see Chapter 1).[148] These were representatives of the 'seven noble houses' and it was presumably from these same seven families that the king's wives had to be chosen.[149] In Xerxes' case seven chief maids are noticed.[150] The number seems to reflect the number of the Amesha Spentas, the 'beneficent spirits' who include the supreme god Ahura Mazda (see Chapter 3). There were even seven conspirators against Strattis of Chios in 479,[151] though these were Ionians not Persians: the story has perhaps acquired a Persian narrative tic. Several centuries later, Mithridates I of Pontus was, like his ancestor Darius, one of seven conspirators,[152] while Mithridates II claimed descent from another of the Seven against Smerdis.[153]

Many of these advisers were the king's 'friends', and were linked to him by marriage, such as Megabyzus, who married Xerxes' daughter Amytis.[154] Greeks found this relationship difficult to understand; it was described in Persian as *bandaka*, referring to a bond (the word is a cognate) of trust and loyalty (*pistis* in Greek); but Greek expressed this idea of the 'bondsman' with the word *doulos*, meaning 'slave'. All the people of Persia were in a sense the king's slaves, in that they owed him unquestioning loyalty (such as companies today often demand of their employees), and any service could be required; but that does not mean they could be bought and sold as slaves. The limited use of coin as reward for work, and the treatment of pay as 'rations', also recalled to Greeks the condition of slavery: Aristotle[155] remarks that a slave's 'pay' consists of his food (as an animal's does today).

EUNUCHS

One class of staff whose condition did approach that of slaves were the eunuchs.[156] Herodotus remarks that eunuchs are especially noted for their *pistis*, loyalty.[157] Xenophon[158] says the same, and the loyalty of eunuchs was a byword in the Ottoman Empire also.[159] Plutarch[160] has a telling story about King Artaxerxes II and his mother Parysatis playing dice with a eunuch as the prize: 'but first they agreed that each of them might except five of their most trusty (*pistotatoi*) eunuchs, and that out of the rest of them the loser should surrender any that the winner should select'.

One of Xerxes' most loyal eunuchs, and one of his most trusted confidants, was Hermotimus, to whom he entrusted his children for the journey back to Asia after the Battle of Salamis. (Plato mentions care of the royal children as a regular function for eunuchs.)[161] Although loyal to Xerxes, Hermotimus, who came from Caria, perhaps a particularly prolific source of eunuchs, harboured bitter anger against the slave-trader and castrator Panionius, who had made him a eunuch in the first place: he 'made his living by the abominable trade of castrating any good-looking boys he could get hold of, and taking them to Sardis or Ephesus, where he sold them at a high price'.[162] In due time (in a very Herodotean way) the man fell into Hermotimus' power, and he exacted his revenge for his human ruination by forcing the trader to castrate his own sons, and the sons to castrate their father.

The ranks of eunuchs were swelled by an annual tribute from various parts of the empire (since, unlike slaves, they could not be bred). The Ottoman Empire, too, had an annual round-up of boys, the *devşirme*, but the purpose of this was to fill the ranks of the janissaries. The Persian king imported each year 500 boys from Babylonia, 500 every four years from Ethiopia, and 100 boys and 100 girls every two years from Colchis:[163] the echoes of the black eunuchs and the famed white-skinned Circassian women of the Ottomans are unmistakeable. In addition, boys could be taken as booty and castrated, as they were from rebel Ionian cities in 493 BC, the aftermath of the Battle of Lade.[164]

The eunuchs fulfilled many functions, not only that implied by Herodotus' comment that they were the 'best-looking' boys. The word is Greek and means literally 'holder of the bed'; protection of the bedchamber and the women was inevitably an important function. Hegai and Shaashgaz,[165] 'guardians of the bedchamber' of Ahasuerus, are probably eunuchs. Eunuchs escorted the doctor Democedes when he was sent to Darius' women.[166] A prominent eunuch at Xerxes' court was Mithradates his chamberlain.[167] Gadatas, who arranged Cyrus' dinners for him, was a eunuch. When the king had company Gadatas did not even take a seat, but when they were alone he would sit with him to eat and talk.[168]

But eunuchs could also rise to high office in the empire, as they did also in the Byzantine Empire and, to a lesser extent, at the Ottoman court. One named Bagoas was chiliarch to Artaxerxes III,[169] and it was the eunuchs who represented the last stand when Darius and his fellow conspirators murdered Smerdis. Bagoas was also the king-maker to Darius III, while another Bagoas, a dancing boy this time, aroused Alexander's passions to an unusual degree.[170]

It is possible that not all those called eunuchs were eunuchs in the anatomical sense. The word simply means 'bed-bearer', i.e. chamber attendant, and Pierre Briant and others consider it 'unlikely that all were emasculated slaves'.[171] It is linguistically possible that the same word should have two completely different meanings, but it would be surprising. The revisionist argument is that evidence for an anatomical sense is confined to Middle Assyrian texts; it thus depends on rating the negative evidence, the absence of explicit mention of castration in the Old Persian texts, over the clear statements of Herodotus and other Greeks.

Eunuchs came from all over the empire, but the running of the empire was almost exclusively in the hands of Persians. We scarcely encounter an official, or a provincial governor, in the reign of Xerxes, who has a non-Persian name, and even Medes scarcely figure. (But see below on some notable non-Persian high officials.) Information about his vast empire was important to the king, and his spies were everywhere. There was an inspector of the satraps themselves, called *gaušaka*, who went around to ensure their continuing loyalty.[172] This official was often referred to as 'the king's son' or 'the king's brother' or even 'the king's eye'. Greeks reacted with mirth to the solemn title of The King's Eye (there was also a King's Ear), and Aristophanes in *Acharnians* brings a Persian delegation onto the stage: the Persian ambassador solemnly introduces Pseudo-Artabas, the Great King's Eye: we know that the actor wore a special mask with one enormous eye across its front, so that the Athenian interlocutor tells him he looks like a trireme. Pseudo-Artabas turns out to be incapable of speaking Greek properly (he is after all a 'barbarian') and his utterance 'No getti goldi, Nincompoop Iawny' is variously interpreted by those present, the ambassador explaining that he is really referring to 'income-coupons'. (This exchange in B. B. Rogers' Gilbertian translation alters to 'nincompoops' the considerably ruder *chaunoproktas*, 'gape-arsed', but I have been unable to think of a suitable pun. Perhaps something about 'bulging bum-bags'?)[173]

DOCTORS

An exception to the rule that all important officials at court were Persians is made for doctors.[174] Throughout the history of the empire Greek doctors were prominent at the Persian court. Xenophon emphasises the importance of doctors:

> Cyrus encouraged the ablest physicians of the day by his liberal payments, and if ever they recommended an instrument or a drug or a special kind of food or drink, he never failed to procure it and to have it stored in the palace . . . he showed especial gratitude to the doctors if they cured their patients by the help of his own stores.[175]

A rare mention of first aid in battle in ancient literature comes in Herodotus' account of Artemision, so medical learning, at least of a simple kind, was widely disseminated. To begin with Egyptian doctors had a high reputation, and Darius came to rely on one named Udjahorresnet, whose surviving biography describes how Darius sent him to establish a medical school (House of Life) in the Nile Valley.[176] Other Egyptian doctors, however, were found wanting when Darius sprained his ankle: their treatment was too violent and the pain kept him awake for seven nights, until the Greek doctor Democedes was summoned from among the prisoners and restored him completely. He was rewarded with an estate and the title of Tablemate. Later he treated Queen Atossa for an abscess in her breast. Eventually he obtained permission to return home to his native Croton, where he married the daughter of the celebrated wrestler Milo.[177] Curiously, we hear nothing of Xerxes' doctors, but his successor Artaxerxes I (464–424) cultivated Greek doctors assiduously. Hippocrates famously refused his invitation, accompanied by gold and silver, when the army was suffering from 'plague', replying 'I have enough food, clothing, shelter and all substance sufficient for life. It is not proper that I should enjoy Persian opulence or save Persians from disease, since they are enemies of the Greeks. Be well!'[178] Others were less haughty. Apollonides lived at the court for many years and saved Megabyzus from dying of wounds sustained when he took part in the assassination of Xerxes. But later Apollonides attempted to seduce Megabyzus' wife Amytis, who was Xerxes' daughter, when she was suffering from an inflammation of the womb. He attempted to persuade her that the best cure would be repeated sexual intercourse with him; when the remedy did not work, Amytis complained, Apollonides was tortured on the rack for two months and then buried alive.[179]

The story may be no more than a folk tale, and Apollonides certainly did not have the excuse that Nectanebo had for his deception, since the latter had to fulfil certain Egyptian theological requirements for the birth of

Alexander.[180] There are several such stories about employees and the boss's wife in Boccaccio: Day 3.2, the groom seduces the wife of King Agilulf; Day 4.2, Friar Alberto pretends to be the Angel Gabriel; Day 7.3 Friar Rinaldo, caught in bed with his godchild's mother, claims to be chasing away the child's worms. Nearer to the Persian period, the *Life of Aesop* revolves around the slave's affair with his philosopher-master's wife, who falls for him when she catches him masturbating. Such stories go back to the dawn of story-telling, and Ctesias certainly picked up some good ones in Persia.[181]

Despite Apollonides' gruesome fate, the later king Artaxerxes II continued to be able to attract Greek doctors. One of those who did come, Polycritus, is a name only,[182] but another, Ctesias of Cnidus, is of paramount importance to us because his access to the court enabled him to write a book that is one of the most extensive (if wayward) sources for Persian history. Ctesias came from Cnidus, home of one of the great rival medical schools, the other being Cos. His book includes references to fifteen different diseases, as well as drugs, poisons and wounds; he discusses the long dying of Darius I and Darius II, as well as Amytis' trouble with her womb.[183]

People in the Middle East have always looked westwards for their doctors, even today (though people now fly from London to Budapest to get their teeth looked after, and Turkish clinics advertise for IVF clients). Shah Abbas was no different. When Thomas Herbert was at his court in Isfahan he was treated by a Persian doctor for an attack of dysentery: 'He did me little good, albeit I took what he prescribed (part of which I well remember were pomegranate pills, barberries, sloes in broth, rice and sundry other things) and returned what he expected: so that it was hard to judge whether my spirits or gold decayed faster.'[184] Abbas knew that his doctors' remedies were inadequate and asked another of his European visitors 'to do everything possible to bring a Christian doctor with me when I returned, because he did not dare entrust his life to Mahommedans'.[185] The Ottoman sultans were similarly receptive to European medicine. The Levant Company's 'factory' at Smyrna maintained its own doctor; and in Constantinople the Italian doctor Giovanni Mascellini treated the sultan and grand vizier and their families, as well as being summoned to Crete to look after the general Ahmed Köprülü, to whom he in due course dedicated his book, *Artis medicae . . . summarium*, published in Vienna in 1673.[186]

The Achaemenid enthusiasm for Greek doctors perhaps began when Darius' usual Egyptian doctor failed to improve the sprained ankle. Besides these professionals, Persian kings turned to the Magi for medical assistance, but their treatment focused around astrology and the use of magic stones.

When we read some of these prescriptions, we can be fairly sure that they did not work. Pliny, for example,[187] refers to stones used by Zoroastrians, and later books of stone lore started from the remedies of the Magi.[188] 'Of all people who ever lived, the Persians were perhaps most remarkable for their unshaken credulity on amulets, spells, periapts, and similar charms, framed, it was said, under the influence of particular planets, and bestowing high medical powers, as well as the means of advancing men's fortunes in various manners.'[189] Walter Scott's comment is belied by the kings' more rational approach, but it is no doubt true of popular medicine, as is evident from the plethora of stone-books that were written in later years referring to 'Zoroastrian' sources. Pliny the Elder's *Natural History* is our oldest informant for many of these, for example, the astriotes or 'star stone': 'Zoroaster proclaimed the remarkable merits of this stone when used in the practice of magic'; 'The Magi falsely claim that the amethyst prevents drunkenness' (the stone's name actually means 'non-drunken'). Chalk is supposed to improve wet-nurses' flow of milk; hyena stones (extracted from the eyes of hyenas), if placed under the tongue, enable a man to foretell the future, while haematite cures diseases of the eyes and liver. 'Zoraniscaea is said to be a gem found in the river Indus and used by the Magi' (for what, he is unable to say). 'I can only suppose,' Pliny sneers, 'that the Magi, in committing these statements to writing, express a derisive contempt for mankind.'[190]

Derisive or not – and Pliny's list of non-magian prescriptions contains many things no less absurd – stone-books had a long subsequent history in Greek literature. One such book, which came to be attributed to Aristotle, was current in the Middle Ages in Arabic, Hebrew and Latin.[191] This contains stones that will induce sleep as well as ones that stop horses from whinnying and ones that assist in king-making. Astrology is as prevalent as medical uses of stones, and the carrying of stones as amulets or talismans was no doubt popular throughout Persia. But the kings were right to encourage doctors who had worked in the Greek tradition. The doctrine of the four humours that was developed by the Hippocratics has left its mark in present-day Persian traditional medicine, which is based on the correct balancing of hot, cold, wet and dry in the diet and in the body generally.[192]

OTHER NON-PERSIANS IN HIGH OFFICE

Throughout the fifth and fourth centuries we find non-Persians appearing sporadically in Persian service.[193] Before hostilities began in the 490s, Miltiades had a tyranny on the Hellespont.[194] One Greek who was important to Xerxes before his expedition against Greece was Demaratus, the exiled king of Sparta, and in the period following his retreat, another Spartan ruler, Pausanias, as well as the exiled Athenian Themistocles, had a role as an adviser, and, in Themistocles' case, official government service.[195] Another Greek who found refuge and honour in Persia was Scythes of Inyx in Sicily, who was briefly tyrant of Zancle (Messina) in 496/5; after his city was conquered by Samos, he sought asylum with Darius I, lived out his days in Persia and became very rich.[196] The use of Greek in Darius' letter to Gadatas (if it is genuine) about the sacred gardens at Sardis suggests that, despite his Persian name, he was a Greek speaker.[197]

Although foreigners were rarely appointed as satraps, there are a few examples, most notably the dynasty of Hecatomnus in Caria, which continued into the fourth century under Mausolus and, in Alexander's time, Ada. Under Artaxerxes II a Babylonian, Belesys or Bel-šunu, rose to be governor of his province or city, though probably subordinate to the satrap himself.[198] Another Babylonian, Iddin-Nergal, was a governor and toll-collector with a Persian title.[199] In some regions Persia trusted loyal native kings to maintain their empire as vassals: this was the case in Cyprus and Cilicia from the time of Cyrus the Great according to Xenophon,[200] and also in Sidon and elsewhere.[201] But a provincial governor could never rise to the top, as so many later did in the Roman Empire.

At a humbler level, Greeks also fought as mercenaries as early as the time of Cambyses[202] but increase in numbers after 479. Many Greeks and other nationalities also worked at Persepolis (see Chapter 6). Egyptians, too, found employment, in such posts as foreman and quarry supervisor.[203]

Slightly better known is the series of Jewish governors of Judah in the fifth and fourth centuries, starting with Tattenai and Zerubbabel under Darius I. Zerubbabel became a renowned figure in Jewish lore. In the apocryphal Book of Esdras he is the wise adviser to the king who comes up with the best answer to the king's poser, 'Which is strongest? – wine, women or the king?' Zerubbabel gives a long discourse on the dangerous power of women, which he illustrates with an account of Cyrus the Great's infatuation with his concubine Apame.[204] In John Gower's retelling of the story in *Confessio Amantis* (VII) the sage continues, rather surprisingly, by recounting the story of Alcestis and Admetus from Greek mythology. But Zerubbabel's punch line is that Truth is stronger than all the contenders, an answer guaranteed to please a Persian king for whom truth-telling was synonymous with virtue. As a result, Zerubbabel wins the favour of Darius for a restoration of property to Jerusalem and the rebuilding of the Temple.

In the early fifth century, perhaps in Xerxes' reign, succeeding Jewish governors were Elnathan, Yeho-ezer and Ahzai, to be followed by the more famous Ezra and Nehemiah under Xerxes' successor Artaxerxes I.

In general, then, the Persian king kept power close to his chest. Social mobility was not part of the deal, and the king's favour counted for everything.

CHAPTER THREE

The Image of a King

The king established himself at Susa or Ecbatana, invisible to all, dwelling in a wondrous palace within a fence gleaming with gold and amber and ivory. . . . So effective was the organization, in particular the system of signal-fires, which formed a chain of beacons from the furthest bounds of the empire to Susa and Ecbatana, that the king received the same day the news of all that was happening in Asia. Now we must suppose that the majesty of the Great King falls as far short of that of the God who possesses the universe, as that of the feeblest and weakest creature is inferior to that of the king of Persia. Thus, if it was beneath the dignity of Xerxes to appear himself to administer all things and to carry out his own wishes and superintend the government of his kingdom, such functions would be still less becoming for a god.

Pseudo-Aristotle, *On the Universe*, 398a12–398b7

The king was a symbol of the empire. Everything he did, at least in public and often in private, was directed at establishing his status as representative of the divine order laid down by Ahura Mazda. His royal progress, his acts of state, his dress and ceremonial, his treatment of petitioners, his mode of dining, his close relationship with the fruitfulness expressed in the idea of the king as gardener, and his administration of justice, all convey the symbolic and religious order of the world. It is hard, as Judith Mossman has shown in the case of Artaxerxes, to penetrate behind the facade to an actual person. It is necessary therefore, first of all, to understand that facade.

A Day at the Court

Because of the extent of the empire, the king had several capitals, the most famous of which now is Persepolis, probably known to Greeks as 'Parsa'. Most of the Greek authors claim that Xerxes spent the summer in mountainous Media, at Ecbatana, and the winter in the humid plains of Susa and/ or Babylon.[1] Polyaenus cites the inscribed menu at Persepolis for information that he commuted between the three, without mentioning Persepolis in the itinerary! Strabo wrote that the king moved from Media to Babylon at the end of summer,[2] but he must mean Susa. In fact, no Greek writer before Alexander's destruction of Persepolis ever mentions the city, though the Persepolis Fortification Tablets show that it was part of the itinerary every year; and no writer before Strabo mentions Babylon. The first author to mention all three capitals is Athenaeus.[3] According to the calendar worked out by Heidemarie Koch,[4] the king spent New Year (that is, the spring equinox) at Persepolis, the first two months at Susa, the hot summer months at Ecbatana (Hamadan), and the last four months at Susa again. Christopher Tuplin[5] argues that the programme was not as rigid as this, though common sense dictated that the burning summer months should be spent in the cooler mountainous region of Ecbatana. In 495/4, for example, building works at Persepolis kept Darius there longer than usual. In each year the king probably spent as much as two months travelling. His whole retinue came with him, as well as the golden plane-tree and a sufficient supply of water from the River Choaspes, for the king would drink no other.[6] (The Hapsburgs, too, took water from Schönbrunn with them wherever they went, and the Queen of England today is always accompanied by a supply of Malvern water.)

People begin their days early in the Middle East, to get through the business at hand before the heat becomes too great. The hardy youth of Persia would set out on their hunting breakfastless until a halt was called in the chase;[7] but perhaps Xerxes began the day with some flat bread, with fruit or preserves – maybe the fine apricots of central Asia, or just some of the ubiquitous nasturtium leaves. Xerxes was once offered some dried Attic figs, but refused them until he was able to pick his own, fresh, in Attica itself.[8] In the absence of any stimulating drink such as tea or coffee, the figs could be washed down with a refreshing draft of *dugh*.

After being dressed by a eunuch attendant in the flowing robes, leggings and soft boots of Persian royalty, the king proceeded to the audience hall. While not as festive as the banqueting hall described in the Book of Esther[9] – 'in the court of the garden of the king's palace, where were white, green

and blue hangings, fastened with cords of fine linen and purple to silver rings
and pillars of marble' – the hall has its own splendour.[10] Whether in one of
his royal palaces, or in a satrapal capital, or on campaign where the court
was a tent (one envisages something like Suleiman's war-tent, captured in the
siege of Vienna and now displayed in Vienna's army museum), the king
ascended his throne of gold and silver, which faced the building's entrance.[11]
(Satraps, too, sat on a golden dais to receive their supplicants and envoys.)[12]

Imposing in his splendour, the king was attended by the *chiliarch*: the
Persian term is thought to be *hazarapatiš*. Although the office is primarily a
military one,[13] he probably functioned as Grand Vizier and master of ceremonies, and had the task of introducing petitioners and councillors to the
royal presence. The 'treasury relief' from Persepolis shows (probably) Xerxes
seated on his throne, hair curled and topped by his distinctive smooth crown
and holding his sceptre in his right hand and, in his left, a bunch of lotus
flowers. His golden throne is accompanied by a matching footstool, both
with bull's feet, and he sits under an ornamental canopy or baldachin. Behind
him stands the crown prince Darius with several courtiers: one, probably a
eunuch, with his head wrapped in a *bashlyk* and carrying his towel of office;
the second is in Median costume and carries a bow case and an ornamental
axe, as well as on his belt a dagger in a scabbard certainly of gold like that in
the Oxus Treasure – a trove of gold objects from the Achaemenid period.
Behind these officials stand two soldiers in Persian dress with cylindrical
hats. Before the king are positioned two small pillars with curious pyramidal
objects on top: these may be small fire altars, or perhaps incense burners.
Approaching Xerxes from the right is (perhaps) the *hazarapatiš* in a Median
cap. He is stooped forward in a slight bow, and raises his hands to his lips,
either to prevent his breath from polluting the presence of the king, or in
the gesture the Greeks called *proskynesis*, literally 'blowing a kiss' of greeting.
Behind him stand two further figures, a guard with a long spear and an
attendant holding some kind of bucket or bag, perhaps containing incense,
or clay tablets ready for note-taking.

Behind those no doubt came the petitioners who were lucky enough to be
admitted that day. Admittance was no easy process, and there were many
stages of access to the royal presence. Like the Ottoman court, access began
at a Gate. The Topkapi Palace, and also Shah Abbas' palace at Isfahan,
consisted of a number of buildings in a park-like setting. Like the Topkapi
(Gun Gate) of the sultan's palace, the Gate of Xerxes was a great deal more
than a five-bar affair. It was a building in its own right, a kind of border
control. Here stood all the 'people of the gate' described by Plutarch in his

Life of Themistocles: two chiliarchs, the king's cousin and others.[14] Here you just had to wait for attention: The Spartan general Callicratidas was stuck there for two days in 406 BC.[15] Some people might spend a long time here before getting any further, as Mordecai did when Esther was newly married to the king.[16] Mordecai was there so long, and was so observant, that he was able to detect a conspiracy of two of the king's chamberlains, and to pass on the news to Esther, who told the king, who had them hanged. Xenophon too describes the process of sitting at the Gate: 'to this day the Asiatics under the Great King wait at the door of their rulers'.[17]

On reaching the royal presence there was an elaborate protocol of obeisance to the king. Herodotus describes the methods of greeting in Persia: if two men are of similar social standing, 'they kiss each other on the lips; if either of them is from a slightly lower rank, they kiss each other on the cheeks; and if one of them is the other's inferior by a long way, he falls to the ground and prostrates himself in front of the other person'.[18] This latter custom of prostration caused much resentment among non-Persians; Mordecai incurred the enmity of Haman by refusing to prostrate himself before him,[19] with the result that Haman decided to exterminate the Jewish population of the empire. Greeks were equally intransigent, and when Spartan ambassadors went to Susa,

> once they gained an audience with the king, Xerxes' guards ordered them, and tried to force them, to fall down and prostrate themselves before the king. Their response to this was to declare that even if the guards were to hurl them headlong down on to the ground they would never do any such thing, not only because it was not the Greek way to prostrate oneself before another human being, but also because that was not what they had come for.[20]

Apparently they got away with it. Isocrates and Xenophon regarded prostration as unbefitting a free man except in the presence of a god; and the Persian king was never a god, even to his own people.[21] Clemency was a characteristic of the Persian king (when it suited him); and Plutarch[22] explains how you could save face by pretending you had dropped a ring as you flung yourself to the floor before the king.

Even Queen Esther had to wait her turn: 'she put on her royal robes and stopped in the inner court of the palace, opposite the royal apartment. The king was seated on his throne in the throne room, facing the building's entrance.'[23] Finally, when the king noticed Queen Esther standing in the court, she won his favour; and the king extended to Esther the gold sceptre that he was holding. Then Esther came up and touched the tip of the sceptre. Now the king asked her what her petition was, and she might at last speak.

One of the 'Additions' to Esther describes the king's appearance at this point: 'He was seated on his royal throne, arrayed in all his splendid attire, all covered with gold and precious stones – a most formidable sight! Raising his face, flushed with colour, he looked at her in fiercest anger. The queen stumbled, turned pale and fainted.'[24] But the king revived her by tapping her on the neck with his sceptre. The overwhelming splendour of the Persian king's appearance is also evoked when the disguised Alexander visits Darius III in his court in the *Alexander Romance*: 'Darius sat still, wearing his crown set with precious stones, his silk robes woven with gold thread in the Babylonian style, his cloak of royal purple and his golden shoes studded with gems which covered his shins. He held a sceptre in either hand. . . .'[25]

Audiences could no doubt go on as long as there were petitioners, or meetings to take part in, or until the king got tired of business.

Gift-Giving

A successful petitioner could become a 'friend', as could a loyal adviser. The relation of king and friend was often marked by elaborate gift-giving:[26] Darius once said to the ruler of Miletus, Histiaeus, that 'the most valuable possession in the world is an intelligent, loyal friend'.[27] Histiaeus' reward on this occasion was to become Darius' regular dinner-companion, but gifts commonly took a more tangible form: coins, gold and silver objects, dinner ware, clothing, furniture and tents and parasols[28] – perhaps even peacocks, if that is the meaning of the expostulation by Dikaiopolis in Aristophanes' *Acharnians* 62–63: 'I'm sick to death of embassies, and all their peacocks and their impositions.'[29] The Book of Esther specifies clothing and a horse as gifts for Mordecai;[30] Ottoman sultans, too, often gave their favoured courtiers suits of clothes. Xenophon states that it was Cyrus who started the custom, and that 'there is no one in all the world whose friends are seen to be as wealthy as the friends of the Persian monarch: no one adorns his followers in such splendour of rich attire, no gifts are so well known as his, the bracelets, and the necklaces, and the chargers with their golden bridles. For in that country no one can have such treasures unless the king has given them.'[31]

When Democedes the doctor cured Darius' sprained ankle, the king 'sent Democedes off to the royal wives. The eunuchs took him there and introduced him as the man who had saved the king's life, whereupon each of the king's wives dipped a cup into a chest full of gold, and gave the cup to Democedes. The gift was on such a generous scale that the house-slave who had come with Democedes, whose name was Sciton, made himself a considerable fortune just from picking up the staters that fell from the cups!'[32] Artaxerxes (which one?), who had a 'high esteem' for Entimus of Gortyn, 'gave him a tent of extraordinary size and beauty, and a couch with silver feet; and he sent him also expensive coverlets, and a man to arrange them, saying that the Greeks did not know how to arrange a couch'.[33]

Even ambassadors were given generous gifts. Aelian lists those received from some unspecified Persian king:[34] a Babylonian talent of silver coins (about 31.5 kilos of silver), two silver cups of the same weight (a struggle at tea-time unless some kind of vast urn is meant), bracelets, a sword and necklace and a robe. Bracelets indeed are ubiquitous, and they are frequently depicted in art as well as found in considerable quantities in the Oxus Treasure, for example.[35] Xerxes sealed pacts of friendship with Acanthus and Abdera with such gifts: a suit of clothing for the people of Acanthus, and a golden dagger and tiara for Abdera.[36]

Xerxes is several times referred to as giving land to those he favoured. An Ionian captain named Phylacus was recognised as a 'king's benefactor' (*orosanges*) and given a large estate on Samos; Xenagoras of Halicarnassus was given the rulership of the whole of Cilicia for his own as a gift from the king, for saving his brother Masistes's life. Darius, too, gave Miltiades' son Metiochus a house, an estate and a Persian wife who bore him several children.[37] At the end of Xerxes' reign, the Athenian Themistocles was given three cities for his sustenance (see Chapter 9). So it was quite in keeping with Persian practice when Alexander offered a beggar who asked for alms a city. When the poor man protested that there was not much he could do with a city, and would prefer the price of a meal, Alexander's response was that he was considering not what it was suitable for the man to receive, but what was appropriate for him, the Great King, to give.[38]

Gardens

Ask anyone to think of the first word that occurs to them in connection with the word 'Persian', and the chances are that it will be 'carpet'. The weaving of carpets goes back as far as we can trace in Persian history, and one of the earliest carpets ever described was the 'Spring Carpet' that graced the audience hall of the Sassanian king Chosroes II (C7) in his palace in Ctesiphon.[39] Tabari describes it:

> . . . a huge carpet, depicting a garden with streams and paths, trees and
> beautiful spring flowers. The wide border all round showed flower-beds
> of various colouring, the 'flowers' being blue, red, yellow or white stones.
> The ground was yellowish, to look like earth, and it was worked in gold.
> The edges of the streams were worked in stripes, and between them stones
> bright as crystal gave the illusion of water, the size of the pebbles being
> what pearls might be. The stalks and branches were gold or silver, the
> leaves of trees and flowers made of silk, like the rest of the plants, and the
> fruits were coloured stones.[40]

No jewelled carpets now survive, but the garden carpet is a familiar feature
of Persian design, often taking the form of a *chahar bagh*: four gardens
symmetrically divided by streams like the four rivers of Paradise. 'Paradise'
is a Persian word; it comes from Old Persian *paridaida*, Elamite *partetash*,
and gardens in an arid land were always a source of solace and refreshment,
as well as use. The connotations of the term are somewhat hard to disen-
tangle, however, as at various times the Greek word *paradeisos* is used in
our sources to denote a garden of fruits, vegetables and flowers, a grove
or orchard of trees, and a hunting park.[41] Sir William Temple summed up
the range:

> A paradise among them seems to have been a large space of ground,
> adorned and beautified with all sorts of trees, both of fruits and of forest,
> either found there before it was inclosed, or planted after; either culti-
> vated like gardens, for shades and for walks, with fountains or streams,
> and all sorts of plants usual in the climate, and pleasant to the eye, the
> smell, or the taste; or else employed, like our parks, for inclosure and
> harbour of all sorts of wild beasts, as well as for the pleasure of riding
> and walking: and so they were of more or less extent, and of different
> entertainment, according to the several humours of the Princes that
> ordered and inclosed them.[42]

The first known planter of a garden in the Middle East was Yahweh – 'And
the Lord God planted a garden eastward in Eden'.[43] He provided the garden
with both pleasant and useful plants, a river, and trees including the Tree of
Life and the Tree of Knowledge of good and evil. Not long after came the
Garden of Babylon, 'of no slender antiquity', as Sir Thomas Browne wrote,
for 'gardens were before Gardiners, and but some hours after the earth'.[44] The
famous Hanging Garden of Babylon may not have been in Babylon at all, and

not built by Nebuchadnezzar, but by Sennacherib (705–681) in Nineveh, according to a plausible argument developed by Stephanie Dalley;[45] but its purpose was undoubtedly to provide shady walks and a formalised image of the countryside in an urban setting. Sennacherib's passion for gardens and orchards is well attested,[46] and the taste goes back to his semi-legendary predecessor Sargon of Akkad (2300–2284 BC), whose mother was a gardener.[47] Reliefs from the palace of his grandson Ashurbanipal (669–627) depict a garden with palm trees and conifers, but also the vine,[48] suggesting a propensity for collecting non-native plants for cultivation. Later, in the reign of Sennacherib, reliefs show files of attendants bringing bunches of flowers, unfortunately unidentifiable, into the palace, while plant-collecting is reflected in botanical lists and manuals that include reference to the cotton plant, the olive, the sissoo-tree (rosewood), palms from southern Mesopotamia, and possibly sandalwood.[49] Kings themselves delighted in their skill in manual labour, not only bricklaying and bronze-casting, but digging and planting, grafting and pruning.[50] This is perhaps no more than a metaphor: 'the godly chosen one makes the paradeisos bloom, and thus demonstrates that he is the legitimate king as he knows how to preserve the divine order once established on earth'.[51] But symbolic acts may be important even when they are not strenuous: the Prince of Wales takes pride in weeding his paving regularly, though one suspects he has some help.[52] Ecclesiastes speaks in the person of one who possesses the wealth of kings: 'I made me great works; I builded me houses; I planted me vineyards; I made me gardens and orchards, and I planted trees in them of all kind of fruits: I made me pools of water, to water therewith the wood that bringeth forth trees'; but he goes on to conclude, in his usual gloomy fashion, 'then I looked on all the works that my hands had wrought, and on the labour that I had laboured to do: and behold, all was vanity and vexation of spirit, and there was no profit under the sun.'[53] Was this The Preacher's view of all that a king's ransom could buy you: ennui?

Persian kings undoubtedly followed this royal model. Cyrus the Younger – 'not only a Lord of Gardens, but a manuall planter thereof'[54] – was proud to display to the Spartan general Lysander his paradise at Sardis, according to Xenophon:

> Lysander was amazed at the beauty of the trees, all growing in neat rows and of the same height, and the regular layout of the garden, as well as the many sweet scents that accompanied them as they walked around. 'I am amazed at the beauty of all this, Cyrus,' he said, 'and I admire you even more for measuring it all out and arranging it so neatly.' Cyrus was

pleased at this comment, and said 'Yes, Lysander, I measured and laid out all of this, and some of them I planted myself, too.' Lysander looked at him, at the beauty of his robes, and his perfume, the beauty of his bracelets and armlets and all his other jewellery, and said 'What, Cyrus, did you really plant any of this yourself?' Cyrus replied 'Are you surprised, Lysander? I swear to you by Mithras, as long as I am healthy, I can boast that I never dine without working up a sweat either by military exercise or by labouring in the garden or some other activity.' When Lysander heard this he shook him by the hand and said 'You seem to me, Cyrus, to be a genuinely happy person; for you are happy in being a good man.'[55]

Again the resemblance to the Ottoman court is striking. Michael Kritovoulos in his chronicle of Mehmed the Conqueror wrote how

The Sultan, passing the winter at Byzantium, among other interests occupied himself with repopulating and rebuilding the city. Also he finished the palace. . . . On every side extended vast and beautiful gardens, in which grew every imaginable kind of plants and fruits; water, fresh, clear and drinkable, flowed in abundance on every side; flocks of birds, both of the edible and of the singing variety, chattered and warbled; herds of both domestic and wild animals browsed there.[56]

Mehmed himself loved gardening and spent many hours planning, digging and planting his gardens. But mostly the Sultans relied on an army of gardeners, who had high rank and were divided into nine classes. They lived in barracks, and in 1739 there were 3,000 of them.[57]

I would like to imagine Xerxes too stripping off his brocaded robes and his golden armlets of gold, to drive a fork into the ground or get down on his knees with a trowel, to sow a row of seeds and to clip the roses and pomegranates to improve their flowering. Unfortunately no ancient Persian secateurs have ever been found by archaeologists. Like Richard II, he sees his kingdom as a garden, but not an unweeded one; in his last dialogue with Rostam, Esfandiyar advises the hero not to sow what he cannot plant, and Rostam says that when order is restored his heart will be happy like a garden that has been cleared of weeds. The only slight hint that Xerxes himself wielded the clippers and trowel comes in the Vulgate version of the Book of Esther, which expands the Greek text by referring to the feast that Ahasuerus held 'in the vestibule of the garden and the woods, which had been planted by the royal hands with a magnificence worthy of them'.[58] But one of his successors, Artaxerxes I, was not ashamed to take on the role of a woodsman:

> At length he came down to a royal halting-place which had admirable parks in elaborate cultivation, although the region round about was bare and treeless; and since it was cold, he gave permission to his soldiers to cut the trees of the park for wood, sparing neither pine nor cypress. And when they hesitated and were inclined to spare the trees on account of their great size and beauty, he took an axe himself and cut down the largest and most beautiful tree.[59]

In the time of Alexander's conquest, the king of Sidon was deposed and replaced by a distant relative, Abdalonymus, who was working as a market gardener. 'Two noblemen came without notice into his garden, which Abdalonymus happened to be clearing of weeds, carrying the robe with its royal insignia. . . . The whole thing was like a dream to Abdalonymus.'[60] This may not be as bizarre as it sounds, if a king was required to be proficient in such arts of life as horticulture. Abdalonymus also had a hunting park, in which the conqueror was invited to go hunting, if we are to take at face value the scenes depicted on his sarcophagus, now in the Istanbul Museum.

But there were risks. In ca. 1860 BC Enlil-Bani the gardener was created 'substitute king' to ward off omened evil from the real king. The usual fate of the substitute king was to be put to death after his job was done, but Enlil-Bani managed to grab the throne and it was the original king who died instead.[61]

Five gardens have been identified by archaeologists in the Persian realm,[62] and several more are known only from references on the clay tablets from Persepolis:[63] at Pasargadae the palaces stood in a vast garden on the *chaharbagh* (four divisions) plan. The foundations of pavilions and remains of watercourses are still apparent, though now there is scarcely a blade of grass in the whole site, while the margins of the nearby River Pulvar remain green. There was also a walled garden surrounding Cyrus' Tomb at Pasargadae, perhaps 200 x 170 metres, the βασιλικὸς παραδεισός, as is also described by Arrian[64] on the occasion of Alexander's arrival there: the tomb stood in a grove of trees surrounded by a greensward. There were two gardens at Susa, one with porticoes overlooking a river, the other a platform fronting the palace, which is likely to have been a garden. And finally, at Persepolis itself, an open area 60 x 31 metres seems most likely to have been laid out as a garden.

What grew in these gardens? They cannot have been on the scale of the palm grove and 'balsam paradise' that Strabo describes at Jericho,[65] for the palm-tree park is 100 stadia long (about 12 miles) and watered by rivers and full of scattered dwellings. As Xenophon explains, 'these paradises in which the king spends his time must contain a fine stock of trees and all other beautiful things that the soil produces'.[66] The most vivid evocation of what Greeks thought of as a pleasure garden is that described by the novelist Achilles Tatius in the fictional garden of Leucippe's father at Tyre:

> She was in a formal garden adjoining the house. It was in fact a grove of very pleasant aspect, encloistered by a sufficiently high wall and a chorus line of columns that together formed a covered portico on all four sides of the garden. Protected within the columns stood a populous assembly of trees. A network of sturdy branches interlaced to form an intricate pattern wherein petals gently embraced their neighbours, leaves wound round other leaves, and fruits rubbed softly on other fruits. Thus far the world of plants knows intercourse.
>
> Ivy and bindweed ravelled their way around some of the massy trunks: the bindweed clung to the plane tree by a soft reticulation of tendrils, while the ivy spiralled intimately among the pine boughs . . . . Grapes grew on trellises on either side of the tree, thick-leaved, ripe with fruit whose clusters tumbled through the trelliswork like locks of curly hair. . . . The flowers of various colours displayed their beauty in turn – violet, narcissus, rose – the earth's dyed stuffs. . . . Among the flowers, a spring bubbled up within a rectangular pool constructed to contain the flow. The flowers were reflected in the water as in a mirror, so that the entire grove was doubled – the realm of truth confronting its shadowy other.[67]

Achilles populates his garden with songbirds, crickets and swallows, as well as peacocks, swans and parrots. The garden sounds quite like those evoked by medieval Persian writers. The garden on a small scale, as depicted on carpets, is a part of Persian culture. Sa'adi's poems are collected in the Gulistan (Rose Garden) and the Bostan (Orchard); and Sa'adi's memorial in Shiraz is a garden of roses; there is another for Hafez. For Rumi, 'the colours of the planting and the breath of the birds will endow us with the water of life, when we go together into the garden, you and I'.[68] Here the garden is a metaphor for the Paradise that waits in the other world; but Persians have always built paradises to enjoy in the here and now.

The planting of Leucippe's garden is noteworthy. Trees for shade and vines for fruit are first emphasised, but also remarkably are ivy and bindweed, which I at least spend much of my afternoons trying to eliminate from my garden. Yet Greeks loved ivy, the sacred plant of Dionysus, and Alexander's renegade treasurer Harpalus spent many hours trying to get it to grow in his pleasance at Babylon. The bindweed, fortunately, is a mistranslation by the admirable John Winkler, for the Greek is actually *smilax*, an attractive plant whose small flowers turn to vivid red berries, which still grows freely in Asia Minor, though it is rather apt to create impenetrable tangles in woodland. (Like so many plants, it started life as a nymph: she fell in love with a mortal youth, Crocus, but for this transgression was transformed into a plant: now she still clings to mortals, but more indiscriminately, as they wander through the undergrowth.) Of flowers there are few, since Western gardeners had no inkling of the profusion that would in later millennia be brought from China or the Americas. One might have expected poppy, iris, anemone or Adonis; but these are likely to need plentiful watering if not growing wild; or the herbs like rosemary, thyme and fennel that characterise the Roman garden. Persians certainly grew roses.[69]

But Achilles' is not, of course, a literal description of a Persian garden from the age of Xerxes, six centuries before his time. Despite the need for shady groves for recreation, there was always an emphasis, in larger-scale plantations, on useful plants. The Persian king instructed his satraps always to have a care for the proper cultivation of their territories. From the jewel of the rose garden to the acres of the pistachio plantation, proper use of the soil is an aspect of adherence to the Right. Gardening is a metaphor of government (and executions are a form of pruning).[70]

A letter in Greek preserved on stone near Magnesia on the Maeander[71] purports to be a missive from Darius I to Gadatas, the satrap of Ionia,[72] reproving him for aspects of his stewardship of the king's land but praising others:

Without doubt you exercise care in cultivating the land that belongs to me, since you transplant into the regions of Lower Asia trees that grow on the other side of the Euphrates: on this point, I praise your intent, and, for that, there will be great recognition in the king's house. But, on the other hand, since you choose to disregard my desires as regards the gods, I shall cause you to experience, if you do not change, my wrath excited by an injury. The sacred gardeners of Apollo have been subjected by you to tribute and required to work profane land; that is to disregard the sentiments of my ancestors toward the god . . . .

Gardening, then, is good, but the god's employees are not to be deflected to mere economic activity. The gift of something as simple as a fine pomegranate was a way to impress the king.[73]

Satrapal gardens are referred to elsewhere, too: the king's representative shared his responsibility for cultivation of the fruits of the earth. Tissaphernes was so overwhelmed by the flatteries of the renegade Athenian Alcibiades that he reciprocated by naming a park after him: 'the most beautiful park he had, on account of its healthful waters and lawns, with resorts and retreats decked out in regal and extravagant fashion'.[74] The Thracian king Kotys had a 'beautifully planted grove . . . wherever he discovered places shaded with trees and watered with running streams, he turned these into banqueting-places; and visiting them in turn, as chance led him, he would offer sacrifices to the gods and hold court'.[75]

The garden was not just a horticultural paradise. There were extensive parks designed for hunting, like those laid out at Dascyleion to surround the palace of the satrap of the Hellespont and Phrygia.[76] A lake provided the focus of the estate,[77] now Lake Manyas near Ergili. A tomb relief in the museum at Çanakkale depicts a hunter in a landscape, and may have come from Dascyleion (see p. 49 above). Unfortunately no other such estates have been identified on the ground, though there are possible remains of a satrapal palace near Erzincan, and a memory of the hunting park at the satrapal residence of Celaenae is preserved in the place's present name, Geyikli ('full of deer'). A number of others are known from literary sources, including one in Syria and one at Sittake on the River Tigris.[78] Xenophon, a keen huntsman, had an eye for such places. They were familiar enough to provide the inspiration for part of Diodorus' description of the imaginary island of Atlantis.[79] Hunting parks, like gardens, had a long Mesopotamian history, and are often depicted in Assyrian palace reliefs; six hundred years after the fall of the Achaemenid Empire, a Sassanian king of Persia still depicted himself hunting in his pleasure groves, on the impressive cave-relief at Taq-e-Bostan.

Such hunting parks, it seems, were in general enclosed by a wall.[80] Enclosure turned a mere pleasance into a sacred space, where a king like Kotys could conduct his regular sacrifices. Such a conception explains the reverence shown by Xerxes to the beautiful plane tree he encountered at Sardis. Herodotus says that the tree was 'of such beauty that the king was moved to decorate it with golden ornaments and to leave behind one of the Immortals to guard it'. An alternative version had it that a plane tree metamorphosed miraculously into an olive.[81] Aelian, like other writers, saw this devotion as somewhat ridiculous, remarking that the tree was in no way benefited or ennobled by this attention.[82] Louis Couperus makes Xerxes' reverence for this tree the occasion of a comic scene:[83] one of the Immortals is left to stand guard over it, but is then forgotten for months on end; eventually a caravan comes by and the Immortal, in rage, joins it, stripping the tree of its golden armlets and ornaments to pay the caravan leader for safe conduct. 'You god-damn plane-tree, you!' he snarls as the caravan moves away:

> The plane-tree made no reply. It did not even seem to notice that it had been stripped of all the decorations of honour bestowed on it by the King of Kings, and, quite unmoved, omnipotent in its beauty and power, it flung out its broad crown of leaves to the skies.[84]

This reverence for the tree surely indicates an enduring habit of tree cult, as Pierre Briant argues.[85] He draws attention to several Persepolis seals depicting the king making an offering of a crown to a tree, which takes the form of a 'tree of life'. Similar scenes also occur on Assyrian reliefs of Ashurbanipal. On one seal, a pair of Immortals guard a palm tree over which hovers the winged disc, clearly indicating that a god is present where the tree stands. In the Babylonian *Contest of the Tamarisk and the Palm* the tamarisk exults over its rival, 'At the place of Sin's offering . . . . Where I am not present the king does not libate . . . . My rites are performed, and my twigs are heaped up on the ground.' And again, 'I am the exorcist and purify the temple . . . I have no rival among the gods'.[86] At the very least this shows reverence for trees for their gifts to mankind: Strabo knew of a Persian song 'wherein are enumerated three hundred and sixty uses of the palm tree'.[87] (It must have been rather monotonous, though perhaps useful as a mnemonic for the days of the year.) There is a continuing reverence in the Middle East for fine trees, which sometimes become 'prayer-trees'. Ottoman rulers, later, if they encountered a particularly beautiful tree, were accustomed to plant flowers around it to honour it.[88] This reverence also explains the golden vine at Susa, under which the Persian kings held court, 'with its clusters of green crystals and rubies from India and other gems of every description'[89] – the Achaemenid version of the jewelled carpet-garden of a later century.

DINNER

At the end of the day dinner would be served; often the king 'sat down to dinner' with 15,000 people.[90] (See Chapter 1 for the menu recorded by Polyaenus.) Clearly the reference is to the whole of his staff, and with gardeners, cooks, serving staff, harem attendants and so on, the numbers would be considerable. It chances that Athenaeus lists the staff responsible for the king's dinner at Damascus when he was on campaign against Alexander,[91] and thus not in one of his own palaces: 277 cooks, 29 kitchen assistants, 13 cooks specialising in dairy products, 17 drink preparers, 70 wine filterers, and in addition 329 concubine musicians, 46 chaplet weavers and 40 perfumiers. All the serving staff were freshly bathed and dressed all in white.[92]

Xenophon approves of this division of labour:

> When there is work enough for one man to boil the pot, and another to roast the meat, and a third to stew the fish, and a fourth to fry it, while at the same time someone else must bake the bread . . . it is obvious, I think, that in this way a far higher standard of excellence will be attained.[93]

Xenophon also describes the seating plan at Cyrus' court:

> Gadatas was the chief of the mace-bearers, and the whole household was arranged as he advised. . . . As the guests entered, Gadatas would show each man to his seat, and the places were chosen with care: the friend whom Cyrus honoured most was placed on his left hand (for that was the side most open to attack), the second on his right, the third next to the left-hand guest, and the fourth next to the right, and so on.[94]

The guests were served on golden plates and with golden cups; the king's cup was reserved for him, and a taster would always sip the wine before it was served to the king in case of poison (which the cup-bearer was thus best placed to administer, as in the story of Alexander's alleged poisoning).

The atmosphere is one of extreme luxury, and that too is part of the king's image. Athenaeus devotes two chapters to luxury at the Persian court, where the king walked on carpets from Sardis on which no one else might tread; and he quotes Clearchus:

> While he gave to all those who could invent him any new kind of food, prizes for their invention, he did not, while loading them with honours, allow the food which they had invented to be set before them, but enjoyed it all himself.[95]

Alexander, a hardy Macedonian, professed to be shocked by such luxury; but Hellenistic rulers adopted the style. Chief exponents were the Ptolemies of

Egypt, who in turn incurred the mockery of the hardy Romans before the latter were themselves, in time, 'corrupted'.

CRUELTY

The king also had to administer justice and to punish wrongdoing. A notable feature of Persian punishments is their extreme cruelty.[96] The Persians inherited from their Near Eastern predecessors a multiplicity of cruel punishments, and their Sassanian successors were just as inventive, as exemplified by the case of the prophet Mani, flayed alive by Shapur II. But unlike their predecessors, the Persians did not depict such punishments in their more formalist art, which so often evokes an almost hieratic calm.

It has sometimes seemed that the women were even more cruel than the men.[97] ('A man can never be as cruel as a woman,' opined the philosopher Kierkegaard.)[98] A predominant feature of Amestris's treatment of her rival in love (see Chapter 8) is her cruelty. As portrayed by Herodotus, her treatment of Masistes' wife seems to go far beyond normal vengefulness, even when making allowances for the predominance of mutilation as a punishment in the Persian Empire. Later, after Xerxes' death, Amestris badgered her son Artaxerxes for five years for the head of the Egyptian rebel Inaros; when she eventually got her hands on Inaros, she had him impaled on three stakes.

It is easy to multiply examples of cruelty attributed to women by Greek authors. Plutarch tells of Artaxerxes' wife Parysatis dicing with her son for the life of a eunuch; when she wins, she has the victim flayed alive.[99] Parysatis is the protagonist of another unpleasant story when she poisons Stateira by the intriguing method of cutting an apple with a knife on one side only of which poison had been smeared. There is no particular reason to disbelieve such stories, which can be paralleled many times in history from Lucrezia Borgia to the Ottoman court.[100]

Amestris' daughter Amytis was no better; when she had been tricked into having sex with her doctor Apollonides, she insisted that her mother take revenge on him. This time Amestris had the culprit buried alive. An earlier Amytis, the wife of Cyrus the Great, had a eunuch blinded, flayed alive and crucified. To 'kill' a victim several times over in this way seems to have been frequently the aim. A Carian who boasted of having killed Cyrus the Younger, when he had merely been the first to wound him, was racked on the wheel for ten days, then had his eyes gouged out, and then had molten bronze dropped into his ears until he died.[101]

XERXES.

A
TRAGEDY.

As it is Acted at the

THEATRE-ROYAL,

IN

LINCOLN's-INN-FIELDS.

Written by COLLEY CIBBER, *Esq*;

Quot Homines, Tot Sententiæ.

L O N D O N:
Printed for W. FEALES, at *Rowe's-Head,* over-
againſt *St. Clement's Church* in the *Strand,*
M. DCC. XXXVI.

1 Frontispiece to Colley Cibber, Xerxes (London 1736).

2 The Treasury Relief, Tehran Museum. The king (probably Xerxes, but possibly Darius), seated, receives petitioners. Behind him stand a guard and a priest.

3 The petitioner, perhaps the *hazarapatiš*, or another court dignitary.

4 Pasargadae: view from Tell-i-Takht. The Zendan-i-Suleiman is in the nearer distance, and in the far distance the Tomb of Cyrus.

5 The Zendan-i-Suleiman (Prison of Solomon) at Pasargadae. The purpose of the building is unknown but it may have been used in coronation ceremonies.

6 The Qa'aba of Zoroaster at Naqsh-i-Rustam, near Persepolis. This building, which stands before the tombs of the kings, is a better-preserved version of the Zendan-i-Suleiman at Pasargadae. Its purpose is likewise obscure.

7 Relief from the Tripylon at Persepolis: lion attacking bull, possibly a symbol of *Now Ruz*, the spring festival when the sun enters Taurus.

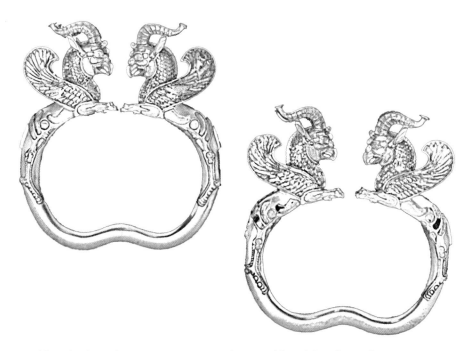

8 A gold armlet from the Oxus Treasure, an Achaemenid hoard found near the River Oxus in the 1870s; now in the British Museum. Such armlets were favourite gift items and are frequently depicted on the Persepolis reliefs.

9 Gold rhyton (pouring vessel), Achaemenid or later.

10 Hunting relief from Celaenae, now in the Çanakkale Museum.

11 Relief of musician and warriors from the 'Polyxena tomb', now in the Çanakkale Museum.

12 Taşkule, the 'stone tower'; an Achaemenid-period tomb hewn from solid rock outside the town of Foça (Phocaea), Turkey. Perhaps it was the tomb of a satrap?

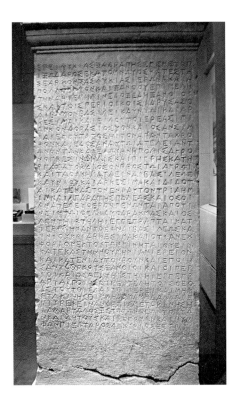

13 The Greek face of the trilingual inscription from the Letoön (sanctuary of Leto) near Xanthos, Turkey. It records a dedication in Greek by the king of Kaunos in 337 BC.

14 Coins of the Persian Empire.
(a) Silver siglos depicting the king as archer.
(b) Silver coin of Shapur I: reverse, depicting a fire-altar.
(c) Coin of Mazaeus, the satrap of Babylon who surrendered to Alexander the Great; reverse, with the lion and bull motif.

15 Tiled floor in the palace of Darius I at Susa.

16 The tomb of Cyrus at Pasargadae.

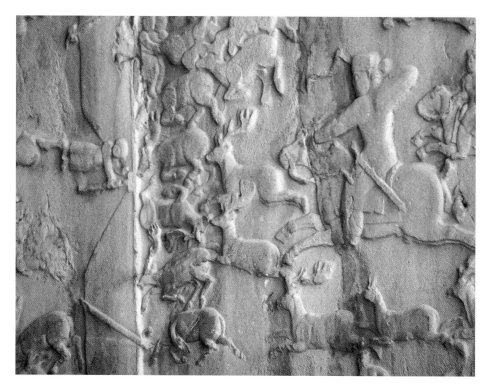

17 Hunting relief from Taq-e-Bostan near Kermanshah; Sassanian period.

18 A Magus, or Zoroastrian priest, wearing a bashlik (hooded cap) and carrying a barsom (bundle of twigs).

19 The king before a fire-altar: from the tomb of Darius I at Naqsh-e-Rustam.

20 This cypress tree at Abarkuh, allegedly planted by Zoroaster (like the one that once grew at Persepolis), is still the object of, not reverence exactly, but excursions to admire its beauty.

21 Xerxes' 'daeva-inscription', in which he asserts 'I made proclamation: "the demons shall not be worshipped!"'.

22 A winged disk from a pilaster at Persepolis.

Flaying alive was a regular punishment in the Persian Empire, for example when Cambyses flayed Sisamnes,[102] but when attributed to kings it is always an act of punishment, not spite. Walter Ralegh, to be sure, made Xerxes himself a cruel man – 'foolish and a coward, and consequently merciless', but cruelty becomes a kind of leitmotif for Persian queens. The bait is easily swallowed by Louis Couperus, who introduces Atossa with her whip, lashing out systematically at a slave girl who has been unfortunate enough to fall into a vat of boiling fruit.[103] Even the fictional Esther is vengeful enough to have Haman and his sons not just executed, but their corpses displayed in public.[104] The motif may show, not so much that Persian queens indulged their passions, but that they wielded a power equal to their menfolk in punishing infringement of their status.

The cruelty of Persian punishments can lead one to nausea, and Greek writers seem to have reacted in the same way, to judge from the horrified fascination with which they recorded it.[105] Greeks too used torture, and a slave's evidence was inadmissible in court unless he had been 'tortured' first; but in practice Greek torture consisted of beatings, and did not engage in the refinement of cruelty that Persian punishments exhibit. One of the simplest is the crushing of the head of a poisoner between two stones,[106] which was employed for the maidservant of Parysatis who actually prepared the poisoned knife, while one of the most repulsive is the torture of the boats, described in Plutarch's *Life of Artaxerxes*.[107]

The victim is laid in a wooden boat or trough, and another is fitted closely over him and fixed down in such a way that the victim's head, hands and feet are left projecting. The executioners pour over the man's face and into his mouth a quantity of milk and honey (honey is a product of the bee, an evil being for Zoroastrians); this attracts flies and other vermin, which settle on his face and hide it completely. But as time goes by the man must of necessity pass water and void his bowels; this attracts further flies and maggots, which eat into his flesh within its wooden prison, until his entire body turns to a mass of putrefaction; and so he dies. This is the punishment that was inflicted on Mithridates, who had killed the rebel Cyrus the Younger in battle, and boasted of it in such a way as to discredit the king's claim that he himself had slain the rebel. It took Mithridates seventeen days to die.

The motivation for such punishment becomes a little easier to understand when one considers that torture has a symbolic dimension. Michel Foucault began his book *Discipline and Punish* with the reflection that what is perhaps abnormal is the leniency of modern European punishments. He descants on the 'glory' of torture, and its symbolism as a 'quantitative art of pain', in terms that recall the commandant of Kafka's story, 'In the Penal Colony':

> Torture rests on a whole quantitative art of pain. But there is more to it: this production of pain is regulated. Torture correlates the type of corporal effect, the quality, intensity, duration of pain, with the gravity of the crime, the person of the criminal, the rank of his victims. . . . Even if its function is to 'purge' the crime, torture does not reconcile; it traces around, or rather, on the very body of the condemned man signs that must not be effaced. . . . Public torture and execution must be spectacular, it must be seen by all almost as its triumph. The very excess of the violence employed is one of the elements of its glory: the fact that the guilty man should moan and cry out under the blows is not a shameful side-effect, it is the very ceremonial of justice being expressed in all its force.[108]

Kafka's story in fact expresses something of the Persian attitude to torture, that it not only 'fits the crime', but inscribes an image of the malefactor's misdeed on his very body:

> How quiet he grows at just about the sixth hour! Enlightenment comes to the most dull-witted. It begins around the eyes. From there it radiates. A moment that might tempt one to get under the Harrow with him. Nothing more happens after that, the man only begins to understand the inscription, he purses his mouth as if he were listening. You have seen how difficult it is to decipher the script with one's eyes; but our man deciphers it with his wounds. To be sure, that is a hard task; he needs six hours to accomplish it. By that time the Harrow has pierced him quite through and casts him into the grave . . . . [When stuck] the face of the corpse . . . was as it had been in life; no sign was visible of the promised redemp-tion; what the others had found in the machine the officer had not found; the lips were firmly pressed together, the eyes were open, with the same expression as in life, their look was calm and convinced, through the forehead went the point of the great iron spike.[109]

The Inquisition followed similar methods, in for example the piercing of the tongue that has spoken heresy, and the burning of the body to purge away matter and thus sin. (The Macedonian conquerors of Athens put Hyperides to death, but only after cutting out the tongue that had made so many speeches against them.) The Elizabethan punishment of hanging, drawing and quartering, by contrast, seems simply designed to demonstrate to the victim how much indignity a body can suffer; it seems as vengeful as the reputed saying of the Emperor Caligula, 'let him feel that he is dying'. American torture of Iraqi prisoners, still more inexplicably, was stated by its perpetrators to be 'for fun'.[110] Persian punishments are more like those of the Inquisition in symbolic power.

In the torture of the boats, as Bruce Lincoln has argued, the enveloping of the criminal's body in his own excrement and putrefaction symbolises his reduction to matter, to the condition of the evil power that contends with light for mastery of the world. Digestion is an Ahrimanic process; among the numerous Persian terms for evil, the commonest of which are the Lie and rebelliousness, there is also the epithet 'stinking'.[111] The use of this vile punishment thus becomes, rather surprisingly, an argument in support of the Zoroastrian orthodoxy of the Achaemenid kings.

Amestris' revenge on Masistes' wife makes more sense if viewed from these perspectives. The mutilations inflicted on the latter are those that are commonly inflicted on rebel leaders, a good example being Alexander's treatment of Bessus a century later, which again startled the Greek writers.[112] (Another example of Persian influence on Alexander might be his experiment with napalm, when he tests it on a slave to see if it kills him – which it does, excruciatingly.) Herodotus' story may, accordingly, have distorted the narrative sequence of events: Masistes' attempt at rebellion should have preceded the punishment by mutilation.[113] Masistes might, in fact, be simply a title (*mathista*, 'greatest') and conceal the character Ariamenes, the ruler of Bactria; an attempt at usurpation by Xerxes' brother would not be unexpected at this point in his reign.[114]

We may thus, in a sense, exonerate Amestris from pure vengefulness. Nonetheless, the punishment she inflicted, even if it was 'justified', is seen by Herodotus as a fatal step in the process that led to Xerxes' eventual downfall.

The king, then, was a remote being to his subjects, with powers little different from those of a god, though he was never worshipped as one. He gave and withheld as he saw fit; he made the plants grow and the earth blossom; he pruned the trees and plucked the weeds, while his punishments of malefactors made clear the power of Truth to prevail over the stinking lies of brute matter. Pseudo-Aristotle was right to name both God and Xerxes in the same sentence. What it felt like to be a god on earth is truly difficult to determine.

CHAPTER FOUR

The Religion of Xerxes

Among those countries there was a place where previously false gods were worshipped. Afterwards, by the favour of Ahura Mazda, I destroyed that sanctuary of the demons, and I made proclamation, 'The demons shall not be worshipped!' Where previously the demons were worshipped, there I worshipped Ahura Mazda and Arta reverently.

XPh 35–41

The Shah's son [Esfandiyar] went –
A hero-slaying swordsman – with his host
To all the nations. Over Rum he passed
And Hindustan, passed Ocean and the Gloom,
And published the evangel by command
Of God, the All-provider. When folk learned
About the good faith, they received its rites,
Adorned themselves therewith, and sought instruction.
They burned the idols on their thrones, they kindled
The Fire in stead thereof, and all dispatched
This letter to the Shah: 'We have accepted
The faith delivered by Esfandiyar,
And donned the girdle. He hath ordered all.
Thou shouldst not now ask tribute of us, we
Have been converted and profess the Faith.
Send us the Zandavasta of Zardusht.'

Firdausi, *Shahnama*, tr. Warner and Warner, V. 76–77

Now that I have sought vengeance, adorned the world with splendour,
killed those who rose against God and whom it was necessary to kill,
there is not a place on earth which does not recognise my authority.
Kai Khosrow in Ferdowsi, *Shahnameh*, tr. Dick Davis, 348

THE QUESTION OF ZOROASTER

The inscription quoted above presents Xerxes as a strongly religious king,
even a man with missionary zeal. It may even be evidence that Darius and his
son represented religious revolution in Iran. To understand the significance
of the statement we must go a long way around, and explore the intractable
problems surrounding the prophet Zoroaster.

The religion of the Achaemenid kings is controversial. Their tombs are
adorned with the same figure of a bearded male in flight on a winged disk
('Ahura Mazda on his bicycle', as I once heard someone describe him) – but
he probably represents the king's royal glory, his *farr* (in modern Persian) or
khvarenah (Old Persian), not the god, as seen on modern Zoroastrian fire
temples. But were the kings Zoroastrians in the modern sense?[1] The question
is bound up with the date of the prophet Zoroaster, about which scholars
have held and continue to hold widely differing opinions. No one now thinks
he is purely a figure of legend: his name, meaning something like Old Camel,
is too prosaic for that, and his family lineage, of the Spitamas who are inde-
pendently attested, is too specific. One may begin, however, by discounting
the assertion in several Greek writers that he lived 6,000 years before Plato.[2]
This is the result of confusion with the Zoroastrian doctrine of 3,000-year
world cycles.

Among more rational opinions, one extreme is represented by Mary
Boyce,[3] who places the career of the prophet early in the second millennium
BC, between 1700 and 1000 – a period which begins in the Stone Age – a
view rejected as wildly improbable by Heidemarie Koch.[4] Gherardo Gnoli
offers a less extreme view, placing him around 1000 BC, on the basis of the
archaic quality of the language of the *Gathas*, perhaps the only religious
texts that can be attributed to Zoroaster himself.[5] A rather earlier date in
the Bronze Age is favoured by Paul Kriwaczek.[6] Warwick Ball[7] puts him a
bit later, 'before 800', which allows him plenty of time to influence the
theology of Isaiah.

If Zoroaster lived at any of these dates, before the rise of the Persian
Empire, then it is quite possible for his ideas to have influenced formative
Judaism among the exiles in Babylon and Susa, after they came under Persian

rule in the mid-sixth century. Influence is clearer from the sixth century onwards. Second Isaiah (45.1) refers to Cyrus, and if such passages as 42.3–4 and 45.8 and 12 are thought to convey Zoroastrian ideas,[8] then this would make the Persians Zoroastrians already in the time of Cyrus (ca. 560). Influence has also been detected on the Greek philosophers of the sixth century, Heraclitus and Anaximander. Heraclitus regards fire as the fundamental element in the universe and makes interesting remarks about the exposure of the dead; Anaximander's idea of cosmic justice seems to have something in common with the eternal cyclical conflict of good and evil in the Zoroastrian universe. Empedocles, too, echoes Zoroastrian tradition when he claims, like Zoroaster, to have pre-existed as, among other things, a bush.[9] But influence on these Greek philosophers, flourishing around 500 BC, is compatible with a late sixth-century dating of Zoroaster.

Zoroastrian tradition, however, is clear in the opinion that Zoroaster lived '258 years before Alexander'. This is given, for example in the *Arda Viraf Namag*, an account of a descent into hell by the eponymous Arda Viraf, and it also penetrated the Arabic chronicles such as that of Mas'udi.[10] If 'Alexander' is shorthand for 'Alexander's sack of Persepolis' in 330 BC, then that puts the prophet's *floruit* in 588. If we assume that this was when he was around forty, and that his life lasted seventy-seven years, as is also traditional, then his dates would be 628–551 BC.[11] This would place Zoroaster firmly in the 'Axial Age' that also ushered in the teaching of the Buddha, Confucius and the Pre-Socratic philosophers, the sixth and early fifth centuries BC. His ethical teaching transformed the character of the Indo-Iranian polytheism from which it derived, turning it into Mazdaean henotheism,[12] which comes close to monotheism – though the one God Ahura Mazda, the 'Wise Lord',[13] is almost equally balanced by the evil Ahriman – and introducing a regard for personal purity and morality that we do not find in any text of the Bronze Age. Ernst Herzfeld went so far as to assert 'The Persian Empire is the turning-point in the history of all religions.'[14]

Zoroaster's birth is described in the *Fravardin Yasht*:[15] 'Let us rejoice, for a priestly man is born, the Spitamid Zarathustra. From now on . . . Mithra will promote all supreme authorities of the nations and will pacify those in revolt.' (The hymn goes on to say the same of a long series of gods, first among them Apam Napat, the god of the waters.)

Persian tradition makes Zoroaster (Zardusht in Persian) a contemporary of the Kayanian King Gushtasp or Vishtaspa, who ruled in Balkh. Zoroaster's family name is Spitama, and his origin is variously placed in Azerbaijan (Qazvini) or Rayy. He is deemed to have come to the court of Gushtasp and converted him to the purified religion that he preached. E. G. Browne in the 1880s[16] encountered a Zoroastrian who identified himself as 'Zardushti, Kayani', i.e. of the race of the ancient Kayanian dynasty. One of the sacred books of Iran, the *Vishtasp Yasht*,[17] begins:

> 'I am a pious man, who speaks words of blessing', thus said Zarathustra to the young king Vishtaspa. – 'She appears to me full of Glory, O Zarathustra!' – 'O young king Vishtaspa! I bless thee with the living of a good life, of an exalted life, of a long life. May thy men live long! May thy women live long! May sons be born unto thee of thy own body!
>
> 2. 'Mayest thou thyself be holy, like Zarathustra! Mayest thou be rich in cattle, like an Athwayanide![18] Mayest thou be rich in horses, like Purushaspa! Mayest thou have a good share of bliss, like King Husravah! Mayest thou have strength to reach the Rangha, whose way lies afar!'[19]

Another sacred book, the Yasna,[20] puts praise of Vishtaspa in the mouth of Zoroaster:

> That insight the Kavi Vishtaspa, with his control of the rite, attained by the paths of Good Thought, the one which he meditated with Right, to proclaim for us as we desired, 'Bounteous is the Mindful Lord'.[21]

Zoroaster's preaching begins from the common ground of Indo-Aryan religion which is also known from the Vedas, but his attitude to tradition is reformist or even revolutionary. The religion he was combating was a traditional polytheism comparable to that of Vedic India, and deriving from a time before the Indo-Iranian culture split into two branches. It is easy to collect the points in common. A number of the gods have almost identical names: Iranian Mithra is Indian Mitra, such gods as Indra, Nasatya and Sarva appear in Zoroastrian texts as demons or *daevas*. Both religions regard fire as sacred, and both practise the consumption of a sacred drink that produces a mild ecstasy, *soma* for the Vedas, *homa* for the Iranians. Horse sacrifice is integral to Brahmanic religion, and there was a sacrifice of horses at the funeral of Cyrus.[22] Like the Buddha, Zoroaster looked at the world around him and saw it full of suffering and corruption. The conclusion he drew was that the world is the realm of evil, and humankind must escape it for the world of the good.[23]

The keys to his doctrine are reverence for the elements, Fire, Water and Earth (and also Air), a central focus on the Cow, the heart of the life of the pastoral Iranians, and an insistence on the right behaviour of the faithful.[24] 'All night long, address the heavenly Wisdom. Three times a day raise thyself up and go to take care of the beneficent cattle.' 'Have no bad priests . . . though thou wish to sacrifice, it will be to the Amesha Spentas as if no sacrifice had been offered.'[25] The Amesha Spentas are the beneficent spirits or 'bounteous immortals', aspects of the supreme god, and they are seven in number.[26] They are Aša, Right; Vohu Manah, Good Thought; Armati, Piety; Spenta manyu, Bounteous Will; Xšaθra, Dominion; Haurvetat, Wholeness; and Ameretat, Immortality. However, all these are merely aspects of the one Supreme God, so that Zoroaster has replaced the Vedic polytheism with a henotheistic position. It is henotheistic not monotheistic, because there is also an eternal Spirit of Evil, Ahriman or Angra Mainyu, whose realm is 'The Lie'. Zoroastrianism also includes belief in an afterlife and the coming some time in the future of a Saviour, Saoshyants, whose functions resemble those of the Jewish Messiah to whose coming Isaiah looks forward.

Zoroaster composed (like Homer, in a dialect so archaic that some have been tempted to place his lifespan six hundred years earlier) a series of hymns or *Gathas* in which he propounded his new religion of a single beneficent god constantly at war with an equally mighty power of evil; it is up to men to give every support to the good and to minimise the effect of evil in the world. Mani, in the third century AD, was to preach a similar doctrine of dualism, giving his name to the long-enduring tradition of Manichaeism.[27] Although the idea is similar, the social setting of Zoroaster's revelation is very different. But like Mani, Zoroaster set out to reform the religion of the Magi, the hereditary priestly caste of the Persians (like the Levites in Judaism).

Zoroaster gave the daevas the status of demons (in a bad sense) and made the *ahuras* the true objects of worship, chief among them Ahura Mazda, translated by M. L. West as 'The Mindful Lord'. This information concurs with the statement of the Greek historian Diodorus Siculus[28] that Zoroaster introduced the *Agathos Daimon* or 'Good Spirit'. His teaching reflects the conditions of a pastoral society, as Hymn 33 makes clear:

> He that is best to the righteous one, whether with clan or village
> Or tribe, or by tending the cow with care,
> Will be in the pasture of Right and Good Thought.
> I that by worship will seek to keep from Thee, Mindful One,

disregard and bad thought
And the clan's arrogance and the village's closest neighbour, Wrong,
And the detractors in the tribe, and from the cow's pasture the worst
counsellor . . .
I long, Mindful Lord, to see Thee and confer with Thee.[29]

The position of the other Indo-Iranian gods in Zoroaster's system is something of a puzzle. Notably Mithra, who became so important in later centuries, seems to have no place in this system and ought, by its logic, to be no
more than a daeva. Yet there is a *Yasht* addressed to Mithra, which begins:

> Ahura Mazda spake unto Spitama Zarathustra, saying, 'Verily, when I
> created Mithra, the lord of wide pastures, o Spitama! I created him as
> worthy of sacrifice, as worthy of prayer as myself, Ahura Mazda.'[30]

The *Yasht* seems to be modifying the single-mindedness of Zoroaster, and
the fact that the *Yashts* are addressed to a great variety of divine beings,
including the angel Ordibehesht, the Sun and Moon, the Earth and the star
Vega (Vanant), suggests that the religion as it developed found room for a
plurality of objects of worship, much as Catholic Christianity accommo-
dates a variety of saints. Other major deities include Apam Napat, God of
the waters, who appears in a relief at Cyrus' Pasargadae, but not in later
Achaemenid times, and the Semitic goddess Anahita, who is occluded until
the reign of Artaxerxes I, after Xerxes' death.

The impact of Zoroaster's arrival is evoked in Abolqasem Ferdowsi's
Book of Kings (completed in 1010, the year of his death: he was born in 940),
in a passage that he said was revealed to him by his predecessor, Abu Mansur
Ahmed Daqiqi (ca. 932–976), in a dream. It should for this reason incorporate tradition much older than Ferdowsi. Gushtasp had not long been
enthroned in Balkh when the prophet appeared:

> Thus passed a while, and then a Tree appeared[31]
> On earth within the palace of Gushtasp
> And grew up to the roof – a Tree whose roots
> Spread far and wide, a Tree with many branches,
> Its leafage precept and its fruitage wisdom:
> How shall one die who eateth of such fruit?
> A Tree right fortunate and named Zardhusht,
> The slayer of malignant Ahriman.

Thus said he to the monarch of the world:
'I am a prophet and thy guide to God.'
He brought a censer, filled with fire, and said: –
'This have I brought with me from Paradise
The Maker of the world said: "Take thou this,
And look upon the heaven and the earth,
Because I made them not of dust and water:
Behold herein how I created them . . ."
Receive his good religion from the speaker,
And learn from him his usage and the way.
See that thou do as he directeth thee,
Choose wisdom, recognise this world as vile,
And learn the system of the good religion,
For kingship is not well when faith is lacking.'[32]

The echoes of the Book of Genesis are intriguing: Zoroaster is a Tree of Knowledge of good and evil who will not cause the Fall of Man but will lead to immortal life; and God has created the world not, as the God of the Jews created Adam, from dust, but from fire. Around 500 BC in Ephesus the 'dark philosopher' Heraclitus also taught that the world consisted of 'the turnings of fire', which would end in a universal conflagration and (perhaps) a phoenix-like recreation of the world. An influence from Persia on a thinker who lived on the fringes of Darius' empire is far from improbable.

The tree was felled by the Muslim ruler al-Mutawakkil in 861.[33] It was sliced into logs and brought to Baghdad, though the people of Persepolis offered 50,000 gold pieces to save it. However, the Caliph was murdered the day after the logs' arrival. This information, from the seventeenth-century *Dabestan*, also states that the tree was planted 1,450 years earlier, i.e. in 589 BC, a neat coincidence with the regular tradition on the dating of Zoroaster's arrival 258 years before Alexander.

The tradition is consistent. The Arab historian al-Tabari (tenth century AD)[34] says that 'Bishtasb (i.e. Gushtasp, Vishtaspa) and his father Luhrasb embraced the religion of the Sabians, until Sami[35] and Zoroaster came to Bishtasb with their tenets. This occurred after thirty years of his reign [of 150 years] had elapsed.' (The Sabians may be identifiable with the modern Mandaeans, though in Tabari's time the term applied to a star-worshipping sect centred on Harran.) Mir Khwand,[36] too (284–286) brings Zoroaster to the court of Gushtasp; unlike Ferdowsi, he writes from a strongly Muslim viewpoint and refers to Zoroaster as a follower of Iblis (the Devil). He also tells us that Zoroaster had previously been a tree,[37] and a cow, and that he laughed at the moment of his birth. He further attributes to him the writing down of the Avesta on a set of golden ox-hides that were said to have been kept at Persepolis until Alexander destroyed them.[38]

GUSHTASP AND DARIUS

The name of Gushtasp is the same as that of Hystaspes, the father of Darius, and it is tempting to make connections. This Gushtasp, however, is ruler in Balkh, nowhere near Fars where the Achaemenid kings have their origins. Furthermore, his son is Esfandiyar and there is no mention of Darius. The problem, as was already outlined in the introduction, is that the part of the *Shahnameh* which ought to be telling the story of the Achaemenid kings, between the outright legendary rulers from creation onwards, and the arrival of Alexander the Great in Persia, shows no cognisance whatever of any Achaemenid stories. Instead, the stories are east Iranian in their setting and probably derive from Parthian tradition. Whether the Parthians enfolded into their legends some dimly remembered stories of their predecessors is of course another question. It seems not impossible, though such stories would probably have survived only in the form of romantic tales about the court (such as we find in Ctesias). Nothing could be more natural than that the Parthian *gosan*s (storytellers) should retell these stories but give them more familiar settings in their homeland of Khorasan. That is what the author of *Vamiq o 'Adhra* did to the Greek novel of Metiochus and Parthenope,[39] and that is what the compilers of the *One Thousand and One Nights* did with stories that came from the most varied of sources, from Greece to Persia.[40]

It is, however, possible that Darius' family did come from Bactria, even though he came to power as satrap of Hyrcania. There is a hint in Plutarch's *Sayings of Kings and Commanders*,[41] when dispute arises over who is to succeed Darius: 'Ariamenes, the brother of Xerxes, was on his way down from the Bactrian country.' He was presumably one of the elder brothers from Darius' previous marriage, born before he became king. If Darius came from Bactria, he could have married there and had his first children before his rise in the Persian bureaucracy began. Perhaps his father really was ruler in Balkh. (However, Artaxerxes' brother Hystaspes was also governor in Balkh at the time of his father's assassination: perhaps it was a post regularly allotted to a son of the ruling king?)

There is further support for the Bactrian connection in the Roman historian Ammianus Marcellinus:

Hystaspes in pursuit of knowledge, having penetrated into the remote parts of Northern India, reached a secluded place amidst forests, the calm retreats of which were inhabited by Brahmins of the most exalted order: being counselled by them, he directed his utmost attention to learning the principles of the motions of the universe and the stars, also the pure forms of worship. A part of what he had thus acquired he inculcated on the minds of the Magi; which they handed down to their posterity, in conjunction with the science of foretelling future events.[42]

For Ammianus, then, Gushtasp had sought a guru in Bactria and brought back his teaching to his kingdom. Also in Ferdowsi, Gushtasp, rejected by his father, goes to India (and Rum! – the name denotes the Byzantine Empire) before coming back with a Rumi wife.[43] Her name is Nahid, i.e. Anahita. This seems to be purely fantasy. In the *Yashts*, by contrast, Gushtasp's sister-wife is Hutaosa, or as the Greeks pronounced it Atossa, and she is the mother of Esfandiyar,[44] while Greek sources make her the mother of Xerxes.

There is a good chance, then, that the Gushtasp of Persian tradition is really the same man as the historical Vishtaspa/Hystaspes who was Darius' father. The argument is not neat, as Darius does not feature at all in the tradition and many of the acts of Gushtasp have to be aligned with the historical deeds of Darius. (Not least among these is his son, Esfandiyar, who holds the place that Xerxes should occupy in this legendary genealogy.)[45] Further, Gushtasp in Ferdowsi built a great palace which seems to be that at Persepolis, around the cypress tree planted by Zoroaster:

> When it had sent aloft full many a bough
> Gushtasp raised over it a goodly palace,
> Whereof the height and breadth were forty cubits;
> He used no clay or water in the building.
> When he had reared the palace of pure gold,
> With silvern earth and dust of ambergris,
> He painted there a picture of Jamshid,
> Engaged in worshipping the sun and moon,
> Commanded too a picture to be drawn
> Of Faridun armed with the ox-head mace,
> And limned there all the potentates . . .[46]

Jamshid, the legendary founder of Persepolis, is here assumed to be the subject portrayed in the winged disc, while the 'potentates' are clearly the delegates who eternally process up the great staircase to the royal presence.

There may be a dynastic link between Zoroaster and Darius, too. Ctesias provides us with the following genealogy:

Ctesias says that when Cyrus conquered Media, Astyages went into hiding with Amytis and her husband Spitamas.[47] After Spitamas was killed on Cyrus' orders, Amytis married Cyrus. Her sons were Spitakes and Megabernes.[48]

Darius was at best a descendant of Teispes, the great-grandfather of Cyrus, and thus his claim to the throne was weak. Can it be that Darius and Zoroaster joined forces after the death of Cambyses? Darius married Atossa and thus became a relative by marriage (half-brother-in-law) of Spitakes. Thus the lineages of Cyrus and Astyages combine in Darius. If Zoroaster is really this dynastic intriguer, the character seems at odds with that of the other-worldly prophet. But, as Bruce Lincoln observes,[49]

Table 4 The Families of Spitama and Cyrus

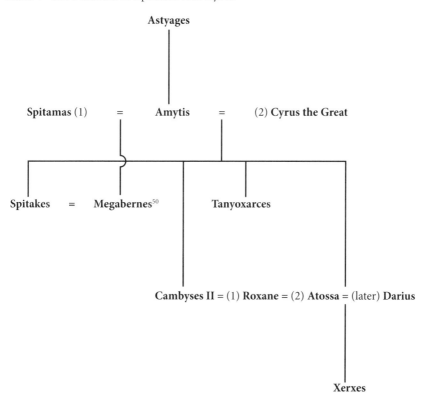

Darius refers to Ahura Mazda no fewer than seventy-six times in his Bisutun inscription: 'he made an effort to plead his cause in dynastic terms, but, like most usurpers, he was more inclined to stress the charismatic side of the argument'.

Herzfeld interprets the Revolt of the Magi (better, the usurpation of the magus) as a 'strike of the civil service' but perhaps more importantly as an eastern Iranian revolt against the Achaemenids, an attempt to secure what they saw as the legitimate succession of a Kayanid.[51] Gaumata's populist overtures would be an attempt to overturn the new social order.[52] On the wrongness of social revolution, Dick Davis draws attention to a parallel case in Ferdowsi, where 'Mazdak preaches a kind of proto-communism, saying that wealth and women should be held in common. Qobad is swayed by Mazdak's eloquence, but his son Anushirvan will have none of it. . . . Mazdak's followers are killed by having their heads buried in the ground; after being shown this edifying sight Mazdak is strung up on a gallows and shot full of arrows.'[53]

So the rise of Zoroaster is not just a religious revolution but in part a political one: the accession of Darius is not the rise of an interloper from Fars but the result of the Bactrian dynasty of Hystaspes making common cause with that of the Spitamas clan against the line of Cambyses. Historically, Darius' father Hystaspes is supposed to have been satrap of Hyrcania, within striking distance of the other branch of the family in Balkh.

Real confusion is introduced by Ctesias who refers to Gomata, 'the false Smerdis', as Sphendadates. This name is almost certainly that which was preserved in later tradition as Esfandiyar. But the role is completely wrong. No doubt Sphendadates came into the story somewhere, and Ctesias has misremembered just how.

Problems with the Attribution of Zoroastrianism
to the Persian Kings

Mary Boyce believed that all the Achaemenid kings, from Cyrus the Great onwards, were Zoroastrians in more or less the modern sense. Such a view naturally depends on a relatively early dating of Zoroaster, at least before Cyrus, if not, as Boyce proposed, in the second millennium BC. A more prevalent view has been that, as the tradition tells us, the religion came in with Darius, who rejected important aspects of the religion of Cyrus. This could be symbolised by the non-reappearance of the fish-clad deity Apam Napat, who appears on pillars at Susa but is not found thereafter. Cyrus' tomb is of a quite different design from those of the later Achaemenid kings, and there was also a horse sacrifice at his funeral, which would not be an acceptable rite for Zoroastrians. But there are problems with the identification even of Darius' and Xerxes' religion as Zoroastrian as distinct from Mazdaean. Some scholars have thought that throughout their reigns, Zoroastrianism was just one religion among many in the Persian lands.[54] (In the whole empire, of course, there were always many religions.) In the reign after Xerxes', that of Artaxerxes I, there seems to be a re-emergence of non-Zoroastrian deities such as Anahita; at the same time, a reform of the calendar under Artaxerxes I gave all the months the names of Zoroastrian angels, which they still bear today, suggesting that this might be the period at which Zoroastrianism became fully entrenched.

Albert De Jong has made a helpful distinction between three possible views of the history of Achaemenid religion: the 'fragmentising' approach, which supposes a number of different and mutually exclusive religions in Persia; the 'harmonising' approach, which allows for only one, highly conservative and unchanging tradition of Zoroastrian belief and practice; and the 'diversity' view, which allows for historical change and development in the religion: on this last view, the *Gathas* are not the origin of all Zoroastrian doctrine, and other gods can win and lose adherence over time within the overall dualist framework.[55]

The main arguments against the Zoroastrianism of Darius and Xerxes depend on taking the strong, 'harmonising' view of Zoroastrian history. They are as follows.

First, there seems little evidence of dualism in their inscriptions, all of which refer to Ahura Mazda alone as the supreme, good god. Zoroastrianism, however, teaches that the world is an endless battlefield between good and evil, the latter represented by Ahriman or Angra-Mainyu. But there was no need for the king to refer to the evil principle: all Darius needs to announce is that he is Ahura Mazda's agent. Furthermore, Darius' inscribed pronouncements are insistent about his rejection of 'The Lie': this term for all that is evil is congruent with the attitude to Ahriman shown in Zoroastrian literature. The fact that Greek authors rarely refer to Ahriman has been taken to indicate that this deity was not significant for the Achaemenids. Herodotus never mentions him, though Plutarch in his *Life of Themistocles*, writing some 600 years later, does. Does this mean that the dualism in this form came in between the time of Herodotus, or his informants, and that of Plutarch?

The second and most obvious difference from modern Zoroastrianism is that there is no evidence for exposure of the dead. For Zoroastrians, the elements of earth, water and fire are all holy and must not be polluted by death, so bodies are exposed until the flesh falls away and the clean bones are placed in an ossuary. But how can we know in what condition the kings were laid to rest? Were they embalmed before being entombed, or had their bodies too been exposed to the elements and the birds of the air to be picked clean before bones alone were laid to rest? As all the tombs are empty, we cannot know. But there is one hint from a rock-cut tomb at Limyra in Lycia, which the Greek inscription calls a τάφος, 'tomb', while the Aramaic counterpart refers to it by the Persian word *astōdana*, meaning an ossuary.[56] This might suggest that, here at least, the dead man was excarnated by the birds of the air before his bones were entombed. Aristobulus says that the dead were exposed in this way at Taxila in Swat, on the fringes of the Achaemenid realm.[57] A further consideration is that, according to Herodotus and Strabo, only the Magi were excarnated.[58] Agathias also refers to this as a practice of the Magi alone, rather than something done by everyone.[59] So it may be that ordinary people were buried,[60] whereas the kings were mummified and/or entombed. It is also likely that the practice changed between the time of Cyrus and Darius.[61] Cyrus' body was laid to rest in a huge tomb, while the kings from Darius onwards were placed in rock-cut tombs with small loculi for the bodies; they did not have the viewing facilities that Cyrus' tomb provided. Ernst Herzfeld deduced from this that Darius' religion differed from that of Cyrus: Darius was a Zoroastrian.

Third, no securely identified fire temples have been found prior to the Parthian period,[62] and this is consonant with Herodotus' observation that the Persians had no temples but their priests, the Magi, conducted ceremonies in the open air. (Greeks tended to interpret this as sun worship.)[63] What seem to be fire altars, however, are frequently represented on the tombs of Darius and later kings.[64] The gold plaques from the Oxus Treasure depict figures who seem to be Zoroastrian priests, sometimes with masked faces, holding the bundles of sticks known as *barsoms*,[65] and there are masked figures also on the reliefs at Persepolis.

Furthermore, several anecdotes about the Persian kings seem inconsistent with the reverence for the elements preached by Zoroaster. If the stories about Cyrus' capture of Croesus and his plan to burn him alive on a pyre have any historical validity, they should suggest that Cyrus cannot have been a Zoroastrian. Cambyses' burning of the Egyptian pharaoh Amasis is said to have distressed the Persian elite,[66] and similarly implies that this king had no reverence for fire. Again, Xerxes' flogging of the Hellespont was seen by Diogenes Laertius as essentially un-Zoroastrian; but this may be explained by the fact that the victim here was salt water.[67] Persians, who had rarely seen the sea in their central Asian homeland, revered above all the life-giving fresh waters: salt water would be the province of the evil Ahriman. The burial alive of young people at Nine Ways as a sacrifice[68] seems also to be un-Zoroastrian, and to show lack of reverence for the element of earth; but against that, burial alive occurs not infrequently as a method of execution in Persia.

The horse sacrifice at Cyrus' tomb seems also to be non-Zoroastrian, though it fits well with earlier Indo-Aryan practice. Xenophon supposed that horse-sacrifice was a 'normal' part of the ritual of the Achaemenid kings, for he describes a sacrifice of both horses and cattle to the Sun, in *Cyropaedia*.[69]

Another problem is the use of the intoxicant or stimulant *homa*. Zoroaster inveighs against the use of this drug, but the Persepolis treasury relief from the reign of Xerxes depicts a pestle and mortar, presumably used for pounding the plant from which *homa* is made.[70] Ugo Bianchi's response would be that what Zoroaster opposes is the unbridled use of the stimulant.[71] (The identity of *homa*, incidentally, has been a perennial puzzle. It is made by pounding the stems of a plant to make a drink: the plant is addressed in one of the *Yashts* as a kind of god, brilliantly bright and yellow-gold in colour: 'we worship the yellow lofty one'.[72] The procedure of preparation is too brief to permit the fermentation that would be necessary if it were wine, as Herzfeld proposed. Other theories include rhubarb – but the kind that grows in my garden is red, not yellow – coffee (even more improbable), cannabis, mandrake, magic mushrooms and ginseng. The most plausible candidate seems to be Joint Pine, *ephedra fragilis*, a plant with stiff stems, rather like broom, clad in tufts of bright yellow flowers. Texts refer to its 'stems and shoots'. It is the plant from which the stimulant ephedrine is made, making it the ideal candidate for a consciousness-enhancing drink for religious use.)[73]

All these problems can be explained away if we assume that the kings are somehow special: their burial rites might be different, and anyway tyrants can express their power by flouting norms. Philip Kreyenbroek echoes others in proposing a non-essentialist interpretation of Zoroastrianism;[74] far from being immutable, as for Boyce, it is a religion constantly in process of formation, not least in the first century or so of its existence. We should not expect religious practice of 2,500 years ago to be the same as that of the present day. I think we are entitled to regard Darius as the introducer of the revelation of

Zoroaster to the people of Persia.[75] Cyrus, whatever exactly his religion was, had not benefited from the revelation of Zoroaster.

THE MAGI

The essence of Persian religion, for Greek and Roman writers, was the role of the Magi.[76] In Herodotus they are the functionaries of all the religious rites of the Persian kings:

> They do not anthropomorphize their gods as the Greeks do. Their worship of Zeus consists in going up to the highest mountain peaks and performing sacrifices; they call the whole vault of heaven Zeus. They also sacrifice to the sun and the moon, and to earth, fire, water and the winds. . . . They do not construct altars or light fires when they are going to perform a sacrifice, nor do they use libations, reed-pipes, garlands or barley. . . . Once he has chopped up the limbs of the sacrificial victim into pieces and boiled the meat, he spreads out the freshest grass he can find . . . and places all the meat on it. When this arrangement is in place, a Magus comes up and chants a theogony – at least, that is what they say the song is about. There always has to be a Magus present for a sacrifice to take place.[77]

In this passage Herodotus, as usual, defines Persian practice largely by its difference from that of the Greeks. This may explain why he says the Magi do not 'light fires': they do not need to, because the sacred fire never goes out! The passage cannot be used as an argument that there were no fire-altars in his day. Herodotus makes clear that he did not understand everything about the ceremony – and perhaps he had never seen one – when he mentions that he has only been told that the hymn (a *Yasht*?) is a 'theogony'. The centrality of the Magi is, however, a datum for him, as for most later Greek authors. Magi are also well known for their role as prophets,[78] though Herodotus was clear that they were less good at their trade than Greek diviners.[79]

The Magi were a priestly tribe or caste, from Media, comparable with the Levites among the Jews and the Brahmans in India.[80] It is tempting to see them as the representatives of the malpractices that Zoroaster combats, and the fantasy of F. Marion Crawford, in his novel *Zoroaster* (1885), pushes this to an extreme. In this novel, Zoroaster is summoned from self-imposed exile to give advice to King Darius on the reform of the Mazdaean religion as conducted by the Magi. The sensitive Darius is repelled by the extravagant behaviour of these Magi ('half of them are black,' complains his wife Atossa, drawing attention to the consanguinity of the Iranian Magi with the Indian Brahmans) and their over-indulgence in the intoxicating *homa*. At a climactic scene in the supposed 'Temple of Ahura Mazda' at Persepolis,

> Ever more and more they drank, repeating the verses of the hymn without order or sequence. One man repeated a verse over and over again in ear-piercing shrieks, swaying his body to and fro till he dropped forward upon the ground, foaming at the mouth, his features distorted with a wild convulsion, and his limbs as rigid as stone. Here, a band of five locked their arms together, and, back to back, whirled madly round, screaming out the names of the archangels, in an indiscriminate rage of sound and broken syllables. One, less enduring than the rest, relaxed his hold upon his fellow's arm and fell headlong on the pavement, while the remaining four were carried on by the force of their whirling, and fell together against others who steadied themselves against the wall, swaying their heads and arms from side to side. Overthrown by the fall of their compan-ions, these in their turn fell forward upon the others, and in a few moments, the whole company lay grovelling one upon the other, foaming at the mouth, but still howling out detached verses of their hymn – a mass of raging, convulsed humanity, tearing each other in the frenzy of drunk-enness, rolling over and over each other in the twisted contortions of frenzied maniacs.[81]

Whatever the magian religion was like, it is hard to believe it bore much resemblance to this temperance preacher's nightmare. But Crawford's imagi-native approach may nonetheless suggest an interpretative possibility relating to the conflict of king and Magi. Darius' reign began, on 29 September 522 BC, with a conspiracy to place a magus on the throne:[82] as has frequently occurred in Iranian history, it was the priestly caste that threw up the founders of dynasties, like Papak the founder of the Sassanian Empire.[83] After the defeat of the conspiracy, the Magi were murdered – not only those involved, but also any whom people happened to meet in the street, according to Herodotus;[84] furthermore, the event was said to have been commemorated by an annual festival. The information has attracted some doubt,[85] but even if there really was a celebration of the 'Murder of the Magi', there is no doubt that the Magi continued to play a central role in the religious life of Persia for centuries afterwards.

Interpretation of the role of the Magi in the empire has ranged between extremes: for one school they are the villains of the piece, for another they are the main disseminators of Zoroastrianism, more Zoroastrian than anybody.[86] On the former view, this (temporary) suppression of the power of this Median caste of priests might well have been connected with the reformist activities of a king who had fallen under the sway of the prophet Zoroaster. A 'purification' of the national religion would be a good way to establish a ruler whose genealogical credentials were less than perfect.[87] Darius' attack on Gaumata accuses him of 'destroying the holy places'. Heidemarie Koch suggests that we should see here a conflict of the Magi and the fire-priests, whose temples will have been vandalised by Gaumata.[88] But Gherardo Gnoli favours a more limited interpretation of this passage of DB, namely that Darius is simply cleaning up after the collateral damage caused by the uprising. Probably we shall never know exactly what happened, but there seems little doubt that, by the reign of Xerxes, the Magi, like so many Vicars of Bray, had adapted themselves to the prevailing religious climate and were once again central to Persian religion.

It is notable that Ferdowsi never mentions the Magi. In fact he does not dwell on matters of religion at all. He neither mentions the rites of the Persian people, nor, though he is writing for a Muslim patron, does he make any references to Islam. His nationalist stance even excludes Arabic words from his vocabulary, and he goes so far as to make Alexander a Christian (because he is a Rumi, i.e. Byzantine). But the struggle between Darius and the Magi may be reflected in that battle Ferdowsi describes, between Arjasp the Turkmen on the one hand and Gushtasp and 'that old sorcerer' on the other.[89] (The Turkmens are the textbook barbarians for the Persian people.)

In sum, it looks as if a change occurred in Persian religion with the accession of Darius, the first 'Persian' king.[90] The kings of Anshan, Cyrus and Cambyses may have claimed allegiance to Ahura Mazda, but Darius the Persian made them Zoroastrians. The Magi as a tribe may have taken a beating as a result of the victory of Darius in the succession; yet the Magi as a priestly caste hung on and remained central to Iranian religion in its now reformed state.[91]

Darius' vigorous onslaught on 'The Lie', so prominent in his propaganda, finds its mythological counterpart in the binding of the demon-king Zahhak. Stories relating to Zahhak may even have found their way westwards. In Aeschylus' *Prometheus Bound*, Prometheus, the helper of mankind but 'the enemy' of Zeus, is chained like Zahhak on a remote mountain; his liver is chewed daily by an eagle, and bleeds continually, like the heart of Zahhak in

Ferdowsi. Although Zahhak is portrayed as a teacher of repulsive arts and customs, in some texts it is possible to discern him as a helper of humankind, like Prometheus. In this interpretation, the play by 'Aeschylus' (for it is unlikely to be by him) is a dramatisation of what is in many ways an Iranian theme, the endless struggle of good versus evil. But if Zeus is a Persian king, then the liberator has to be a Greek hero, Heracles: the myth is turned on its head.[92]

<h2 style="text-align:center">TOLERATION</h2>

The Persian Empire has acquired the reputation of being a tolerant society.[93] Religious toleration is a more contested matter. The founder, Cyrus, was explicit in a statement of religious toleration. The Cyrus cylinder states the case:

> I am Cyrus, king of the universe, the great king, the powerful king, king of the four quarters of the world, son of Cambyses . . . descendant of Teispes, the great king, king of the city of Anshan. . . . I sought the safety of the city of Babylon and all its sanctuaries . . . the sanctuaries across the river Tigris – whose shrines had earlier become dilapidated, the gods who lived therein, and made permanent sanctuaries for them. I collected together all of their people and returned them to their settlements, and the gods of the land of Sumer and Akkad which Nabonidus – to the fury of the lord of the gods – had brought into Shuanna, at the command of Marduk, the great lord, I returned them unharmed to their cells, in the sanctuaries that make them happy.

Other documents refer to 'Cyrus, who loves Esagila [the temple of Bel in Babylon]'.

As Bruce Lincoln puts it, 'Conceivably the Teispid kings were eclectic and/or opportunistic in their theology, worshipping Marduk in Babylon, YHWH in Jerusalem, Horus and Ra in Memphis, Apollo in Miletus, and so on.'[94] This could be interpreted either as enlightened tolerance or as calculated self-interest. One may cite Darius' concern for the sacred gardeners of Apollo at Aulai (see Chapter 3), or for the Temple in Jerusalem. Josephus asserts that Xerxes was 'pious to Yahweh'[95] – but the king in Josephus' account is in fact Artaxerxes I.[96] The pogrom in Susa that drives the plot of Esther might, however, be taken as evidence against toleration, while during the Ionian revolt, it seems, sanctuaries were systematically destroyed as punishment.[97] The situation in Greece is more complex, as a later discussion will make clear. Toleration as such may be an anachronistic concept,[98] but these passages do show a concern for the maintenance of established religions.

XERXES AND THE DAEVAS

Xerxes himself, however, has been seen as a king with a mission to establish Zoroastrianism to the exclusion of all other religions. One of his own inscriptions states:

> Among these countries there was [a place] where previously false gods were worshipped. Afterwards, by the favour of Ahura Mazda, I destroyed that sanctuary of the demons, and I made proclamation, 'The demons shall not be worshipped!' Where previously the demons were worshipped, there I worshipped Ahuramazda and Arta [Justice] reverently.[99]

Interestingly, Esfandiyar speaks in rather similar terms in the *History of the Early Kings of Persia* by Mir Khwand:

> I am Esfandiyar, the son of Gushtasp, who have cleansed the face of the earth from the polluted existence of the wicked; quelled whatever tumults have arisen in the four quarters; freed the world from the treason of the idolatrous and reprobate; and confirmed the true worshippers in the service of the Almighty.[100]

He goes on to speak in praise of Zardusht, Zoroaster. The account is a summary of the longer narrative in Ferdowsi,[101] in which Esfandiyar carries the faith of Zoroaster far and wide, even as far as Rum (equivalent to the Byzantine Empire, and thus including Greece) and Hindustan: he burns the idols and sends copies of the Zend Avesta to the benighted nations.[102] Even in the 1970s, the Shah of Iran believed that he had a divine mission, like that of Jamshid. Messages from God had helped him 'save' his country.[103] (Mind you, the American president thought the same.)

'The place' referred to in Xerxes' inscription could be anywhere, of course, but it has sometimes been thought to be Babylon. Herodotus says that, after suppressing a revolt in Babylon soon after his accession, Xerxes carried off a statue of solid gold, fifteen feet high, from the temple of Bel, and killed the priest who tried to prevent him.[104] This was not the cult statue itself, but the sacrilege recalls the stories of Cambyses' desecration in

Egypt – and, later, of Xerxes' removal of artistic treasures from Athens. However, it is only Alexander's propaganda that made Xerxes the destroyer of E-sagila, so that he himself could pose as its restorer.[105]

Xerxes' proclamation could with equal plausibility be taken as describing the Athenian Acropolis. Religious zeal has sometimes been counted among the motives for the invasion, but this is inconsistent with Xerxes' veneration of, for example, the temple of Athena at Troy. The key consideration seems to be whether an enemy submits gracefully or has to be beaten into submission in battle; in the latter case, the gods are treated as enemies just like the humans they protect, and come in for similar destruction.[106]

A more 'religious' assessment of Xerxes' campaign has been based by some authors on interpretation of this 'daeva-inscription', quoted above.[107] In this argument Xerxes is credited with a missionary zeal to bring over the whole world to his own creed.[108] The question was examined thoroughly in an important article by Ugo Bianchi, in which he argues for a purely 'local' interpretation of the daeva-inscription.[109] The daevas, in this view, are not foreign gods, who could not be described as 'the other gods who are', but gods of the popular religion at a lower level than Ahura Mazda. (Nor do they include, for example, Mithras, who retains his status alongside Ahura Mazda.) It should be noted that the Persepolis Fortification Tablets, dating from the reigns of Darius and Xerxes, contain mention of many deities, as well as of the *lan* sacrifice which seems, whatever it is, not to be a fire-rite. Marduk, for example, could not be one of the daevas, since he is sometimes seen as simply the Babylonian name for Ahura Mazda. In the *Gathas* this term is used for the gods of Zoroaster's ancestors, the 'idols'. Drug and Aeshma, Lie and Violence, are also demons in this sense. Heleen Sancisi-Weerdenburg[110] went further and argued that the inscription is entirely generic and does not contain a 'personal' statement. It is simply a statement of religious orthodoxy. 'The worship of Ahura Mazda is a metaphor for loyalty to the king',[111] and, as a corollary, daeva-worship is a metonym for rebellion.[112] The emphasis is on the fact that 'where false gods were worshipped, *I* worshipped Ahura Mazda': i.e. Xerxes brought right thinking to places of The Lie; but he did not impose it permanently. He improved these places by performing Zoroastrian rituals in them. This view has now come to be accepted, but it is nonetheless a forceful statement of the religious underpinning of Persian rule.[113] The most recent statement, by Wouter Henkelman,[114] draws attention to an inscription of the Elamite king Tepti-Huban-Insušnak some seventy to ninety years before Xerxes, which asserts the dominant religion in similar terms. Xerxes' inscription is, for him, 'an ideological manifesto dealing with the eternal ruler, the *pax Achaemenidica* guaranteed by Auramazda and his representative, the King of Kings'. On this reading, Xerxes is a faithful Zoroastrian but not a missionary or proselytiser. His expeditions against both Babylon and Greece had more central motives than the religious.

CHAPTER FIVE

Invasion (I): The Cornerstone of Greek Freedom

The king with half the east at heel is marched from lands of morning.
His armies drink the rivers up, his shafts benight the air
And he that stands will die for nought, and home there's no returning;
The Spartans on the sea-wet rock sat down and combed their hair.
A. E. Housman

& oon the merveile that ever I dede reede,
Grettist & unkouth pleynli onto me,
Is how Xerxes, kynge off Perse & Mede,
For to shewe a special syngulerte,
Out off Asie, ouer the Grete se,
As seith myn auctour, whom I dar alegge,
Into Europe made a myhti bregge.
John Lydgate, *Fall of Princes*, IV, 2255–61

The Problem of the West: Egypt and Babylon

When Darius died in 486 BC, Xerxes inherited his problems with his kingdom. Perhaps he was always under the shadow of his great father; much of his reign seems to consist of dealing with Darius' unfinished business. In order to live up to his great father he must prove himself a great conqueror: 'I need victories,' Gore Vidal has him say on his accession, echoing Xerxes' own claim in Herodotus that God is guiding him to glory and the conquest of new lands.[1] In this he resembles Esfandiyar in the *Shahnameh*, who remains under the thumb of his father Gushtasp all his life – so much so that Gushtasp eventually imprisons him on suspicion of conspiracy. Plainly the latter episode has nothing to do with the historical Xerxes, but Dick Davis draws attention to a recurring pattern in the *Shahnameh* in which the old order is constantly reasserted against the new: the father destroys the son.[2] Should we think that it was following Darius' example that led Xerxes to disaster? Xerxes admits to immaturity[3] and frequently vacillates; but his conduct of the Greek invasion was not irrational. However, Greece was not his first concern.

First among Xerxes' duties was the recovery of Egypt, which he undertook 'in the year after Darius death' (485/4).[4] It seems to have been an easy campaign, and all that Herodotus otherwise tells us is that Xerxes installed his full brother Achaemenes as ruler of Egypt, which he governed for some twenty years. (He was murdered in another revolt that began in 464, the year after Xerxes' death.) The implication is that Xerxes abandoned his predecessors' Egyptianising approach for direct control of this, his most westerly dominion.[5] Herodotus speaks of the Egyptians being 'enslaved'.

An opaque reference in the Book of Ezra runs 'the people of the land weakened the hands of the people of Judah, and troubled them in building [sc. the Temple] . . . . And in the reign of Ahasuerus, in the beginning of his reign, wrote they unto him an accusation against the inhabitants of Judah and Jerusalem.'[6] The account continues with specific reference to Artaxerxes, Xerxes' successor: a letter is sent to him that results in the mission of Ezra to Jerusalem. The parallel account in Esdras puts the disturbance in the time of Zerubbabel,[7] i.e. in the reign of Darius. One possible interpretation of these passages is that there was a revolt, or civil conflict, in Judah at the beginning of Xerxes' reign, which caused the Temple to be delayed and/or damaged, and only restored under Ezra in the 440s. However, the chronological indications are so contradictory, the names of the kings so muddled, and the description of the troubles so vague, that it is unwise to base much upon them. We cannot safely say that Xerxes' troubles in the west extended to Judah.[8]

There was, however, almost certainly a serious revolt in Babylon, as is stated by Ctesias.[9] The catalyst may have been increased taxation.[10] A document from Babylon dated to August 482/1 names Belšimanni as 'king of Babylon'.[11] It has been thought that he may have remained in power as little as two weeks, but probably his revolt began in 484. There may in fact have been two usurpations in Babylon in Xerxes' Year 2, to judge from the interruptions in the archives.[12] Ctesias says that the Babylonians murdered their governor Zopyrus, but Herodotus makes this Zopyrus a general of Darius I who devised a remarkable ruse to induce the Babylonians to open their gates to the Persian army in 522/1.[13] Zopyrus went so far as to mutilate himself and announce to the Babylonians that it was Darius who had removed his nose and ears, and that therefore he was in rebellion against his king. When the Babylonians believed him and let in Zopyrus' troops, it turned out that this was the imperial Persian army; and thus Babylon was retaken. Darius' army is said to have destroyed the city wall and torn down the gates, and impaled 3,000 men.[14] If this can be believed, Zopyrus then remained in Babylon as governor, despite his disfigurement, until he was murdered in the revolt of Belšimanni.

Ctesias, we are told by Photius, set the whole story in the next generation: when Zopyrus was overthrown, his son Megabyzus mutilated himself, went to the Babylonians to blame King Xerxes for his disfigurement, etc. 'So Babylon was taken thanks to Megabyzus.' Xerxes made him a present of what Ctesias calls a golden millstone, 'which is the most esteemed royal gift of all amongst the Persians'.[15]

Whichever general it was who captured Babylon, Xerxes certainly went there himself and saw 'the tomb of Belitanas', the king who had been Semiramis' gardener and had succeeded her when she died. Aelian paraphrases Ctesias:

> Xerxes, son of Darius, dug his way into[16] the tomb of the ancient god Belus and found a glass sarcophagus, in which the body lay in olive oil. The sarcophagus was not full, the oil was perhaps an inch short of the rim. Nearby lay a small stele with the inscription: 'For the man who opens the tomb and does not fill the sarcophagus, it will not be so good.'[17] When Xerxes read this he was afraid and gave orders to pour in oil at once. But the sarcophagus did not fill up. He gave the order to pour once again. But the level did not rise, and he gave up after wasting to no avail what was poured in. Closing the tomb, he retreated in dismay. The inscription did not fail in its prediction: for having assembled 700,000 men against the Greeks he came off badly, and on his return he suffered a most shameful death, murdered one night in bed by his son.[18]

The story reinforces the Greek picture of Xerxes as prey to fears as well as giving up his task in despair. To modern readers the first impression is perhaps of credulity in the face of an 'omen'; but there is no reason to doubt the implicit belief of the ancients in omens and oracles of all kinds. In

Babylon, of all places, divination had first been turned into an art and there were few phenomena that could not be interpreted by the Chaldaeans as containing an omen. But did Xerxes actually believe such things? If we envisage him as a Zoroastrian zealot, all these omens will have been mere mumbo-jumbo. If he did try to fill the sarcophagus to placate his hosts, it would not be surprising if he gave up in impatience when he discovered it leaked.

Aelian confuses Beletanas with Bel-Marduk, the chief god of Babylon whose death and resurrection were celebrated every year. Strabo informs us that Xerxes did destroy the tomb of Belus, which was 'a quadrangular pyramid of baked brick, not only being a stadium (ca 200 m) in height but also having sides a stadium in length'.[19] Alexander later claimed to have restored E-sagila, but the evidence for destruction is controversial and may have been entirely invented as propaganda for Alexander as the 'good cop' reflection of Xerxes.[20] The ransacking of Etemenanki might, however, explain how Nebuchadnezzar's clay cylinder came to be at Susa, where it was found in the twentieth century.

The story about the tomb is clearly a folk tale, perhaps invented by the Babylonians on this occasion, about 'the evil foreigner outwitted by the kings of old'. It has been supposed that Xerxes' destruction in Babylon was extensive, and that this explains why Herodotus' account of Babylon makes no mention of the Ishtar Gate for example (he is supposed to have been unable to reach it because Xerxes had diverted the river), or of the ziggurat (because it had been severely lopped by Xerxes' troops). The alternative explanation is that Herodotus never actually went to Babylon at all![21] Destruction can be a loose term: Sennacherib claimed to have destroyed the Temple of Marduk, and flattened the whole of Babylon, less than a hundred years earlier; but people can, and do, rebuild their cities in a short space of time.[22] Daily life and business were to some extent disrupted, as the interruptions in the archives show, but it seems likely that Xerxes did not loot or flatten his rebellious subject city.

A Debate in Susa

Greece was much further away than Babylon, but there was pressure on Xerxes from many sides to do something to recoup the indignity of Marathon, as well as the Athenian sack of Sardis,[23] and to secure the revenues of the Greeks of Europe as well as those of Ionia. Persia might feel that it had a good claim to Greece, since Cleisthenes' ambassadors in 507 had given earth and water to the king's representative. Perhaps they understood this as a polite token of welcome, but to Persians it was an explicit assertion of subjection to the Great King.[24]

Ctesias has an odd set of reasons: Xerxes marched against the Greeks because the Chalcedonians had tried to set the bridge over the Bosphorus adrift, and because they destroyed the altar that Darius had set up; and because the Athenians killed Datis, the commander at Marathon, and did not return his corpse.[25] The 'altar' is not mentioned elsewhere, though Herodotus says that he erected two pillars by the Bosphorus, inscribed in 'Assyrian' and Greek respectively with lists of the tribes and peoples who made up his army;[26] the pillars were removed by the people of Byzantium and used to build an altar of Artemis the Saviour.

A. T. Olmstead characterised Xerxes' invasion as 'insane', and if those had been his overriding motives perhaps it would have been. Perhaps Olmstead was over-influenced by the words of Darius' ghost in Aeschylus' *The Persians*, describing his son as 'uncomprehending in his youthful audacity. . . . Surely some disease of the mind had seized my son?'[27] No less insane, perhaps, would have been to approach the war in the spirit that Louis Couperus envisages:

> Asia was his. Europe would be his. His was the earth, and the skies were
> his to be. His would be the winds, obedient to his sceptre. His would be
> the grain, and its ears would bow to him in their fullness. Those Greeks,
> that wretched little people yonder, he would tread in the dust. An immeasurable emotion swelled within him and caused him to smile silently.[28]

So far the novelist; but when we look at the more powerful arguments that were presented to Xerxes, the invasion may seem less 'insane'.

In Herodotus' account self-interest of the various parties was paramount. First of all, Xerxes' cousin Mardonius, the son of Darius' sister who had married Gobryas (one of the 'Seven' who had placed Darius on the throne), exercised a strong influence over the king. (We do not know the Persian form of his name, though it contains the element 'mard', 'a man'.) Herodotus writes: 'he wanted to stir things up and he wanted to become governor of Greece'.[29] So he urged Xerxes to attack Greece, both to enhance his reputation and to set an example to any other parts of the empire that might be thinking of rebelling. According to Diodorus, Mardonius put Xerxes up to it out of rivalry with the Carthaginians.[30] In addition he kept telling Xerxes that Greece was a beautiful and fertile country where every imaginable plant grew luxuriantly. One wonders whether he was just making this up, or whether his view sprang from genuine ignorance about the arid climate of Greece, which few would characterise as fertile: from earliest times Greece had to secure grain supplies from Egypt and the Black Sea simply to feed its population. The appeal to the 'gardener' in the king is patent. Still, the historian Deinon tells us that Xerxes was passionate about Attic figs,[31] so perhaps he was playing on receptive ears – though Xerxes cannot ever have tasted an Attic fig, other than a dried one, before he reached Attica: they would never have withstood the journey to Persia. (Nonetheless King Bindusara in India also wanted to be sent some Greek figs, and a Greek philosopher. Neither was forthcoming.)[32] Anyway, the king only ate food that was produced inside his empire, so he must have gone by reputation alone.[33]

To the temptation of luscious produce were added diplomatic representations. The ruling family of Thessaly, the Aleuadae, sent a mission encouraging Xerxes to take over, no doubt with an eye to their own advantage, and the Pisistratids, the exiled Athenian tyrant family, reasoned that if Xerxes were to conquer Greece he would restore them to power and put down the incipient democracy. To strengthen their case they brought with them a purveyor of oracles, Onomacritus, who had gathered prophecies from all over Greece and was persuaded to declaim to the king only those that offered a favourable outcome for Persia: in particular he had one which told that a 'man of Persia' would build a bridge across the Hellespont.[34] Another motive was the unfinished business of Xerxes' father: Darius had desired revenge on Athens ever since the burning of Sardis.[35] For one modern historian, this makes Xerxes' decision a 'rational one', while another sees him as 'carried away by emotion'.[36] Prestige, honour, custom and the desire for revenge and punishment all came into the mix;[37] whether these are rational impulses is perhaps debatable, but they are certainly political ones.

A combination of economic reasons and nationalist anger is usually enough to get a war going, even without the argument of a threat from the victim. For an expansionist empire, these reasons were sufficient. Still, as George Cawkwell says, suggesting that the debate is all Herodotus' invention, 'there is no real evidence for why the Persians invaded Greece in 480'.[38] Only the military argument might have given Xerxes pause, since the Persian defeat at Marathon had come as such a surprise. Again, Mardonius was ready with abundant misinformation about the Greek fighting style.[39] Mardonius then did as was expected of him, no doubt standing on his gold brick, as was required of anyone who addressed the Persian king: '"Master," he said, "you are the greatest Persian there has ever been, nor will there ever be anyone to equal you in the future either.'"[40] After such an auspicious beginning, Xerxes was bound to believe what Mardonius told him about the Greeks, who 'usually wage war in an extremely stupid fashion, because they're ignorant and incompetent':[41] they choose a flat plain to fight in and carry on until nearly everyone is dead, instead of using subterfuge. The implication is that the Persians could win simply by superior numbers, and that was surely what the king expected – as Darius III did when Alexander's army invaded.

No one at the meeting dared to contradict these two powerful men, until Xerxes' uncle Artabanus spoke up,[42] prefacing his remarks with the comment that weighing up alternative proposals is always helpful. The spirit of democratic debate that informed Greek deliberations is in the historian's mind, but it was applicable to a ruling elite too – if we could only believe that Herodotus actually knew what was said on this occasion. Nevertheless, Artabanus' arguments are reasoned ones. Darius had been defeated by the Scythians, and the Greeks are better fighters than the Scythians. The danger is that Xerxes will be cut off in Greece while Greek ships prevent his return by dismantling the bridge (just as the Scythians had done on the Danube in Darius' reign). Artabanus also proposed that Mardonius should go on his own if he was so keen; there was no need for the king to go.[43]

Artabanus then plays the god card. The gods have it in for those who are arrogant and trust in their own superiority: 'the god does not allow anyone but himself to feel pride'. Again the sentiment is Greek rather than Persian, and it is the beginning of one of the leitmotifs of later interpretation of Xerxes, his defiance not just of the Greeks, but of the gods and the elements. It also offers an opportunity for Xerxes to display another of his vices, anger. He flies into a rage; like many a politician, he didn't really want a discussion at all, he wanted everyone to agree with him and was offended when they didn't.

The gods now took a hand, in Herodotus' account. Despite his rage, Xerxes was having misgivings. But that night the king had a dream 'or so the Persians say'. Is Herodotus really recounting something he heard from a Persian informant? Perhaps: many of the details look like what we know of Persian storytelling. In Xenophon's *Education of Cyrus* the king is visited by a dream at a crucial moment of decision: an unnamed apparition, larger than life-size, tells Cyrus it is time to set his affairs in order for his death is imminent.[44] Now Greeks too dreamt dreams like this: the most famous is the apparition to Achilles of his dead friend Patroclus in the *Iliad*; but dream divination was a Near Eastern speciality. Babylonians in particular had perfected the art of seeking dreams in moments of decision. A tablet of Ashurbanipal (r. 669–640 BC) describes the procedure:

> In the extreme darkness of the night in which I appealed to her a certain seer lay down and beheld an ominous dream. Ishtar caused him to see a vision of the night which he repeated to me saying, 'Ishtar who dwells in Babylon entered . . . . Before her thou didst stand; she even as a begetting mother spoke with thee, Ishtar exalted among gods cried unto thee and counselled thee saying, 'Look thou up for making battle'.[45]

Note that the king actively seeks the dream, though it appears not to him but to his seer. Xerxes simply chances to dream, in the Persian story, but he then sends Artabanus to seek a dream (see below), which confirms the first. There are few sought dreams in Greek literature, though Nectanebo in the *Alexander Romance* actively summons two to go to Philip and Olympias. Artemidorus' dream book is entirely concerned with the interpretation of the kind of dreams that well up from the subconscious. So the story of Xerxes' dreams looks set fair to be a genuine Persian one. As Ferdowsi wrote:

> Take care not to consider visions as senseless
> Regard dreams as divine messages
> Bright souls see in dream all acts of Fate
> Exactly as reflection of fire in water.[46]

In the Greek version of Esther, Mordecai has a dream that seems obliquely to foretell the action, but it is not an epiphany (more of a cinemascope vision of dragons, thunderstorms and earthquakes) and it does not precipitate it.

The 'tall, handsome man' who appeared to Xerxes in the dream told him to have the courage of his convictions and make war on Greece. When Xerxes announced to his advisers his change of mind, that he would not attack Greece, he had the dream again the following night. Now he decided to test the validity of the dream by getting Artabanus to dress in his clothes and sleep on his throne in his place. (A curious detail, it puts one in mind of the Babylonian 'substitute king' ritual that was used to avert danger to the royal person.) Sure enough, the same figure appeared to Artabanus: 'So you're the one who has been trying to discourage Xerxes from attacking Greece, are you? . . . Well, you will not escape punishment, either now or in the future, for trying to deflect the inevitable.' And Artabanus also dreamt that the phantom was on the point of burning his eyes out with red-hot skewers. Now Artabanus came round to the opinion that favoured the Greek expedition.

Xerxes was trapped. What he was about to do was, as the phantom had said, 'inevitable'. As Herodotus often explains the course of events, 'what was going to happen, happened'. It was in the decrees of fate that Xerxes would march on Greece, and that he would be defeated, and that this would lead to his ruin. If the story of the dream is Persian, this 'tragic' understanding of human destiny is Greek through and through; it is actually more tragic than Aeschylus' presentation of Xerxes' humiliation, since Aeschylus does not suggest that it was predestined. Xerxes is like Oedipus, doomed by the gods to destroy himself.

Another more encouraging dream also came to Xerxes, that he was wearing a garland made of sprigs of an olive tree whose branches overshadowed the whole world. He was dreaming of the wonderful Greek olives. But the garland disappeared. This time it was the Magi who explained his dream. (In Herodotus the Magi always get it wrong; they do not have the skill of Greeks at seeing into the future.)[47] They were sure it meant he would achieve dominion over the whole human race, though on what interpretative principles they based this is not stated.[48]

Having set up the divine apparatus and the political debate that will doom Xerxes to his fate, Herodotus moves on to the practical details of the expedition. In the absence of other sources, and in view of the circumstantial and detailed account he provides, we must assume that he is retailing reliable information. Louis Couperus hazards a different interpretation, that it was the Magi who pushed Xerxes into war; and that they were playing a double game, and had set him up for destruction.[49] There is as little evidence for this as for Sir Walter Ralegh's suggestion that 'the vision appearing to Xerxes was from God himself, who had formerly disposed of those things, ordaining the subversion of the Persian monarchy by the Greeks'.[50]

Human intervention may also have played a part. Demaratus, the exiled king of Sparta, was presumably present in Susa at the time of the debate over the invasion, since he had arrived there before Xerxes' accession and was with him again during the expedition,[51] but Herodotus makes no mention of any participation by him in these discussions. However, according to Herodotus, as soon as the decision to invade had been made, Demaratus found a way to send a secret message to the Spartans forewarning them.[52] He sent a slave with a wax tablet on which the message was not written, as usual, on the wax with a burin, but on the wood underneath the wax. When this mysterious communication arrived in Sparta, no one knew what to make of it until Gorgo, the wife of Leonidas, suggested scraping off the wax. (Even as a child of nine, Gorgo had been a canny player, telling her father Cleomenes to send away the rebel Aristagoras when he came to call in – probably – 498, before his bribes became too tempting.)[53] And thus the Spartans knew that the Persians were on the way. The story, however, seems out of keeping with Demaratus' otherwise loyal attitude to Xerxes in Herodotus, and it may be a fabrication.

Spring in Sardis

It was spring 480 when the army of Xerxes departed from Sardis for the attack on Greece. The intervening three years had been devoted to exhaustive preparations. Not least among them was the construction of a canal across the peninsula of Mt Athos (which was in subject territory), to obviate the disaster that had afflicted Darius' fleet when it was wrecked as it rounded the dangerous cape. Bridges were also built across the River Strymon to enable the army to advance without delay through Thrace. The aim was without doubt to polish off Greece in a single season.

Sardis was the westernmost centre of Persian power, the capital of the satrapy of Lydia, from which power also extended over the neighbouring provinces of Phrygia to the north (a satrap's palace has been identified at Dascyleion), Ionia to the west and Caria to the south; Caria was later to become a semi-autonomous region under the dynasty of the Hecatomnids that culminated in the reign of Mausolus, and later that of Alexander's patroness Ada; but at this time it was ruled by a governor in the capital city of Mylasa. In 499 the Carians had been ruled by Pixodarus, son of an earlier Mausolus, and had joined in the Ionian Revolt against Persian rule.[54] During that revolt the Ionians, led by Miletus, had enlisted the assistance of the Athenian fleet and had conquered Sardis without encountering any opposition. They burned the city, most of the buildings of which were made of reeds, but had no time to plunder it because the inhabitants, hemmed in by the flames, gathered in the marketplace and defended themselves furiously.[55] Among the buildings destroyed by the fire was the temple of Cybebe (Cybele), 'and it was this that the Persians used as their excuse later when they in their turn burned the temples of the Greeks',[56] regarding the Athenians as in large part responsible.

Probably it was only the roofs that were made of reeds, since the excavators found some traces of these but also of stone foundations.[57] Sardis was dominated by an acropolis with a wall protected by the gods and built in the

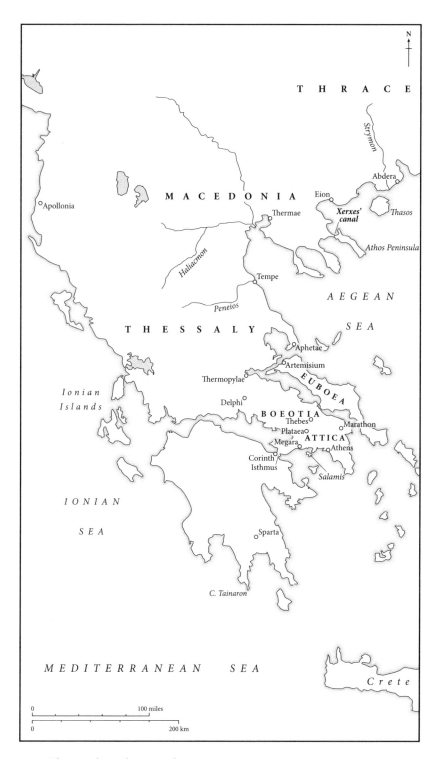

Map 2 The Road to Thermopylae 1

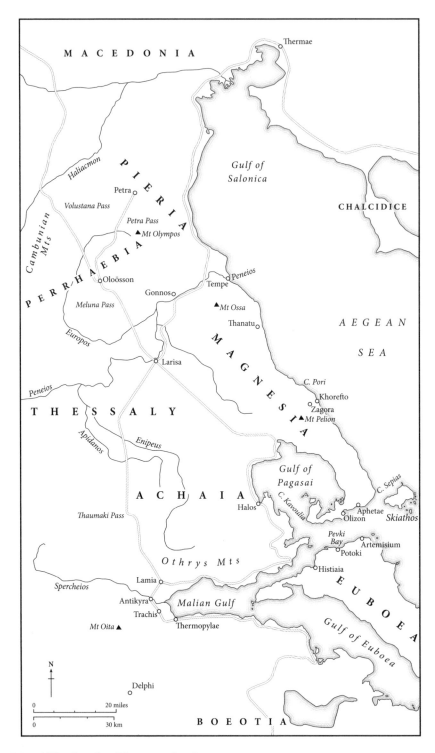

Map 3 The Road to Thermopylae 2

eighth century BC. There was probably a palace on the acropolis as well as one in the city itself. The palace of Croesus took the form of a megaron with gaily painted gables, probably built mainly of mud brick but faced with terracotta friezes: the relief of Pegasus found on the citadel formed part of one of these. Croesus' palace was taken over by the Persian rulers as the seat of the satrap. Of the rest of the city, little can be said; it was probably built too early to have any kind of orderly street plan such as the Achaemenids introduced.

Sardis was the beginning of the Persian Royal Road that led all the way to Susa, and whose importance for the efficient running of the empire is emphasised by Herodotus.[58] It was along this royal road that Xerxes brought his army from Susa to the west. For the first part of the journey the army marched northwards through the level lands east of the Tigris towards Nineveh. Herodotus says that the Gyndes and Zab had to be crossed by ferry and that the road led into Armenia. Both the Tigris and Euphrates had also to be crossed by ferry, the latter perhaps rather high up, soon after the river emerges from its gorges, probably at Thapsacus. (This city has never been identified, though some think it is the place later known as Zeugma.)[59] The road then goes through Cilicia and turns north through Cappadocia to the River Halys (Kizilirmak), the famed border of Croesus' empire, by crossing which he provoked Cyrus into the conquest of Lydia. (This was more or less the route that the younger Cyrus followed in reverse when he revolted against his brother Artaxerxes II in 400; but Alexander followed a quite different route in his attack on Persia.)

Xerxes assembled his forces at Sardis, consisting of 60,000 troops plus the 1,000 Immortals, as well as between 9,000 and 10,000 cavalry. The ferry crossings of the Halys alone will have taken up to a week each, as did that of the Hellespont later. With a minimum ninety days of marching as well, his forces must have marched throughout the summer in order to reach Sardis from Susa by autumn 481. The army and court wintered there. The king would have been accompanied by his whole retinue, his wife and concubines and chancellery, and ruled from the west for six months.

In the spring of 480 they were ready to advance. All the indications are that the Persian army began to move towards the Hellespont around the end of April, after devoting the usual several days to celebrating the spring equinox festival of *Now Ruz*.

Xerxes only conducted a review of his troops, according to Herodotus, once he had reached Doriscus in Thrace.[60] But the army that set out from Sardis was in all essentials the same, and though Herodotus says it consisted of

1,700,000 men, that total is undoubtedly exaggerated. Modern estimates make it closer to 200,000 or even less;[61] and at no point, not even at Thermopylae, did the Greeks encounter the entire Persian army. Xerxes counted his troops by picking out 10,000, building a wall around them to enclose them tightly, and then fitting further groups of men into the space until he had worked through them all. The troops were divided into units according to nationality. The practical advantages of this were obvious, in that the members of each contingent would speak the same language; but there was also a tactical disadvantage in that soldiers with similar skills were distributed among different units.[62] This difficulty will have been only partly offset by the fact that many national groups used distinctive kinds of weaponry, such as the Lycians with their sickle-ended swords.

Besides the Persian and Median sections of the army, clad in colourful sleeved tunics and trousers, felt caps and fish-scale armour, and each carrying bow and arrows as well as a spear and a dagger, with a wickerwork shield for protection, there were dozens of other ethnic groups represented. Kissians (or Elamites) and Hyrcanians (from Gurgan) were armed in a similar way to the Persians. The troops also included Assyrians, Bactrians, Scythians and Indians, Areians (from the Herat region), Parthians and Chorasmians (from east of the Aral Sea), Sogdians (from modern Uzbekistan), Gandarians (from Gandhara in Pakistan), Caspians and other central Asian groups. There were Arabians with long bows and dressed in *zeiras* – which resembled the modern *gallabiya*, but fastened at the waist with a belt. The Ethiopians made a vivid sight, dressed in leopard- and lion-skins, with their bodies painted half white and half yellow, and carrying bows two metres long and arrows tipped with stone instead of bronze. The Libyans wore leather and carried javelins. Numerous groups from Asia Minor were similarly armed with javelins and daggers, small shields, plaited helmets and sturdy boots. Lydians, Greeks from Ionia and Mysians all carried javelins, as did the Thracians (who must have joined the army after the crossing of the Hellespont), who wore deerskin clothing (not surprisingly in that region) and brightly coloured *zeiras*. There were also troops from the Black Sea region.

Herodotus probably had access to a list from the Persian archives, since his information is so detailed, though the colourful details may be from another source.[63] He also gives us the names of the commanders of many of the units. No fewer than twelve of Darius' sons, brothers and half-brothers of Xerxes, were included among them.[64] The High Command consisted of Mardonius, Tritantaichmes the son of Artabanus – Herodotus says they were both nephews of Darius – as well as Smerdomenes and Anaphes, who were brothers of

Xerxes' queen Amestris and therefore his cousins, Masistes (a son of Darius and Atossa and thus a full brother of the king), Gergis, son of Ariazos, and Megabyzus, the son of Zopyros, who was married to Xerxes' daughter Amytis. In addition there were Ariabignes, Xerxes' half-brother, son of the daughter of Gobryas and commander of the fleet; his full brother Achaemenes, also a naval commander; and two others, Prexaspes and Hydarnes. 'Also serving as generals over sub-groups were: Xerxes' half-brothers Gobryas, Arsames, Arsamenes and Ariomaidos; his brother-in-law Artochmes; and Artaphrenes the Younger, the king's nephew.'[65] Other generals included Xerxes' cousin Pharandatis as well as further members of his extended family

Herodotus also has the details of the fleet.[66] He says that there were 1,207 triremes, and a total of 3,000 ships, and gives the breakdown of the peoples who supplied them: Phoenicia and Palestine (300 each), Egypt (200), Cyprus (150), Cilicia (100) – the sailors wore woollen tunics – Pamphylia (30), Lycia (50), whose troops carried bows and arrows besides their billhooks and daggers, and wore goatskin capes and feathered headdresses,[67] Dorians of Asia (30), Caria (70), Ionia (100), Aegean islanders (17), Aeolians (the coast and islands close to Mytilene: 60), and the communities of the Hellespont (100). The presence of all these Asia Minor troops is in marked contrast to the invasion of Darius, in which none had been deployed.[68]

Herodotus was also fascinated by the presence of a woman among the naval commanders, Artemisia the ruler of Halicarnassus in Caria, Herodotus' home town. She was the daughter of Lygdamis (the name is the same as that of the tyrant of Naxos) and a descendant of hers was another Lygdamis, under whose rule Herodotus was forced to leave his city. A later Artemisia was the wife of the dynast Mausolus whose father Hecatomnus established a virtual royal line in Caria – a notable example of the way that Persian rule employed vassal kings as well as Persian satraps. Artemisia gained a reputation as a wise adviser to the king, even though he did not always follow her advice (e.g. at Salamis). A tomb chamber close to the Mausoleum at Bodrum is somewhat unconvincingly said to be hers. She was immortalised by a statue in the Persian Stoa at Athens after the war ended.[69]

In addition to the regular army there was the famous elite division known as the Immortals, commanded by Hydarnes.[70] This regiment of (no doubt) aristocrats was so-called because whenever one was killed in battle another picked warrior was drafted in to take his place. They travelled with their own provision trains of camels and oxen, their own slaves and a supply of concubines in covered wagons, shielded from the leering gaze of the private soldiers. They were portrayed on friezes of glazed bricks at Susa, so we know that they carried spears and bows, and wore long robes with wide sleeves and appliquéd badges, all in yellow and blue, and woven headbands; their shoes were also of yellow leather, a Persian fashion also mentioned by Aeschylus when he has Queen Atossa evoke the ghost of Darius, 'raising the yellow-dyed slippers on your feet'. (In fact the Persian king wore blue shoes, and the nobles wore yellow.) They also wore masses of gold jewellery, notably the torques and armbands that were marks of honour at the Persian court, and apparently kept them on even in the thick of battle,[71] providing rich spoils for the Greeks after Plataea.

It has been said that while amateurs talk tactics, professionals talk logistics. On that basis, Xerxes' arrangements could not be faulted. His army was well provisioned, his supply lines were covered (until the retreat after Salamis), and his army and fleet many times outnumbered the Greek forces. He managed to intercept several grain ships at Abydos, stating simply 'they are ours'.[72] Did this lead him into a sense of over-confidence, the famous arrogance of the Persian king? The Greek campaign does seem to be a case where tactics won the day against a superior army. Greeks later liked to portray Alexander's army in the same way, outwitting the massive Persian force by skill, flexibility and quick thinking. But that is to neglect the central role of logistics in Alexander's planning throughout his immense march. Except in the Hindu Kush and Gedrosia, his supply lines never failed. He needed superiority in both logistics and tactics; Xerxes' experience should be a lesson that the one is insufficient without the other.

The Greeks were well aware of his preparations, whether or not they had been warned by Demaratus' concealed letter. Already in the previous summer (481) representatives of the chief Greek states had met at the Isthmus of Corinth to discuss their resistance. These *Probouloi* included representatives of Athens, Sparta and the Peloponnesian League, but invitations were sent to a number of other states, including those of Crete.[73] Corcyra (Corfu) and Syracuse in Sicily were invited to join forces, no doubt because of their powerful fleets, but by the time war came Gelon of Syracuse was embroiled in a war of his own with the Carthaginians: his final victory against Carthage at Himera was said to have taken place on the same day as the Greeks defeated Persia at Plataea. Some Greek states, notably Thebes and the strategically important region of Thessaly, would not get involved but openly supported Persia, while Argos was ostentatiously neutral (but quietly supported Persia). In the end the main players on the Greek side were Sparta, under their regent Pausanias and King Leotychidas as well as the former's uncle Leonidas, and Athens under Aristides and, especially, Themistocles, who became the dominant figure on the Greek side.

The Probouloi reconvened at the Isthmus in spring 480. At this time the Thessalians asked the Greeks to occupy the pass of Tempe. Ten thousand hoplites were sent to Tempe in May 480, but were then retired – a mark of indecision and dissidence on the Greek side, at which point the Thessalians decided to throw in their lot with Persia. Greek freedom was by no means a universal slogan, and some may have seen greater advantage in belonging to a larger empire.

XERXES REVIEWS HIS TROOPS

Xerxes' army, after setting out from Sardis, soon reached the point where the Hellespont had to be crossed. According to Herodotus the king paused his army at Troy, scene of the first epic military encounter between Greeks and an 'oriental' people, where the local guides told him the whole story of the Trojan War.[74] He sacrificed a thousand cattle to the goddess Athena, while the Magi poured libations to the dead heroes. Almost two thousand years later, in 1462, another more successful conqueror of Greece, Mehmet II, visited the ruins of Troy, and recalled the poems of Homer, to which he had been introduced by the Italian humanist Cyriac of Ancona:

> Then, it is said, he pronounced these words: 'It is to me that Allah has given to avenge this city and its people: I have overcome their enemies, ravaged their cities and made a Mysian prey of their riches. Indeed it was the Greeks who before devastated this city, and it is their descendants who after so many years have paid me the debt which their boundless pride had contracted – and often afterwards – towards us, the peoples of Asia.'[75]

While Mehmet's visit is well authenticated, one wonders whether Xerxes' visit is a neat imagining by Herodotus. The historian also takes the opportunity to suggest that Xerxes' advance preparations were already being shown up as inadequate, since he says they had brought insufficient water, and the army drank the River Scamander dry.[76]

The moment is also the first sounding of a theme that Herodotus points up repeatedly in the rest of the campaign, that the gods are fighting with the Greeks against the invader.[77] Here the extravagant sacrifice only leads to a panic attack in the Persian army.[78] Athena seemed to be making the point that the sacrifice was not accepted, as she later reacted to the Persian destruction of the Acropolis of Athens by causing her olive tree to sprout afresh within twenty-four hours.[79] The other gods too played their part: the Persians propitiated Thetis at her home on Cape Sepias, but that was just where their ships soon met with disaster in the run-up to the Battle of Artemision,[80] where the North Wind also played a part.[81] Apollo drove the troops away from Delphi,[82] the ghostly sound of an Eleusinian procession troubled the troops before Salamis;[83] and when the Persians were retreating from Greece, floods at Potidaea seemed to be the revenge of Poseidon for their sacrilege against him.[84] As Themistocles insisted,[85] it was the gods and heroes who accomplished the defeat of the Persians, 'because they did not want to see a single man ruling both Asia and Europe'.

TEARS AT THE HELLESPONT

Oblivious of the marshalling of the Greek gods against him, Xerxes arranged games and competitions for his army and fleet, which he watched from a dais of white stone that had been previously erected for him on a hill above Abydos, on the Asian side:

> The sight of the Hellespont completely covered by his ships, and the coast and plains of Abydos totally overrun by men first gave Xerxes a feeling of deep self-satisfaction, but later he began to weep. When his uncle Artabanus . . . noticed that Xerxes was crying he said, 'My lord, a short while ago you were feeling happy with your situation and now you are weeping. What a total change of mood!' 'Yes,' Xerxes answered. 'I was reflecting on things and it occurred to me how short the sum total of human life is, which made me feel compassion. Look at all these people – but not one of them will be alive in a hundred years' time.'[86]

Xerxes' moment of insight into the *lacrimae rerum* speaks of a spirit that chafes against the constraints of human existence.[87] That may be a good or a bad thing. A man's reach should exceed his grasp, but every Greek knew that there is no point in longing for the impossible. 'My soul, seek not for immortal life,' wrote Pindar,[88] summing up the Greek pessimism that is so often set against oriental arrogance. Artabanus' reply to Xerxes seems totally Greek in spirit:

> Its not just that life is short, but also that there's no one on earth, including these men, whose happiness is such that he won't sometimes wish he were dead rather than alive – and this is a thought that occurs frequently during one's lifetime, not just once. We are so overwhelmed by tragic accidents

and illness that, however, short life actually is, it seems long. So people look forward to dying, as an excellent way to escape from life with all its troubles. And this just goes to show how grudging the god is, because all we get is a taste of how sweet life may be.[89]

Walter Ralegh paraphrased Artabanus' speech with an infusion of his own melancholy:

> That which is more lamentable than the dissolution of this great troop within that number of years by the king remembered, is, that the life itself which we enjoy is yet more miserable than the end thereof; for in those few days given us in the world, there is no man among all these, nor elsewhere, that ever found himself so accompanied with happiness, but that he oftentimes pleased himself better with the desire and hope of death, than of living; the incident calamities, diseases, and sorrows whereto mankind is subject being so many and inevitable, that the shortest life doth oftentimes appear to us over-long; to avoid all which, there is neither refuge nor rest, but in desired death alone.[90]

The moral Artabanus draws is the same as the one used by Solon in his warning to Croesus in the opening book of Herodotus' history, that one should call no man happy until he is dead. The idea is such a leitmotif of Greek thought that it is difficult not to think that this exchange is Herodotus' own composition (and, indeed, who would have reported it to him?). However, the moral Artabanus draws is not the same as Xerxes': Xerxes speaks like a Persian.[91]

Persian writers often reflect in a similar way on the fragility of human existence. Farid ud-Din Attar describes the long pilgrimage of the birds to seek enlightenment under the guidance of the hoopoe:

> Of all the army that set out, how few
> Survived the way; of that great retinue
> A handful lived until the voyage was done –
> Of every thousand there remained but one.[92]

Much of Persian literature depicts a 'culture of mourning . . . . We destroyed our future and imprisoned ourselves in the past, eroticizing pain and suffering, and celebrating nothing that is not past.'[93] That predilection for mourning is still evident in the particular cast of Shia Islam, with its focus on the death of

Hussein. A sudden access of pessimism may be part of the Persian character, and need not imply a lack of confidence in the larger scheme of things. It is not a reason for inaction.

Artabanus goes on to tell Xerxes that he himself is 'out of his mind with fear'; and he worries that Xerxes is relying on his own tremendous preparations while discounting the enmity of two entities, the land and the sea. Again the note of inadequacy is sounded, with the suggestion that even the elements are taking the side of the Greeks. Xerxes may have been acknowledging his own uncertainties by making offerings to the Hellespont, however brash his outward demeanour.[94]

Ralegh understood that Artabanus' advice was correct:

> These cautions were exceeding weighty, if Xerxes' obstinacy had not misprised them. For to invade by sea upon a perilous coast, being neither in possession of any port, nor succoured by any party, may better fit a prince presuming on his fortune, than enriched with understanding. Such was the enterprise of Philip the Second upon England in the year 1588, who had belike never heard of this counsel of Artabanus to Xerxes, or had forgotten it.[95]

At all events, Xerxes sent Artabanus back to Susa to act as regent. Much better to get the demoralising influence out of the way without delay.

THE CROSSING INTO EUROPE

The next task was the crossing of the Hellespont. The bridge of boats had been completed earlier in the spring, and repaired after a storm. It consisted in fact of two bridges: the eastern line comprised a series of ships anchored fore and aft at right angles to the line of the bridge, facing towards the Black Sea, while the ships of the western line were anchored at an angle to it, allowing for the changing direction of the current as it sweeps down from the Marmara to the Aegean. The line ran from Abydos to the coast opposite at Bigali fort, and from Nagara Burnu to a headland a little south of Bigali. This is not the narrowest part of the Dardanelles: the shortest direct line is that taken by the modern ferry between Çanakkale and Kilit Bahir, but the very narrowness of the strait here means that the current is faster and more turbulent than it is to the north, and is made more complicated by the sharp bend in the straits just west of Abydos. So Xerxes' engineers picked a spot where the flow of water would be less hostile to the ships. The distance here is about 2,000 metres today, but Xenophon, a century later, estimated it as no more than eight stades (about 1,500 metres): the difference between then and now may be explained by erosion of the level southern coastline by currents and by the rise in the level of the Aegean Sea since antiquity, by about five feet (1.5 metres).[96]

Once the ships were anchored to form pontoons, cables of flax and papyrus were stretched from one shore to the other across the top of the boats. The immense length of cable required would have been very heavy and hard to move if it was brought from elsewhere, so instead the cables were constructed in situ, using capstans to twist the fibres into ropes: these must have been attached to the shore by stanchions. Roman engineers would have attached the ships together with these cables, but it appears that the Persians did not do so. Instead, a roadway was constructed of planks, cut the full width of the tree trunks, and laid on top of the cables, to which they were tied. Palisades were also erected on the edges of the planks. On these planks both men and horses, and animals pulling wagons, could cross, with the roadway shifting less than if it had been fastened to the ships.

The plan was an excellent one, but not good enough for the gods. Soon after it was completed, a violent storm arose; the wind and the heaving sea together tore the ships from their moorings and the cables snapped. Xerxes, understandably annoyed and frustrated, had the chief engineers executed; one is reminded of Reza Shah who, on driving along a newly built road and finding it had a bump in it, had the head of the engineering company executed.[97] More remarkably, Xerxes 'ordered his men to give the Hellespont three hundred lashes and to sink a pair of shackles into the sea. I once heard that he dispatched men to brand the Hellespont as well.'[98] The episode lends itself to interpretation as an illustration of the unbridled arrogance of the king, who expects even wind and waves to obey him. But it is consonant with an ideology in which the 'King of All Lands' is king not only of its people but of its elements. As representative of the Wise Lord on earth, any opposition must be that of demons. Salt water, in Iranian belief, was sweet water contaminated by the forces of the Lie, and the 'punishment' of the sea was a way of taming the enemy.[99] The Greeks, however, could think that the winds were on their side, as they did later when Boreas intervened to wreck much of the fleet before Artemision (see below).

Work was begun again with, as far as we are told, no change in method. This time the bridges held, and the army crossed the Hellespont in seven days[100] (though some have argued that it must have taken them a month). The bridges were still there when the last of the Persian army retreated at the end of the following year (479 BC), and Aeschylus, who took part in the siege of Sestos that took place at that time, and had seen the bridges, described how

> The king's army, which annihilates cities [*perseptolis*], has already crossed over to the neighbouring land opposite, passing over the strait named after Helle the daughter of Athamas on a raft bound with ropes of flax, throwing around the neck of the sea as a yoke a roadway connected with many bolts.[101]

An episode that occurred at this time may shed light on the character of Xerxes. According to Herodotus there was an eclipse of the sun just as the army was leaving Sardis, which the Magi interpreted as meaning that the Persian army (the moon) was about to overwhelm the Greeks (the sun).[102] Xerxes is said to have been convinced by this rather unlikely interpretation. His confidence at this stage of the expedition is repeatedly emphasised by Herodotus: he laughs at the Greeks' preparations, and their presumption in resisting at all, despite Demaratus' warnings.[103] The fact that there was no solar eclipse in this vicinity at any time during 480 (though there had been one in Sardis a year earlier) suggests that the story was Herodotus' invention or at least that the sequel is to be placed much earlier.

The sequel involved Pythius of Lydia, who was the richest man in the world after Xerxes, and whose father Atys had given Darius the golden plane tree and vine that were the ornament of the palace at Susa. Pythius told Xerxes in Celaenae (shortly before he reached Sardis) that he would like to help finance the war and offered the king just short of 4 million gold daric staters. Xerxes, however, could not be upstaged and offered instead to make up Pythius' fortune to the full 4 million, while providing the additional funds for the war from his own treasury. The king's gift giving was legendary and also a part of traditional behaviour among the Persian nobility. 'Do make sure that you never change,' said Xerxes. 'I can tell you that you will never regret this kind of behaviour, now or in the future.'[104] Pythius was naturally grateful for this sign of favour and, when the alleged eclipse took place, was emboldened to ask for a boon from the king. He was filled with anxiety and asked the king to exempt one of his five sons from military service, 'so that he can look after me in my old age and manage my property as well'. A reasonable request, one might think; but Xerxes flew into a rage and pulled rank by pointing out that the entire population of his empire were no more than slaves (as the Greeks saw it). That is, gifts to the king never imposed any reciprocal obligation, unlike among Greeks. Xerxes agreed to spare four of

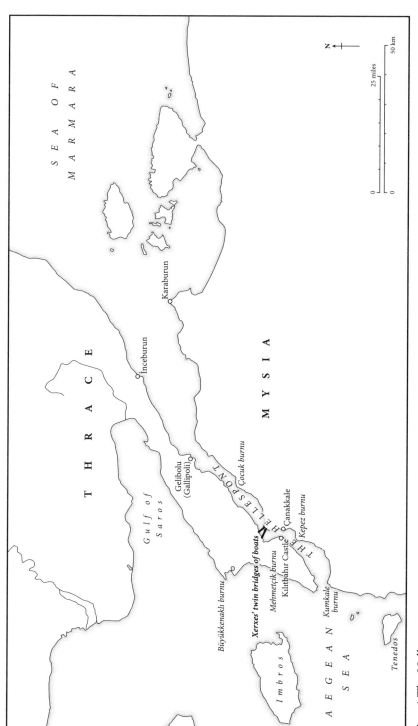

Map 4 The Hellespont

the sons of Pythius, but the fifth, the eldest, was seized to become a human sacrifice for the prosperity of the expedition. The young man was cut in half, and the army marched between the two halves as it set off for the Hellespont. The story is almost a doublet of the beginning of Darius' expedition in 484. Furthermore, it recalls the custom of the Macedonian army which, when departing on campaign, would march between the severed halves of a dog. The Hittites, too, conducted such a ritual with a human sacrifice in order to cleanse a defeated army. So we may be encountering a good story made out of a repulsive local ritual practice.[105] If such a sacrifice did indeed take place, it may not have been in the context of such an ungrateful rage as Herodotus depicts; but in the absence of other evidence it is hard to say more.

At Nine Ways on the Strymon the Magi again sacrificed horses to the gods as well as, we are told, making a human sacrifice of nine youths and nine maidens who were buried alive.[106] The behaviour seems strikingly un-Zoroastrian, but this is not the only account of burial alive in Xerxes' reign: consider the story of Amytis. The army had now reached the friendly Greek territory of Macedon, where it seems to have halted for some time in early summer. Perhaps Xerxes stayed with the ruler, Alexander I, in Aegae: it was a last chance for diplomatic manoeuvres before launching a full-scale invasion. Perhaps it was now, as Polyaenus tells us, that Xerxes showed his cleverness by sending messages to all the Greek states claiming that the others were ready to betray them.[107]

XERXES' PLAN

The fleet and the army rejoined each other at Thermae and began the march south into Greece. From this point on the chronology of the advance becomes crucial, but as the arguments are rather technical I have relegated them to an appendix. Xerxes advanced full of confidence towards his first encounter with a Greek army. He relied on his superiority in numbers and did not hurry.[108] He expected the Greeks to be fragmented and to fail to get together a serious defence. He devoted time to improving the roads southward. He seems also to have found no need to worry about supplies. If Xerxes' army consisted, as Herodotus tells us, of 2,370,610 men plus, from Europe, 240,000 sailors and 300,000 soldiers, and an appropriate quantity of service train personnel, then the total size of the expedition was well over 5 million. T. Cuyler Young has calculated that an army of just half this size would need, daily, 117,300 tons of grain, 63,750 tons of fodder for animals, and 453,033,000 litres of water.[109] Jack Balcer draws the reasonable conclusion that the army must have been much smaller than this. Nevertheless, the food requirements of a large expedition must have put an intolerable strain on the friendly lands they passed through. (An Abderan citizen expressed heartfelt thanks that Xerxes was not accustomed to eat lunch.)[110] The natural response of a local population, however friendly, to an army's requisitioning, is to hide as much as possible of its own resources. The Thessalians surely did so, though they could not hide the rivers, which the army duly drank dry.

When expressed in these terms, the scale of the requirements poses the question: what was the purpose of Xerxes' fleet? The sources uniformly describe it as a fighting force, and perhaps even more as a defensive force partly to neutralise the well-known strength of the Greek fleet; but Herodotus does also refer to supply ships carrying grain, and such was Xerxes' confidence that he let some Athenian grain ships go by without intercepting them.[111] Such supplies would not last forever: Xerxes did not have time to spare. His delay at Thermae is therefore puzzling.[112]

The Greeks, meanwhile, had been wasting time in disputes and trying to assemble alliances.[113] July went by and nothing was done. Some of the Peloponnesian states preferred to rely on a wall at the Isthmus (which Herodotus regarded as useless),[114] while the Council decided against this in favour of the defence of the Vale of Tempe.[115] This Isthmus Wall would prevent the Persians from entering the Peloponnese, but it would mean abandoning Athens to its fate. Tactically it was a less sound plan to fortify an Isthmus six kilometres wide than to defend a pass only a few metres wide, namely that at Thermopylae. When Xerxes was known to be only a few days from the pass of Thermopylae, the Spartan king Leonidas finally moved into action.

Born in the 540s and king since 489, Leonidas was already in his sixties but still a tough warrior – 'of chevalrie called the lode-sterre,/The sunne of knythood, that shon so briht and sheene', as John Lydgate called him.[116] Although the festival of the Carneia had begun (10 August), during which time no Spartan army could go into the field, Leonidas as king overrode the taboo, with plentiful sacrifices to Apollo Karneios, and led a picked task force of 300 northwards, collecting reinforcements from allied states as he went.[117] No man was chosen for this taskforce unless he had a living son to carry on his line. The small size of the force gave Leonidas the added advantage of speed over the march of some 210 miles (360 km) from Sparta to the pass, which cannot have taken much less than ten days. On arrival at the pass they set to work repairing the old Phocian wall that ran parallel to the pass, to protect defenders. Its height is unknown, but unless it was well over six feet high it would pose only a slight obstacle to lightly clad Persian soldiers.

When Xerxes was in sight of the pass, he halted; according to Herodotus, he stood idle for four days, apparently in the expectation that the Greeks would take fright on seeing the size of his army, and simply run away. The Greeks thus gained some of the time they had lost, and further troops were able now to leave Sparta and head for the pass. By the time the assault began the Greek force was about 7,000 hoplites. It was not unreasonable to suppose that, if they could hold the pass for long enough, they could starve the Persians into going home in disorder.[118] It was a battle Leonidas could not win, but it would – and did – gain time for the Greeks. The Spartans devoted some time to gymnastic exercises, and to combing the long hair of which they were so proud, like Red Indian braves. Xerxes was further enraged by this insouciant display, and confident at the prospect of conquering what Paul Cartledge imagines he saw as 'a bunch of gym-mad cissies'.[119] Demaratus' warning made no impact on him: he just laughed at the Greeks' confidence.[120]

The plain of Thermopylae stretches about five miles from west to east, with mountains on the south and the sea to the north. The present-day coastline is some miles from the ancient line, consisting mainly of salt flats; in antiquity the defile between the mountains and the sea was only a few metres wide, and punctuated by three 'gates'. At the middle gate the Greeks took up their position, sheer cliffs to the left and the sea to their right. Confident in his numbers, Xerxes sent the command to the Greeks to surrender their arms, to which Leonidas sent the famous reply, 'Come and get them!', *molōn labe* in Greek.

The two armies that faced each other were very different in appearance. The Persians wore tight trousers and long tunics, with leather boots and felt caps. They did not wear armour, except rarely a padded jerkin, and the shields they carried were made of wicker. (These are not as useless as they sound; they are easily penetrated, but also trap enemy arrows and spears so that they cannot be reused.)[121] Their chief weapon was the bow, which was intended *en masse* to wipe out an enemy by aerial bombardment before the armies ever engaged. The Greeks, by contrast, relied on the hoplite phalanx. The men wore heavy metal breastplates and kilts, greaves and helmets, and carried a spear and a short thrusting sword. The tactic was to form the troops into a tight block which was impenetrable to assault, and which would advance steadily, remorselessly, like a gigantic rugby scrum, until it trampled and crushed whatever stood in its path.[122] In particular, horses, which the

Persians relied on heavily after the initial bombardment, will not charge at a solid object such as the phalanx presented, and so a cavalry charge would be fragmented.

Many of the troops on the Persian side were differently armed from the Persians, as we have seen, and more equipped for hand-to-hand combat. After a Persian volley of arrows that darkened the sky and, as a Spartan named Dianeces remarked, enabled the Greeks to fight in the shade,[123] and after an attack by the Medes, who died in large numbers, Xerxes' decision was to send in the Immortals, troops unsuited for close combat. Their spears were shorter than Greek ones.[124] Two days went by while the two sides grappled with one another, neither gaining the advantage. Xerxes had set up a seat to watch the battle, 'like a man come to watch an entertainment',[125] but 'three times during the fighting he leapt out of his seat with fear for his own army',[126] like an excited spectator at a deadly football game. But then Xerxes had a lucky break. A local shepherd offered to show the army a 'secret' path over behind the towering mountain so that the army could come down on the Greeks from behind. It is notable that neither side had any advance intelligence about this path. Some 150 years later, Alexander's approach to leading an army into foreign territory would be much more sophisticated.

The Greek force now divided in order to send the bulk of the troops to fight the detachment that crossed the mountain in the night. Battle was engaged 'about the time the market begins to fill up', presumably about nine in the morning. Leonidas moved his 300 men into the wider part of the pass so that the entire force could be deployed at once. He instructed them to eat a good breakfast, as they would be dining together in Hades.[127] What charisma he must have had, to gain assent to such an order – like that of Mustafa Kemal at Gallipoli in 1915 to his forces, 'I am not ordering you to fight, I am ordering you to die.' Sacrifices were made to the gods; the shrill screeching of the *aulos* began, and then the little force moved forward as one in deadly silence.[128]

Persian casualties were high, and many more were trampled to death by their comrades in the confined space. The Greeks fought 'with reckless disregard for their lives', using their swords once all their spears were broken. At the end of the onslaught all the Spartans were dead, including Leonidas.[129]

Herodotus says that he knows the names of all the 300 Spartans who died. But other groups suffered greater losses on that day, including the Thespians who lost 700 men. According to Herodotus, the Persians lost 20,000 men in the assault. Among them were two of his own brothers, Abrocomes and Hyperanthes.[130] Xerxes quickly had all but 1,000 of these men buried, while leaving all the Greek dead in heaps for his own men to exult over – both the army and the fleet, which now came up again with the army. Leonidas' body was mutilated and his head fixed to a pole. Although it was a defeat for the Greek defenders, it had the crucial effect of delaying the Persian advance, giving the Greeks a second chance, and enabling the gods to intervene in the worsening weather of the last days of summer. The heroic self-sacrifice of the Spartans was remembered in the perfect epitaph for their tomb composed by the poet Simonides:

> Go tell it to the Spartans, passer-by,
> That here obedient to their laws we lie.[131]

Xerxes called his advisers together to ask for their advice.[132] Demaratus suggested that he divide his fleet and send part of it to Cythera to use the island as the base for a land attack on the Peloponnese from the south. But Xerxes' brother Achaemenes was against dividing the fleet; as always, the Persians relied on massive numerical force to achieve their ends. The debate was to recur after the sack of Athens, with the same result. Xerxes elected to keep his forces together.

THE BATTLE OF ARTEMISION

The Persian fleet had suffered its own travails. After leaving Therma, probably around 10 August, it had arrived closer to Cape Sepias. The leading ships were moored just offshore, while the rest rode at anchor further out.[133] But in the morning the wind rose and for three days the ships were battered by a 'Hellespontine wind', plainly the *meltemi*, which characteristically blows in July and August for periods of three days at a time. Any sea captain will seek a lee shore in these conditions. (I have spent a bumpy night in the lee of Icaria, watching the wind at morning howling down the cliffs and raising sea-spray into rainbows.) At Cape Sepias the ships were completely exposed; a few were hauled ashore, but those at anchor were at the mercy of the storm. 'It was a monster of a storm, quite impossible to ride out.' When the three days and nights were over, 400 of the total fleet of 1,207 triremes had been destroyed, as well as an 'untold number of supply ships, carrying grain'.[134]

The Magi performed sacrifices to soothe the angry gods, but the storm died down, as such storms do, on the fourth day. Greeks knew that the gods were backing them in this case, since 'the Athenians had appealed for help to

Boreas, the north wind, as result of an oracle urging them to appeal for help to their son-in-law. Now, according to Greek legend, Boreas, the north wind, is married to Orithyia, the daughter of Erechtheus – that is, a woman from Attica'.[135] So the Greeks had sacrificed to Boreas and called on him for help. It was not of course Boreas but his north-easterly brother who sent the wind, but this was not a moment for quibbling about compass points (see Appendix 3).

The Greek fleet of 271 ships was waiting at Artemision, eight hours' rowing from Thermopylae, the aim being to prevent the Persian fleet joining with the land forces at Thermopylae.[136] By the time the battered and demoralised Persian fleet caught up with the army at Artemision, more bad weather was impending. The howling wind was now bringing rain.[137] Leonidas knew it from watching the stars; and sure enough, when the Greek and Persian fleets engaged at Artemision, a night of storms immediately followed. It was about 2 September when the sea-battle began. Despite their sufferings, the Persian complement of ships was still vast and the Greeks were alarmed, and ready to abandon their position at Artemision.[138] The people of Euboea, fearful of being left at the mercy of the Persians, gave a quantity of money to the Athenian commander Themistocles, who used part of it to bribe Eurybiades, the Spartan commander, to stay put.

The tactics were a repeat of those at Thermopylae. A small number of Greek ships formed a tight circle, prows outward, which the surrounding Persian ships were unable to demolish by side-ramming.[139] Numbers here succumbed to tactics, and there was no possibility of a flanking movement like that via the pass at Thermopylae. Some Persian ships tried it, but were spotted and sunk. The Persian fleet was pushed back, and further demoralised by the night of storm and rain that followed. More ships were wrecked on the rocky coast: 'this all happened by divine will, to reduce the Persians' numerical advantage and bring their forces down to the level of the Greeks'.[140]

The fighting at Artemision continued for three days, though Herodotus gives few further details. Themistocles employed diplomacy as well, carving messages on the rocks wherever there was drinking water, urging the Ionian sailors in the Persian fleet not to fight against their fellow Greeks but to join the Greek side. Xerxes had a sharp response to this diplomacy-by-graffiti. He sent a message to the fleet inviting them to come to Thermopylae and view the heaps of slain. 'Friends and allies, there are some people in the world who are foolish enough to think they can overcome the might of King Xerxes. If any of you want to go and see how we deal in battle with such

people, the king grants you permission to leave your station and do so.'
(Herodotus calls this 'a ridiculous trick'.)[141]

The Persians technically won the battle, but their losses were so heavy
that Xerxes now had no choice but to follow Achaemenes' advice about
keeping all the fleet together,[142] so that the Greeks gained enormous advantage for their own very different style of tactics. Six hundred years later,
Plutarch visited the shore, and waded through piles of ash where the ships
and the dead had been burnt.[143]

It was said that the Battle of Himera, in which a Greek force defeated the
Carthaginians off the north coast of Sicily, had taken place on the same day.
But of course no one in Greece knew that at the time. However ambiguous
the outcome of Artemision, it was an absolutely right judgement by Pindar
that called the battle 'the cornerstone of Greek freedom'.[144]

CHAPTER SIX

Invasion (II): The Wooden Walls

The daring Greeks deride the martial shew
And heap their vallies with the gaudy foe.
Th'insulted sea with humbler thoughts he gains,
A single skiff to speed his flight remains;
Th'incumber'd oar scarce leaves the dreaded coast
Through purple billows and a floating host.
Samuel Johnson, *The Vanity of Human Wishes,* 234–40

Think on Salamis;
In that deep sea the Persian honour sunk.
'Twas there our dazzling Sun, great Xerxes' glory,
Set for ever.
Colley Cibber, *Xerxes,* I

THE SACK OF ATHENS

Xerxes remained confident despite the battering of his fleet and his considerable losses at Thermopylae. He still relied on the size of his immense
army, and pressed on eagerly to his major goal, the hated city of Athens. The
Greek fleet, meanwhile, withdrew to the south, since it was clear that the
Persian advance, though slowed, had not been halted, and the next battle
would be for Athens.

The Persian army swept through Phocis, which alone in northern Greece
was standing out against the Persians because of the Phocians' feud with

pro-Persian Thessaly.[1] The army destroyed and plundered the sanctuary of Apollo at Abae, leaving it in flames and pursuing the defenders, including women; when they caught up with them 'some of the women from this party were gang-raped until they died'.[2] At Panopes the army divided and, while Xerxes with the bulk of the army made for Athens, a division bore down on Delphi, the greatest of the Greek sanctuaries, to plunder it. 'O hatful serpent of hih presumpcioun' – wrote John Lydgate, summing up the collective view of his Greek sources – 'Ay onstaunchable with gredi usurping . . . Xerxes . . . / Purposed hath with odious appareil/The temple of goddis contagiously tassaile'.[3] But here the god himself, it seemed, took a hand in the war. Instructing the people of Delphi not to panic, and not to bury the treasure, since he was perfectly capable of defending himself, the god (or his father Zeus) sent a thunderbolt that caused two crags to break off from Mount Parnassus. In the resulting avalanche many of the Persians were killed and the rest turned tail and fled, pursued by the giant phantoms of the heroes Phylacus and Autonous.

As the Persians advanced, they found Boeotia an easy victim. The Boeotian leaders threw in their lot with the invaders, but there was no question of surrender for Xerxes' main target, Athens. When the Persians reached Attica, they ravaged the countryside, 'razed Athens to the ground and sent up in flames the temples of the gods'.[4] For the Greeks this must have been the most cataclysmic event of the whole campaign – the complete destruction of a city already adorned with spectacular temples and statues, though nothing like those that arose in the aftermath of the war. It was the first wholesale destruction of buildings and property on Greek soil. All the inhabitants of Athens had been evacuated some time before,[5] except for a few who still believed that the 'wooden wall' to which the oracles had referred was a stockade around the Acropolis rather than the fleet. As Plutarch put it, 'the whole city of Athens put to sea'.[6]

A decree inscribed in the third century BC but already referred to by the orator Aeschines in 348 purports to be an order issued by Themistocles to evacuate the city except for the Acropolis;[7] the form of the decree means that it cannot be a verbatim report, but it is likely to contain the substance of Themistocles' proposal. It must have been issued before the manning of Thermopylae, perhaps as early as late June,[8] even if it was carried out somewhat later. It also enjoins the manning of positions at Salamis: the fact that this is what was actually done does not mean that it was not envisaged a few months before. Themistocles' strategy had been long meditated. Civilians may have left Athens even earlier,[9] so that when the Persians arrived they found what Napoleon found in Moscow, a shell of a city.[10] Peter Green vividly evokes the tensions that this evacuation must have aroused: the conservatives did not want to abandon Athens, as Plutarch tells us:[11] 'it was *their* estates, *their* investments, *their* beliefs and prejudices which the iconoclast from Phrearri wanted thrown to the hungry Persian wolves'. But Themistocles demonstrated that the goddess's sacred snake had evacuated the city, and all the citizens could do was follow. Pets had to be left behind, but Pericles' father's dog swam after his ship until it could swim no more: it was buried on the promontory of Cynossema ('dog's tomb').

The Persians stationed themselves on the Areopagus and began to bombard the fortress with burning arrows, but their attempts to mount the steep ascent to the citadel were thwarted by the defenders – priests plus a small garrison – rolling down boulders onto them. Here for the first time Xerxes began to doubt himself: how was this siege to be concluded?[12] Eventually a few of the besiegers discovered a way up the Acropolis beside the sanctuary of Aglaurus, on the east face of the rock, and though it was 'so steep that no one could have expected a human being to climb up it, some Persians did just that'.[13] The defenders now despaired: some threw themselves from the cliff to their deaths (like the watchman who was on duty when the German invaders reached the Athenian acropolis on 28 April 1941). Others took sanctuary in the temples, where they were sought out and slaughtered by the invaders. The Persians then looted everything of value and set fire to the Acropolis.

Xerxes was able to despatch a messenger to Susa with the news that Athens had fallen and the mission of revenge for the burning of the temple in Sardis in 494 had been accomplished. But the next day, Herodotus tells us, Xerxes summoned all the Athenian exiles in his own party, 'and told them to climb the Acropolis and sacrifice victims in their own manner'.[14] Herodotus was puzzled as to why he did this, and interpreted it as remorse for the sacrilegious acts of the previous day. Later interpreters, too, have found it hard to square this action with the supposed mission of Xerxes to wipe out other gods and impose Zoroastrianism in his dominions. But this supposed intolerance would be inconsistent, too, with many of his other acts, such as his sacrifices to Athena at Troy at the beginning of the expedition. In fact the evidence for Xerxes' hostility to Greek gods is as shaky as that for his father's supposed devotion to Apollo (especially at Didyma) and Artemis (at Ephesus).[15] Greek and Roman authors, looking to the destruction of Greek sanctuaries, put it down either to the natural savagery and impiety of barbarians or to a belief that the gods could not dwell in buildings of stone and must be liberated from their prisons: 'Xerxes ordered the temples of the

Athenians to be burned, because he thought that it was sinful for the gods, whose home is the whole world, to be shut in by walls.'[16] The explanation seems to be the much simpler one that, where peoples surrendered and acknowledged Persian rule, their gods were spared; where they resisted, the gods were interpreted as being just as hostile as their worshippers, and were attacked equally as enemies.[17]

The destruction of sanctuaries was one of the most shocking memories that the Greeks held of the Persian invasion, and the recovery of looted statues was an important part of Alexander's war of revenge in the 330s. Stories attached themselves to many sadly remembered cult images, including that of Artemis at Brauron and that of Apollo at Branchidae (Didyma):[18] Pausanias knew stories that both of these had been carried off by Xerxes,[19] even though that at Branchidae had certainly been removed during the earlier plunder by Darius' army in 494. Statues that definitely were taken to Persia at this time include the bronze tyrannicides[20] and the statue of Artemis Kelkaia.[21] A marble statue of Penelope that was found in the treasury at Persepolis and smashed by Alexander's soldiers is made of Thasian marble and may have been seized at an earlier time, or even have been presented by the islanders to the Persian king.[22]

Archaeology has produced more precise detail of what was destroyed on the Acropolis: the archaic temple of Athena was pulled down, 'the sculptures from the Gigantomachy pediment crashing to the ground and piles of Athena's sacred *peploi*, accumulated over many years of Panathenaiai, being tossed on to a bonfire'.[23] The Older Parthenon was destroyed by fire, its stones cracking in the heat, and the sanctuary of Athena Nike was pulled down and all its contents were destroyed. Many bronzes were simply melted down, while marble statues including the Antenor *kore* and the Monument of Kallimachos that commemorated Marathon were broken to pieces. Probably there were hundreds of statues on the Acropolis at this time. Those that were carried off were few and choice, and most were simply smashed. That little statue of Brauronian Artemis that went missing at this time was probably not given the honours of transport to Susa, but simply destroyed. Somehow the *korai*, votive statues of young women with haunting archaic smiles, survived despite fire damage and were buried soon afterwards, if they had not been buried before the fire for protection.[24]

THE BATTLE OF SALAMIS

The flight of the Athenians may not have been prompted solely by the Themistocles decree. Delphi had at an unspecified time (though Herodotus implies that it was soon after Xerxes set out from Sardis)[25] produced a prophecy of doom for the Athenians:

> Wretches, why sit ye here? Fly, fly to the ends of creation,
> Quitting your homes, and the crags which your city crowns
> with her circlet . . .
> All – all ruined and lost. Since fire, and impetuous Ares,
> Speeding along in a Syrian chariot, hastes to destroy her . . .

According to Herodotus, the Athenians were so disheartened by this that they returned to the oracle in the attitude of suppliants, bearing olive branches, and begging for a better future. This time the god gave some hints of salvation, even though Zeus would not give way to Athena's pleas:

> When the foe shall have taken whatever the limit of Cecrops
> Holds within it, and all which divine Cithaeron shelters,
> Then far-seeing Zeus grants this to the prayers of Athena;
> Safe shall the wooden wall continue for thee and thy children.
> Wait not for the tramp of the horse, nor the footmen mightily moving
> Over the land, but turn your back to the foe, and retire ye.
> Yet shall a day arrive when ye shall meet him in battle.
> Holy Salamis, thou shalt destroy the offspring of women,
> When men scatter the seed, or when they gather the harvest.[26]

The god's words provided a subject of intense debate in the assembly at Athens. One party interpreted the oracle as meaning that the Acropolis should be protected by a wooden stockade, as it had been in the past; but Themistocles, who was the leading politician in Athens at this time, persuaded the people that the 'wooden wall' was a metaphor for ships, and that the fleet recently constructed with the revenues of the silver mines at Laurion should be used to stand against the Persian invaders. The problem was that, if Salamis was to be the death of many men, it hardly seemed a good recommendation to build a fleet and fight the enemy there. Here Themistocles cunningly pointed out that the god had called Salamis 'holy' and not, for instance, 'cruel', so the men who were to die must be Persians.

The episode is a textbook case of the use of oracles in political debate. The god's words are ambiguous and must be interpreted; democratic debate provides the opportunity, the oracle the focus of discussion, and the outcome is a policy decision.[27] Accepting that the city itself could not be defended against a large army, the Athenians determined to draw the Persians into a sea battle. Themistocles' plan is clearly expressed by Herodotus.[28] Themistocles insists on fighting the Persians by sea at Salamis, the last piece of unconquered Attic territory, even though the League majority voted for defending the Isthmus with a wall.[29] It was Salamis that was to be the saviour of the Greeks.

Why did Xerxes let himself be drawn into this sea battle? Several alternative strategies were discussed among the high command. Demaratus, the exiled king of Sparta, had already recommended sending a part of the fleet to occupy the island of Cythera and use it as a base for an attack on the Peloponnese[30] – 'whereby that ancient speech of Chilon the Lacedaemonian should be verified, that it were better for his countrymen to have that isle drowned in the sea, than stand so inconveniently for them as it did'.[31] He could even have captured unwalled Sparta. Xerxes' brother Achaemenes, however, insisted that the fleet should not be divided. Mardonius was sent to consult all the naval commanders for their opinion, and they were all for engaging the enemy in a sea battle with their entire forces. The only dissenter was Artemisia, the queen of Caria:[32] she pointed out that all Xerxes needed to do was wait, and the Greeks would not have the resources to hold out for a long time; whereas if he engaged in battle on that unfamiliar element, the sea, he was likely to lose. Artemisia was right; there was no need to engage the Greek fleet that lay at Salamis if Xerxes could enter the Peloponnese by other means. He should simply have bottled up the fleet at Salamis and continued the land invasion. Sir Walter Ralegh commented that the advice of the other generals 'would questionless have been the same which Artemisia gave, had not fear and flattery made all the captains utter that, as out of their own judgment, which they thought most conformable to their prince's determination'.[33] Peter Green, too, was clear that this 'two-pronged strategy of divide-and-rule' was the right course of action:[34] it would be the best use of superior numbers; Achaemenes' anxiety about the reduced size of the fleet simply shows how important Artemision had been to the Greek survival.

But Xerxes was not simply being arrogant, or stupid, in making up his own mind in the teeth of consultation. The problem, again, was one of resources: Xerxes did not have the time, as autumn shaded into winter and his supply routes became more difficult to maintain, to play a waiting game. Furthermore, most of his supplies were seaborne, and he could not afford to have them cut off.[35] So his decision was to engage the Greek fleet at sea, relying again on superior numbers and the fact that the Greeks had, apparently, hemmed themselves into a place where they could be confined and overwhelmed. Meanwhile, the army moved towards the Isthmus, but this can have been no more than a feint, since it could achieve nothing without the fleet's support.[36]

As we have seen, according to Herodotus the Persian fleet numbered 1,207 triremes, precisely the same number as was given by Aeschylus in *Persians* some decades earlier.[37] However, 400 had been lost in the days preceding Artemision, and another 200 on the first day, so that the strength of the fleet had been halved or more. It still considerably outnumbered the Greek contingent, which Herodotus states to have been 380 ships at Salamis (though the numbers he gives for the individual states actually add up to 365).[38]

The Persians entered the straits of Salamis expecting to find a divided and disordered Greek opposition. Themistocles had managed to supply some disinformation to the Persian commanders,[39] to the effect that the Greek alliance was breaking up and Xerxes had better strike while the iron was hot, and attack quickly. It seems surprising that the Persian command believed the story; but Greeks in the north had, after all, changed sides readily, and Persians always had a predisposition to prefer peaceful conquest if possible.

A story in Plutarch, given on the authority of a writer called Phanias of Lesbos,[40] has it that Themistocles also carried out a vicious act at this juncture: while Xerxes was seated on his golden throne overlooking the straits, the Greek general was conducting sacrifices alongside the admiral's trireme:

> There three prisoners of war were brought to him, of visage most beautiful to behold, conspicuously adorned with raiment and with gold. They were said to be the sons of Sandauce, the King's sister, and Artayctus. When Euphrantides the seer caught sight of them, since at one and the same moment a great and glaring flame shot up from the sacrificial victims and a sneeze gave forth its good omen on the right, he clasped Themistocles by the hand and bade him consecrate the youths, and sacrifice them all to Dionysus Carnivorous, with prayers of supplication.

Peter Green thinks that the story is a smear against Themistocles spread by his opponents, but if it did take place, and in sight of the boys' uncle, this may have enraged the king into swift action.

The battle of Salamis is 'one of the worst-documented battles in the whole history of naval warfare',[41] and a writer as great as Ralegh remarked that he could find no remarkable events to build a narrative around. Only the general outlines of the action can be recovered.

On the morning of the battle, 30 September (see Appendix 3), the Persians entered the straits where the Greek fleet appeared to be fleeing north to the Bay of Eleusis.[42]

> It was not in flight (the Persian messenger tells the queen) that the Greeks were singing the sacred paean, but rushing into battle with courage and confidence. A trumpet fired their whole fleet on with its sound. . . . We could hear a great shout: 'O sons of the Greeks, come on, liberate your fatherland, liberate your children, your wives, the shrines of your ancestral gods and the graves of your forefathers!'

But as the Persians excitedly pushed forward to shut the Greeks up in the gap, the Aeginetans and Megarians appeared from hiding on their left. Although the Greek ships were slower, the Persian rowers were tired. The morning swell that began about 9 a.m. further hampered the Persians' movements. As Aeschylus described it,[43] the whole fleet followed the right wing, and after an initial clash moved on through the Persian lines, curving around to surround them, in the manoeuvre known as the *diekplous*.[44] The Phoenician ships, in the tightest corner of the straits, had little room for manoeuvre and were quickly destroyed.[45] The Phoenician commanders blamed the Ionians, next in line, for letting them down. However that may be, the Persian fleet was crucially weakened. The fighting was confused and consisted mainly of encounters between individual ships. The usual tactics of direct ramming, and shearing off of oars, were used to disable ships which would lead to hand-to-hand fighting. Casualties on the Persian side were huge, and it appears that many of the Persians could not swim.[46]

Xerxes had, as usual, arranged a grandstand view of the conflict for himself, setting up a throne on the hill Aigaleos above the straits on the mainland:

> A king sate on the rocky brow
> Which looks o'er sea-borne Salamis
> And ships by thousands lay below
> And men in nations – all were his!
> He counted them at break of day
> And when the sun set where were they?[47]

This grandstanding was a source of amazement to Greek writers, as had been that of the general Datis at Marathon: Aristophanes describes the latter 'wanking in the noonday sun'.[48] Datis 'of the savage cry' was present at Salamis too, though his role is unknown.[49] Scribes sat beside Xerxes to record the detailed progress of events. He could hardly believe his eyes as the disaster unfolded. Although he was increasingly impressed by the behaviour of Artemisia (she ran down one of her own side, but from a distance Xerxes thought it was an enemy soldier), a number of the other commanders were killed, including Xerxes' brother Ariabignes. Polyaenus explains Artemisia's action as a stratagem to deceive the commander of an approaching Greek ship into thinking hers was one of his own ships, and thus to escape: Xerxes presented her with a complete suit of Greek armour as a reward, but gave the captain of the scuppered ship a distaff and spindle:[50]

> The Greek ships encircled the Persians and made their strike; ships' hulls were turned upside down, and it was no longer possible to glimpse the sea, which was brimming with wrecked ships and dead men. The shores and reefs were filled with corpses. . . . They kept on striking and splitting us open with broken oars and fragments of the wreckage as if we were tunny or a net of fish. At the same time groaning and shrieking spread over the sea, until the black visage of night brought it to an end.[51]

The Greeks believed that the gods intervened here too:

> A bright light blazed out from the direction of Eleusis, and a noise – a cry – echoed over the Thriasian Plain and down to the sea. It sounded as though a large crowd of people was escorting the mystic Iacchus in the procession. Then a cloud appeared to rise gradually up into the sky from the shouting throng before sinking down again and setting on the triremes. Others seemed to see apparitions, the ghosts of armed men coming from Aegina with their hands held out to protect the Greek warships; they took these armed men to be the Aeacidae, to whom prayers for help had been offered before the start of the battle.[52]

The wind moved round to the north and washed up Persian corpses on the shore of Salamis. The Greek pursuit continued as far as the island of Andros. At least as important was the hoplite battle that followed, according to Aeschylus:[53]

> Xerxes wailed aloud as he saw the depth of the disaster. For he had a seat with a clear view of the whole army, a high hill close to the salty sea. He

tore his robes and shrilly screamed, and straightaway gave an order to his
infantry, so that they rushed away in disorder.

Should Xerxes have ignored Themistocles' ruse and delayed his attack until
the Greeks had fallen prey to further Persian divisions?[54] It was a risky
calculation, and Xerxes had made a rational decision, but the outcome
was unexpected. Dissension now arose between the Persian commanders,
Mardonius still insisting on total conquest, the others, notably Artemisia,
feeling that enough was enough. Thucydides puts in the mouth of Athenian
envoys, many years later, the argument that 'Xerxes, once defeated at
sea, realised that his power was diminished and quickly retreated with the
bulk of his army.'[55]

The defeat made Xerxes even more anxious about his escape route, since
it was clear he could not maintain his army in Greece over the winter. He
feared that the Greeks might demolish the bridges on the Hellespont,[56] and
he would be cut off in hostile territory. To cover the course of action he had
settled on, namely retreat, he began to build a causeway between the mainland and Salamis, as if he intended to fight another sea battle.[57] Ctesias and
Strabo concur in describing this puzzling manoeuvre, of no obvious strategic
value, and Herodotus may be right in interpreting it simply as a feint. Some
historians[58] think that Herodotus has misplaced the manoeuvre, and that it
occurred at the same time as the army was moving towards the Isthmus.
Certainly there was no question now of advancing by land and facing the
Isthmus Wall.

The king sent a messenger to Susa with news of the defeat. It arrived so
soon after the previous message, reporting the fall of Athens, that rejoicing
turned to weeping.[59] The defeat was bad enough, but the real concern of the
Persians was for the safety of their king: for unless the king were preserved,
the state and the empire were in danger of collapse. It was incumbent on
Xerxes to return home and restore confidence by his appearance, and to
renew the solidity of the kingdom by the necessary rituals of safe return.
This was Artemisia's advice, and this time he accepted it with relief and
pleasure.[60]

THE RETREAT

In fact the bridges were still intact, though by the end of winter they were
destroyed by storms. Plans for any further land campaigns, as suggested by
Mardonius, were aborted and Mardonius with part of the army retreated to

Thessaly for the winter.[61] Artemisia advised this course of action and Xerxes was happy to leave it to Mardonius to crush the Greeks for good in the next campaigning season. A further reason may have been to keep Mardonius in position to cover the retreat of the king's forces.[62] Mardonius was expendable, the king was not.

The army was, technically, still undefeated.[63] When Xerxes had already reached Thessaly, a herald arrived from the Spartans quoting an oracle that instructed them to demand compensation from the Persians for the death of Leonidas and his 300 men. 'Xerxes burst out laughing and then, after a long pause, he pointed to Mardonius, who happened to be standing by his side, and said, "All right, then, here's Mardonius. He'll pay them what they deserve."'[64] This was Xerxes' final act of war against the Greeks, and it was to be proved true, in the way of oracles, in a manner very different from what he imagined: for next year Mardonius was to pay with his life for what he had done to the Spartans.

The army that returned to Persia suffered considerable privations on the march from Thessaly to the Hellespont, many dying of shortage of food and of disease;[65] others drowned crossing the frozen River Strymon, which cracked beneath their weight,[66] and Herodotus reports that when they reached Abydos the troops gorged themselves and died of overeating, and of bad water. Tradition says that Xerxes and his entourage were entertained at Abdera by the father of the philosopher Democritus: but it must have been a brief respite for a mere few. Democritus himself was born some twenty years later, but maybe his father's stories of the Great King's visit inspired the philosopher's love of travel.

Xerxes' march from Thessaly took altogether forty-five days, so it must have been late November 480 when the army reached Abydos.[67] Perhaps because of the lack of supplies on land, Xerxes is supposed to have taken ship from Eion on the Strymon back to Asia. But a storm sprang up, with a wind from the north, and the ship seemed in danger of foundering. (Most modern sailors would think twice before taking a boat out in late November in the northern Aegean.) The captain said that the ship was overloaded. Xerxes said to the passengers, 'Now you have an opportunity to show how much you care for the safety of your king.' At once most of the passengers jumped overboard and were drowned; much lightened, the ship reached Asia safely. Xerxes gave the captain a gold crown for saving the life of his king, and then had him executed for causing the deaths of a shipload of Persians.

This strange story, if true, throws emphasis on the importance of the physical safety of the king for the continuance of the realm. The symbolism of the successive reward and execution of the captain needs to be borne in mind in considering the cruel acts that come to the fore in the later stages of Xerxes' reign: the acts of the king are not occasioned by reasonable human sympathy, or even by considerations of balanced justice,[68] but by their symbolic meaning. Xerxes' subjects were ciphers for the enactment of symbolic rituals.

Herodotus may have been wrong to disbelieve this story,[69] though the unspecific nature of the route from Eion to 'Asia' is suspicious. Herodotus decides that Xerxes in fact went by road like the rest of the army; and from Sardis there is no doubt that he did so. But it may well be that he took an honoured place on a ship that brought him, avoiding the rigours of the march, with a north wind behind him, from Eion to somewhere near Smyrna, where he would be in one of his own satrapies again.

Xerxes then remained at Sardis for nearly a year, until after the Battle of Mycale in July or August 479. The representation of the king by Aeschylus, who has him return to Susa, graphically clothed in rags, to bring news of the defeat at Salamis, is thus quite unhistorical. He did not 'flee like a coward', as Lydgate reads the situation, but he preserved his kingdom by his continued existence.[70]

For Xerxes, the story of the invasion of Greece ends here. But there is of course an aftermath. Mardonius remained in Thessaly with an army of 300,000 men, virtually the satrap of Greece. Artemisia summed up the strategic calculus by saying:

> If Mardonius succeeds in the conquests he has set himself and things go as he intends, the achievement is yours, because it was your slaves who did it. But if things go wrong for Mardonius, it will be no great disaster as regards your survival and the prosperity of your house . . . . If anything happens to Mardonius, it doesn't really matter; if the Greeks win, it won't be an important victory, because they will only have destroyed one of your slaves. The whole point of this campaign was to burn Athens to the ground; you've done that, so now you can leave.[71]

Artemisia's words sound ruthless, but in fact this was a realistic summing up of the situation. Although Herodotus uses the tendentious word 'slave' to translate the Persian, which means something more like a feudal bondsman, the point is sound: as long as the king is safe, the empire is unharmed.

So when disaster came to the Persians for a second time at Plataea in 479 BC, it made no immediate impact on Xerxes and his court. He was by this

time embroiled in the Masistes affair, when the king fell in love first with the
wife of his brother Masistes and then with their daughter. (The affair is more
fully described in Chapter 8, pp. 184–5.) Herodotus presents this as simply
an erotic entanglement.[72] But the punishment meted out to Masistes' wife is
that appropriate to a traitor. This leads to the suspicion that there was more
to the quarrel with Masistes than simply a love affair indulged in by an all-
powerful tyrant; it may have been the first stirrings of a movement to replace
Xerxes as king, in the belief that his failure at Salamis disqualified him for
rule. If that was the case, Xerxes rode it out: it is his last appearance in
Herodotus' history, and for the rest of his story we are dependent on scraps
in a miscellany of authors.

MARDONIUS' CAMPAIGN

The last stages of the Greek campaign had repercussions in Susa, even though
Xerxes was not present. In Greece, Xerxes' agents had resumed diplomatic
activity to induce the Greeks to surrender. Alexander, king of Macedon,
whose sister was married to a Persian man and who owned the city of
Alabanda, personally delivered to Athens a letter from Xerxes offering an
amnesty if the Athenians would surrender. Alexander himself argued that
'the king has incredible power at his command and a very long reach':[73] in the
long term, they would be unable to hold out. There was an element of bluff
to this communiqué, since Xerxes had already retreated from the scene and
only Mardonius remained all out for war against Greece.

In early summer the general once again invaded the independent states
of Greece from his base in Thessaly. He advanced in May or June, and sent
a messenger with a repeat of the message already delivered by Alexander.
The Council was still divided about how to react; but one of its members,
Lycides, who spoke in favour of accepting Mardonius' proposals, was stoned
to death. Now the Athenians again evacuated their population to Salamis
and the Persians sacked what was left of the city for a second time. The
Spartans, meanwhile, were nowhere to be seen, as they were celebrating the
festival of the Hyacinthia, and even when it was over they continued to
delay a decision for ten days, perhaps trusting in the Isthmus Wall that was
now nearly finished.

Mardonius' next move is puzzling. Instead of forging on towards the
Peloponnese, he retreated to Boeotia. He had expected the Athenians to
submit to his terms when he destroyed their city a second time; when they did
not, he was nonplussed, particularly as the Spartans had finally taken action

and were moving north towards the Isthmus. The reason Herodotus gives for his withdrawal is that he did not want to fight a cavalry battle in Attica, and that his escape route was a narrow pass;[74] so he withdrew his forces to Thebes, which was a friendly city, and waited for the Greek troops to meet him there. It was probably late July.[75]

THE BATTLE OF PLATAEA

In 1932 a farmer in the Attic countryside came upon an inscription that recorded the details of an oath sworn by the Athenians before the Battle of Plataea, which ran in part 'I shall fight as long as I am alive, and I shall not value living above my being free . . . I shall not quit the field unless the commanders lead me away, and I shall do whatever the Generals order . . . and I shall not destroy Athens or Sparta or Plataea or any of the cities which have fought as our allies . . . whether they be friends or at war.' It seemed like a historian's dream: first-hand evidence of Athenian tempers at the moment of the greatest battle for Greek freedom. But it is very doubtful whether the document is authentic. To begin with, the letter forms indicate a date a century and a half after the event, about 335–300 BC. That need not be an objection, since there could have been good reasons for reinscribing the oath at this time, as a memento of a great occasion of Greek cooperation, just when cooperation was needed again against the new imperial enemy, Macedon under Alexander III.[76] A more extreme view is that of Paul Cartledge;[77] he regards the oath as an outright invention of the later period, by Athenians embroidering an admittedly glorious past, but one in which the main credit for victory at Plataea undoubtedly belonged to the Spartans. Whichever it was, all the Greek armies knew that this was a defining moment in their history.

Mardonius had a long wait. He did nothing to prevent the Greeks from emerging from the pass at Hysiae. As always, he wanted to use numbers to defeat the enemy,[78] so preferred to wait until he had the whole army in an open plain where he could deploy all his forces, rather than pick them off as they came. The Persians camped behind a wooden stockade on the north banks of the River Asopos; after eleven days they were still waiting for their opponents to materialise. The Persians stood on good cavalry country, while the Greeks waited in terrain more suitable for infantry. Artabanus proposed that the army fall back on Thebes, but again time was running out for the Persian army, and there was always the question of supplies.

In the end, though the omens taken by Hegesistratus advised the Persians to go on waiting,[79] Mardonius followed the 'custom' of the Persians (the law of the Medes and Persians, which changeth not) and attacked anyway. Pausanias, the Spartan commander, forced him into an attack by feigning a retreat. Greeks could thus believe that the Persian commander had failed because he ignored the advice of the gods.[80]

When the armies eventually engaged, it has been calculated that the total numbers on the Persian side may have been about 100,000 (including medising Greeks; Herodotus gives a surely inflated 350,000); on the Greek side Herodotus' numbers add up to 41,400 hoplites and 74,000 light-armed troops. The total number of troops was then considerably something over 200,000, comparable to the numbers that fought at Waterloo and higher than the total at Gettysburg.[81]

Relying on his cavalry, Mardonius aimed to encircle and disrupt the Greek lines; but with great effort the Greek hoplite forces held their positions. At one point the Persians came close to winning, when they were able to prevent Greek access to the vital springs of water. But in the end the infantry proved the key to the battle; holding their positions they were able to withstand the Persian infantry (inferior weaponry)[82] and eventually put them to flight. The spear of the Greeks prevailed over the bow of the Persians.[83] In the final phase of the battle Mardonius himself, riding high on his white horse, was killed by a stone slung by a Spartan soldier, and the Persians fled back in disorder to their stockade. Artabazus was at last approaching with a further 40,000 troops, but when he saw Mardonius' force in retreat, he decided to turn back and head for the Hellespont, which he reached some weeks later after losing a great many men to hunger, exhaustion and attacks by Thracians.

The Greeks now poured into the Persian camp and a massacre ensued – though Herodotus' figure of 270,000 dead defies belief. Valuables were looted, including the bronze manger from which Mardonius' horses had fed. The golden items that the Persians carried with them to the battlefield are itemised by Herodotus: pavilions, couches, bowls and cups, all of gold, sacks of gold, armbands and daggers were removed from the bodies of the dead, again gleaming with gold.[84] Although the Aeginetans bought most of this cheaply from the Spartan helots who looted it, a tenth was reserved for dedication at Delphi, a tenth at Olympia, and a tenth at the Isthmus: Apollo had fought for the Greeks, Zeus Olympius had presided over their survival, and Poseidon was lord of the Isthmus where the Persians would never have been able to pass. The rest of the gold, the animals and women were divided among those who had fought at Plataea. King Pausanias of Sparta joked about all this wealth in the way that Alexander was to do when he captured the pavilions of Darius at Issus. The furnishings of Mardonius' pavilion were those that had been Xerxes' own when he marched into Greece, so Pausanias could claim to have captured a genuine royal household. Laying the tables with gold and silver plate, he ordered Mardonius' cooks to prepare a typical Persian meal, and alongside he laid out a typical Spartan meal. The bowls of 'black broth' contrasted piquantly with the meats, dairy products, wines and fancy loaves of the Persian kitchen. Afterwards, however, Pausanias developed a taste for Persian luxury and took to going about in Persian robes,[85] which antagonised the rest of the Greeks and inclined them to regard the Athenians as the leaders of their alliance.

A proposal from Lampon of Aegina that the body of Mardonius be mutilated, and his head displayed on a pole, as Leonidas' had been, was rejected indignantly by Pausanias.[86] In fact the body of Mardonius, according to Herodotus, mysteriously disappeared, and was never found.

On the same day as the Persians were defeated at Plataea, it was said, the Persian naval force that had gone ashore at Mycale was routed by the Greek fleet,[87] which had moved to Samos as Xerxes began his retreat, in an abortive plan to instigate a revolt against Xerxes in Sardis, promoted by opponents of the ruling Persian governor, Theomestor. It must have been obvious to every Greek that this was impossible and that the only ones to gain would be the Samian enemies of Theomestor.[88] Massive forces would have been required for the Greeks to take on the Persian Empire on its own territory – an enterprise that would not be undertaken until Alexander was able to deploy a united force nearly 150 years later. The episode perhaps demonstrates that for the first time Greeks were entertaining the possibility of liberation from Persia; the king was not invincible. The Greek fleet did make its way as far as Samos; but the Persian fleet immediately determined not to engage with them and slipped away to the mainland, where they fortified a base at Mount Mycale.

The ships and the stockade were set alight, and most of the defenders were massacred. The remainder made their way back to Sardis. Among those who got away was Xerxes' brother Masistes (son of Darius). Somewhere along the way he started a violent quarrel with the commander, Artayntes, abusing him roundly for the failure of his defence. At last they came to blows, and when Artayntes was on the point of plunging his dagger into the king's brother, a man from Halicarnassus named Xenagoras caught Artayntes in a wrestling hold and dashed him to the ground. In gratitude for saving his brother, Xerxes made Xenagoras governor of Cilicia. Xerxes' gratitude for the safe preservation of his brother may have been premature, as the sequel shows.

The story of the Persian invasion of Greece thus comes to a close. Xerxes was able to leave Sardis and return home, possibly via Babylon.[89] It was probably in the course of this gloomy journey home that Megabyzus pillaged Didyma.[90]

Encouraged by the success of their resistance, the Greeks now began a war of attrition against Persian positions on the coast of Asia Minor. To begin with, the Athenians laid siege to Sestos. As autumn wore on, the population were reduced to starvation. The governor Artayctes and some henchmen escaped but were captured. With remarkable cruelty, the Athenian besiegers crucified Artayctes on a plank of wood, and then stoned his son to death before his eyes. Such nipping at the ankles of the Persians in Asia Minor was to go on intermittently for another twenty years.

Reactions in Persia and Greece

Truth-loving Persians do not dwell upon
The trivial skirmish fought near Marathon.
As for the Greek theatrical tradition
Which represents that summer's expedition
Not as a mere reconnaissance in force
By three brigades of foot and one of horse . . .
But as a grandiose, ill-starred attempt
To conquer Greece – they treat it with contempt
Robert Graves, 'The Persian Version'

The poet's irony is somewhat marred by the conflation of Marathon and Salamis, ten years apart, but the point that the triumphalism of the Greeks must have had a corresponding Persian response is a sound one, and draws attention to the one-sidedness of our sources. True, Dio Chrysostom, seven hundred years after the event, once met a man from Persia who told him that Salamis had been a great Persian victory.[91] Colley Cibber's play presents a Xerxes who conducts a triumph on his return home, including a procession of conquered kings, like Tamburlaine. Perhaps he did, for the Persian Empire was hardly damaged by this failed expedition.

There were no Persian historians to record the course of the war except in the most laconic, annalistic way, but clearly there was some kind of oral tradition, perhaps even an epic tradition, like the songs that were sung about the deeds of Cyrus the Great,[92] which would have immortalised the events of this brief year in the history of the Persian Empire. It does not take long for a legend to get established that bears little relation to historical fact (consider the Alexander legends), and after seven centuries there was plenty of time for changes. But perhaps the campaign of Salamis and Plataea really was a victory in Persian lore.

The only echo the whole campaign makes in the Persian sources is that Xerxes' title of 'King of All Lands' changes to 'King of Many Lands'.[93]

Edward Said castigated Aeschylus for giving the King's Mother a voice, in *Persians*, that was imposed on her by a Greek. Perhaps one would do better to castigate Persia for not providing her with a voice. Persia, in committing the stories of its great leaders to oral tradition, lost the war in written record as much as on the battlefield. Greeks, by contrast, wrote in droves about the famous victories of Marathon and Salamis. The chorus of Aristophanes' *Wasps*, jurors of mature age with a nasty sting in their tails, remember how

> the barbarian came, smoking out all the city [like a wasps' nest] and putting it to the torch, with the intention of destroying our hives by force. At once we ran out with spears and shields to fight them, sharp honey in our mouths, standing side by side and chewing our lips with ferocity. The sky could not be seen for the arrows flying overhead. . . . But an owl [Athena's bird] flew over the army before we joined battle, and then we pursued them with our harpoons into the traps. They fled from our jabs in their faces and foreheads, and even now the barbarians are accustomed to say that there is nothing more manly than an Athenian wasp.[94]

The lines, written soon after the appearance of Herodotus' history, conflate the clouds of arrows he associates with Thermopylae with the spearing of the drowning sailors at Salamis as they are hemmed in by the Greek ships; the owl, too, was observed at Salamis.

In general it was Salamis that loomed largest in Attic literature from the campaign of 480–479, because it was there that Athenian naval expertise had carried the day. The largely Spartan victory of Plataea carried less resonance for Athenians. Writing about the war began almost immediately after Mardonius' retreat.[95] Most famous were the official poems of mourning composed by Simonides to commemorate all three of the great conflicts: the epigram for the fallen at Thermopylae, the 'Battle of Salamis', known by its title only, and the 'Battle of Artemision', of which four words survive: but later scholars tell us that Simonides wrote elegiac poems on 'the kingdom of Cambyses and Darius, the sea battle of Xerxes and the sea battle at Artemision, as well as a lyric poem on Salamis'.[96] In the Artemision poem he mentioned Orithyia; as this nymph was a victim of the lusts of the North Wind, Boreas, he undoubtedly described the part which that god played in the defeat of the Persians. In recent years his poem on the Battle of Plataea, again an elegiac memorial, has been discovered on papyrus.[97]

In 476, probably, the playwright Phrynichus put on his *Phoenician Women*; it does not survive, but we know that it was set in Susa and had something to do with the Persian Wars: perhaps it represented the mourning of Phoenician wives for their disgraced husbands at Salamis. An earlier play, *The Sack of Miletus* of 492, had caused consternation because it represented a disaster that afflicted the Greeks of Ionia; this later play must have redressed the balance. But the Miletus play must have been to some extent the inspiration for the most famous reaction to the Persian defeat, Aeschylus' *Persians* of 472.

In fact *Persians* does contain some hints that Xerxes' extraordinary return to Persepolis, in rags and weeping, is not simply a picture of demoralised defeat. Richard Seaford argues that part of the purpose of the concluding scene of the play is the re-establishment of the kingdom.[98] The king is back in his palace. Alexander historians criticised Darius III for fleeing at the end of every battle; but this was not a sign of cowardice, or even of defeat as such; rather, the king must survive and return to his throne to ensure the survival of the kingdom. Louis XIV did exactly the same in the Flanders campaign of 1693.[99] 'L'état c'est moi' is equally true of both kings. Aeschylus understood the role of the king better than some of his critics: the conclusion of the play is an extended lament, but as he enters the palace it is also a reaffirmation that the king is in his place and order will return.[100]

The epic conflict provided poets with material for the next two hundred years. Most problematic is the assertion of Diogenes Laertius that Empedocles the philosopher (ca. 492–432) wrote a *Persica* in hexameter verse,[101] which however was burnt by his daughter after his death because it had remained unfinished. It is most probable that this report is an error, resulting from the confusion of the words *persica* and *physica*;[102] but David Sider, placing great weight on Aristotle's knowledge of the title, has argued that one of the fragments of Empedocles (B134) could be from a poem about Persians because of its description of an unidentified god:[103] 'he boasts not a human head upon his body, two branches spring not from his shoulders, no feet has he, no swift knees, no shaggy parts; rather is he only a holy, unspeakable mind, darting with swift thoughts over the whole world.' The statement resembles that of an earlier Pre-Socratic philosopher, Xenophanes of Colophon, about the bodiless nature of the divine, and becomes familiar in Neo-Platonic discourse of the third century AD; but these early poets may well have been reflecting Persian ideas about the transcendent otherness of Ahura Mazda, so unlike the lively and quasi-human nature of Greek gods.

In the later fifth century, Choerilus of Samos wrote an epic poem, *Persica*, which was of high quality and was still being read in the third century.[104] Aristotle criticised it for its obscure and mannered style, but the few lines we have suggest a competent poet. It included in Homeric fashion a catalogue of the peoples who fought on the Persian side: among them 'the sheep-pasturing Sacae, Scythians by race; they dwelt in barley-bearing Asia, and they were an outpost of a nomad people, men who live by laws' and 'far from them lived a people wondrous to behold, uttering the speech of the Phoenicians from their mouths, but living among the Solymian mountains by a broad lake;[105] their young men shave the crowns of their heads, but on top of their heads they wore horses' scalps, dried by smoke'.[106] It was probably the mass of barbarian troops who 'crowded around the springs of Arethusa [metonymy for water] like swarms of bees in their thousands', perhaps at Celaenae. Like Simonides, Choerilus told the Orithyia story. He also mentions 'a Samian ship that looked like a pig'.[107]

Between 419 and 396 Timotheus wrote an elaborate lyric composition, *Persians*, which dilated on the scene of Salamis in an almost Shakespearean way: 'the emerald-haired sea was reddened in its furrows by the drops from the ships. Shouts combined with wailing across the waters. The shipborne army of the barbarians was carried again to mingle with the fish-garlanded, rock-winged bosom of Amphitrite.'[108] Much of the poem is taken up with the speeches of drowning Persians, lamenting that they will never return to their native lands. 'O heavy fate that led me to the land of the Greeks' (201–02). The broken Greek of one Persian, from Celaenae, is represented in almost comic fashion (150–61). One passage (72–97) strongly recalls Aeschylus' treatment. The king commands the wealth to be carried away, and the tents to be burnt, after the defeat – a precaution for which there was no opportunity after the later battle at Plataea. The poem ends with the Greeks setting up trophies and singing a paean of victory to Apollo, with whose praises the poem concludes. Like Aeschylus' play, Timotheus' poem focuses on the sorrows of the defeated enemy more than on the Greek achievement as such. Like Herodotus, Timotheus emphasises the inability of the Persians to swim. His poem was very popular and we know of another performance as late as 205 BC by one Pylades at the Nemean Games.

Licymnius of Chios, some time in the fourth century, wrote a poem, 'Nanis', about an earlier episode of the conflict, the sack of Sardis in 498 BC.[109] The plot of the poem revolved around a daughter of Croesus, Nanis, who fell in love with the Persian commander, Cyrus, and helped him to take the city. This is a story-pattern that is familiar not only from the myth of

Scylla and Minos but also from repeated appearances in Persian stories: in the *Book of the Deeds of Ardashir*, the princess Zijanak betrays her father Ardavan in order to elope with Ardashir, and a similar story, told by Tabari and Mir Khwand, concerns the Sassanian king Shapur and an unnamed princess. Theodor Nöldeke thought that the motif was borrowed from the Greek myth, but it may equally be that the Greek story, like the rest of the myth of Scylla, concerning the princess's passion for her father Nisus, has its origins in Persian tales.[110] Licymnius, living close to the Persian realm in Asia, would be well placed to pick up stories of this kind. The plot hints at the kind of romantic treatment Persian storytellers may have given the exploits of Xerxes, too.[111]

In all these texts there is little sign of sympathy for the defeated enemy, and even where one finds a voice, like the speaker of stumbling Greek from Celaenae as he sinks beneath the waves, it only serves to emphasise the ill-conceived nature of the entire expedition. The Greeks could not have anticipated victory, but they were grateful to their gods. It is only Aeschylus who gives a presentation of Persian mourning sufficiently extended to arouse some sympathy. Yet even here the wretchedness of Xerxes' appearance is so exaggerated that one can hardly empathise. But if Seaford is right that the play somehow presents a re-establishment of the old order in Persia – trauma survived, balance asserted – then the drama is not just a long howl but a slice of historical understanding. Strangely, Louis Couperus thought that Xerxes would have liked the play. 'For Xerxes was prone to aesthetic impulses . . . Xerxes would have admired Aeschylus' *The Persians* if the chance to hear and see the tragedy which dealt with his own fate had ever been vouchsafed him.'[112]

In the end, the Greek campaign was a distraction that prevented the king from doing what he might otherwise have done – extend the empire further east.[113] The land-based empire was what Xerxes needed to secure, and the fact that not only Greece but, by the end of his reign, Bactria had slipped from his hands, suggests that his efforts had not been best deployed. But in the meantime, he was back in Susa. Several of his brothers were dead, the Greeks were to remain a thorn in his flesh for fifteen years; but his empire still stood proud as ruler of lands. This was not a demoralised Xerxes who sank into apathy and devoted his time to buildings and women. Rather, the building of Persepolis became his main occupation and must, in a just view, remain his greatest monument.

CHAPTER SEVEN

Persepolis

Where are the kings who exercised dominion
Until the cupbearer of Death gave them to drink of his cup?
How many cities which have been built betwixt the horizons
Lay ruined in the evening, while their dwellers were in the abode
of death?
**Inscribed at Persepolis by 'Ali ibn Sultan Khalid ibn Sultan Khusraw
(1476 CE), and attributed to 'Ali, the successor of the Prophet';
quoted in E. G. Browne 1893 (1984), 277**

This City of War which, in a few short hours,
Hath sprung up here, as if the magic powers
Of Him who, in the twinkling of a star,
Built the high pillar'd halls of Chilminar,
Had conjur'd up, far as the eye can see,
This world of tents, and domes, and sun-bright armoury: –
Princely pavilions, screen'd by many a fold
Of crimson cloth, and topp'd with balls of gold: –
Steeds, with their housings of rich silver spun,
Their chains and poitrels glitt'ring in the sun;
And camels, tufted o'er with Yemen's shells,
Shaking in every breeze their light-ton'd bells!
Thomas Moore, *Lalla Rookh* (1817)

PERSEPOLIS AND ITS GHOSTS

Persepolis became one of the most famous ruins of antiquity. Begun by Darius I about 515 BC, continued by Xerxes who was responsible for the most extensive building programme on the site, and still expanding in the reign of Artaxerxes III (359–338 BC), it was destroyed by one of the best documented fires in history, set by the army of Alexander the Great in 330 BC. Although it was Darius' conception, as an ensemble Persepolis is the work of Xerxes, and it is his true monument. Never rebuilt after Alexander's destruction, it became a place of legend and ghosts for the local population of Pars.[1]

Diodorus Siculus is the only Greek historian to provide a description of what the site was like before the destruction by Alexander. Diodorus had certainly never been there – in fact no Greek writer whose work survives ever went there, though Xenophon knew of it[2] – and the description is presumably lifted from one of Alexander's own writers:

> The citadel is a noteworthy one, and is surrounded by a triple wall. The first part of this is built over an elaborate foundation. It is sixteen cubits in height and is topped by battlements. The second wall is in all respects like the first but of twice the height. The third circuit is rectangular in plan, and is sixty cubits in height, built of a stone hard and naturally durable. Each of the sides contains a gate with bronze doors, beside each of which stand bronze poles twenty cubits high; these were intended to catch the eye of the beholder, but the gates were for security.
>
> At the eastern side of the terrace at a distance of four *plethra* [Diodorus does not make clear what it is distant from] is the so-called royal hill in which were the graves of the kings. This was a smooth rock hollowed out into many chambers in which were the sepulchres of the dead kings. These have no other access but receive the sarcophagi of the dead, which are lifted by certain mechanical hoists. Scattered about the royal terrace were residences of the kings and members of the royal family as well as quarters for the great nobles, all luxuriously furnished, and buildings suitably made for guarding the royal treasure.[3]

Greeks uniformly describe Persepolis as a *polis*, a 'city', but it is the palace area alone (Diodorus' 'citadel') that has been excavated, though traces of the surrounding buildings are clearly visible. The 'triple wall' may be a garbled recollection of three levels of the site – plain, terrace and eastern fortification.[4]

Diodorus effectively conveys the awe-inspiring height of the terrace as you approach from the south.

Diodorus describes the sack of the city:

> It was the richest city under the sun and the private houses had been furnished with every sort of wealth over the years. The Macedonians raced into it slaughtering all the men whom they met and plundering the residences; many of the houses belonged to the common people [this seems to contradict what Diodorus says in the previously quoted passage, that the homes were those of nobles] and were abundantly supplied with furniture and wearing apparel of every kind. Here much silver was carried off and no little gold, and many rich dresses gay with sea purple or with gold embroidery became the prize of the victors. The enormous palaces, famed throughout the whole civilized world, fell victim to insult and utter destruction.[5]

A story in Plutarch tells that

> On beholding a colossal statue of Xerxes which had been rudely over-thrown by the huge crowd of people that forced its way into the palace, Alexander stopped before it, and accosting it as if it had been alive, said: 'Shall I pass on and leave you lying there, because of your expedition against the Hellenes, or, because of your noble spirit and excellence in other respects, shall I set you up again?' But finally, after communing with himself for a long time in silence, he passed on.[6]

The statue of Xerxes, whichever one it was, represented the heart of the glory of Persepolis, as an allusion in the *Alexander Romance* makes clear. Darius sits brooding as Alexander makes his escape from a visit to his court in disguise: 'Then he saw an evil omen. A statue of King Xerxes, of which he was particularly fond because of its high artistic quality, suddenly fell through the ceiling.'[7]

I have wondered whether the fabled city of Iram of the Columns, built by Shaddad of Ad to rival paradise on earth and described in the *Arabian Nights* as well as in the Qur'an,[8] may not be a remembrance of Persepolis. Iram is most often localised at 'Ubar in Oman, with the main rival candidate being Damascus; but a story in al-Mas'udi says that Alexandria was built by Alexander to be an exact copy of Iram – not that Alexandria in any way resembled either 'Ubar or Persepolis. Still, there was no place in the lands the

Arabs conquered that had more or taller columns than Persepolis. This might even explain why in the seventeenth century the local Carmelite friars informed a German traveller that Persepolis had been built by Alexander![9] Be that as it may, Persepolis was a mysterious ruin for Muslims and local Christians alike, until Western travellers, the first of whom was Pietro della Valle, followed by Sir Thomas Herbert and Jean Chardin, began to arrive with a background of reading in ancient history to explain the remains.

The site of Persepolis has been much praised. F. Marion Crawford runs to the extreme in lush description:

Stakhar itself was a mighty fortress, in the valley of the Araxes, rising dark and forbidding from the banks of the little river, crowned with towers and turrets and massive battlements, that overlooked the fertile extent of gardens, as a stern schoolmaster frowning over a crowd of fair young children. But Darius had chosen the site of his palace at some distance from the stronghold; where the river bent suddenly round a spur of the mountain, and watered a wider extent of land. The spur of the hill ran down, by an easy gradation, into the valley; and beyond it the hills separated into the wide plain of Merodasht that stretched southward many farsangs to the southern pass. Upon this promontory the king had caused to be built a huge platform which was ascended by the broadest flight of steps in the world, so easy of gradation that a man might easily have ridden up and then down again without danger to his horse. Upon the platform was raised the palace, a mighty structure resting on the vast columned porticoes and halls, built entirely of polished black marble, that contrasted strangely with the green slopes of the hills above and with the bright colours of the rose-gardens. Endless buildings rose behind the palace, and stretched far down towards the river below it. Most prominent of those above was the great temple of Auramazda, where the ceremonies were performed which gave Darius so much anxiety. It was a massive, square building, lower than the palace, consisting of stone walls surrounded by a deep portico of polished columns. . . . The walls and the cornices and the capitals of the pillars were richly sculptured with sacrificial processions, and long trains of soldiers and captives, with great inscriptions of wedge-shaped letters, and with animals of all sorts. The work was executed by Egyptian captives . . . .[10]

We'll come back to the 'Egyptian captives'. The 'temple of Ahura Mazda' is a product of Crawford's imagination, created to fit his plot, but the rest of

his description concurs well with ancient reports. Sir Thomas Herbert had
done his homework when he described the palace:

> Built at the east end of a spacious vale, upon a rock or rising ground four
> hundred paces from the city, the plot containing fifty acres of ground or
> thereabouts. The walls on either side were elaborately carved with figures
> of men and beasts. The second storey was of porphyry mixed with marble
> of other several colours, embellished with costly stones in mosaic sort;
> but the architrave, frieze, and most part of the arches were studded with
> gold, being flat and terraced at the top. Towards the east it had a high and
> stately tower . . . . From the summit of that tower the Kings had not only
> a delightful prospect over all the city that spread itself below, but (notwith-
> standing the hills that surround the plain) as it were an unlimited horizon,
> uncircumscribed save by heaven itself. Adjoining this was a mount, which
> contained about four acres of ground, and built after the noblest manner.
> It was the mausoleum in which and in the contiguous hills were entombed
> several of the Persian kings. The roof and casements (says an old author)
> [unidentified][11] were of gold, silver, amber and ivory, and the walls were
> polished marbles of several colours.[12]

Herbert went on to praise the location of the palace, which 'gave itself a full
prospect to the city below, not unlike the view we have of Windsor Castle
from Eton' – a description heartily mocked by a later visitor, George Nathaniel
Curzon: 'I confess that I cannot imagine two objects more dissimilar; nor do
I know of any site or structure in the world, with the single exception of the
platform at Baalbec, in Syria, with which Persepolis can at all fairly be
compared.'[13]

Pierre Loti in early May found the plain covered in white poppies and
green barley, giving way to 'la prairie sauvage, tapissée de menthes et
d'immortelles jaunes', succeeded then by a 'dead village at the foot of a dead
mountain', where he indulged his melancholy with predictable observations
that 'these mute ruins tell their own history and that of the world through
innumerable inscriptions; the smallest block could speak, to anyone who
knew how to read these primitive writings.'[14]

XERXES' GRAND DESIGN

Enthusing is easy at this marvellous site, but it is time to set about understanding it, and making use of those 'primitive writings' that are too much

trouble for the aesthete. Persepolis is the greatest of Xerxes' 'grand designs', the 'great deeds' that a Persian king had to undertake to impress contemporaries and posterity.[15] The Athos canal was one such deed, rivalling the canal completed by Darius in Egypt,[16] and the bridge of boats on the Hellespont emulated Darius' similar bridge into Scythia, which Atossa urged him to build to show his greatness as king.[17] Most Near Eastern rulers left monuments for posterity in some huge feat of engineering; for Nitocris it was hydraulic works in Assyria,[18] for Nebuchadnezzar it was the Hanging Gardens of Babylon, one of the Seven Wonders of the World.[19] Darius felt the same impulse, and it fell to his son Xerxes to make his own what his father had begun. Persepolis perhaps only failed in becoming the eighth wonder of the world because the first lists of Seven Wonders were only compiled, by Hellenistic poets, after Persepolis had already been destroyed.[20]

The first excavations at Persepolis took place in 1874 and 1891; Ernst Herzfeld was invited to survey the site in 1929 and dug there from 1931 to 1934 for the University of Chicago, until he was succeeded by Erich Schmidt from 1935 until 1939. Further excavations took place under Ali-Akbar Tajwidi in the late 1960s, while a restoration programme began in 1965, directed by the Italian Giuseppe Tilia. In 1973 A. Shapur Shabazi established the Institute of Achaemenid Research at Persepolis. The Elamite clay tablets found in the treasury and in the north fortification were exhaustively studied by Mark Garrison and Margaret Cool Root, transforming our understanding of Achaemenid government and economy. In 2002 UNESCO became involved with the renewal of the Institute as the Foundation for Parsa-Pasargadae Research. It is to the scholarly endeavours of all these bodies and individuals that our understanding of the building history of the site is largely due.

The region of Parsa was settled during the sixth century BC. Building work began, as previously remarked, in the reign of Darius the Great (522–586?), at the foot of Mount Mithra, and the progress of works can be traced in the series of inscriptions, most of which are collected in R. G. Kent's *Old Persian: Grammar, Texts, Lexicon* (1950).[21] First comes DPa (i.e. 'Darius, Persepolis, a', in the elegant shorthand of scholarship): 'Darius, the Great King, King of Kings, son of Hystaspes, an Achaemenian, who built this palace'. DPc notes that one of the window-frames is the work of Darius, and DPi asserts the same of a door-knob; DPd prays for aid from Ahura Mazda in protecting the land from The Lie, and DPe lists the lands that make up Darius' empire. Little detail there, then, from which to construct a building history. Archaeologists, however, have been able to determine that the earliest buildings are the great stairway and the apadana, or audience hall; the terrace itself was begun between 490 and 480. Most of the rest belongs to the reign of Xerxes, including the Palace of Xerxes and his so-called Harem, the hall of 100 columns (completed by Artaxerxes I) and the Palace of Artaxerxes I, which was begun by Xerxes. What we see when visiting Persepolis is, apart from the monumental approach (described in Chapter 2), largely the work of Xerxes with some sometimes confusing overlays.[22] When Alexander came here, he was able to distinguish, and to single out for destruction, exclusively the buildings that had been erected by Xerxes.[23]

THE BUILDINGS

The terrace on which Persepolis is built is 300 metres wide and 455 metres long, faced by a battlemented retaining wall 15 metres high. Its stone is the local grey limestone, from nearby quarries,[24] as well as a darker grey limestone from 40 kilometres away. Much of the interior construction, roof beams and maybe panelled walls were made of cedar wood,[25] which is why it burnt so splendidly when Alexander's men set their torches to it.

At the south and east there is a curtain wall 7 metres high with towers that rise a further 5 metres above it. Darius' plans included the palace, apadana, treasury and an entrance gate, where the foundation inscription was placed; probably also gardens, since there are traces of canals running from several miles to the north-west where they are fed by the spring Hakemi; garden plants (cypress trees, lotuses, roses) are also depicted on the reliefs. There is also a well, 26 metres deep, and the drains still work. From 499 BC, the Treasury Tablets reveal, there were hundreds of additional workers employed at the site, under a clerk of works named Farnaka (Greeks would call him Pharnaces) who was Darius' uncle[26] and who, unlike the court, stayed on site for most of the year. The oldest building on the site is the Palace of Darius above the apadana, and its frontage provided the model for the tomb facade later created on the cliff face beyond.

Xerxes, however, had a more grandiose vision for the site. Gore Vidal's narrator reckoned that, after Salamis, the king 'had lost all curiosity about the world. He had turned in upon himself. He cared for nothing but the harem and the completion of those buildings that he had begun in his youth.'[27] The sneer is probably undeserved. To leave a great monument to posterity may be a better thing to do than conquer a truculent people in an arid land. Xerxes might equally be regarded as the king under whom the Persian Empire reached its peak of glory.[28] His building programme would create a city of a truly Persian kind, which would increasingly be the nerve-centre of the empire. Here the archives would be kept, the court would have its most extensive quarters. Here the kings would be buried, and here, perhaps, the New Year festival would be annually carried out. If coronations took place at Pasargadae, that could be regarded as simply an outpost of Persepolis, a Westminster Abbey to Persepolis' Windsor Castle (to revisit that improbable similitude).

Xerxes made his mark on the plan of Persepolis as soon as he took over the works. He may have begun construction only after the Greek expedition was over, but it is more likely that work continued uninterrupted immediately after his accession, as Vidal imagined.[29] One scholar supposed that the entire complex was a building site, unusable as a palace, until the reign of Artaxerxes,[30] but this seems most unlikely. Xerxes blocked the south entrance built by Darius, with its 14-metre stair, and created a new north-western stair, with gentle steps, which Ernst Herzfeld called 'perhaps the most perfect flight of stairs ever built'.[31] Sixty-three steps with long low rises lead to a 90-degree turning; a further forty-eight such steps enabled the dignitaries of the Persian court to ascend, without getting out of breath or having to hitch up their colourful robes, to a grand entrance, the Gateway of All Lands through which one still enters the complex.

The name is given by Xerxes' inscriptions (XPa, XPe); but the Gateway, notably, leads nowhere. In fact Gate is something of a misnomer, since the building has the form of a roofed hall with a bench. It is a 'gate' like this in which Mordecai is depicted in the Book of Esther (2.19–20) waiting for audience, while eunuchs stand guard on either side. The visitor, then as now, was greeted by the massive guardian bulls that flank the eastern doorway at the top of the stairs. Inside, the cedar beams of the roof were supported on columns 16.5 metres high; the walls were tiled with designs of rosettes and palm trees. Each doorway bears the same inscription: 'By the grace of Ahura Mazda, this Gateway of All Lands I made; much else that is beautiful was done throughout Parsa which I did and which my father did; whatever work seems beautiful, all that we did by the grace of Ahura Mazda.'[32]

Mahmud Hamadani's *Book of Wonders* (1194 CE), referring to the entire complex as the 'Palace of Darius', described this gateway:

> Two great bulls have been carved, with hoofs as a bull, and a beard as a man, twelve cubits long and high, and of what weight God only knows, one on one side, and another on the opposite side, such as in the present age no man could erect. If it be said that a *djinn* or *peri* had made it, this would be acceptable to the intellect.[33]

Once inside the Gateway, you must turn right to the south door, whence you see the northern side of the apadana. This audience hall is a vast building, 22 metres high, 60 metres square, and with thirty-six columns as well as three porticoes of twelve columns each, bringing the total to seventy-two columns, on which rested cedar beams; the doors were plated with gold. Such audience halls are characteristic of Persian architecture. Although they represent a departure from the park-like residence of Cyrus at Pasargadae, the audience hall is found also at Susa, and later at the palace of Ardashir at Firuzabad as well as at the nineteenth-century Golestan Palace in Tehran. The hall at Persepolis, it has been estimated, could accommodate 10,000 people. Darius deposited a foundation inscription beneath each of the four corners. Along with several contemporary Greek and Lydian coins there are gold and silver plaques stating the dimensions of Darius' kingdom, 'from the Scythians that are beyond Sogdiana, to Ethiopia, and from Sind to Sardis'.[34] This most splendid structure is approached by two staircases, on the north and east sides, which bear inscriptions of Xerxes on glazed bricks stating how he added to Darius' original building: 'Proclaims Xerxes, the Great King: By the favour of Ahura Mazda, Darius the king my father built and ordered to be built much that is beautiful, and similarly, by the will of Ahura Mazda, I added to that work and built more.'[35] The stairways of the apadana bear images of processions of guards and dignitaries, and delegations of gift bearers from all over the empire, which have already been described in Chapter 2.

The architectural programme of the east side was copied in mirror view on the north west, and a portico added to the north.[36] All this seems to have been done in some haste, though the new facade looks very impressive. The door frames carry images of the enthroned king, accompanied by attendants with fly whisks, but without the crown prince standing behind him.

One of the most important images of the sculptural programme of the apadana was what is called the Treasury Relief: this block, which depicts the king on his throne with the crown prince behind, originally occupied a central position in the eastern staircase of the apadana,[37] and there was a mirror image of it on the northern staircase. On his throne is spread a carpet whose pattern is of a similar design to that of the *pazyryk* carpet from Siberia: the latter, dating from Sassanian times, is one of the oldest 'Persian carpets' in existence, and shows how much continuity of style there is between Achaemenid and Sassanid art (and indeed modern carpet design). The two reliefs were removed in antiquity and brought to the Treasury, where they were found by the excavators: one remains there, while the other is in the Tehran Museum.

The prevailing view is that the block depicts Darius enthroned, the builder of the staircase on which it was placed occupying a central position in his edifice. Thus Xerxes will have had the block moved when he became king, though why he should have dumped this magnificent work of art in a room in the Treasury remains unclear. An alternative view is that of Shapur Shahbazi, that the relief actually depicts Xerxes enthroned, with his son the crown prince Darius (who never ruled) standing behind him.[38] The main reason for this identification is that the seated king wears an upright tiara, such as Xerxes wears in other reliefs that are uncontroversially depictions of him, while Darius is normally represented wearing a crenellated headpiece. The relief would then have been removed and hidden away in a storeroom following the assassination of Xerxes and his eldest son, early in the reign of his successor Artaxerxes I. Needless to say, there is no conclusion to be drawn from the features of the kings depicted; they all look identical, emblems of royalty that entirely overlay their individuality.

If Shahbazi is right, the figure of King Xerxes dominated the scene as the visitor came closer to the royal presence, as his throne itself, with his living presence, dominated the room from the moment you came through the door. 'The king was seated on his throne in the throne room, facing the building's entrance', as the author of the Book of Esther (5.1) describes the scene at Susa. People could stand for a long time in the crowd, waiting for the chance of a word with the king. Even Queen Esther took some time to attract her husband's attention in the press, until he 'extended to Esther the gold sceptre that he was holding. Esther came up and touched the tip of the sceptre. The king then asked her, "What is your petition?"'

The last of the major public buildings on the site stands next to the apadana (east of the courtyard): this is the Hall of a Hundred Columns, the second largest building at Persepolis, 68.5 metres square with ten rows of ten columns, 14 metres high: the door frames carry images of the king on his throne, without the crown prince but accompanied by an attendant with a fly whisk. The building was only completed after Xerxes' death by his successor. 'This house is the one that Xerxes the king, my father, laid its foundations in the protection of Ahura Mazda: I, Artaxerxes the king, built and brought it to completion.'[39] 'Everywhere charred remains of palace items and of cedar beams evidence a frightful fire. Even the colour and texture of the stone are altered.'[40] The purpose of this magnificent hall cannot be stated with certainty, but it would be an ideal location for those week-long banquets the king liked to offer to his court.[41] If this is where Alexander and his officers and courtesans held a giant party to celebrate their conquest of the symbolic city – and where they found the bronze inscribed menu preserved by Polyaenus[42] – it would explain why it is the building most severely damaged by fire. The overturned candelabra caught the tablecloths, the carpets and the cedar wood beams, and soon the whole place was ablaze. The fire, perhaps accidental in its origins, suddenly seemed an appropriate symbol of conquest, and the Athenian courtesan Thais, drunk and dishevelled, led the men in a riot to spread it to other parts of Xerxes' palace:

> Behold how they toss their torches on high,
> How they point to the Persian abodes,
> And glitt'ring temples of their hostile Gods!
> The princes applaud with a furious joy,
> And the king seized a flambeau with zeal to destroy.
> Thais led the way
> To light him to his prey,
> And like another Helen, she fir'd another Troy.[43]

Alexander's inferno was carried from the Hall to the Palace of Xerxes, and also to the Treasury, where the heat of the conflagration contributed to the preservation of the huge archive of inscribed clay tablets giving information about the administration of the empire (see below).

THE PRIVATE BUILDINGS

South of the apadana, and adjoining it, is the *tachara* or Palace of Darius, an elegant building 40 × 30 metres: it had twelve columns in the main hall with two adjoining smaller rooms; on the south was a columned portico and several smaller chambers. The building has five doors and sixteen windows, each of which bears the inscription DPc: 'stone window-frame, made in the house of king Darius'. The door-jambs of the smaller chambers depict Persian lance-bearers and attendants with what appear to be folded towels and perfume bottles, or a Persian 'royal hero' in single combat with a rearing lion. Further inscriptions, DPa and DPb, identify the figures of Darius and Xerxes respectively positioned as if entering the palace.[44]

A staircase links the tachara to the south courtyard; the inner walls of the stairway have representations of attendants, dressed alternately in Median and Persian costumes, carrying food and utensils. Others lead sacrificial animals such as goats. Their mouths are covered in the manner of Zoroastrian priests, suggesting that rituals and animal sacrifices may have taken place here. The name of Darius appears everywhere on this building, while DPa identifies an image of Darius. On the west jamb a king's garment is inscribed 'Darius' while on the east is 'Xerxes' (XPk) as crown prince (he has no royal title). The crowns, armlets and other ornaments of both kings were covered with sheets of gold, while their beards were picked out in lapis lazuli.[45]

In front of the palace of Darius a staircase leads up from the courtyard to the palace of Xerxes (also called *hadish* in one of its inscriptions): 'Saith Xerxes the Great King: By the favour of Ahura Mazda this palace I built . . .' (XPd). To rub the point home, a slightly different inscription – 'Saith Xerxes the King: this palace I built' (XPj) – appears in a hundred places! This palace was twice the size of that of Darius, and had a thirty-six-columned square hall with a panoramic view out over the plain. Two double staircases, similar to those on the tachara, carry sculptures that also resemble those on the earlier building. The door jambs again show images of the king entering; though one is labelled 'Xerxes', another is marked 'Darius' (north-west doorway), suggesting that the building was begun during the life of Xerxes' father, when Xerxes was still crown prince and successor designate. Here too there are reliefs of people, this time leading goats or carrying utensils.

The adjoining 'harem'[46] bears one of the longest of Xerxes' inscriptions, XPf. This describes how Darius chose Xerxes during his lifetime as 'the greatest after himself', and thus identifies Xerxes as his legitimate successor. Its layout compels the deduction that its purpose was residential, but there is of course no reason to suppose that it was really a harem as that is known from the Ottoman Empire; this is simply an extrapolation from the idea that the Persian king had 360 concubines (one for each night of the year) and that Xerxes' only interests after being humiliated by the Greeks were sex and architecture, here conveniently combined in a single structure. The jambs show Xerxes, accompanied by two attendants, one of them a eunuch: the king wears a flowing pleated gown and a skirt on which patterns of flowers, stars and walking lions are incised (EI 12). Again, on the eastern door jambs, Persian royal heroes fight respectively a lion and horned griffin. Shahrokh Razmjou points out that the building has a similar plan and dimensions to the tachara and suggests that it might be a second tachara: more residential quarters but without being exclusively reserved for women.

Then there is the smaller Central Palace or Tripylon, the work of both Xerxes and his successor Artaxerxes I, with its depiction of a festival procession. On the jambs of the eastern doorway are sculptured images of the king seated under the royal canopy, above which hovers the figure of the Royal

Glory in the winged disc. Artaxerxes is shown on all four door jambs that lead to the two porticoes.

The Treasury is an extensive structure, 120 × 60 metres, and is one of the most important buildings from a historian's point of view. It was here that a large store of clay tablets was found, written in Old Persian and Elamite, dating from 492–458 BC, and supplying a great deal of information about life in Achaemenid Iran. More tablets were found in the northern fortifications, mostly in Elamite, and are known as the Fortification Tablets. There are more than 2,500 of these, dating from 509 to 494 BC; though many of these have been read and published, work is still continuing. They give information on 'the supply, transfer and distribution of natural produce . . . issued as daily, monthly or sometimes extra rations to individuals or groups of workers, and also for the upkeep of animals'. All in all there is information here about the maintenance of 15,000 individuals in over a hundred localities.[47]

Xerxes carried out significant alterations to the building, cutting off the western parts for the 'harem', and creating a new entrance on the east side. The heavily fortified entrance at the south-east was now the main access. A complex series of interconnections between the various rooms must have given the Treasury the air of a labyrinth: did the ancient Persians have exit signs? It must have been easy to get lost in this bureaucratic building! If it is the Treasury, it is here that Alexander discovered the treasure of 120,000 talents in gold and silver, all of which he took away with him, sending for quantities of mules as well as 3,000 camels to carry it off.[48]

An unfinished gate to the north was to lead to the garrison quarter and the eastern fortifications and the tombs of Artaxerxes II and III.

THE ART OF PERSEPOLIS

There has been considerable debate about the nature of the art of Persepolis: is it essentially Near Eastern in style or should it be categorised along with contemporary Greek sculpture? For Ernst Herzfeld (in the 1920s), Achaemenid art was Near Eastern through and through, while in 1946 Gisela Richter vigorously proposed that the art of the Persian kings was 'created' by Greeks. Her view was controverted by A. D. Momigliano,[49] but has been strongly reasserted by John Boardman (2000), taking issue with the classic account by Margaret Cool Root (1979). In part the disputants are at cross-purposes, since Boardman is considering style and technique, which undoubtedly betray the influence of Greek developments especially in Lydia and Ionia,

while Root is speaking of substance. Portrayals of the king trampling his
enemies, for example, are commonly found in Mesopotamian art, while
Greek art has nothing of the kind. Some of the argument comes down to
styles of drapery, and the matter of nudity and body contours, present in
Greek art but absent in Persia. In fact the style is eclectic[50] as is much of the
small-scale art: for example, the chariot from the Oxus Treasure, depicting
an Achaemenid warrior, is also adorned with a head of the grotesque
Egyptian god Bes. Column bases and capitals sometimes recall Egyptian as
much as Greek models.

The aesthetic value of the art of Persepolis has also been controversial.
Attacks began in the eighteenth century with Diderot's *Encyclopédie*, in
which he described the palace as 'ill-proportioned and badly designed
with grotesque ornaments . . . magnificent but in bad taste'. Warwick Ball
describes the buildings of Persepolis as 'committee architecture'.[51] George
Curzon found the palace monotonous, Robert Byron found it soulless.[52] 'No
one can wander over the Persepolis platform . . . no one can contemplate the
1200 human figures that still move in solemn reduplication upon the stone,
without being struck with a sense of monotony, and fatigue. It is all the
same, and the same again, and yet again.'[53] 'Certainly they are not mechan-
ical figures; nor are they guilty of elaboration for its own sake; nor are they
cheap in the sense of lacking technical skill. But they are what the French call
faux bons. They have art, but not spontaneous art, and certainly not great
art. Instead of mind or feeling they exhale a soulless refinement, a veneer
adopted by the Asiatic whose artistic instinct has been fettered and devital-
ised by contact with the Mediterranean.'[54] Byron preferred the Assyrians![55]
Boardman ends by agreeing with these writers: Achaemenid art is prescrip-
tive, the product of an idea not of experience, it evinces grandeur but
no 'organic' life;[56] but he accepts the summation of Root that Persian art
(and the empire as a whole) is 'a culmination of all that had gone before – a
final packaging for posterity of the pre-hellenic historical and cultural
experience'. Bruno Jacobs too regards the art of Persepolis as a mechanistic
and unimaginative reproduction of the livelier art of Assyria.[57] But despite
the repetitive nature of the processions on the apadana and tripylon reliefs,
they are full of precisely observed detail, from the variety of the offerings
brought by the tribute-bearers to the little moments when one courtier
turns to speak to another: one can imagine the conversations, the scent of
the flowers they hold, the anxious concern about etiquette, the pride in the
beautifully realised beasts they lead. The varieties of dress of the tribute-
bearers are recorded in loving detail, even if the men (they are all men) are

types not individuals. Like Egyptian art, the effect is pictorial; if it does not have the humanist perfection of classical Greece, still I could stare at it for hours.

Ryszard Kapuscinski[58] could not help wondering about the fate of the builders: 'their pain, their broken backs, their eyes gouged out by errant splinters of stone. . . . Could these wonders have come into being without that suffering? Without the overseer's whip, the slave's fear, the ruler's vanity? In short, was not the monumentality of past epochs created by that which is negative and evil in man? And yet, does not that monumentality owe its existence to some conviction that what is negative and weak in man can be vanquished only by beauty, only through the effort and will of his creation?' Is Persepolis just a monument of cruelty and oppression or is it rather the encapsulation of a vision of a world whose peoples are unified by a common purpose? At least that is how its architects must have thought of it.

Gore Vidal's narrator has an intriguing take on the place:

Over the years, I was to watch Xerxes create at Persepolis the most beautiful complex of unfinished buildings in the world. When Callias came to Persia for the peace negotiations, I took him to Persepolis. Elpinice tells me that he was so awed by what Xerxes had built that he ordered one of his slaves to make drawings of the principal buildings. At this very moment, the Athenians are busily imitating Xerxes' work. Fortunately, I have seen the originals. Fortunately, I shall never see Phidias' crude copies.[59]

The 'Peace of Callias' may be a historical figment, but whenever he came to Persia – if he did – it was before 447 BC when the Parthenon was begun.[60] However, the traffic may have gone the other way, with Greek workmen at Persepolis rather than imitators of Persia in Athens. Xerxes, though he would never see the finest achievements of classical Greek art, had seen the great temples of the West, the Artemision at Ephesus and perhaps the Temple of Hera on Samos; he had seen the archaic temples of Athens and could have admired the early masterpieces of figurative sculpture including the three-bodied daemon of the Old Parthenon and the figure of Athena lunging forward, her snake-fringed aegis swinging, to quell the rebellion of the Giants. The Acropolis in 479 BC was a forest of statues. Surely the king had observed the enigmatic smiles of the *korai*:

On Attic stelae, did not the circumspection of human gesture
amaze you?[61] – those steles
where the dying
are changed to stone on a gesture of curved air
lingering in an infinite departure.[62]

Rainer Maria Rilke's poem 'Archaic Torso of Apollo' ends with the words, 'You must change your life.' There is no sign that Xerxes changed his life as a result of exposure to Greek art. He probably saw Persepolis as the pinnacle of art, as Vidal's narrator suggests.

There is no doubt that workers at Persepolis came from all over the empire,[63] as Darius states in the gate inscription, though the style is essentially Median: the halls and porticoes can be compared with those of Hasanlu (Nush-e-Jan). There are Greek masons' graffiti at Persepolis: one says 'I am the boundary', the other 'I am by Pytharchos'. A third says 'Nikon wrote me'. A couple of graffiti of human figures are entirely Greek in style.[64] Stone-cutters at Susa came from Ionia and Sardis,[65] and it is likely that the same was the case at Persepolis, while Treasury tablets also refer to stone-cutters from Caria and Babylon; Persepolis, being built mainly of stone, will have needed many more stone-cutters than predominantly brick-built Susa. The woodworkers at Susa came from Lydia and Egypt (EI 15), the goldsmiths and the decorators of the walls (perhaps those who glazed the bricks?) were from Media and Egypt. There was one quarry manager from Greece.[66] There were also Greeks in the secretariat, since one (just one) tablet is actually written in Greek.[67] The Egyptian craftsmen whom Crawford saw as predominating at Persepolis come from Diodorus, who says that Cambyses used Egyptian captives for palace building in Persia;[68] but Cambyses had no hand in Persepolis. Eight hundred Greek craftsmen were liberated by Alexander, who found them near Persepolis:[69] all of them had been deliberately maimed, leaving them only the limbs used in their specialist crafts – an extreme example of division of labour.

We know nothing of the numbers of workmen employed to build Persepolis, but Michael Roaf has calculated some of the man-hours involved. It would have taken a mason two to three days to carve the head of one of the smaller figures on the staircase reliefs, and the work seems to have been shared by two masons; the north wing of the east side of the apadana would have taken at least twelve months, perhaps two or three times as long depending on the number of workers involved. Three masons would take three months to complete the torus of just one of the hundreds of columns that tower even now like a forest of trees over the visitor.

It was in the setting of the palace complex that was largely his creation that Xerxes chose to erect his major statement of purpose, XPh, the so-called *daeva* inscription:

A great god is Ahura Mazda, who created this earth, who created yonder heaven, who created man, who created blissful happiness for man, who made Xerxes king . . . I am Xerxes the great king, king of kings . . . these are the countries of which I was king outside Persia; I ruled them, they bore me tribute. . . . The law that was mine, that held them firm: Media, Elam, Arachosia, Armenia, Drangiana, Parthia, Areia, Bactria, Sogdiana, Chorasmia, Babylonia, Assyria, Sattagydia, Lydia, Egypt, Ionians who dwell by the sea and those who dwell beyond the sea, the Maka people, Arabia, Gandara, Indus, Cappadocia, Dahae, Scythians who drink haoma, Scythians who wear pointed hats, Thrace, the Akaufaka people, Libyans, Carians, Nubians.[70]

Compare this list with that from the *Vendidad*, quoted in Chapter 2, and note that Xerxes includes the mainland Greeks among those under his sway, despite recent events at Plataea. Compare also his Babylonian titulature, 'king of the land of Persis, king of Media, king of Babylon, king of the lands', a form created by Babylonian scribes on the model of the kings of Akkad, *šar mat Šumer u Akkadi*.[71]

Xerxes continues with his statement against the daevas, which has been discussed above, and a general assertion that 'what has been done wrong, I have put right': he concludes with praises of Ahura Mazda and by enjoining on 'you, who shall be hereafter' to obey the law of Ahura Mazda.

This text was inscribed in Old Persian (two copies), Elamite and Babylonian on limestone slabs that were found in the garrison quarters at Persepolis; a copy in Old Persian alone was erected somewhere at Pasargadae, but when found it had been reused to cover a drain. There is no knowing where the Persepolis version was originally placed. It was written not just for Xerxes' subjects, but for posterity: but who was expected to read it? We cannot know since its original position is unknown. This quandary is just part of the wider problem of determining the purpose of this astonishing assemblage of buildings.

THE PURPOSE OF PERSEPOLIS

What was this huge palace for? The buildings are 'a vast statement of royal power,' writes Robin Lane Fox, 'where for nearly two hundred years, the power of Persia had met in Persepolis for its annual festival'.[72] Ali Mousavi also sees the complex as predominantly a ritual centre for the celebration of *Now Ruz*.[73] At the very least the presence here of the sacred cypress tree of Zoroaster marked the city out as like no other in the empire.[74]

Shahrokh Razmjou revisits all the identifications of the buildings at Persepolis[75] and returns to a line of interpretation, already ridiculed by Curzon,[76] that sees the entire complex in religious and sacral terms. Razmjou sees the tachara, for example, as a sanctuary, drawing attention to the cognate Armenian term *tajar*, meaning 'temple' (cf. Georgian *tadzari*). He pointedly asks, if this was a palace, where was the kitchen? He notes that Xerxes' own term for the building was *hadish*, which is cognate with the Latin *aedes*, meaning 'temple': 'By the grace of Ahura Mazda this *hadish* Darius the king made, who was my father'.[77] A ritual use seems undeniable, but this need not exclude the possibility that Darius also slept and ate in the main building: the king was a sacral figure, and kitchens have often been located far from residential quarters.

For Razmjou, there are no residential buildings on the platforms at all (which goes against the implications of Diodorus' description): all are ceremonial, for official meetings and for religious rituals. Certainly it is no bad thing to emphasise the religious dimension of Persepolis: Xerxes does as much in all his inscriptions, and the constant hovering presence of the *farr* in his winged disc shows that Ahura Mazda's divine protection is never absent.

However, a purely sacral interpretation involves turning a blind eye to many of the most impressive buildings on the site. Other minimalist interpretations of the complex are that it was an administrative centre and, as it were, the central bank of the empire, where those 120,000 talents of precious metal were stored. Or it was simply a stronghold like a medieval castle, whose central importance made it the prime target for Alexander's campaign of revenge for the destruction of the buildings on Athens' Acropolis. Yet another line has it that the whole thing is a Persian Stonehenge whose main purpose is to mark the passing of the seasons: a calendar and an observatory in one.

None of these alone seems sufficient explanation, and one is put in mind of a monumental site on another continent, Chaco Canyon in New Mexico, where undeniable precise calendrical functions incorporated in the buildings are allied with a road system, and huge storerooms, that connote a sophisticated communications system that controlled the bringing of tribute from as far afield as what is now Guatemala.[78]

Margaret Cool Root most persuasively puts forward the obvious interpretation, consonant with the ancient sources' information about the king's peripatetic rule, that Persepolis was one of several 'capital cities' of the empire, where the king held court and received suppliants in his audience chamber: Shahbazi cites Xenophon's description of the court of Cyrus as a way of imagining what went on here.[79] It will be clear from what I have written above that I share this view.

George Curzon's is perhaps the most eloquent summing up of the meaning of Persepolis:

> To Persepolis, which boasted a middle temperature, he (the king) appears only to have come at springtime, to receive the first-fruit offerings of his people, the reports of his officers, and the tribute of his subjects. The great platform, with its palaces and halls, was a place of ceremonial resort rather than of habitual occupation; but its proximity to the Pasargadae of Cyrus, and its own associations, rendered it a site of peculiar importance. There its kings sat in state; there they worshipped at the fire-altars of the Magian faith; there, according to tradition, Darius laid up the Avesta, written in gold and silver letters upon 12,000 tanned ox-hides; and there six of the Achaemenian monarchs were laid to rest. But while the platform was devoted to the pomp and the residence of the sovereign, around it, and far over the adjoining plain, must have stretched the city of the shopkeepers, the middle and lower classes, and the artisans.[80]

The conclusion seems inviting that the reliefs of delegations are a permanent memento of an event that took place regularly, perhaps every year, when 'foreign ambassadors and suppliants would come for an audience with the King of Kings'.[81] Paul Kriwaczek follows a line of interpretation that makes the bringing of tribute part of a festival to celebrate the New Year beginning on the spring equinox,[82] at which time the king was resident in Parsa (see Chapter 2). *Now Ruz* is still a major festival in Iran, taking up ten days of festivities. The link to this ancient Zoroastrian festival was made already by Herzfeld and is reiterated by Shahbazi, who points out that the frequent symbolism of the lion in combat with the bull to be found in the sculpture aligns with the entry of the Sun into Taurus on 21 March.[83] As spring begins, the demon king is defeated anew by, in one myth, Esfandiyar, in another Fereidun: the world is created afresh and nourished with fresh rain and milk.[84]

Beyzavi, in his *Nizam al-Tawarikh* (AD 1275), assumed that the palace was built by Jamshid to celebrate *Now Ruz*:[85]

> Jamshid constructed an immense edifice in Istakhr, of which the columns and other vestiges remain to this day, and it is called Chehel Menar. No one has ever seen such an edifice in this world. When Jamshid completed this monument, he assembled all the rulers and chiefs of different countries, and at the hour of vernal equinox seated himself on his throne in that palace. He offered justice and clemency, and that day has since been called nowrouz . . .

Gushtasp's palace built around the cypress tree of Zoroaster, described in Ferdowsi, seems to bear the features of Persepolis, with its 'picture of Jamshid/Engaged in worshipping the sun and moon . . . and all the potentates'.[86] Solomon was sometimes identified with the legendary Jamshid,[87] introducer of most of the arts of civilisation to Iran, and both of them were supposed to be flown around by the djinns to wherever they wanted to go. So the building of Persepolis was often attributed directly to Jamshid, and this is reflected in the name by which it was known from around 1700, Takht-e-Jamshid, 'Throne of Jamshid';[88] before that it seems to have been, more prosaically, Chehel-minar, 'Forty Columns', which is what Sir Thomas Herbert calls it.

Root, however, prefers to interpret the reliefs as a 'symbolic encomium', an abstract presentation of the idea of empire, rather than a portrayal of a regular event.[89] An annual procession of all those offerings and animals does indeed stretch credibility.

Robin Lane Fox accepts the idea of an annual festival but does not commit himself as to whether it was identical with *Now Ruz*.[90] Here, the timing of Alexander's stay in Persepolis is significant. He arrived here in the cold of winter and was here until at least late March. We know from Curtius that he made a sortie from Persepolis 'at the time of the setting of the Pleiades',[91] which must refer to the evening setting of that constellation in April.[92] Curtius says that his expedition at this time was hindered by 'heavy rains and almost unbearable weather', and that it came to a desolate region where the road was covered with permanent snow; but this must have been high in the Zagros Mountains, not on the plain around Persepolis.

No ancient source refers to *Now Ruz*, but it is not impossible that Alexander lingered four months in Persepolis[93] in the expectation of being acknowledged as the new Great King on the occasion of the festival. Peter

Green points out that this sojourn was much longer than was justified by military considerations, even though it began in the depths of winter.[94] Brian Bosworth assumes that Alexander was waiting for the winter snows to disperse[95]– though this did not stop him making the arduous incursion into the Zagros mentioned above. But when exactly did those four months begin and end? Green says Alexander arrived on 31 January 330, J. R. Hamilton in early February. Four months would bring his departure to the end of May, or April if Plutarch was counting inclusively in the Greek manner. 'There was only one motive that could possibly have kept him in Persepolis until April and beyond: the Persian New Year festival.' The destruction by the Macedonian army had been kept under control; 'in other words, the New Year festival could still be held. Perhaps after such a lesson, Alexander argued, these proud nobles and priests might change their minds . . . . But March passed into April, and soon it became clear that Persepolis would see no procession that year, no ritual renewal of kingship. About 20 April Alexander finally gave up hope.' After his Zagros expedition, 'Alexander returned to Persepolis in late May, his mind finally made up. The city must be destroyed.'[96] The story has plausibility: his burning of the palace could then have been revenge, not only for Athens and for E-sagila in Babylon, but for the failure of the Persian nobility to be as compliant as he had hoped.

To return to Xerxes: the Persepolis he built was the expression of everything that Achaemenid royalty stood for: the king throned in splendour in his golden halls, watched over by the *farr* or royal fortune symbolised by the man in the winged disc; the assemblage of peoples bringing gifts from every corner of his vast empire; and above all the grace of Ahura Mazda by which the king exercised his rule. Around the edges of the palace were the settlements of the people who lived and farmed there, the workers who maintained the palace, while the houses of the nobles, as Diodorus tells us, filled the further edges of the platform. All the people who lived there derived their existence in some way from the palace.

Xerxes was proud of his achievement: 'Me may Ahura Mazda together with the gods protect, and my kingdom, and what has been built by me' (XPb).

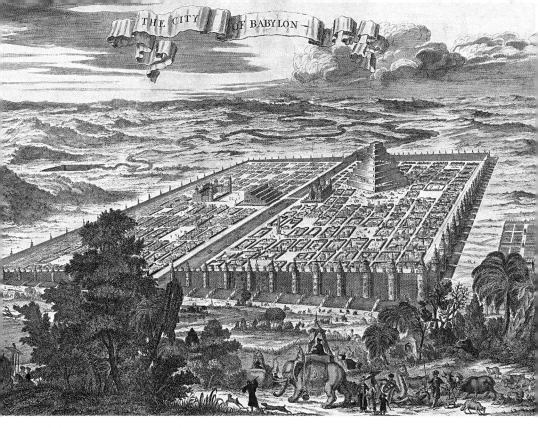

23 Babylon: an engraving by H. Fletcher, 1690.

24 The Hellespont: view from the south. In the distance can be seen its narrowest point, where Xerxes' bridge of boats was constructed.

25 Thermopylae: the Leonidas monument.

26 Thermopylae: general view.

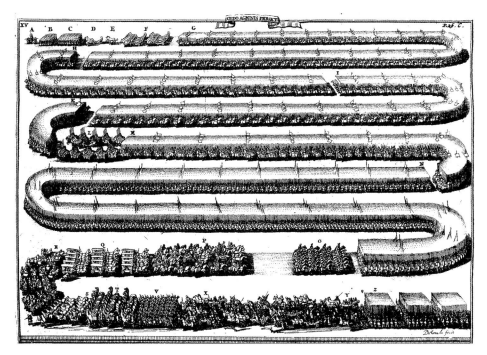

27 The Persian army: engraving from Samuel Pitiscus' edition of Q. Curtius Rufus, *Historia Alexandri Magni*, Utrecht 1683.

28 The present-day ruins of Sardis. Nothing remains from the Achaemenid period.

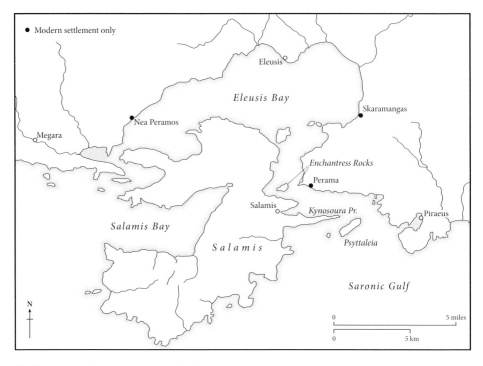

29 Map of the island and straits of Salamis.

30 The battlefield of Plataea: view to the north.

31 The approach to Persepolis.

32 Gateway of All Lands.

33 Ganj-nameh ('Treasure Book') on the outskirts of Hamadan, Iran. Inscription of Xerxes stating 'Ahura Mazda is a great god . . . I am Xerxes, the Great King, King of Kings, king of the lands of many people, king of this great earth far and wide, son of Daris the king, the Achaemenid'. The inscription of Xerxes is to the right of a similar inscription by Darius I. Were they inscribed simultaneously (by the same sculptor), or was Xerxes keen to add his contribution when he came to the throne?

34 Reliefs from the Apadana (audience hall) at Persepolis. Courtiers in conversation. Note the garden setting of roses and cypresses.

35 Detail of a Bactrian with an urn.

36 View of Persepolis from Kuh-i-Rahmat (Mountain of Mercy): top left is the Palace of Xerxes.

37 The king and attendants depicted on a door jamb of the Palace of Xerxes.

38 A somewhat imaginative rendering of the Gateway of All Lands. Engraving by Johan van den Avele from Pitiscus' edition of Q. Curtius (above).

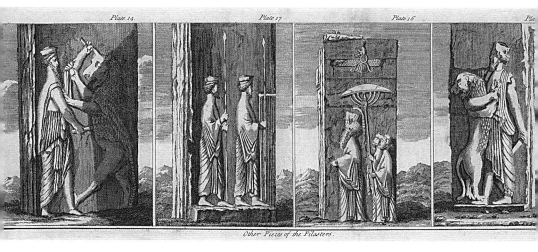

Plate 14. Plate 17. Plate 16. Plate

Other Pieces of the Pilasters.

39 One of Cornelius De Bruyn's magnificent series of engravings from *Travels in the Levant*, 1698.

40 Darius' 'original plan' for Persepolis, as imaginatively realized by Charles Chipiez (1835–1901).

41 Old photograph of Persepolis before excavation by Mirza Hassan Akasbashi, 1859. A very Ozymandian scene.

42 Old photograph of the Apadana after excavation, 1933. It looks better without the modern roof.

43 Esther before King Ahasuerus with Haman being sent to the gallows beyond.

44 The Tomb of Xerxes at Naqsh-e-Rustam.

CHAPTER EIGHT

Family Romances

Xerxes: Ma pur che dirà Amastre, e l'offeso suo padre del mio imeneo, del mio novella amore.

Amastre: Saprà delle mie offese ben vendicarsi il cor. Colui che l'ira accese proverà il mio furor?

Silvio Stampiglia and G. F. Handel, *Serse* I. xi and I. xiii

It seemed like a dream. Now he had returned and all was as before. The Persian empire, enormous, immeasurable, just as everything about him was immeasurable, Susa, his capital city, nothing was changed.

Louis Couperus, *Arrogance: The Conquests of Xerxes* (1930), 229

Sometimes what tortures us most upon our return home are the ways in which we, and our home, have remained exactly the way we remember them.

Gohar Homayounpour, *Doing Psychoanalysis in Tehran* (2012), 101

If Persepolis was Xerxes' triumph, his love life was his downfall. For Gore Vidal, both passions were equally symbols of his failure as a king. The narrator says 'He had lost all curiosity about the world. He had turned in upon himself. He cared for nothing but the harem and the completion of those buildings that he had begun in his youth.'[1] In words attributed to him by Gore Vidal, the king himself says ' "I've not added so much as a handful of earth or a cupful of water to my father's realm. All I have done is build." '[2]

He covered his feelings of inadequacy at the failed conquest by giving way to lust. Later, the narrator says Xerxes' ennui, or *accidie*, is enhanced by his sense of failure, of coming home to the scenes that reminded him of a father whose triumphs were far greater, and of three brothers who had died in his unsuccessful campaign in Greece.[3]

The enormous 'harem' that Xerxes built at Persepolis seems to betray a king who gave in to the pleasures of a 'court of women', as Colley Cibber's play *Xerxes* calls it. 'Enter Xerxes, follow'd by a train of ladies.'[4] There follows a 'masque of luxury' in which Indifference speaks:

> Indifference is the happiest state
> On which no care or sorrows wait;
> Nothing hating, nought admiring,
> Never wanting, ne'er requiring;

And then Venus chimes in:

> Would you know the sweetest joys,
> Which Virtue wisely keeps from fools,
> Then steal a mistress, break all ties,
> That would confine your love to rules.[5]

Later in the play, Xerxes' 'search for new pleasures' leads him to murder a series of virgins.[6]

Ridiculous as all this is, it embodies a judgement that can also be found in the historians and moralists. Even naturalists get in on the act, like Aelian in his *Inquiry into Animals* when he informs us that the wrasse, 'the most jealous of all fishes', lives just like the Persian king: 'the refinement in their mating, and the propensity which they enjoy for having many wives one might describe as characteristic of barbarians who luxuriate in the pleasures of the bed, and (if one may jest on serious subjects) as living like the Medes and Persians'.[7] Yet the picture is at odds with much of the evidence for Xerxes' relations with women, at least until the last years of his life. Unlike his polygamous father, Xerxes spent his life married to a single woman, Amestris, the daughter of Otanes, who was the commander of the Persian troops on the march to Greece.[8] She was thus of pure Persian blood, and the three sons she bore him (Darius, Hystaspes and Artaxerxes) had an unimpeachable claim to the succession, while their daughter Amytis also carried with her the highest dynastic kudos, as the later actions of her husband

Megabyzus were to show. Of a second daughter, Rodogyne, little is known. Another daughter, Ratahshah, was an infant in 486.

Even by modern bourgeois standards of love and fidelity, Xerxes seems to score quite highly here. That Persian kings could be regarded as paragons of devotion is shown by a long story in Aelian's *Historical Miscellany* about Cyrus the Younger and his love for a Greek woman, Aspasia, who came from Phocaea on the coast of Asia Minor. When growing up her friends called her Milto, 'Scarlet' because of her attractive blushing complexion. 'His love for Aspasia was celebrated in Ionia and the whole of Greece; the Peloponnese was full of reports about the love of Cyrus and Aspasia, and their fame even reached the Great King. It was really believed that after her Cyrus would not wish to have anything to do with any other woman.' When Cyrus was killed in battle by his brother Artaxerxes, Aspasia was among the captives, and it was Artaxerxes' turn to fall in love with her. He went so far as to make her his 'senior wife', a remarkable honour for a non-native Persian. Her grief for Cyrus made her slow to switch her affections to her new master, but a turning point came when Artaxerxes' favourite eunuch, Tiridates, died. Artaxerxes was inconsolable, but Aspasia did her best to cheer him up. 'The Persian was greatly encouraged by her sympathy and asked her to go to the bedroom and wait for him, which she did. When he came back he put the eunuch's black cloak over Aspasia's black dress. Somehow the young man's clothing suited her, and her beauty struck her lover even more powerfully.'[9] The upshot was that the young lady *travesti* did more to console Artaxerxes than she had done in her own person.

The story brings together several leitmotifs of Greek thinking about Persian erotic habits: not only the long-term devotion of the initial couple, but the seductiveness and sympathy of the (Greek) girl, the prevalence of eunuchs at the Persian court and their use, as the Greeks supposed, as additional sexual partners for the king; and finally the almost comic role-inversion which, however, leads to no mixed feelings (unlike those of Orsino for the disguised Viola in Shakespeare's *Twelfth Night*). We should like to know where Aelian got this story from: he gives no source, but it is certainly of the same kind as the stories that Ctesias likes to retell about the Persian court in the fifth and fourth centuries. Maybe the source was Greek – one of those people who told it in all of Greece and the Peloponnese – but I suspect it was a tale that was told at the Persian court ('even the Great King' knew the story, though this may not be so surprising as he was the young man's father), and that Ctesias (who else could it have been?) picked it up and wrote it down. The story, then, is not just a Greek interpretation of events, but reflects the way the Persians liked to regard their own amours.

CHASING LOLITA IN SUSA

Xerxes' own fidelity only collapsed in the last days of the expedition to Greece. Herodotus tells the story in masterly detail; whether all those details are true is another matter.[10] While in Sardis he fell for the wife of his full brother Masistes. She, however, would have nothing to do with him, and Xerxes' own respect for his brother prevented him from pushing his suit too forcefully. What he did next was to arrange a marriage between Masistes' daughter and his own son Darius. If Darius was, as it appears, his eldest son, he must have been born while Xerxes was still crown prince. If these events took place, as Herodotus implies, in 479, Xerxes was now about forty years old and his son might be, say, twenty. Herodotus says that his purpose in arranging this marriage was to improve his access to the woman he desired. The next act in the story, however, suggests that it was the daughter, whether a Lolita or somewhat older, whom the middle-aged king had his eye on. Once back in Susa and formally married to Darius, the girl, whose name was Artaynte, became a member of the royal household. Xerxes turned his attentions to his niece 'and he was successful with her'.[11]

Both parties managed to keep their affair a secret until Xerxes did a foolish thing. His wife Amestris had woven a beautiful shawl as a present for the king (thus implicitly disproving Herodotus' claim that it was shameful for Persian women to weave textiles). Xerxes wore it when he went to visit Artaynte, and she conceived a great liking for it. The continuation is predictable, for, as in all good folk tales, the girl now insinuatingly asks the king whether he will give her whatever she wants. Kings should know better than to say 'yes' to requests like that, but Xerxes had not the benefit of two thousand years of scholarship on folk-tale motifs and story patterns, so he agreed. Of course it was the shawl she wanted. (Silly girl.) The king's robe was more than just a garment, it was a symbol or talisman of his royal authority;[12] so to give it away was not just an insult to his wife but, implicitly, an act of surrendering the kingship. This is the first sign that this story is about something more than an old man's infatuation, for it conceals a story of rebellion.

When Amestris saw Artaynte wearing the shawl, her anger knew no bounds. But instead of taking it out on her husband's niece, she assumed that it was Masistes' wife who had set up the whole thing. Amestris' reasoning is unclear, but her actions were anything but. It was her turn to ask Xerxes, wheedlingly, for a gift.[13] She made her request at the major festival of the king's birthday, when he could not refuse her. The gift was to be Masistes' wife. Xerxes did as she asked; Masistes' wife was seized and taken to the queen. Xerxes summoned Masistes and made him an offer: divorce his present wife and accept Xerxes' daughter instead. Masistes was horrified; he was another of those uxorious Persians, and he loved his wife. Besides, he seems to imply, Xerxes' daughter would be much too young for him (as presumably Artaynte was much too young for Xerxes). Xerxes now went into one of his fits of rage: 'I withdraw the offer of marriage to my daughter, and you're not going to live with your wife a moment longer either.'

The fate of the latter was, of course, out of his hands by now. As soon as Amestris had got the woman in her grasp, she sent for Xerxes' personal guard and with their help she mutilated Masistes' wife. 'She cut off her breasts and threw them to the dogs, cut off her nose, ears, lips and tongue, and then sent her back home, totally disfigured.'[14] Masistes, out of his mind with rage, fled to Bactria with the aim of raising an insurrection against his brother who had let all this happen to him; but Xerxes was quicker. He sent an army after him and killed Masistes, his sons and all his troops. His throne was safe, for the time being.

The story is a rich one, introducing such themes as the rage and cruelty of Persian queens as well as their capacity for independent action, the customary nature of sexual relations with close relatives such as nieces (and even daughters), the role of torture in the Persian Empire, and the motives and punishments for revolts against the king. It may be that nothing in this story is quite what it seems. Let us look at each element in turn.

WOMEN AT THE PERSIAN COURT: QUEENS AND NOBLES

The first thing that strikes a reader is the polygamy of the Persian kings. Darius married all the available women of Cyrus' line,[15] the aim being to ensure that all the bloodline of the kingship was concentrated in him and his descendants. In the case of Xerxes, it was the eldest son who succeeded, whether 'born in the purple' or not.[16] Many of the actions of Persian queens are best interpreted as directed at preserving the purity of the bloodline, as well as the succession of their own sons.[17] This aim was intensified by a practice that was common in Persia but struck Athenians and others as particularly strange, namely marriage of kings (and others?) with close relatives, including daughters, sisters and nieces.[18] Euripides' character Hermione saw the practice as a mark of the 'barbarian': 'thus the entire barbarian race: the father has intercourse with his daughter, the child with its mother and the girl with her brother'.[19] Stories of mothers who conceived a passion for their sons were also current, including the Assyrian queen Semiramis' passion for her son Ninyas, as well as Parysatis for her son Artaxerxes.[20] This practice of marrying close relatives, in Persian *xwēdōdah* (OP *khvaētvadatha*), ensured that there were no rival family claimants to the throne and, in the absence of an understanding of the genetic effects, it was widely accepted. Nevertheless, the practice was treated by Western writers, for example Bardaisan of Edessa, as an example of the truth that there are no universal cultural norms: even incest, which is 'universally' abhorred, is current among the Persians 'up to now in Media, and in Egypt, Phrygia and Galatia'.[21] Ps-Clement goes even further: 'it is customary among Persians to take mothers and sisters in wedlock, and all Persians under the open heaven marry in this incestuous way'.[22] The author of the Malay version of the *Alexander Romance* (which stems from the Arabic tradition) remarks à propos the marriage of Bahman and Homay that it is quite acceptable among Zoroastrians to marry one's daughter.[23] Such alliances are quite common in Persian literature, from the Sassanian *Karnamag-e-Ardashir* to the medieval *Vis o Ramin*.[24] Xerxes' attachment to his niece Artaynte is paralleled in his father's marriage to his own niece Phratagune, which according to Brosius[25] was designed to concentrate the family's wealth further because she would bring with her the riches of her father Artanes.[26]

Thus Cambyses married his sister[27] as many pharaohs did, though Herodotus regarded this as exceptional. The Jewish philosopher Philo more or less grasped the point: 'Those of the Persians who are in high office marry their own mothers; they consider those who are born from these unions to be of superior birth and, as it is said, think them worthy of the highest sovereignty.'[28] It is an extreme corollary of the fact that, it appears, only pure-blooded Persians could be wives, as distinct from concubines.[29] Strabo adds the information that the king normally married his wives at the spring equinox (i.e. at *Now Ruz*, though this feast is never named in ancient authors), and that on that day the groom would eat nothing but either an apple or a camel's marrow.[30] (I know which I'd choose.)

Preservation of the bloodline was crucial also to the longevity of the Ottoman Empire, a dynasty that survived unbroken through thirty-six sultans. But Ottoman rulers did not marry their sisters; their solution was not to marry wives at all, which under Islamic law would inevitably have diluted the family's property. Instead, they took concubines from neighbouring nations, all of whom were in fact slaves, as were all the officials of the Ottoman court. Some sultans became particularly attached to just one concubine, as Suleyman did to the Polish lady whom Western observers called Roxelana; but the usual rule was that, as soon as a concubine had produced a son, she was retired. A series of concubines produced plenty of princes to act as provincial governors (sometimes from the age of ten), one of whom would eventually become the next Sultan. His brothers would then all be executed. The last case of this shocking practice was in 1574, when Murad III's funeral was quickly followed by that of nineteen of his sons, an event that so overwhelmed the people that the custom was abandoned. The mass fratricide, like Persian incest, exemplifies the lengths to which an absolute ruler must go to preserve his bloodline intact.[31]

But not all the king's women were his wives. He also had, according to Herodotus, 'numberless' concubines.[32] In fact there is quite a gradation of the king's paramours, including not only these high-status, but not noble or Persian, companions, whose sons could in principle become king.[33] Darius II, for example, was the son of a Babylonian concubine. Artaxerxes I had eighteen sons by his concubines, while Artaxerxes II apparently had 150 by his. Still, for a non-Persian like Esther to become 'queen' must be an extreme case. Concubines were not to be confused with courtesans, prostitutes or mistresses, still less with 'dancing-girls' or other musical entertainers.[34] Some of these were the product of 'finishing schools', according to Pierre Briant.[35]

Greeks also believed that the Persian king had a vast number of women available to satisfy what Louis Couperus calls his 'pelvic ardours'.[36] Commonly there were said to be 360 women, one for every night of the year, a conception paralleled in the basic plot of the *Arabian Nights*, where the sultan executes a girl after each night of pleasure, until Sheherezade thinks of a way to preserve her life by telling stories and ending each evening with a cliff-hanger. Pierre Briant cautiously accepts the information, and suggests that each king on his accession picked a new set of 360, though it is unclear what happened to the previous set.[37] Diodorus says that the girls had to line up on parade each night for the king to make his choice.[38] The idea recurs in the elaborate procedure for selecting Esther as Ahasuerus' queen; and the Book of Judith also makes clear how much care had to go into a girl's appearance before she presented herself to her master. The concubines, it seems, would have to be non-Persians, since Spithridates was indignant when Pharnabazus proposed taking the former's daughter as a concubine.[39]

Greeks were very struck by the much greater social prominence of women in Persia, compared with the secluded state in which most Athenian women lived (other Greek states, especially Sparta, had different customs). For example, Persian women dined with the men, as Herodotus noted,[40] and as a

funny story in the apocryphal III Esdras makes clear:[41] Apame was sitting to
the right of her husband Darius when she snatched his crown, put it on
her own head, and boxed his ears. The king just gaped at her. The courtier
Zerubbabel drew the moral that 'nothing is stronger than a woman'.[42]
Plutarch writes 'The lawful wives of the Persian kings sit beside them at
dinner and eat with them. But when the kings wish to be merry and get drunk,
they send their wives away, and send for their music-girls and concubines.'[43]

Women also hunted alongside men, not only the king's wives but also his
chief concubines.[44] (Lloyd Llewellyn-Jones points out that they might have
been screened off in the hunting park, like Mughal women.) A famous female
archer is mentioned by Ctesias.[45]

Some authors contradicted Herodotus' picture, for example Plutarch
(writing 600 years later) when he refers to Persian women and queens being
kept in virtual purdah:

Non-Greek races in general, and the Persians in particular, are fiercely –
even savagely – protective of their womenfolk. They keep a strict watch
over not only their wives, but even their slaves and concubines, who are
consequently never seen by strangers, but live their lives in seclusion at
home, and when they go outside travel on wagons under awnings with
curtains drawn all around them.[46]

The Book of Esther, too, opposes Herodotus' picture, since Queen Vashti
refuses Ahasuerus' request to join him in public, which leads to his rejection
of her for a new queen. The picture is somewhat confused but may be resolved
by making a distinction between segregation and seclusion. Noble women
were not shut away but, as in the modern Middle East, led separate lives for
much of the time and would be visible only to their close kin.

Women were also able (again like Spartan women) to own property in
their own right. Darius' wife Irtašduna (Artystone) possessed three estates,
and Amestris owned vast amounts of property – enough to put the wealth-
iest of Athenians in the shade – while the revenues of one Egyptian village
went to keep another queen in shoes.[47] Ottoman queens were likewise maintained through land grants and tax concessions as well as a direct stipend,[48]
which of course would lapse on their deaths and the revenues revert to the
sultan. These queens could also undertake public works such as the building
of mosques and baths. In the Persian case, 'Plato' represents Socrates as
saying to Alcibiades:

Yet the Spartan wealth, though great in comparison of the wealth of the other Hellenes, is as nothing in comparison of that of the Persians and their kings. Why, I have been informed by a credible person who went up to the king (at Susa), that he passed through a large tract of excellent land, extending for nearly a day's journey, which the people of the country called the queen's girdle, and another, which they called her veil; and several other fair and fertile districts, which were reserved for the adornment of the queen, and are named after her several habiliments. Now, I cannot help thinking to myself, What if someone were to go to Amestris, the wife of Xerxes and mother of Artaxerxes, and say to her, There is a certain Dinomache, whose whole wardrobe is not worth fifty minae – and that will be more than the value – and she has a son who is possessed of a three-hundred acre patch at Erchiae, and he has a mind to go to war with your son – would she not wonder to what this Alcibiades trusts for success in the conflict?[49]

In the next generation, Parysatis was able to supply her son Cyrus with troops from her estates in Syria, and that was only part of her holdings since she owned land in Media as well.[50]

Economic importance was paralleled by the greater political influence of royal women. The Queen Mother was always powerful, as also in the Ottoman Empire, where she might even take the reins of government for an underage son, especially if he was appointed to govern a province at the age of ten.[51] Irdabama, the mother (it appears) of Darius I, had considerable estates, was able to oversee payment of food supplies, and commanded a large army of servants and workers at Shiraz and elsewhere.[52] She was even able to deputise for the king and to hold audience in her own right. The evidence for Irdabama's power, drawn from the documentary evidence of the Persepolis tablets, suggests that Herodotus' depiction of the power of Atossa may not be as far removed from reality as has sometimes been supposed. The mother of Darius III, too, played a role in negotiations with Alexander after her son's death, though perhaps not as great as the *Alexander Romance* supposes (let alone Terence Rattigan in his play about Alexander, *Adventure Story*). The position of the Queen Mother would be analogous to that of later harem-based empires such as the Ottoman and the Abbasid. In the court of Shah Abbas, it was in fact his paternal aunt, Zainab Begum, who ruled the roost, and was included in his Council of State.[53] In Louis Couperus, Atossa keeps the women under control with her whip.[54]

Achaemenid queens, however, did not hold direct political power, despite Ctesias' implications of 'petticoat government'.[55] They could not, for example, act as regent, as Seleucus' wife Apame was able to do in the third century BC. One of the best-known satrapies of the empire, Caria, seems however to provide an exception to this rule. This was the home of Xerxes' naval commander Artemisia, who was also queen of Caria. A later Artemisia, the wife of Mausolus, ruled as queen after his death; and a descendant, Ada, who was exiled by her brother, regained power under Alexander and became queen in her own right.[56] Such things never happened in the Persian heartland.

Other noble women could also wield political influence, especially through intercession with the king. A well-known example is Esther's plea for her threatened compatriots; but historical examples are also ready to hand. Intaphernes burst in on the king (Darius) when he was in bed with a girl, and was sentenced to death along with all male members of his family.[57] His wife interceded with the king, who said that he would spare the life of one male member of her family. Faced with such a choice, she famously chose her brother, reasoning like Antigone that she could get another husband, but never another brother. Darius, impressed, spared not only the brother but her eldest son; yet Intaphernes had to die.[58]

Another case involved Sataspes, who was accused of having raped the daughter of a nobleman, Zopyrus.[59] Sataspes' mother interceded with the king – this time Xerxes – and was given the privilege of altering his sentence. She set him the task of sailing round Libya; but when he failed, the original sentence was imposed and Sataspes was impaled.

Xerxes was faced with another angry mother, his sister Sandace or Mandane[60] whose three sons had all lost their lives at Salamis. When she learnt that Themistocles, the architect of the Persian defeat, was present in Susa, she went to the king and demanded his execution. The king paid her no heed – for reasons not given – so she raised a mob to storm the palace. Xerxes then agreed to put the Athenian on trial. However, Diodorus tells us, the preparation took so long that Themistocles was able to learn fluent Persian in the interim, and defended himself with such success that he was acquitted.

Themistocles provides another instance of the importance of the ruler's women. When he offended the ruler of Sardis by rashly requesting the return of a statue to Athens, it was by sweet-talking the satrap's concubines that he saved his skin.[61]

THE HAREM

Much dispute has raged around the question of whether the female component of the Persian court should be termed a harem, and if so whether there was a building that could be called a 'harem' at Persepolis. The two questions have been effectively disentangled by Lloyd Llewellyn-Jones. As he points out, the word 'conjures up the popular image of a closely guarded pleasure palace filled with scantily clad nubile courtesans idling away their days in languid preparation for nights of sexual adventure in a sultan's bed. It is a world of scatter cushions, jewels in the bellybutton, and fluttering eyelashes set above gauzy yashmaks.'[62]

A harem, in the correct sense of the word (as it applies for example to the portion of the Topkapi Palace set aside for the sultan's women in the Ottoman Empire), is a place of seclusion – the word means 'forbidden' – where the women of the palace live without access to the rest of the court and under the guardianship of eunuchs. The sultan's quarters, it should be noted, were also a 'harem' in this sense. The women, even those with great political influence, never emerged from these suites but, like many women in the Muslim world today, exercised their influence over their menfolk from their own domain. Princes were brought up in the harem and did not see the wider world until one became the next sultan, at which point he put all rival claimants (his brothers) to death. The atmosphere, according to observers, was more like a nunnery than a brothel![63]

But the term also is applied more generally to the women associated with the king. In the latter sense, there is no doubt that the Persian king had a 'harem'. It may be that the new king simply inherited his father's women, with the necessary changes of position of the Queen Mother, chief wives, and so on; but it may also be that all 360 women were dismissed and replaced by a new set chosen by the new king. If so, they may have retired to special quarters, as Ottoman harems did.[64] We do not know.

It is clear that no systematic seclusion of women took place in the Achaemenid Empire, despite Plutarch's assertion to the contrary (above). But this is not to say that there was no separation of men and women, as in the modern Middle East. Hierarchy and division were all-important at the Persian court. But given the political and social influence of the women at court it seems misguided to deny the existence of a harem in the wider sense, though several great scholars do just this.[65]

However, the question of whether there is a building or suite of rooms to be identified as the 'harem' in the strong sense is another matter. Neither Plutarch nor Herodotus implies that there was a special building on the Ottoman model for the womenfolk. The building at Persepolis called Xerxes' harem may be quite misnamed. A. T. Olmstead's evocation of the building is vivid:

To the west of the final treasury building, and separated from it by a street, was the harem which Xerxes completed for his imperious queen, Amestris. Surrounded by the guard rooms of the watchful eunuchs was a tier of six apartments to house the royal ladies. Each tier consisted of a tiny hall whose roof was upheld by only four columns, and a bedroom so minute that even with a single occupant the atmosphere would have been stifling.[66]

But he concedes that these apartments were connected with the main palace by long corridors. The identification of the building as a harem has come into dispute, though it is difficult to come up with a convincing alternative view. Llewellyn-Jones points out that the apartments as a whole are not as tiny as all that.[67] There are twenty-two of them, each about 10 × 10 metres and consisting of several rooms. But whether they were or were not the women's quarters, the women were free to come and go, to hold audience, to manage their staff in a way quite different from that of the Ottomans.

The parallel with the Ottoman harem is again instructive. The sultana herself had magnificent quarters adjoining those of the sultan, 'and one can go through secret rooms from the one to the other . . . . The chambers of the Sultana are very splendid, with chapels, baths, gardens and other amenities, not only for herself, but for her maids as well, of which she keeps as many as one hundred.'[68] But the accommodation of retired and widowed princesses might be a great deal less splendid: the non-elite were confined to cramped, dark rooms and corridors, as contemporary witnesses make clear.[69]

THE BOOK OF ESTHER: IS IT HISTORY?

Besides the dalliance with his niece in his last years, Xerxes' name is linked with another woman whom he preferred to his wife: Queen Esther. The Jewish tale of Esther is certainly fiction, but it is fiction with a purpose and is set at the court of Xerxes, whom the Jews called Ahasuerus (see Chapter 2). No other source refers to a wife of Xerxes called anything like Vashti (Aste in Josephus) or to his affection for a beautiful Jewess called Esther. The tenth-century historian al-Tabari, attempting to reconcile his sources, states that the mother of Bahman, son of Esfandiyar, was 'a Jewess from the house of Saul', but does not name her.[70] The Book of Esther, probably written much earlier than the Book of Judith, about 400 BC, reflects a period when there are numerous Jews living in Susa, who have not taken part in the Return to Judah. It is a tale that reflects tensions at Susa, and perhaps also the concerns about 'marrying out' that disturbed Malachi around the end of Xerxes' reign. The same theme permeates the Book of Ruth.

There is no doubt that Esther is full of information about the Persian court, much of it corroborated from other sources.[71] The geographical extent of Xerxes' empire is correctly given, the description of the palace at Susa matches information from archaeology, as well as the description of the luxurious dining room given by Alexander's chamberlain Chares;[72] Xerxes' character is portrayed in a way consonant with our other information – he is fond of parties, lavish with gifts, but has a tendency to lose his temper. The seven advisers of the king are a historical detail, as is the reliability of the postal system, the custom of prostration, the use of hanging as a form of execution, the observance of lucky days. A good many Persian words appear in the text. The Greek Additions to the Book of Esther, too, betray a knowledge of Hellenistic chancellery style.[73] Addition D has Esther overwhelmed by the king's splendour as Judith was by that of Holofernes, and the Alexander of the *Romance* by that of Darius. But, as Carey Moore rightly says, all this amounts to is proof that the author was familiar with the Persian Empire – and that the author of the Additions knew about Hellenistic letter-writing – not that the story is historical.[74]

Even the appearance of an accountant named Marduka at Susa in the first year of Xerxes does not make our Mordecai a real person.[75] There are serious contradictions between the Book of Esther and our other sources, most notably the statement that Esther was queen between the seventh and twelfth years of Xerxes' reign,[76] while Herodotus makes it clear that Amestris was queen at this time; furthermore, in the seventh year of his reign (480 BC) Xerxes was leading an expedition in Greece, and was thus away for two of the four years that it allegedly took him to find Esther.[77] There would be no difficulty in attributing polygamy to Xerxes, as to his father, but one would expect some record of his other wives to appear elsewhere, even if Esther, as an insignificant Jewess, could not be a full wife but only a concubine. Perhaps the best that Esther's supporters can hope for is that her original was one of the 360 anonymous bedfellows, raised to heights of influence by an enthusiastic Jewish author.

But probably there is even less historical basis to Esther than that. An ingenious study by Stephanie Dalley has developed the argument that the plot is a reworking of a Babylonian sacred tale about the gods Ishtar and Marduk (Esther and Mordecai), while Haman is the chief god of Susa, Humban.[78] His ten sons bear the names of Elamite daevas, or demons.[79] The original setting is seventh-century Assyria and was adapted in a later rewriting to the conditions of the Achaemenid court. The possibility of using the Book of Esther as historical evidence thus evaporates, but its role as a mediator of Jewish opinion about the Persian court remains. It is full of circumstantial details, as we have seen in Chapter 2; but Esther, alas, is not to be counted among the ladies who graced Xerxes' bed.

Nonetheless, the encounter between Esther and Ahasuerus has caught the imagination of many writers and artists since, not least because of the lively picture it evokes of the Persian court and its splendour. For Jews it is the origin of the festival of Purim, the liveliest and most fun-filled of Jewish feasts, since Haman had cast the lots for their destruction on the 14th and 15th of Adar.[80] Fiction or no, Esther is the supreme example of the power of women at the Persian court.

CHAPTER NINE

Assassination

'Abu, 14+x [i.e. 4–8 August 465 BC] Xerxes' son killed him.'
Babylonian tablet BM 32234 (Kuhrt I. 306. See also Aelian *VH* 13.3)

This Artaban was provost off his hous
And an officer most especial, –
With his seuene sonys strong and despitous,
Vpon a nyht furious and fatal,
Fell vpon Xerxes in his palace roial.
And in his stori as it is remembrid,
On pecis smale thei han hym al dismembrid.
This was off Xerxes the laste final meede
Off his hih pride the funeral guerdoun;
From his too kyngdamys off Perse & [eek] Mede
Froward Fortune hath hym plucked doun.
John Lydgate, *Fall of Princes* III. 2528–38

MORE TROUBLE IN GREECE

Xerxes' authority at court had been weakened by his disastrous affair with his niece. At the same time, events in the west had taken a turn for the worse, and Greece seemed to be slipping from Xerxes' grasp. Since the Persian withdrawal from Greece in 479 the Greek states had returned to their usual fissiparous habits. Sparta and Athens both went their own ways, Sparta developing its position as the leading land power in Greece while Athens rapidly achieved dominance of the seas. Athens kept up a war of attrition that moved to a new level of intensity with the career of Cimon, whose victory at the River Eurymedon, probably in 469 BC,[1] was a decisive stage in the relations of Greece and Persia.

Pausanias, who had commanded the Hellenic forces at Plataea, was sent out to continue the liberation of the eastern Greeks. First he conducted a successful campaign in Cyprus, and then continued to Byzantium; here he expelled the Persian garrison, but it seemed to the Greek population that they had merely exchanged one oppressor for another. Pausanias was seduced by Persian ways, connived at the escape of a number of prominent Persians, and began to identify with the Persian cause to the extent of wearing Persian dress. Seeing an opportunity for personal self-advancement, he engaged in intrigues with the enemy and even pursued a plan to marry Xerxes' daughter. Xerxes welcomed this evidence that a Greek had seen the superior advantages of Persian rule; but before the plan could go further, Pausanias was recalled by a dissatisfied Sparta. Pausanias now hired a trireme on his own account and resumed control of Byzantium; he quickly took over Sestos, but this was too much for the Athenians, who sent the general Cimon to drive him out. Pausanias set up a new base of operations in the Troad, but the Spartans sent a herald to fetch him back. He was put on trial after an informer handed over a letter he had written to Artabazus, the new governor of Dascyleion and a cousin of Xerxes;[2] Pausanias fled to sanctuary in the Temple of Athena of the Brazen House. The Spartan authorities promptly blockaded him there and starved him to death (probably 467/6 BC). Thus came to an end the career of one whom Xerxes might have seen as a fifth columnist in the west.

THEMISTOCLES

Another Greek who began to feel the allure of Persia in the years after Plataea was Themistocles. After his triumph at Salamis he spent time roaming the islands of the Aegean collecting monetary contributions for the defence of Greece. This display of avarice made him unpopular, and he found himself in conflict with the other leading politician of Athens, Aristides. Themistocles was ostracised from an ungrateful Athens and moved to Argos. At the same time he was in correspondence with Pausanias, and when the Spartan ephors discovered the treasonable activities of Pausanias, Themistocles was implicated too. Diodorus says that the Spartans 'engineered' a plot against him by accusing him of having conspired with the Spartan king Pausanias to betray Greece to Xerxes.³ Themistocles fled – this was probably in 471 BC – first to Corcyra and then to Admetus, the king of Molossia, who received him kindly; but when the Spartans threatened to make war on Admetus he sent Themistocles away. He gave him a quantity of gold and helped him to escape in secret, until he arrived at the mountain town of Aegae in Aeolis, in Persian territory. Here Themistocles was given refuge by a man called either Lysitheides or Nicogenes,⁴ who was a friend of the king. 'When Themistocles asked that he lead him to Xerxes, at first he demurred, explaining that Themistocles would be punished because of his past actions against the Persians; later, however, when he realized that it was for the best, he acceded, and unexpectedly and without harm he got him through safe to Persia.'⁵ Themistocles travelled in disguise, dressed as a woman and riding in a covered carriage. A letter from the fictional composition *Letters of Themistocles*, probably composed about 100 CE, describes the journey vividly:

> On the way I passed through a few hills and a deep valley. I saw and traversed great flat plains. The edges of them were inhabited and well worked. The desert part nourished wild beasts and herds of other animals. I sailed down many rivers and visited all kinds of people. From my fellow travellers I learned the Persian language, and the journey was no longer unusually troublesome or tiring to me.⁶

When Themistocles reached Susa he sought audience with the king, first applying to the chamberlain, Artabanus.⁷ But which king? Thucydides and Charon of Lampsacus said that Artaxerxes was already on the throne when Themistocles reached Susa; Thucydides puts the arrival of Themistocles in Susa in the early days of the reign of Artaxerxes I,⁸ some fourteen years after the Persian repulse from Greece. Plutarch claims to find that Thucydides' chronology works better, but then goes on to follow the alternative version, which he, like Diodorus, found in Ephorus, Dinon, Cleitarchus and Heraclides, that it was Xerxes to whom Themistocles came.⁹ Certainly if, as Plutarch says, Themistocles lived 'a long time' in Magnesia, it seems likely that he arrived in the empire before the death of Xerxes. Thucydides' statement may be explained by assuming that he was misled by the fact that Themistocles' Persian career concluded under the later king. Themistocles seems, at any rate, to have behaved himself in his Persian years and not to have given Xerxes cause for dissatisfaction; but still he found it prudent to keep the unpredictable king at arm's length.

Many scholars prefer Thucydides' version, especially Arthur Keaveney, who puts Themistocles' arrival at the turn of the year 464/3:[10] thus he had been on the run for seven years. Keaveney calls it a 'slow, not noisy' progress. A decision is impossible such is the state of the evidence, but nothing prevents the supposition that he arrived under Xerxes and continued to enjoy favour under his successor. It certainly makes a better story! – as Pietro Metastasio found when he concocted the libretto of his much-loved opera, *Temistocle*.[11] Here the king is won over by the Athenian's devotion, but temporarily turns against him when he, Xerxes, falls in love with a maid of his wife's who turns out to be Themistocles' daughter; yet she refuses him. Eventually Xerxes learns the virtues of a good king, pardons everybody and yields the daughter to her own true love.

Themistocles began by introducing himself merely as 'a Greek'. Artabanus warned him that he would have to prostrate himself if he wanted to speak to the king, and Themistocles swallowed his pride and said that he would make no bones about that. Xerxes had perhaps been to some extent fooled by the devious messages that the Athenian had sent him before Salamis, and regarded him as someone he could work with. At all events, the enemy of Xerxes' enemy could be, at least temporarily, the king's friend, and he was given refuge at court. Xerxes gloated over his success: 'I have Themistocles the Athenian!' he cried, celebrating with a few drinks, and prayed that 'Ahriman would never stop influencing his enemies' thinking in this way, so that they banished their best men'.[12]

Themistocles learnt Persian and survived a campaign for his execution by the king's sister; Xerxes then honoured him with the gift of a Persian wife (Diodorus is the only source, but it does not seem implausible), provided him with a multitude of slaves, and presented him with several estates to provide him with an income:[13] Magnesia on the Maeander for his grain, Myus for meat and fish, and Lampsacus for its vineyards.[14] Themistocles went hunting regularly with the king, and even became a friend of the Queen Mother and 'a student of the Magi'.

At Lampsacus, Themistocles was honoured with a festival,[15] perhaps because he 'freed the city from tribute'. (The phrase comes from one of the 'Letters of Themistocles', a concoction made several centuries after the hero's death, but by an author who seems to have had access to now lost historians.)[16] He began to issue his own coins. If he arrived in Susa after the Battle of the Eurymedon, as Keaveney's argument requires, it is perhaps surprising that these western cities were still Xerxes' to give him.[17]

Themistocles took the opportunity to travel widely in Asia Minor: probably he was employed by the king as a useful source of information about what was happening in his Greek-speaking territories. Once, when visiting Sardis, he spotted in the temple of the Great Mother a bronze statue of a girl, known as the 'water-carrier', which he had himself set up when he was superintendent of the water supply in Athens. This statue was one of the spoils that Xerxes had taken from Athens and deposited in Sardis. He made so bold as to ask the satrap of Lydia whether it might be returned to Athens. The satrap became very angry, and it was only by sweet-talking his concubines that Themistocles managed to mollify him. He now decided to settle far from the centre of royal power, on his estate at Magnesia. He even built a temple of the Great Mother there, and lived 'a trouble-free life for a long time',[18] outliving his benefactor Xerxes by several years.

Themistocles went native; his son Cleophantus had a thoroughly Persian education.[19] Themistocles is said to have done a favour to Demaratus,[20] who was still living in Persia. Demaratus had been king of Sparta from 515 to 491, so was born perhaps around 535. In 465 he would have been seventy, and very old if all this took place under Artaxerxes.

'Some historians say,' continues Diodorus, that Xerxes had not yet given up his plan of conquest of Greece.[21] He invited Themistocles, now about sixty-five, to command a fresh expedition (the nub of Metastasio's plot); the latter agreed, but then committed suicide by downing a cup of bull's blood (which is supposed to congeal rapidly and thus choke the victim; this is false).[22] Xerxes abandoned the plan as unworkable without Themistocles, who thus 'by his voluntary death left the best possible defence that he had played the part of a good citizen in all matters affecting the interests of Greece'. Plutarch links the episode with Cimon's triumph at the Eurymedon (see below). But the story cannot be historical if Themistocles actually became governor of Magnesia under Artaxerxes, after 465, and is probably untrue anyway. He most likely died in about 460. John Marr suggests that the story of his refusal of Xerxes' appointment was concocted by Themistocles' sons on their return to Athens in the 450s.[23]

When Themistocles died, at the age of sixty-five, a magnificent tomb was erected for him in Magnesia, as Plutarch reports from information given him by his friend Themistocles, a descendant of the great general. (The 'tomb of Themistocles' at Piraeus, accordingly, must be falsely named, though Thucydides claims that his bones were secretly brought to Athens after his death.)

Xerxes' Last Greek Campaign

The careers of these two men, unsatisfactory as they were, suggest that Xerxes had by no means lost interest in the west. Although he wished to continue his mission of control by diplomatic means, the two players he found were too few to carry the day, and things moved too slowly to be effective. A story about the general Cimon suggests that they were not the only players in the diplomatic game. A Persian called Rhoesaces, 'who had defected from the king's cause'[24] (or, no doubt, claimed that he had), came to Athens with a great deal of money and took refuge at Cimon's house, placing before him bowls full of gold and silver darics. Cimon asked whether he wished to have Cimon as an employee or a friend. 'As a friend,' replied Rhoesaces; whereupon Cimon told him to keep his money, since he would be able to make use of a friend's resources whenever he had need. Cimon was not for sale. The apophthegm recalls one attributed to Xerxes' doppelgänger Esfandiyar by Mir Khwand, 'devout gratitude is better than bestowing gifts; for the effect of the former is permanent, but that of the latter transitory'.[25] Perhaps Xerxes' took Rhoesaces' rebuff to heart.

The Athenians were determined to eliminate the Persian threat by military means, and entrusted the incorruptible Cimon with the prosecution of the campaign to liberate the Greek cities. After driving Pausanias out of Sestos and Byzantium, he turned his attention to Eion, at the mouth of the River Strymon. The Persian commander Boges put up a fierce defence; when the food supplies were exhausted he decided on a grand gesture: he erected a vast funeral pyre, killed his wives and children, slaves and concubines, and threw them all into the flames; he then cast all his gold and silver into the Strymon, and finally leapt himself into the flames. Such episodes are told so many times in Greek history, in several authors,[26] that one wonders whether they can really all be historical. But there is no doubt that Athens benefited from control of this important city, which provided access both to forests for timber and mines for silver (as well as the treasure that Boges had thrown into the Strymon).

A campaign against pirates on Scyros was not directly aimed at Persian power, but perhaps shows the level of instability in the Aegean that had been created by the years of warfare, as well as Themistocles' cash-collecting activities. On Scyros, Cimon found the gigantic bones of the hero Theseus, which the Delphic oracle had told him he must recover and bring to Athens. These sacred relics brought the general immense kudos.

By this time Xerxes had equipped a new army. If this was the army that he invited Themistocles to control, the story of Themistocles' suicide must be false. But Themistocles certainly did not command it, for the commanders were Xerxes' illegitimate son Tithraustes (for the fleet),[27] and his nephew Pherendates (for the army).[28] (The king was perhaps running short of male relatives to hold important military commands.) According to Plutarch, the supreme commander was Ariomandes, son of Gobryas: he was presumably a younger brother of the dead Mardonius. In addition to the army, Xerxes had had a new fleet built, or assembled, from Phoenicia, Cyprus and Cilicia.[29] This combined force came together near the mouth of the River Eurymedon in Pamphylia, early in 466 BC.[30]

Cimon set about making the seas west of Pamphylia impassable for Persian ships. He had redesigned and strengthened the fleet of 300 triremes that had been created by Themistocles, and liberated the coastal towns of Caria in a two-pronged attack: the Greek cities readily revolted, but the bilingual cities that still had Persian garrisons had to be besieged. Cimon made his base at the harbour of Cnidus. It is somewhat hard to reconcile the narratives of Plutarch and Diodorus,[31] but the order of events was probably as follows. By similar tactics to those he had used in Caria, Cimon first compelled the Lycians, whose cities had not been settled from Greece and whose inhabitants saw themselves as Persian subjects, to become members of the recently founded Athenian League.[32] He then came to Phaselis, on the borders of Lycia and Pamphylia: the inhabitants here were Greek, but refused to secede from Persia. In the end they were subdued: Plutarch says that Chian troops in the Greek fleet talked them over by firing arrows with messages attached to them into the besieged city. Cimon now bore down on the assembled Persian force at the Eurymedon.

Again, Plutarch's and Diodorus' narratives are incompatible. According to Diodorus, Cimon disguised his own troops in the clothing of Persians captured earlier in the campaign, so that the Persians received them as if they were their own. When night fell, the Greeks left the ships and slaughtered the Persian army, including one of the commanders, Xerxes' nephew Pherendates. As Diodorus also says that these ships had been captured off Cyprus, 125 miles away, on the same day, and his narrative of the treacherous night-time slaughter has all the marks of a set-piece, it is perhaps wiser to follow Plutarch, who admits that his own sources (Ephorus and Phanodemus) differed on details. Cimon was eager to join battle before Persian reinforcements arrived from Cyprus, and the result was that the Persian fleet made straight for land and the troops fled ashore. More than 200 triremes were captured. The Greek force now pressed ashore and the hoplites, already tired from the sea battle, charged on an enemy whose numbers were superior. But

hoplite tactics won the day, the Persians were massacred and the camp was
looted of its valuables. Thus Cimon was victorious both by land and by sea
on a single day. Xerxes' entire fleet was lost.

It was now, if ever, that Xerxes had reason to feel humiliated – defeated
on what he regarded as his own territory. Plutarch writes:

> These victories of Cimon humbled the king's pride so much that he
> undertook, in the terms of the famous peace, always to keep at least a
> day's ride away from the Greek sea, and not to bring any long ship or
> bronze-rammed ship beyond the Cyanean Islands and the Chelidonian
> Islands.[33]

The existence of this alleged peace is a great crux of historical scholarship.
The evidence is so contradictory that it can never be solved,[34] but it seems
best to remain sceptical. As Plutarch goes on to say, what happened in practice was what he describes: the king's fleet made no further forays into Greek
waters. In the circumstances, it seems unlikely that Xerxes had the heart to
try a further land campaign under the command of Themistocles. Anyway,
his time was running out.

It looks as if this latest failure in warfare may have led to insurrectionist
tendencies at the court. 'After the disastrous war he had waged against
Greece, Xerxes ... began to be despised even by his own people.'[35] His
empire was fraying at the edges. Lycia was sliced off by the Athenians some-
time before 452 when it entered the Athenian League, which was rapidly
becoming an empire; Bactria was soon to slip away, though Xerxes' son
Hystaspes was satrap there at this time; and Egypt raised a revolt as soon as
Artaxerxes was on the throne.

THE DEATH OF XERXES

As usual, the accounts of Xerxes' death as told by the historians vary,[36]
though there is little doubt that Xerxes was slain in his bed. As Xenophon
pointed out (perhaps with Xerxes' case in mind), his hero the great Cyrus
'knew well enough that a man can most easily be assassinated at his meals,
or in his bath, or in bed, or when he is asleep, and asked himself who were
most to be trusted of those he had about him'.[37] If that is genuine Persian
wisdom, then Xerxes had let his guard slip.

In all three of the historians' accounts, those of Justin, Ctesias and
Diodorus, the key figure is Artabanus or Artapanus, the son of Artasyras, a

Hyrcanian and an important adviser of Xerxes. (This is not the same man as Artabanus, the son of Hystaspes and therefore Xerxes' uncle, who had opposed the Greek invasion at the outset.) This man – Justin calls him Xerxes' 'prefect' – decided to murder the king and assume the kingship himself. He got the eunuch chamberlain who was called either Aspamitres (Ctesias) or Mithridates (Diodorus) on his side, and the two of them burst into Xerxes' chamber one night and stabbed him in his bed. Justin, however, says that the crime was carried out by Artabanus and his seven sons.

The seven sons cause one to raise an eyebrow, given the prevalence of the number seven in stories of the Persian court, and not least the seven conspirators who brought Darius to the throne.[38] Certainly Artabanus can have had as little genuine dynastic claim to rule as Darius had had when he carried out his coup.

Now it was necessary to deal with Xerxes' sons. Hystaspes, who was either the youngest or the middle son, was away from the court since he was satrap of Bactria. Artabanus went to Artaxerxes and told him that his elder brother Darius had just murdered his father: all three historians agree on this. Artaxerxes leaps into action, and with his bodyguard goes straight to Darius' room and kills his sleeping brother. Ctesias, however, says that Artaxerxes summoned Darius to his presence and then had him put to death. According to Diodorus, Artabanus immediately summoned his own sons and they set upon Artaxerxes; but the latter fought them all off, slew Artabanus, and became king of Persia.[39] This train of events provides the plot of Metastasio's opera libretto, *Artaserse*.[40]

Our other sources allow Artaxerxes time to be acknowledged as king, and bring in a further character, Megabyzus (Baccabasus in Justin),[41] whom Artabanus takes into his confidence, but who soon reveals Artabanus' treacherous plot to the king. For Ctesias, Megabyzus is disaffected with Xerxes because he believes his wife Amytis is having an adulterous affair (presumably with the king, though Ctesias does not say so). In Justin, however, 'Baccabasus' had no interest in regime change and revealed all to Artaxerxes. Artaxerxes was afraid of the numerous sons of Artabanus (even though he had beaten them all single-handed in a night-time fight), and assembled the entire army. 'The king then pretended his armour was too short and ordered Artabanus to exchange it with his. Once he had withdrawn and was naked, the king stabbed him with his sword; then he had his sons arrested. In this way, this excellent young man avenged the murder of his father and death of his brother, as well as delivering himself from Artabanus' trap.'

The final act, reported only by Ctesias, is that following Artabanus'
execution, the eunuch Aspamitres was also arrested and put to death by
the torture of the boats. The fact that Justin calls this man Mithridates, the
name of the man who in Plutarch's *Life of Artaxerxes* was put to death by
this torture,[42] on a quite different occasion, arouses suspicion.

Even more confusion is imported by a brief allusion in Aristotle's *Politics*,
explaining how conspiracies can have their roots in fear:

> Artapanes [sic] conspired against Xerxes and slew him, fearing that he
> would be accused of hanging Darius against his orders – he having been
> under the impression that Xerxes would forget what he had said in the
> middle of a meal, and that the offence would be forgiven.[43]

The passage is so allusive as to defy satisfactory interpretation. Does it imply
a version in which Darius tried to kill the king, after which Artapanus gained
the impression that Xerxes wanted him dead – 'who will rid me of this turbulent son?', he might have said, and then regretted it? Artapanus killed the
king to save his own skin.

What, if any, of all this are we to believe? Perhaps the answer is 'nothing',
given the evidence of the very laconic Babylonian tablet quoted at the head
of this chapter: 'Xerxes' son killed him'.[44] The date given for Xerxes' death,
between 4 and 8 August 465, can be relied on given the accuracy of Babylonian
timekeeping, but what has happened to Artabanus? Is the entire story about
his conspiracy a fiction or was the Babylonian chronicler just ill-informed, or
working simply from the end result, that Xerxes' son *succeeded* him?

Perhaps it is best to start from questions of interest: who would have
wanted what? We should also consider which stories, in the oral tradition
that conveyed all Persian history to later writers, would have been of benefit
to the only successful actor in the drama, namely Artaxerxes.

It is difficult to believe that Artabanus could have harboured strong hopes
of making himself king in the teeth of three existing legitimate sons of
Xerxes. Accordingly, let us suppose that his part as originator of the plot
was an invention to deflect blame from the successful heir, Artaxerxes. No
doubt expressions of dissatisfaction with the king's conduct of the Greek
war were drifting around the palace. Xerxes' affair with his niece was an
unconstructive and perhaps shameful aberration, and it certainly seems to
have set his own wife against him. It would also have annoyed his son Darius,
who was married to the woman. It was Amestris who stood to gain most
from the whole affair. She would be rid of an unfaithful husband and would

be the Queen Mother of a king who, as it turned out, had a successful reign of over forty years; and still Amestris outlived him, growing old in comfort and honour.

Amestris might have engineered the murder of her own husband by the man who had best access to him as he slept, leading him to suppose that she would support a bid by him to become king. But did she also set up her eldest son Darius as a victim? The plot required that one of them should die (Hystaspes, miles away in Bactria, could be sorted out later), and we must presume that she chose the one son she loved and trusted best to survive. It is also possible that the plot was concocted by Darius and Amestris between them: in this sense Darius would be the murderer, and avenger of his wife's honour, even if the hand he hired to do it was that of Artabanus. This would 'save' the Babylonian evidence, which, it should be noted, does not specify *which* son killed the king. Artaxerxes' murder of his brother would then be an act of filial piety, and Amestris, reckoning one son on the throne was better than none, would swallow the succession of the second in line, Artaxerxes.

If the eunuch Mithridates, who dies by the torture of the boats, is the same man as became Amestris' victim much later in Plutarch, it seems that she bided her time before disposing of the man who knew the truth. Ctesias, writing in the reign of Artaxerxes, was bemused by the disinformation floating around the court (and perhaps further confused in Photius' summary), but he knew that Aspamitres' later death was just an excuse, and that is why he narrates it as part of the assassination story. The other divergences of the accounts are more or less incidental.

A further possibility is that Artabanus is a complete invention. The fact that he shares his name and court function with the better-known adviser from Herodotus[45] – only his father and country are different – raises some suspicion that he is one of those confusing doppelgänger who haunt Persian succession plots. In this case the Babylonian chronicler would be telling the literal truth, that Darius killed his father, which is the story that Artabanus is said to have put about. The invention of Artabanus, however, seems to serve Artaxerxes' purposes less well than his employment as a historical scapegoat.

One has to feel sorry for Xerxes, hoping for a quiet time in his fifties with a pretty young girl as his bedfellow, and trying to forget about the wretched Greeks who had done so much to spoil his life. Amestris was made of sterner stuff. For Louis Couperus, this moment had been coming ever since Xerxes returned from Greece. In a melodramatic scene, Xerxes 'asks himself how it can be possible. His brothers Abrocomes and Hyperanthes at Thermopylae, his brother Ariabignes and his nephews and brothers-in-law at Salamis, Tigranes – how tall and splendid he was! – and Mardonius at Plataea and Mycale, Artayntes, Ithametres, all dead! Woe, woe! All dead!' Suddenly,

> Framed in the unclosed door, in front of a half-drawn curtain in the entrance between the giant spearmen of enamel and glazed stone, human figures are visible. They are six officers of the royal bodyguard. Their commander – Artabanus is his name – leads them. Their swords are drawn, they have regicide in mind. They have been dissatisfied with the war. Artabanus, son of Artabanus, Xerxes' nephew [this relationship is a convenient invention by the author to improve Artabanus' motive], himself is eager to wear the Persian crown. Seen together, they will murder Xerxes as Darius and the six Persians once murdered pseudo-Smerdis. . . . For some minutes the ambitious conspirators hesitate. They consider, they vacillate. But the grief of the women rings in their ears, and it unnerves the covetous daring of the men. 'No, no!' whispers Artabanus, son of Artabanus, 'later, later'.[46]

In this dramatic scenario the plot has been brewing for something like fourteen years before it is carried out. This is of course not to be taken seriously, even though the author has noted several of the features of the eventual plot, not least the repetition of the number seven.

More illumination may possibly be gained from another work of fiction, the *Shahnameh* of Ferdowsi, the repository of the legends of the Persian kings from the creation to the end of the Sassanian Empire. As was noted in the Introduction and elsewhere, there is a strange lapse in the genealogy of the Persian kings of this period as recounted by Ferdowsi. As we have seen, Gushtasp (Hystaspes) corresponds in important ways to Darius I. Darius' son, however, is called Esfandiyar, which recalls the name of the conspirator Sphendadates, not that of Xerxes, whose deeds are largely absent from this *Book of Kings*. But the son who succeeds him is Ardashir of the Long Arms, undoubtedly to be identified with Artaxerxes Makrocheir or Longomannus of the classical sources, although he also has the alternative name of Bahman. (The epithet is said by Mir Khwand to be an allusion to his reach across all the seven climes.)[47] Bahman is said by Mas'udi to be the son of Esfandiyar and a Jewess of the House of Saul:[48] the Book of Esther has given him the details of the mother, and her consort is thus identified with Xerxes. In the Persian sources, it is Bahman who, after reigning for 120 years (the approximate time

between the death of Xerxes and the accession of Darius III in 336), hands
over the kingdom to his daughter Homay; she bears him a son, Darab, whose
son is Dara, the Darius III of the Alexander story where the *Shahnameh*
begins at last to converge with history. Persian tradition remembered a few
other correct facts about Ardashir, for example his connection with the physician 'Bokrat';[49] the great Greek doctor Hippocrates was in fact invited by
Artaxerxes to come to be his court physician, but declined the invitation.
Why is Xerxes so completely forgotten? The usual explanation is that Parthian
tales have overlaid the Persian core, but perhaps Amestris had a hand in this
too, ensuring that Xerxes' name was forgotten in favour of his more heroic
son. For Esfandiyar, heroic though he is, is a failure.

His final end comes when, rejected by his father, he faces the great hero
Rostam in battle. 'Then, as the Simorgh ordered him, Rostam drew back his
bow. Aiming at Esfandiyar's eyes he released the arrow, and for the Persian
prince the world was turned to darkness.'[50] This sounds like instant death,
but Esfandiyar, unlike Xerxes, has time for some last words to his brother
Pashutan:

> Do not torment yourself for me . . . . Where now are Feraydun, Hushang
> and Jamshid? They came on the wind and were gone with a breath. . . . I
> have travelled the earth and known its wonders, both those that are clear
> and those that are hidden, trying to establish the ways of God, taking
> wisdom as my guide; and now that my words have gone forth and the
> hands of Ahriman are tied, Fate stretches out its lion claws for me.[51]

The dying hero turns to Rostam:

> All that happened happened as Fate willed.[52]
> Not you, your arrow, or the Simorgh
> Killed me here: Goshtasp's, my father's enmity
> Made you the means by which to murder me.[53]

Esfandiyar's lament is echoed by his daughters, Beh Afarid and Homay, who
reproach the king, Gushtasp, who 'sent him to Sistan, filling him with
specious talk so that he'd give up his life for the sake of your crown . . . you
killed your son for the sake of greed'.

Clearly none of this matches Xerxes' case in any significant way, though
Rostam's letter of apology to Gushtasp is worth noting: 'As God is my
witness, and as Pashutan can testify, I said many times to Esfandiyar that he

should lay aside all enmity and desire for war. I told him I would give him
land and wealth, but he chose otherwise; Fate willed that he ignored my
pleas, and who can oppose what the heavens bring about?' (Herodotus would
have agreed.)

The rites for the burial of the king no doubt went something like those for
Esfandiyar:

> Now when the mother
> And sisters of Esfandiyar had heard,
> They came forth from the palace with their daughters,
> Unveiled, with dust-fouled feet, and raiment rent.
> When Pashutan came weeping on his way,
> And after him the coffin and black steed,
> The women hung on him, wept tears of blood,
> And cried: 'undo this narrow coffin's lid,
> Let us too see the body of the slain.'. . .
> When the mother
> And sisters of Esfandiyar beheld
> His visage steeped in musk, and sable beard,
> The hearts of those chaste ladies crisp of lock
> Fill'd to o'erflowing, and they swooned away.[54]

Louis Couperus has the conspirators, when they hover at Xerxes' door,
wonder, 'Is this not the moment, the moment that must be improved, the
moment to commit the murder? And then to keep it secret while the corpse
is laid on the *dakhma*, the "Tower of Silence", for the vultures.'[55] And so
may we. Was Xerxes' body exposed in the Zoroastrian manner to have his
bones pecked clean by the birds of the air, before entombment in the
sepulchre that had been prepared for him on the cliff at Naqsh-e-Rostam,
close to Persepolis? All we know about the rites that followed the death
of a Persian king is what Diodorus tells us of the arrangements made by
Alexander for the dead Hephaestion: the sacred fires were quenched 'until
such time as the funeral should be ended. This was the custom of the Persians
when their kings died.'[56]

A period of mourning was decreed; the people, or at least the members of
the court, shaved their heads, and the bier was accompanied to its resting
place by loud wailing.[57] The body was waxed (i.e. make-up was applied?),
and possibly embalmed, and the bier placed on a magnificent chariot. The
accession of the king followed, perhaps after a decent delay, and Artaxerxes

had all the murderers of his father executed, dismissed many of the court officials, and appointed his own choices in their places.[58] In due course, the relief depicting Xerxes was removed from its position of honour on the walls of Persepolis, and deposited in a back room of the treasury. The king was dead, and the new king would indeed live long – though not as long as the 120 years attributed to him by Mir Khwand. Artaxerxes was to reign for forty years and though he saw attrition at the edges of his empire his rule was a period of stability for Persia. The foundations of that stability had been in important ways laid by Xerxes. The preoccupations of the Greek writers who would portray him as a tottering king in charge of a battered empire are exposed by the long reign of his successor.

Conclusion

Think, in this batter'd Caravanserai
Whose Portals are alternate Night and Day,
How Sultan after Sultan with his Pomp
Abode his destin'd Hour, and went his way.
Edward Fitzgerald, *Rubaiyat of Omar Khayyam* (later version)

'In Persian sources we do not find any evidence that can be used for constructing a psychological portrait of Xerxes, or of any of the other rulers of the Persian Empire.'
Heleen Sancisi-Weerdenburg (2002)

AN ELUSIVE PERSONALITY

Apart from Herodotus, Xerxes received a bad press from Greek historians, and his counterpart Esfandiyar did not do much better from his chroniclers. Are Herodotus, Amestris and Alexander to blame for everything that has been said about him over the centuries? Although we have not enough to construct a psychological narrative of Xerxes' life, there is sufficient to construct a character sketch, even though, as with Plutarch's life of Artaxerxes, the personality often gets swamped by the official persona.

Heleen Sancisi-Weerdenburg in an important essay, 'The Personality of Xerxes' (2002), tabulated the characteristics that previous writers had used to construct a portrait of the man. A hundred years ago, Dunlop saw him as bigoted, passionate and neurasthenic. Fifty years ago, Nyberg saw him as a womaniser who lost interest in everything except his harem. For Immerwahr, he lived by passion not reason. Others made Xerxes a religious fanatic, a monster of self-righteousness or a slave to indolence. Some made him a tough and brutal leader, others a prey to fits of weeping and hysteria. Richard N. Frye, like others, saw him living in the shadow of his greater father. All these writers based their interpretations essentially on the narrative of Herodotus. The latter did a good job, for he has not made it easy for us. His method is often to narrate an event from two different succeeding perspectives, like that of the sea captain in the northern Aegean during the retreat from Greece:[1] first he tells a story that seems to show the king in a bad light, then he doubts that it could possibly have happened. Herodotus does not overtly interpret – except in what he has selected, and we have no way of knowing what he has omitted – but he provides the materials for an interpretation. The fact that such diverse character assessments can be based on this single source shows how polyvalent Herodotus' text is. Can we do any better?

Sancisi-Weerdenburg shows how forcefully all these views have been controverted or inverted by the progress of scholarship. Too often Persian customs are interpreted, even by Herodotus, as acts of personal whim – the mutilation of Masistes' wife, the incest, the destruction of Greek temples. She ends, of course, in a revisionist view that makes Xerxes a king who listens to his advisers (sometimes), has a strong sense of his role as king, and may in fact have represented the high point of the Achaemenid Empire. The Greek, Western, view has in the end to be set aside to achieve an under-standing that fits the Eastern perspective. That is why I have given some scope to later Persian writings that seem to illuminate particular characteristics of our ancient subject.

How far should we allow modern, or even ancient, moral judgements to guide our interpretation? Ancient writers were clear that biography had a moral purpose. Examples of tyrannical behaviour and anger, luxury, lust and incontinence, are set against magnanimity and clemency, liberality, bravery and other such virtues. The modern biographer is more concerned to understand than to judge, and a modern writer is more in danger of applying anachronistic values to ancient actions. Persian royal incest is a case in point, a matter in which we are, as so often, heirs of the Greeks and find it difficult to contemplate such marriages dispassionately. Imagine what the tabloid newspapers would say if a modern prince were to have sexual relations with his sister or daughter! Cruelty is another example of tyrannical behaviour, though Herodotus seems to have taken this in his stride.

A SENSE OF POSITION

We should start with the public persona. When we first meet Xerxes he is debating with his advisers whether to invade Greece: his reasons for doing so are a sense of tradition and the demands it imposes on him, the unfinished business of his father, the claims that his position makes on him. He has to live up to people's expectations of him: not only those of his dead father, but those of his people and his advisers.[2] He changes his mind several times in this long discussion, at one point admitting that his own judgement is immature. His advisers pull him this way and that, impelled by their own ambitions. (The same happens in the Book of Esther.)[3] The supernatural is deployed to help him clarify his thought. In the end the decision he makes is the 'wrong' one; but would he have done better, as Rostam said of Esfandiyar,[4] to stay quietly at home?

Later in the expedition Xerxes learns to know his own mind. He listens to his advisers, Mardonius, Artabanus and Artemisia, but the decisions he takes are his own.[5] One wonders why he is so impressed by Artemisia. Is he operating under the influence of a strong-minded woman, like his own mother? Even Alexander was strongly influenced by his own mother Olympias, while in Tarsusi's *Darabnameh* the fictional Alexander (Iskandar) flaps about while his wife Burandokht wins all the victories. Xerxes' decisions may still be the wrong ones – since Artemisia gave the best advice[6] – but he accepts his own responsibility. He has learnt the lesson that anyone today, even the managing director of a small company, has to learn, that you take advice and then make up your own mind. The buck stops here.

If Xerxes had decided to stay quietly at home, whittling bits of wood and listening to courtiers reading him stories from the annals of the empire, he would have failed in a duty that was as important as that of decision-making, namely, of carrying out a Great Deed. Persepolis was to be his ultimate Grand Design, but before that the duty of exacting vengeance on Athens was an equally important mission. In working himself up to the decision to invade, Xerxes certainly overemphasised the importance of Athenian participation in the sack of Sardis. His father Darius, years before, had been told by his wife that he needed to undertake some 'significant achievement . . . to make the Persians understand that their ruler is a real man, but also to keep them ground down by warfare and too busy to conspire against you'. Darius replied, 'Wife, your words echo my plans. I've decided to build a bridge from our continent to the next and to invade Scythia.'[7] Xerxes too built a bridge, across the Hellespont, and he also built a canal, which was twice as big as it needed to be (why did it need room for two triremes to pass each other?) and superfluous anyway since a path for dragging the ships would have done the job as well.[8]

The Greek for Grand Designs is *megalophrosyne*, 'thinking big'. Thinking big can be a good thing when it moves in the direction of magnanimity: Aristotle's 'great-souled man', though perhaps unattractive to us today, is a type admired by Greeks. But thinking big is also the vice of the tyrant and a kind of arrogance. It comes close at the other end of its spectrum to *hybris*, that determinant of fate which the Greeks rated among the most terrible of all. So a Grand Design, fit for a king, was inevitably going to be seen by Greeks as not just arrogance, but a claim to a station higher than the human. As a tyrant, Xerxes deserved his comeuppance. But as a king, and a Persian king, he was doing the right thing.

The grandeur of a king drives him to acts of conspicuous displays of power and superiority. These may be acts of stupendous cruelty or they can be acts of flamboyant clemency (sparing the heralds from Sparta, when the Spartans had killed his)[9] or the giving of vast gifts (see Chapter 3). The frightful treatment of Pythius, who gave Xerxes all his wealth for the Greek campaign and then had the temerity to ask that the king spare his youngest son from going to war – as we saw, Xerxes had the young man killed and sliced in half in front of his father, and then marched his army through the halves – shows that a king brooks no half-measures. A Persian monarch demands 'total commitment' (to borrow another phrase from the vocabulary of managing directors).

Emily Baragwanath has shown how some of Xerxes' actions parallel those of the 'mad' king Cambyses.[10] The latter, too, had sliced a father's favourite son in half, but Herodotus finds no palliative words for his act. When Xerxes fell for his brother's wife he did not use force against her, unlike Cambyses who is a rapist and thus a typical tyrant.[11] Herodotus tries to understand Xerxes while he simply presents Cambyses as a monster. Colley Cibber's play modelled Xerxes as a rapist tyrant as if there were nothing to choose between the two kings. Perhaps there wasn't; but Herodotus gives us the chance to think there was.

It is Xerxes' sense – nay, his conviction – of superiority that makes him unable to take the Greek resistance seriously. When he takes advice from Demaratus, it repeatedly induces laughter at the thought that Greeks could even consider resistance: 'Xerxes laughed and said "Demaratus, what words you've uttered, that a thousand men would fight with so great an army as this!"'[12] As the armies assemble at Thermopylae and Xerxes' scout reports back that the Spartans are sitting combing their hair in preparation for battle, Xerxes does not laugh, but he expresses incredulity. Demaratus reminds him of his earlier laughter and tries to make him understand that the Greeks are no pushover. (But what would Xerxes have done differently if he had assessed the Spartan attitude correctly? He won anyway. Would an immediate attack have made any difference?) If laughter is always a harbinger of doom in the *Histories*, because it indicates arrogance or self-delusion,[13] then Xerxes' laughter at least had some justification in his own eyes. A small Greek army could not seem like a serious threat, any more than Alexander's small army did to Darius III later. Esfandiyar, too, laughs when he first meets Rostam on the battlefield and hears his boast:

> Esfandiyar, when he had heard the words
> Which that old battle-seeking lion spake,
> Laughed and replied: 'Behold, I made me ready
> Or ever I arose from sleep . . .
> God will help me in fight and fortune smile
> Upon mine undertaking.'[14]

The greatness of the king was supported by his pious attitude to his god or gods. The 'daeva-inscription' indicates how important a proper religious attitude was in a Persian king's make-up. The Greeks, of course, had their gods too, and because the event was a Greek victory it was natural for Greeks to assume that their gods had trumped the Persian gods. The Greeks, too, were better at understanding oracles than the Persians, so they had a clearer foreknowledge of the future.[15] The last Shah of Iran also believed that God was on his side (see Chapter 4, p. 106), and perhaps any national leader has to present himself that way, even if he has no belief in the divine right of kings, for example. What for Xerxes was piety was for the Greeks fighting against the gods. In the *Shahnameh*, it was only because the Simurgh assisted Rostam that Esfandiyar was killed.

So much for Xerxes the leader of men. What of his more inward qualities? In Omar Khayyam's *Rubaiyat* the great kings and heroes of the past all carry, in the end, the same message, that human life is fleeting and will not come again. Ruin and decay infect even the most enduring works of man:

> They say the lion and the lizard keep
> The court where Jamshid gloried and drank deep.[16]

In a quatrain not translated by Fitzgerald, which happens to be the first poem
I read in the original after taking up the study of Persian:

> I saw a bird perched upon the battlements of Tus,
>   Before it lay the skull of Kai Kav'us;
>   To the skull it repeated 'alas, alas!'
> Where now is the clangour of the bells, and the clamour of the drums?[17]

Kai Kav'us, Jamshid and Bahram: the legendary heroes are all examples of
the insight that struck Xerxes as he surveyed his troops at the Hellespont. In
a hundred years' time, not one of those heroes was going to be alive.

　If Xerxes was a prey to this very Persian melancholy, is this a way into an
understanding of his character beyond the deeds that set out his royal character? Is this the Plutarchan 'chance saying' to unlock his personality? Gore
Vidal interpreted this melancholy as defeatism and ennui, but it may be a
grander emotion than that. Maybe it is more like the distinctly non-tragic
utterance of Glaucus in Homer's *Iliad*:

> 'Why dost thou so explore',
> Said Glaucus, 'of what race I am, when like the race of leaves
>   The race of man is, that deserves no question; nor receives
>   My being any other breath. The wind in autumn strows
> The earth with old leaves, then the spring the woods with new endows;
>   And so death scatters men on earth, so life puts out again
>   Men's leavy issue'.[18]

Glaucus' moral is 'that I should always bear me well, and my deserts enlarge
Beyond the vulgar, lest I sham'd my race'.[19] A sense of mortality need not
lead to Sardanapalan self-indulgence, but rather to a desire to leave a name
behind. That is what Xerxes did. Glory was the motive he first cited for his
attack on Greece, and the building of Persepolis was an attempt to create
something that would outlast human life.

　I think there may be two other characteristics of Xerxes' personality that
we can detect through the curtain of the sources. First, I see him as sharing
that love of nature that has always characterised Persians, from Xerxes'
decorated plane tree to the roses and nightingales of Hafez. Gardens are
important in an arid land, and Xerxes sought solace in their beauties. Maybe
the adorning of the tree was an expression of a tree cult, but one has to feel
something for trees to want to make a cult of them. The irrigation and

landscaping of Persepolis, as earlier at Pasargadae, or in the Hanging Gardens of Babylon, are not just for productive agriculture, but to make delightful gardens for the court to enjoy. How could one imagine otherwise, even without the evidence of the Book of Esther?[20]

Secondly, we have a glimpse of Xerxes the lover, that aspect brought to the fore in the operas of the eighteenth century including Handel's *Serse* and J. C. Bach's *Temistocle*. His passions are for the most part restrained by his role, and his cleaving to a single wife throughout most of his career is a notable example. It may of course be interpreted as an inability to escape from the dominant influence of his mother, who chose Amestris for him. The sense of being overshadowed by the earlier generation is so pervasive in Persian literature that it may be reasonable to attribute it to Xerxes, as do the scholar Frye and the novelist Vidal. The reverse Oedipus complex may be part of the Persian character.[21] But when passion bursts through in middle age and Xerxes falls for a younger woman, we see a behaviour pattern that is far from unfamiliar. It may be that this is all Persian story-telling, and that that is what the story-makers wanted us to find, to cover up the more sinister story of a revolt in Bactria by his brother. If so, it is at least a Persian glimpse of kingly character as distinct from a Greek gaze.

We should remember, too, that Xerxes probably never learnt to read. That is why on those long journeys in a covered wagon across his vast empire he had to resort to whittling little bits of wood to pass the time. The thought seems frivolous, but the slow pace of journeys across the vast distances of Iran and Anatolia has an impact on character. Coping with boredom is an art, as it is for the guardians of remote sites in Turkey that get maybe one visitor a day! Boredom, however, is not ennui, and Xerxes had plenty of work to do.

Xerxes must also have had plenty of moments for reflection on his lot and role in life. There are few, even among the greatest achievers, who do not sometimes wonder whether it has all been worthwhile. The Alexander of legend certainly seems to have done so, as he won the whole world but lost, not his own soul, but his chance of divinity. Xerxes did indeed maintain a great empire, and build a great city; even if he lost his grip at the end, he had established a foundation for the long and successful reign of his successor. Yet the Preacher from Judaea, perhaps contemporary with the earliest versions of the *Alexander Romance*, but basing his idea of a royal life firmly on the Achaemenid model, would have seen even that as vanity:

I made me great works; I builded me houses; I planted me vineyards: I made me gardens and orchards, and I planted trees in them of all kind of fruits: I made me pools of water, to water therewith the wood that bringeth forth trees: I got me servants and maidens, and had servants born in my house; also I had great possessions of great and small cattle above all that were in Jerusalem before me: I gathered me also silver and gold, and the peculiar treasure of kings and of the provinces: I gate me men singers and women singers, and the delights of the sons of men, as musical instruments, and that of all sorts. So I was great, and increased more than all that were before me in Jerusalem; and my wisdom remained with me. And whatsoever mine eyes desired I kept not from them, I withheld not my heart from any joy; and this was my portion of all my labour. Then I looked on all the works that all my hands had wrought, and on the labour that I had laboured to do: and behold, all was vanity and vexation of spirit, and there was no profit under the sun.[22]

In jaundiced mood, one can fall for the rhetoric of Ecclesiastes, as did the author of the medieval Greek *Phyllada tou Megalexandrou*, who ended his account of the great conqueror Alexander with the words 'All is vanity'; but there is no reason to suppose that the subjects of either tale shared this sense of futility.

Xerxes' legacy is in the works he left behind, at Persepolis. Did he know in his heart that the art of Persepolis was a dead end, doomed to be superseded by the Greek spirit that treasured individualism over magnificence, and that would create an empire on the foundations of his own that came closer than any to binding together east and west, the twain that shall never meet? He had seen the temples of the Greek west, and the smiles of the *korai* on the Acropolis. Did he draw the moral that Rilke drew from the contemplation of the reticent perfection of archaic Greek statuary, 'You must change your life'? I think not. For Xerxes, it must have seemed that he had built a firm foundation for the future of the empire. We know that it was not going to last. It was an experiment that soon gave place to another empire, one that was to influence the history of the world much more profoundly, that of Alexander. But it was by becoming King of Asia, in succession to the Persian monarchs, that Alexander made that empire in the first place.

An exhibition at the British Museum a few years ago about the Achaemenids was entitled 'Forgotten Empire'. Forgotten by whom, I asked myself. The study of ancient Persia is a thriving business, and its characters have figured repeatedly in the arts and literature – not least the operas – of Western Europe. If the Achaemenids do not figure by name in the epics of the Persian nation, the career of Xerxes is an early sounding of a theme that is insistent throughout Persian literature, that death comes even to the greatest and we should not lay too much store by worldly success. 'Bahram, that great hunter – the wild ass Stamps o'er his head, but cannot break his sleep.' And the history of Herodotus teaches by example that even an Evil Empire is led by a human being, and that to understand character and motive is the only way for human beings to live together.

Xerxes in Opera and Drama

Persian themes were prevalent in the drama and opera of the late seventeenth and eighteenth centuries, especially in Italy. Angelo Piemontese has identified some 270 opera libretti on Persian themes, of which 108 originated in Venice, starting in 1640 with a peak in 1691, but fading out after 1736 and the end of the Safavid Empire with its close diplomatic links to Venice, buttressed by their shared antipathy to the Ottoman Empire.[1] Similar themes occur in English and French drama from the beginning of the eighteenth century, perhaps stimulated by the appearance in 1628 of Thomas Herbert's *Travels in Persia* as well as that in 1700 of Thomas Hyde's *History of Persian Religion*. Hyde, a professor of Arabic and then of Hebrew at Oxford, was the first scholar to investigate the history of Zoroastrianism, and had been an interpreter on Persian affairs to the courts of the last Stuarts, and that of William and Mary.[2] Contemporary Persia began to fascinate too. Voltaire mocked Zoroaster in his *Philosophical Dictionary* under the influence of Hyde (not to mention the outlandish behaviour of the Persian ambassadors to Louis XIV in 1715), while Montesquieu's *Persian Letters* of 1721 used Persians as an early version of Craig Rainean Martians to cast an oblique eye on Western manners.

In England, one of the earliest Persian plays was John Banks' (1630–1710) *Cyrus the Great* (1695),[3] which derived from Xenophon's *Education of Cyrus* (translated into English about 1560 by W. Baker, following the French version of 1547). In 1728 Andrew Michael Ramsay (1686–1743) published *Travels of Cyrus* (Dublin), a long novel on the model of François Fénélon, which he styled 'a new *Cyropaedeia*' and dedicated to Lord Lambton. This had perhaps been inspired by the recent appearance of the variorum edition of Xenophon's work by Thomas Hutchinson in 1727. Ramsay's romance fills the gap left by Xenophon between Cyrus' sixteenth and fortieth year, describing his travels in Lycia and Egypt, Greece, Crete, Tyre and Babylon, his meeting with Zoroaster, and his encounter with the prophet Daniel who persuades him that there is only one true religion (his).

The sole English drama to take Xerxes as its central figure is that of Colley Cibber, which ran to a single performance in 1699, and met with 'entire damnation'.[4] In this play Xerxes is an out-and-out villain, as outlined in the Introduction. This may have contributed to its failure, since the successful dramas of the succeeding century were those that presented the Persian kings in a favourable light. However, the equally dismal fate of the next play to be discussed suggests that this is not a sufficient explanation.

In France, the character recurs in Jolyot de Crébillon's *Xerxes* of 1714. This displays the usual formalism of French classical drama, in which the characters address each other in long rhymed speeches, but its plot is well constructed. It begins with Xerxes' decision to make his second son Artaxerxes his successor in preference to his first son the warrior Darius, beloved of the people. As a result Darius' beloved Amestris (a princess) is to be reassigned as the wife of Artaxerxes. (Darius is also loved by another princess, Barsine, who is unhappy.) Preying on the seething passions thus aroused, Xerxes' chief minister Artabanus tricks Darius into lending him his dagger and inveigles the young man into the palace for a secret rendezvous with Amestris. When Artabanus then murders Xerxes in cold blood, Darius is clearly framed. He is about to be led off to execution when Artabanus' confidant Tissaphernes confesses the whole plot, and reveals that he has just dispatched Artabanus. Darius is forgiven and Artaxerxes offers him half his empire. The denouement is as neat as one by Agatha Christie, but Crébillon forgets to reveal who gets the girls. The play did not go down well with its audience, since it, like Cibber's very different play, closed after a single performance.

The real triumph of Persian themes comes in Italian opera. The libretto known to us in Handel's *Serse* (1738) had been written as early as 1654 by Nicola Minato, modified by Silvio Stampiglia, and set five times (see the Introduction). Vivaldi's opera *L'Incoronazione di Dario* (1717) is basically fictional, apart from the name of its hero. Scarlatti's *Cambise* was premiered in 1719. The 1720s and 1730s saw a flurry of Persian operas, mostly to libretti by Pietro Metastasio (1698–1782). Metastasio's libretti dominated opera until the 1750s: in 1730 he became librettist to the Hapsburg court in

Vienna, but when drama superseded opera he ceased to be so popular.[5] Metastasio's libretti are infused with the ideals of the 'Arcadian Academy' in Rome, which set out to promote virtue and discourage vice through drama. Thus many of the heroes experience a notable change of heart, turning from tyranny to beneficence with a grand magnanimous gesture.[6] A happy ending was obligatory.

Metastasio's libretto *Siroe re di persia* of 1726 (about Chosroes II) was followed by *Alessandro nell'Indie* of 1729. The latter, based on a combination of the history of Curtius Rufus and the tragedy of Jean Racine, was dedicated to James II, 'The Old Pretender'; it became the basis of Handel's *Poro* (1731), and was set by eighty other composers up to Pacini in 1824.[7] This popularity was, however, eclipsed by *Artaserse* (1730), another dynastic melodrama. The material of the latter derives from Justin with an admixture of Crébillon's play.[8] This revisits the aftermath of the death of Xerxes and the conflict of the two brothers. The 'Argument' describes the account of events as in Diodorus and the other ancient sources; but in the opera Darius never appears and the suspicion of the murder falls on Artabanus' son Arbaces. As the latter is about to consume poison, Artabanus confesses all, Arbaces is forgiven and Artaxerxes is hailed in a final chorus as a 'great Augustus . . . gentle kind Protector'.

The first opera to use this libretto was that of Leonardo Vinci (ca. 1690–1730). It contained some magnificent arias for the celebrated castrato Carestini as Arbace, worthily followed on record by the counter-tenor Franco Fagioli.[9] Another castrato, bent on revenge on the rival composer Nicola Porpora, may have assisted the success of its premiere by dousing the audience of Porpora's *Siface*, revived the previous evening, with snuff bombs.[10] Vinci died soon after, poisoned by a rival in love with a cup of hot chocolate.

This text was set by over one hundred composers, of whom the best remembered may be G. F. Handel, whose version is entitled *Arbace* (1734), and Thomas Arne, whose version was performed in 1760. Then came *Ciro riconosciuto* (1736), *Temistocle* (1736), and perhaps one should add *Zenobia* (1740) – not the Syrian queen but a fictional Armenian princess. Last came *Il Re Pastore* (1751), which is about the closing days of the Persian Empire during Alexander's campaign. It was set a number of times before Mozart's well-known version of 1775, which made some use of Pietro Alessandro Guglielmi's setting from the previous year.

Temistocle was premiered with music by Caldara in 1736, later (1772) set to music by J. C. Bach, and a century or so after its premiere by Giovanni

Pacini:[11] it represented Xerxes as a magnanimous ruler and ends happily with universal reconciliation, as described in Chapter 9. Gluck took a look at *Temistocle*, but made his debut with an *Artaserse* in 1741.

This avalanche of Italian Persica is the more remarkable as there was in effect no tradition of study of ancient Persia in Italy between the travels of Pietro della Valle (1586–1652) and 1830.[12] Metastasio scoured his classical sources, and the work of older contemporaries, for likely themes that offered the possibility of exotic oriental settings.[13] Other composers and librettists produced both historical and fictional themes with Persian and other oriental settings. Political echoes must form a good part of the *raison d'être* of these works.

Zoroastrian themes gave an added opportunity for drama. Rameau's *Zoroastre* was begun in 1741 and premiered in 1749; originally composed, with the assistance of Voltaire, as a drama about Samson (1732), the plot was recast because of religious objections to the biblical theme. The Zoroastrian theme recurs in Mozart's *The Magic Flute* of 1791.

Both *Serse* (as set by Cavalli and Handel) and *Temistocle* cast Xerxes as a lover. In *Serse* the six characters are largely fictional; in *Temistocle* the king is in love with Themistocles' daughter Aspasia. The latter plot (described in more detail in Chapter 9) makes use of the love triangle that Herodotus describes in Xerxes' last years, but gives different names to the women in question: Xerxes' wife, remarkably, has the name Roxane, which was the name of the wife of Alexander the Great. The drama concludes with a great act of magnanimity by Xerxes in sparing Themistocles and abandoning his love for his daughter to be reconciled with his own wife. A similar theme also formed the plot of Minato and Draghi's *Temistocle in Persia* (1681), which was performed for the emperor Leopold I. But to produce the kind of magnanimous acts that Metastasian opera required, in the case of Xerxes it was necessary to insert a good deal of fiction. For this reason, perhaps, he was a less popular theme than Cyrus or Alexander.

Although Xerxes and his family appear not infrequently, pride of place is given to Cyrus and Alexander. Cyrus, as a 'Sun King' (it was believed that Persians worshipped the sun), had an obvious resonance; while one of the earliest such operas, *La lanterna di Diogene* by Minato and Draghi (1674), was accompanied by a key which explained that Alexander stood for Leopold I, Darius for Louis XIV, Statira for 'Reason of State', two ministers of Darius for the apostolic nuncio and the Venetian ambassador, while the setting in Babylon was an allegory for Alsace. Only Diogenes has no modern counterpart.[14]

The Birth of Persian Kings

Herodotus says he knew four different accounts of the birth of Cyrus the Great. Xenophon's is the blandest: Cyrus is the legitimate son and successor of Cambyses. But in the other versions known to us, Cyrus is an outsider who had to win his place as the acknowledged king. Ctesias made him the son of a bandit. Herodotus' preferred version was that in which the baby Cyrus was exposed by his father Cambyses. Cambyses, a Persian, had married the daughter of the Median king Astyages, named Mandane. Astyages, however, had some disquieting dreams: first, he dreamt that his daughter urinated so copiously that she flooded the whole of Asia; secondly, that a vine grew from her genitals which overspread the whole of Asia. The Magi had no hesitation in interpreting these rather obvious dreams. So, when Cyrus was born, Astyages feared that he would become a son greater than his father (as happened to Peleus, the husband of the sea nymph Thetis in Greek mythology, whose son was Achilles) and his kingdom would be overthrown. Astyages instructed his trusted henchman Harpagus to make away with the baby and expose it to die on a hillside. So far, so like Oedipus. Harpagus then handed the baby over to a herdsman with instructions to do the deed. But the herdsman, and his wife Spaco, or in Greek Kyno (Bitch), instead brought the baby up as their own. So far, so like Romulus and Remus, except that the she-wolf is here a female 'dog'. The story-pattern goes back at least to the legendary Sargon of Akkad, who was said to have been exposed and reared by wild animals.[1]

When the boy reached the age of ten, the truth was revealed because Cyrus displayed his inborn kingly nature in the way he ordered his playmates about. The father of a boy he had been beating complained to Astyages. When the boy was brought before him, Cyrus recognised a family likeness and questioned Harpagus, who broke down and revealed what he had done. So far, so like Ahiqar, whom the king had ordered to be put to death but who reappeared from hiding just when required.[2] Astyages, however, did not yet realise how pleased he was going to be. Instead, he inflicted a horrible punishment on Harpagus, by inviting him to dinner and serving him the flesh of his own son in a stew. So far, so like Tantalus, or Thyestes. But now the Magi step in. Fearful that, if Astyages lets power pass to Cyrus, 'We Medes will be enslaved by the Persians and will become worthless outcasts', they persuade Astyages to send Cyrus back to his true parents in out of-the-way Persia. But Cyrus gets into contact with Harpagus, and between them they combine to overthrow the power of the Medes and establish the rule of Persia over all.

The number of folk-tale motifs, both Indo-European and Near Eastern, in this story, shows that it can hardly be taken as history. Nevertheless, Persians clearly liked the story-pattern, since exactly the same is told about Sasan, the founder of the Sassanian dynasty, in late Sassanian *Karnamag-e-Ardashir* ('Book of the Deeds of Ardashir'). Sasan marries the daughter of Papak, the ruler of Fars, and a son is born – Ardashir. Now the superior king Ardavan sends for Ardashir. He is good at sport (like Cyrus) and one day outdoes Ardavan in hunting.[3] Ardavan's daughter Zijanak falls in love with Ardashir, but when Ardavan consults the astrologers they reveal that Ardashir is likely to overthrow Ardavan. The couple escape and in due course they have a son, Shapur, who falls out with his father. Ardashir makes war against another king, Mithrak; he kills all his sons but a daughter survives and is brought up by a peasant; when she grows up – surprise, surprise – she falls in love with the teenage Shapur. They have a son, Ohrmazd, whom she keeps in hiding until he is seven years old. He is then spotted by Shapur, who recognises him as his son and successor. Ohrmazd grows to maturity and reunites Persia.

It is remarkable that this Sassanian story tells the tale of the hidden son not once but twice. In both this case and that of Cyrus the purpose of the story is to justify the emergence of a new dynasty on the throne of Persia. The king is recognised as the best, and his genealogical claim is treated as important but secondary. But in a third instance the recognition story is applied in a rather different way. Darab marries Homay, but she is already pregnant by her own father; when the son is born she names him Dara, hides him in a basket and sets him adrift on a river. So far, so like Moses. The baby is adopted and brought up by an unnamed emir, but when he grows up he seeks out his father and becomes his heir. The boy's royal blood is thus doubly assured and his virtue shows itself.

The final example of the Persian succession myth has a new twist. Darab takes a Rumi wife, Nahid (=Anahita, like Gushtasp's Rumi wife), the daughter of Filqus of Macedon; but he rejects her because of her bad breath. She goes back home and gives birth to a baby who is named after a herb that is used to cure her stinking breath, which the Greeks call *skandix*, chervil; the lucky child is named after the herb, Iskandar. In due course, as is well known, he overthrows his half-brother Dara and becomes the legitimate king of Persia.[4]

The Chronology of Xerxes' Advance through Greece

The beginning of the march south from Thermae counts as Day 1 of the expedition diary according to the timings given by Herodotus.[1] Herodotus' timings seem to fall apart by Day 30, but for the time being let us try to work with them. On Day 11 the fleet had reached Sepias,[2] and on Day 14 Xerxes with his army was in Trachis, where he waited for four days in the expectation that the Greeks would run away, according to Herodotus' absurd explanation. Thus the two days' fighting at Thermopylae began on Day 18. Meanwhile, the fleet left Thermae on Day 12, according to Herodotus and C. Hignett, but was battered by a 'Hellespontine wind' that blew for three days and destroyed many of the ships.[3] What was left of the fleet reached Aphetai on Day 16; the series of three battles at Artemisium began on Day 20. The fleet then reached Athens on Day 29. Day 30 or 31 should be the date of the Battle of Salamis, which traditionally was held to have taken place on Boedromion 20, to which this corresponds. A firm chronological *point d'appui* is given by the (partial) eclipse of the sun that took place four days after the battle, and which we know to have occurred on 2 October 480.

Now there are a great many more than thirty days between the end of May and the end of September. Into which period should we fit the advance from Thermae to Athens? Much depends on the date of the Olympic Festival of 480. This always began four days after the nine-day Spartan Karneia, which were in progress when Leonidas set out for Thermopylae.[4] Both festivals always ended at the full moon; in this year this must have been that of 21 July or that of 19 August.[5] If the earlier chronology is followed, Thermopylae (Day 18) and Artemision (Day 20) took place around 3 August;

but a problem emerges: what was the Persian army doing from 9 (or 14) August until 23 September when they started the four-day march to Athens?

The earlier chronology is somewhat favoured by the statement of Herodotus that the Battle of Thermopylae took place in *meson theros*, the middle of summer (or 'the middle of the heat', which could denote the hottest time of the year, namely August). But Polyaenus[6] tells us that Leonidas, before Thermopylae, was able to foretell bad weather 'by the movement of a star'. Some scholars have argued that this must refer to the heliacal rising of Sirius (around 23 July), but there is no need to be so specific. Many stars were regarded as prognosticating weather, and if Leonidas was a good astronomer he could predict, not necessarily from the rising of a star, but from its twinkling, what kind of weather was approaching.[7] It would not be in the least surprising to find the meltemi (for that is what a 'Hellespontine wind' is) blowing in the last ten days of August, and this wind typically blows for three days before abating. So Leonidas predicted the storm that was about to devastate the Persian fleet. A few days later, the Battle of Themopylae began, on about 29 August. The resistance at Thermopylae delayed the Persian army and, coupled with the storm damage, allowed the Greeks time to prepare the massive response that awaited the Persians at Artemision. Truly the Athenians could be grateful to the god of the winds, though they were bending the facts in expressing their gratitude to Boreas, the north wind, when it was a nor'easter that had saved them.[8] Herodotus makes this the occasion for a colourful story about Boreas, who, having carried off Orithyia, the daughter of Erechtheus, counted as a 'son-in-law' to the Athenian people:[9] an oracle had told the Athenians to appeal for help against the Persians to their son-in-law. The story has all the marks of one invented after the event, and of glossing over the fact that the Athenians could find no family connection with Apeliotes, the north-east wind.

While 29 August is certainly not 'midsummer' it is still in the middle of the hot season. It was undoubtedly very hot on the day of Thermopylae.[10]

The Persian advance from Thermopylae to Athens, the goal of the expedition, now has a slot of about three weeks. But Herodotus puts Artemision on Days 20–22 (say 2–4 September) and the battle of Salamis on Day 30 or 31, the day after the Persians arrive in Athens. It looks as if Herodotus' counting has gone wrong at this point. The Persians cannot have reached Athens, sacked it, and gone on to Salamis in a single day. We know that Xerxes was present at both events. In fact Herodotus' chronology does not work even in his own terms. The Persians reached Athens, as we are told, in 'early Boedromion'. Boedromion 480 began on 2 September, as we know since Attic months (like Muslim months today) began when the new moon rose.[11] So early Boedromion should mean some time around 8 September, give or take a few days; anyway before the 17 September, mid-month. But the Battle of Salamis took place at the end of September, just a few days before the eclipse of 2 October. So in fact the Persian army devoted a couple of weeks to the sack of Athens while the Greeks made their preparations for the Battle of Salamis. That is not too long a time for the Persian fleet, battered by the meltemi, severely shot up by the Athenians, and further damaged by a storm with rain and thunder that struck on the first night of Artemision, to recover and make its way to Salamis.

Given the implausibility of Herodotus' day-by-day timings at the end of this sequence, it may be wise not to insist on adherence to his 'Days' in the first two weeks of the series. The Persians may not have waited four days before Thermopylae for the Greeks to run away, after all.

TIMETABLE

21 April	*Now Ruz* festival in Sardis
Early May	Crossing of Hellespont
10–19 August	Spartan Karneia; Leonidas advances northwards
12 August	(Day 1) Persian army advances from Thermae
14–19 August	Olympic festival
24 August	(Day 12) Persian fleet battered by three days' meltemi
29–30 August	(Day 18) Battle of Thermopylae
2 September	Attic month Boedromion begins
2–4 September	(Day 20–22) Battle of Artemision; storm
7 September	(Day 25) Persian army reaches Athens: 'early Boedromion'
8–29 September	Sack of Athens
29 September	(Day 29, impossibly) Persian fleet reaches Athens
30 September	(Day 30, impossibly) Battle of Salamis
2 October	Solar eclipse

Abbreviations

I make use of the standard abbreviations for classical authors and their works, as in for example the *Oxford Classical Dictionary* and Liddell and Scott's *Greek-English Lexicon*, except that Herodotus, who appears very frequently, is abbreviated to 'H.'. The names of Persian authors and their works are given in full. Journals are cited according to the conventions of *L'Année Philologique*. The following should also be noted:

AJA	*American Journal of Archaeology*
AMIT	*Archäologische Mitteilungen aus Iran und Turan*
CHI	*Cambridge History of Iran*
EI	*Encyclopaedia of Islam*
E. Ir(anica)	*Encyclopaedia Iranica*
FGrH	Felix Jacoby, *Die Fragmente der griechischen Historiker*
JAOS	*Journal of the American Oriental Society*
JNES	*Journal of Near Eastern Studies*
Kuhrt	Amélie Kuhrt, *The Persian Empire: A Corpus of Sources*, 2 vols (Abingdon: Routledge, 2007)
ML	R. Meiggs and D. Lewis, *Greek Historical Inscriptions* (Oxford: Oxford University Press, 1969)
PMG	*Poetae Melici Graeci*

The inscriptions of the Persian kings are cited according to the system established in Kent 1953 and followed in all subsequent publications. Thus, DNb = Darius Naqsh-e-Rustam, item b; XPh = Xerxes Persepolis, item h, and so on.

Notes

Introduction

1. Quoted in Briant 2002, 515.
2. Stronach 1978, 145.
3. *Essays* iii. 13, 'On experience'.
4. Clearchus F 50 Wehrli, in Athenaeus xii. 13, 539B; see also Valerius Maximus 9.1.3 where it is Xerxes again. Cleitarchus, *FGrH* 137 F 2 (quoted in the same chapter of Athenaeus), told of the legendary king Sardanapalus, whose statue depicted him 'snapping his fingers', as 'nothing but enjoyment was more than that'. The story was already in Ctesias F 1b (quoted in Diod. Sic. II. 23.1–4), emphasising his luxury and self-indulgence, but Cleitarchus used it to draw a contrast with his hardy Macedonian hero.
5. Stoneman 2008, 166–67.
6. The philosopher Maximus of Tyre, however, regards them as being each as bad as the other: *Or.* 14.8, 32.9, 41.3.
7. See Henkelman, Kuhrt, Rollinger and Wiesehöfer 2011. The point is developed fully by S. Müller 2011. Xerxes is often also contrasted with Cyrus the Great, who is remembered for his clemency (to Croesus), and his generosity (to the Jews), as well as for the imagined 'declaration of human rights' represented by the Cyrus Cylinder from Babylon. His portrayal by Xenophon in the *Education of Cyrus* is highly favourable, and contrasted with the decline perceived by Xenophon in his own time – though Cyrus, like Xerxes, is prone to anger. See Wiesehöfer 1996, 42ff.
8. Sancisi-Weerdenburg 1997.
9. H. VII.8; Waterfield 1998, xxxviii.
10. Wiesehöfer 1996, 51; a more nuanced discussion in Baragwanath 2008, 250.
11. Every commentator on *Persians* states that the drama is set in Susa. There are several reasons for rejecting this assumption: 1. The drama is set before the palace and the tombs of the kings, from which the ghost of Darius is conjured up. The tombs of the Achaemenids were at Persepolis. 2. At line 15 the chorus states 'No messenger has come to the Persians' city', ἀστὺ τὸ Περσῶν. The Persian name for Persepolis is Parsa or Bairsha, which is also the name of the region; the city of the Persians must be in the region of Parsa (Fars). (Seaford 2012, 208 also grasps this point.) The name Parsa also appears once on a Greek vase. 3. At line 250 (cf. 646,

1070, 1074) the messenger greets the city on stage, ὦ Πέρσις αἶα, 'O Persian land'. This expression could not be addressed to Susa, which is in Elam (the Greeks seem to have called the region Kissia), not Fars. Arrian (*Ind.* 40.1) explicitly distinguishes the two. 4. None of the references to Susa requires that the speakers be in Susa, except perhaps the ghostly Darius' words at line 761, 'This city of Susa'. (It would be facetious to suggest that Darius does not know where he is, or that ghosts can bilocate.) Line 16 in fact sets Susa and Ecbatana in contrast to the 'Persian city', and lines 115–24 express horror 'lest Susa hear' of the disaster. If we are in Susa, Susa already knows! Lines 730–32 link Susa and Bactria as if they might both be equally distant. It is a curious fact that Persepolis is never named by any Greek writer before the Alexander historians, though the *Alexander Romance* seems to have had a clearer view of the matter in referring to 'the city of Persis' in II. 14. Sometimes they seem to have confused it with Pasargadae, as did Ptolemy. Elam and Media could also be wilfully confused: Dalley 2013, 190. It would be easy to imagine, if one were a distant Greek, that Parsa could not be the name of both city and region, and therefore to assume that the capital which lay in Parsa had another name, such as Susa or Pasargadae. But I think Aeschylus knew what he was doing. On Greek knowledge of Persepolis in general, see Tuplin 1996, 140.

12. Lysias 2.27. On the centrality of Salamis to the Greek (or Athenian) self-image in later centuries, see Ruffing 2006.
13. *Fall of Princes* III. 2241.
14. Ralegh 1676, I. iii. 6.11, 435.
15. English translation, New York 1930.
16. Couperus 1930, 71.
17. Davis 1992–2006, 45.
18. *Shahnameh* tr. Davis 142.
19. In a particularly extreme form this view of oriental decadence was expressed by Walter Wüst, the rector of the University of Munich who presided when the Scholls were arrested. He regarded the decline of Persia as due to Semitic influence: 'It leads to a mixture of races and thence to "degeneration". The inevitable waste of blood of ancient aristocratic families serving in distant outposts of the empire, the "eradication through climate", the "counter-selection" through wars that gradually have to be led by professional armies, the emigration of resident families from their hereditary farms into the capitals and big cities, Susa, Babylon, Ecbatana, and their civilization, and finally the disintegrating influence of the highly developed money economy of natural produce: all that undermined the position of the ruling race and its foundations, "blood and soil".' Cited in Wiesehöfer 1996, 87.
20. H. 8.90.4.
21. See Keaveney 1996, 35–36.
22. Samuel Johnson, *The Vanity of Human Wishes*, lines 231–32, descanting on Juvenal's *Satire* X, lines 173–74.
23. H. VII. 45–46, IX. 16, etc. See ch. 3.
24. B. Dobree, *English Literature in the Early Eighteenth Century, 1700–1740* (Oxford: Oxford University Press, 1959), 240.
25. F. W. Hawkins, *The French Stage in the Eighteenth Century* (1888).
26. Alexander Pope, *Dunciad* I. 236, cruelly attributes to him 'less human genius than God gives an ape'.
27. H. 7.31, Aelian *VH* 2.14 and 9.39 mocks Xerxes for the fact. Couperus 1930, 52, makes a joke of it.
28. There is a recording with René Jacobs, 1986. The libretto used by Cavalli is about four times as long as the one that Handel set: it begins with a prologue on Olympus, in which Apollo, seated on Pegasus, discusses the nature of virtues with the Muses and the god Momus; a great many of the human characters were also eliminated by Handel's librettist in the interests of a tighter plot. They include various magi and

pages, the ambassador of Susiana, and choruses of spirits and of soldiers by the Hellespont. The action takes place in Abydos as Xerxes prepares to invade Greece.

29. The late seventeenth and eighteenth centuries saw a remarkable outpouring of plays and operas on Persian themes, frequently about Xerxes. See Appendix I.

30. Cf. Brosius 2006, 67.

31. As was once observed to me by an English couple who had established a beautiful garden in the Peloponnese, only to be met with incomprehension by the locals because of the lack of the aforementioned vegetables.

32. Baragwanath 2008, 12n.

33. Wilamowitz-Moellendorff 1881, 81.

34. Momigliano 1993, 6.

35. Polybius 10.21.2–3.

36. Cic. *Fam.* 5.12.5. See Hägg 2012, 187.

37. Plut. *Alex.* 1.2.

38. Hägg 2012, 53–54.

39. Mossman 2010.

40. E.g. Jacobs 1994, 97, proposing that we understand the satrapal system 'without the help of Herodotus, since with his help it has been impossible'! Cf. S. West 2011.

41. Georges Bataille in 'L'apprenti sorcier' (1973, I. 526) went so far as to state that truth in itself is meaningless; it must become fiction to be intelligible.

42. Vidal 1981, 615.

43. I have assembled some interesting examples in Appendix 1.

44. Moore 1971, 14, 43, 74.

45. Davis 1992–2006, 97–166.

46. Turgenev 1991, xviii: 'his arrogance seems to epitomise the hubris of all those who challenge fate and bring about their own ruin'.

47. Homayounpour 2012, 54–55.

48. Sancisi-Weerdenburg 1997, 182; see also Müller 2011.

49. Kuhrt I. 300–06; Brosius 2000, 50–54.

50. Kuhrt I. 141ff.

51. Esther: γράμματα μνημόσυνα; Ctesias F 1b para 22: βασιλικαὶ ἀναγραφαί and F 5 para 32.4: δίφθεραι. See Lenfant 2004, xxxvi.

52. Dio Chrys. 11.149; Kuhrt I. 287.

53. Meaning Nineveh: Dalley 2013, 109 and 182–83.

54. See note 4 above.

55. Who compelled Nebuchadnezzar to destroy Jerusalem! – Shahbazi 1981, 135.

56. Identifiable with 'Darius Hystaspes'.

57. *Yasht* 9.26, 15.35 etc.

58. According to Daqiqi.

59. See *Shahnameh* tr. Warners V. 281; Shahbazi 1981, 116, 120.

60. He reached Fars itself in 331.

61. Tabari 1987, 82–84, 87–88. He was born in Persia but wrote in Arabic.

62. A corruption of Nahid.

63. Tha'alibi 1900, 277–376. The corresponding portion of the *Shahnameh* is V. 119ff. in the Warners' translation.

64. Donzel and Schmidt 2010, 97; also 102 and 160 for other sources for this tale.

65. Shayegan 2011.

66. He is unnamed in H. 3. 60ff.

1 Accession

1. Browne 1893/1984, 279.

2. Browne 1893/1984, 258, 265, 375.

3. Tuplin 1998.

4. Ctesias F13 (23); Kuhrt I. 237. In fact Darius had reigned for thirty-six years, not thirty-one: H. 7.1.4.
5. Babylonian texts date both by the reign of Darius and by that of Xerxes in December 486; the news of the old king's death and the new king's accession perhaps travelled slowly and the exact date cannot be determined.
6. DB IV. iv. 52.
7. Koch 1993, 51.
8. The most recent treatment is Schwinghammer 2011.
9. DB I. 13.
10. Justin I. 9. 4–13, Kuhrt I. 165.
11. H. 3.61ff.
12. In a similar way, in the *Shahnameh*, Esfandiyar's brother Pashitan poses as Esfandiyar in a 'Trojan Horse' episode: Shahbazi 1981, 115.
13. Herodotus says Susa, but the whole series of events was surely played out in Persia, not in Elam: Kuhrt I. 160 n.5.
14. DB IV. 4.68.
15. The importance of the number seven in Persian court stories recurs repeatedly. According to the Arabic *Qissat Dhu'l-qarnain* (25) Darius not only was assisted by seven conspirators, but the conspirators he put down also numbered seven. Later, Darius III was murdered by a group of seven ministers. Macedonian kings, too, typically had seven bodyguards: Waterfield 2011, 16.
16. A. *Pers.* 774–75.
17. Ctesias F 13.11–15.
18. The name might be a title of Bardiya ('giver of bounty') rather than a proper name. It is curious that it is a Greek form of the name Esfandiyar, which is the name of Gushtasp's (Hystaspes') son (Esfandiyar) in the later Persian legendary tradition. However, Sphendadates is a Magus whereas Esfandiyar is a zealous Zoroastrian.
19. Kuhrt I. 170.
20. Vidal 1981, 408.
21. Briant 2002, 107ff avoids making a decision about the existence of Gaumata.
22. Vidal 1981, 411.
23. Soudavar 2012, 56.
24. H. I. 125.
25. Vidal 1981, 409.
26. Ctesias F 13 (17).
27. H. 3.84–88.
28. H. 7.5.
29. Justin II. 10.9–10.
30. H. 7.3.
31. Vidal 1981, 411.
32. Athenaeus 12.8.513ff. See further ch. 3.
33. See Introduction, note 9.
34. See ch. 3 for discussion.
35. 'Sayings of Kings and Commanders: Xerxes' 1, *Mor.* 173 BC.
36. Plut. *On Brotherly Love* 488dff.
37. H. 7.187.2.
38. Plut. *Them.* 14.
39. See Appendix 2 for the legends that surrounded the birth of Persian kings.
40. XPf para 4. Kuhrt I. 244.
41. Briant 2002, 520.
42. See Introduction, note 9.
43. *Alcibiades* I. 121 c.
44. H. 1.136.
45. DNb9.

46. Xen. 1.2.3–16.
47. *Laws* 694–95.
48. Strabo 15.3.18.
49. Strabo 15.3.18.
50. Plato *Laws* 695b.
51. Nicholas Denyer's recent edition makes a strong case for authenticity, in the teeth of the opinion of most other scholars.
52. Xen. *Cyrop.* 1.2.10.
53. Xen. *Anab.* 1.9.2–3.
54. Xen. *Anab.* 1.9.12–13.
55. Xen. *Anab.* 1.2.19.
56. Blow 2009, 19.
57. Plut. *Artox.* [sic] 5.1.
58. Vidal 1981, 335.
59. Briant 2002, 522.
60. Briant 2002, 524.
61. Plut. *Artox.* [sic] 2.
62. Nicander *Theriaca* 891.
63. H. 1.118.
64. For the identification see Aelian *VH* 3.39 and Theophrastus HP 4.4.7; Athenaeus 14.61 (649 ce) refers to 'the turpentine tree which the Syrians call πιστάκια'. C. Binder, in his commentary on Plutarch's *Artaxerxes*, argues that the small red berries of the terebinth are also edible, though not very pleasant, and that a handful of these are what the new king had to force down. Llewellyn-Jones and Robson 2010, 167, and Briant 2002, 291, both plump for pistachios. Dalby 2003, 262, notes that pistachio trees are normally grafted on terebinth stock. See also Nicolaus of Damascus fr. 66.
65. Hanaway *EIr* s.v Anahita on the name.
66. Berossus *FGrH* 80 F 11, Kuhrt II. 566–67.
67. Stronach 1978, 138.
68. Binder 2008, 119.
69. Stronach 1978, 132.
70. Boyce 1975.
71. H. 9.110.
72. Cited in Shahbazi 1991, 120–21.
73. Polyaenus 4.3.2.
74. For some corroborative evidence on meals, see Briant 2002, 291.
75. A. De Gouvea, *Relations des grandes guerres* 1646, cited in Blow 2009, 74.
76. See further *EI* s.v. Chess.
77. It was translated into many languages including Catalan and Swedish, as well as appearing in numerous printed editions in Latin (6), German (5), Dutch (3), English, French and Italian (2 each) between 1475 and 1505.
78. Christensen 1936, II.
79. Ferdowsi, *Shahnameh*, 698ff, in Dick Davis' translation.
80. R. Eales, *Chess: The History of a Game* (London: Batsford, 1985), 14–15, 25–27 and 66–67.

2 The Persian Empire

1. It is not known where the Akaufaka lived.
2. Cyrus II Chronicles 36.23.
3. DPh; Kuhrt II. 476.
4. Sancisi-Weerdenburg 1993.
5. Kriwaczek 2010, 250ff.
6. And Xerxes: Moore 1971, 4.

7. DB I. 6.
8. Shown in tabular form in Briant 2002, 172–73. On these lists see Jacobs 1994, 101–12; Ruffing 2009. On the tablets, Koch 1993, 5–48.
9. X *Anab*. 1.7.6, Kuhrt II. 484.
10. Esther 8.9.
11. H. 3.89ff.
12. H. 4.43.
13. Darmesteter 1880/1965, II. 4ff.
14. Cf. the discussion in Gnoli 1980, 63–64.
15. Bailey 1943.
16. *Vendidad* II. 10.
17. Herodotus 3.90 says that the Cilicians paid 360 white horses plus 500 talents of silver.
18. Aelian *VH* 1.31 tells us that whenever the king was on a royal progress, people came out to set forth their produce for him.
19. For examples, Tiepolo's ceiling in Würzburg, or Johann Bergl's in the garden pavilion at Melk Abbey in Austria.
20. H. 3.89.
21. Jursa 2009 and 2011.
22. *CHI* 688–92.
23. See ch. 3.
24. The point is well made by Ball 2010, 23–24.
25. H. 5.52–53; Graf 1994.
26. *Vit. Ap. Ty*. I. 24.1.
27. Aelian *VH* 1.31.
28. Aelian *VH* 10.14.
29. Wiesehöfer 1998, 78, takes an opposite view, arguing that the whole empire was heavily urbanised, but that the buildings were all of mud brick. However, he bases this on the statement in Eratosthenes that Indians and Arianoi are *asteioi*: he takes this to mean 'city-dwellers'; literally the word means this, but the more normal meaning would be 'with cultivated manners'. See Strabo 1.4.9, where the contrast is with 'uncivilized' people. Heraclides Ponticus F 55 Wehrli (Athenaeus 12.512a) makes a contrast between free men who enjoy luxury and labourers who live in 'slavery'.
30. Bulliet 1972, 22.
31. Sancisi-Weerdenburg 1989 and 1998.
32. Strabo 15.3.21.
33. *Oeconomica* 2.1.1–4.
34. See Wiesehöfer 1998, ch. 7, suggesting that workers, though coerced, were nonetheless paid. Aristotle, *Oeconomica* 1344a 36–64, remarks that the salary of a slave is his food; this seems to be the principle on which rations are distributed in Persia.
35. See for example Kuhrt II. 719, Brosius 2000, 115; Hallock 1969 details the rates of, for example, one sheep: 10 BAR (= 100 quarts) of barley; one shekel of silver: 3–3.25 BAR of barley.
36. Kuhrt II. 784.
37. Dusinberre 2014, 88–89.
38. Tuplin 2011, 54.
39. H. 3.96 refers to tribute in coin, and Strabo 11.13.8; Briant 2002, 406.
40. Nehemiah 5:4–6.
41. Kaptan 2002.
42. Ralegh 1829, Book IV, ch. 2; V. 315–18.
43. H. 4.166. In general, Seaford 2004, 125ff.
44. Naster 1970 cited in Seaford 2004, 129n.
45. Wiesehöfer 1998, 90, citing Xenophon.
46. Seaford 2004, 134.
47. Strabo 15.3.21.

48. Xen. *Anab*. 1.5.5.
49. H. 1.153.2; Ruffing 2011.
50. Briant 2002, 407.
51. H. 3.102–5.
52. Curtis 2012, 51.
53. Byron 1937/1981, 166.
54. Boardman 2000, 204–25.
55. Wiesehöfer 1996, 59.
56. Momigliano 1979, 138ff.
57. The classic study is Conybeare, Harris and Lewis 1913. See also Stoneman 1992, Mathys 2010, 294–97, Selden 2012.
58. Momigliano 1979, 151.
59. Briant 2002, 500. Xen. *Oec*. 4.20–23 and *Cyrop*. 8.6.10–12. Plut. *Alcib*. 24 describes its beautiful garden: see p. 81 below.
60. *HG*. 4.1.15.
61. Xen. *Anab*. 1.2.7–9: Kuhrt I. 294: see below 74–82.
62. *HG* 7.8.9–10 and 15.
63. Ind. 39.2–3; Kuhrt II. 877.
64. The Barrington Atlas places Taoce itself inland, at Borazjan, with the alternative name of Tawwaj.
65. Wiesehöfer 1978, 78.
66. Cited from Wiesehöfer, ibid.
67. A thorough survey is Delemen et al. 2007, and there is a masterly comprehensive treatment in Dusinberre 2014. Rollinger and Henkelman 2009 speak of a 'cultural fusion' in the parts of the Greek world dominated by Persia, which may be an overstatement.
68. Jacobs 2002, 385–86, surmises that it was a local decision to ape the distant rulers' style, rather than an imposition from the centre.
69. Briant 2002, 501.
70. Briant 2002, 501–05.
71. Cahill 1988; Dusinberre 2014, 166.
72. Rose 2007.
73. Mellink 1971 and 1973.
74. Ratté 1992.
75. H. 4.88.
76. Dusinberre 2014, 147, 153 and 187–95.
77. Dusinberre 2014, 160 (Lydia), 187 (Cilicia), 182 (Van). Note also the trilingual inscription from the Letoön in the Fethiye Museum.
78. PTT 21 mentions a secretary who is a Yauna, i.e. (Ionian) Greek, while another Yauna assistant appears at PTT 119–20: Lewis 1977 and 1985.
79. H. 4.87; Pliny *NH* 34.68.
80. H. 6.20, 6.119; Miller 1997, 102.
81. Momigliano 1979, 138ff.
82. Selden 2012.
83. H. 7.6.
84. H. 7.43, and also 7.191 at Cape Sepias. See Haubold 2007, 53.
85. Ctesias F 1b = Diod. Sic. 2.22.1.
86. H. 3.89ff, 5.52 and 7.61ff. Jacobs 1994 and 2002 rejects the satrapy list as usable evidence, while S. West 2011 thinks the review of troops too graphic to be from an official document, and surmises borrowing from Hecataeus and even influence from Homer's Catalogue of Ships.
87. Esther 10.2.
88. Stoneman in Stoneman et al. (eds) 2012. There is a similar detail in the fragmentary 'proto-Esther' text from Qumran, 4Q550.

89. *Macrobioi* 14 = Onesicritus *FGrH* 134 F 36.
90. F 9 = Athenaeus 633D; Lenfant 2009, 131–45.
91. Aelian VH 12.48, Dio Chr. 53.6–7.
92. Chares in Athenaeus 12.54; Stoneman 2012.
93. I Esdras 6.21.
94. Esther 2.23; H. 7.100, 8.90 and 8.85.
95. Malachi 3.16.
96. Tuplin 2011a.
97. Selden 2012.
98. Momigliano 1977.
99. Hägg and Utas 2003.
100. Xanthus F 3.
101. Xanthus F 33, DL 8.63). F 11 mentions Artaxerxes: Strabo 1.3.4.
102. Kingsley 1995, 227. F 31 refers to the Magi's custom of incest with their mothers, but in F 32 he wrongly avers that Zoroaster was 6,000 years before Xerxes.
103. Heraclides Ponticus F 69–70, Strabo 2.3.4 and 5.
104. *FGrH* 709; H. 4.44.
105. *Videvdad* 2.5.
106. M. L. West 1971, 87ff.
107. B1 DK on *dike* and *tisis*, 'justice' and 'revenge' or perhaps 'equalling-out and compensation'; cf. Heraclitus B 94, 80, 53.
108. M. L. West 1971, 165–202, surveys the Persian aspects of Heraclitus' thought.
109. DK59A 1–27; Selden 2012.
110. Briant 2002, 588.
111. Pliny *NH* 30.1.8.
112. Mathys 2010. Besides Esther, Daniel's Babylon looks quite Achaemenid. Other books set in the Achaemenid period are Job and Zechariah and Tobit. A contest of the pages at Darius' court is described in III Ezra 3.1–5.6 and in Jos. *AJ* 11.3: at 14.12 the statement that 'Truth rules all' looks very Achaemenid.
113. Mathys 2010, 243–65, prefers a Hellenistic date.
114. 4Q550; Mathys 2010, 286–89.
115. Clines 1984.
116. Luigi Bassano, *Costumi e modi . . . dei Turchi* 18 v. quoted in Peirce 1993, 120–21.
117. Esther 10.2–3.
118. I Esdras, however, gets it right.
119. Tabari 688, IV. 82; cf. Mas'udi II. 127 (cited in Herzfeld 1941, 96): the mother of Bahman, son of Esfandiyar, was a Jewess from the house of Saul.
120. Strabo 15.3.10.
121. Mathys 2010.
122. Momigliano 1979, 138ff.
123. For what follows I am indebted to Grabbe 1992, ch. 2, 'The Persian Period'.
124. Psalms 137.1.
125. Chs 40 and 55.
126. II Chronicles. 36.23.
127. Jos. *cAp.* 2.16, para 165.
128. Ezra 1.8.
129. Haggai. 2.20–23; Zechariah. 3–4.
130. Briant 2002, 115–16.
131. Ezra 7.10.
132. Grabbe 1992, 95–98.
133. Nehemiah 5.2–5.
134. Malachi 2.11.
135. Mathys 2010, 279–82; Schedl 1965.
136. Judith 2.7, 3.8, 10.23 and 12.11.

137. Moore 1985, 50.
138. Judith 12.2.
139. Judith 10.23 and 15.11.
140. Dalley 2007, 17.
141. Heltzer 1989.
142. Moore 1985.
143. Schedl 1965.
144. Diod. Sic. 17.71.8.
145. Blow 2009, 174.
146. Briant 2002, 258.
147. Esther 1.14, cf. Ezra 7.14.
148. H. 3.84; Josephus *AJ* 11.31 says they were representatives of the 'seven houses'.
149. H. 1.135, 3.84, 7.61.
150. Esther 2.9.
151. H. 8.132.
152. Appian, *Mithridatic Wars* 9.
153. Polybius 5.43.1–4, Diod. Sic. 19.40.2. See Shayegan 2011, 310.
154. Ctesias 21, 28, H. 7.82, 121; Briant 2002, 320.
155. *Oeconomica* 1344a 36–b4.
156. Briant 2002, 268–77.
157. H. 8.105.
158. *Cyrop.* 7.5.60.
159. Wheatcroft 1993, 33.
160. Plut. *Artox.* 17.6.
161. Plato, *Alcib.* 121d.
162. H. 8.105.
163. H. 3.97 and 92.
164. H. 6.32.
165. Esther 2.3, 8, 14–15.
166. H. 3.130.
167. Diod. Sic. 11.69.20.
168. Xen. *Cyrop.* 5.2.28, 8.4.2.
169. Diod. Sic. 17.5.3.
170. Briant 2002, 268–77, gives a thorough listing and discussion of eunuchs.
171. Briant 2002, 274; Pirngruber 2011, Mathys 2010, 251.
172. *Cyrop.* 8.6.16, Briant 2002, 343–44. Ps-Aristotle *De Mundo* 398a.
173. Hirsch 1985, 101–39, argues that there was no such official as the King's Eye, but his view has not been generally accepted.
174. Tuplin 2004 is a thorough survey.
175. *Cyrop.* 8.2.24–25 and 3.41.
176. Briant 2002, 473.
177. H. 3.130–32, Briant 2002, 348; Jouanna 1999, 221–22.
178. Pinault 1992, 79–93.
179. Ctesias *FGrH* 688 F 14.42.
180. Stoneman 2008, ch. 1.
181. Stoneman 2012.
182. Plut. *Artox.* 21.3.
183. F 14(44). In general, Lenfant 2004; translation by Llewellyn-Jones and Robson 2012; Tuplin 2004.
184. Cited in Blow 2009, 175.
185. Ibid. On European doctors and the Qajar dynasty, see Wright 1977, 115–27.
186. Anderson 1989, 105–08, 235–36.
187. Pliny *NH* 37.133 and 139.
188. Halleux and Schamp 2003, xxii, xxv.

189. Walter Scott, *The Talisman*, preface; cited in Warner 2012, 226.
190. Pliny, *NH*, 37.133, 124, 162, 169, 185 and 124.
191. Ruska 1912.
192. Browne 1893 (1984), 384; and I have myself heard discussions of the matter in Iran.
193. Briant 2002, 481–90; Miller 1997, 100–05; Brosius 2011.
194. H. 4.137.1 and 6.39–41.
195. Ch. 5 on Demaratus; ch. 8 on Pausanias and Themistocles.
196. H. 6.24, Aelian *VH* 8.17.
197. Briant 2002, 491.
198. Briant 2002, 601–02.
199. Briant 2002, 485.
200. Xen. *Cyrop.* 7.4.12.
201. Briant 2002, 490.
202. H. 3.139.
203. Briant 2002, 481–82.
204. I Esdras, chs 3–4.

3 The Image of a King

1. Athen. 513ff; Plut. *Mor.* 499ab, Aelian *NA* 3.13 and 10.6, Diod. Sic. 6.1; Polyaenus 4.3.32.
2. Strabo 11.13.6.
3. There are ambiguous references in Ctesias *FGrH* 688 F 36 and Deinon *FGrH* 690 F 19, referring to journeys to 'Persas', which could mean either 'the Persians' or Parsa, i.e. Persepolis.
4. Koch 1993, 86–91.
5. Tuplin 1998.
6. Aelian *VH* 1.32; but Artaxerxes II accepts a gift of water from the River Cyrus from a landowner.
7. Xen. *Cyrop.* 1.2.9.
8. Deinon F 12a = Athen. 14.652bc.
9. Esther 1.5–6.
10. See Pseudo-Aristotle *de mundo*, partly quoted at the head of this chapter, on the brilliance of Persian palaces.
11. Esther 5.1.
12. Xen. *HG* 1.5.3.
13. Wiesehöfer 1996, 91.
14. *Life of Themistocles* 26–29; Briant 2002, 327.
15. Xen. *HG* 1.6.6–10.
16. Esther 2.21–22.
17. Xen. *Cyrop.* 8.1.6. Cf. H. 3.120 where two officials find themselves in discussion 'at the entrance to the king's palace'.
18. H. 1.134.
19. Esther 3.5–6.
20. H. 7.136.1.
21. Isoc. 4.151, Xen. *HG* 4.1.35. The row about *proskynesis* at Alexander's court seems to have arisen because the king demanded prostration from his Companions, which was to be followed by a kiss – a rather different procedure from that described by Herodotus. Bosworth 1988, 284–86.
22. Plut. *Artox.* 22.4; also in Aelian *VH* 1.21.
23. Esther 5.1–3.
24. Additions to Esther D 6–7.
25. *Alexander Romance* II. 14.
26. Briant 2002, 301–20; Miller 1997, 100–09, 128–29; Sancisi-Weerdenburg 1998.

27. H. 5.24.
28. See e.g. I Esdras 3.6–7.
29. Ar. *Ach*. 62–63.
30. Esther 6.7–9.
31. Xen. *Cyrop*. 8.2.7–11; at 8.4.24 Cyrus gives such gifts to Tigranes and his wife. Goblets are the prizes in games given by Cyrus: ibid. 8.3.33.
32. H. 3.130. Was Sciton Herodotus' informant?
33. Athen. 2.31, quoting a Peripatetic philosopher called Phanias.
34. *VH* 1.22.
35. Curtis 2012.
36. H. 7.116, 8.120.
37. H. 8.85.2–3, 9.107, 6.41.4.
38. Sen. *de beneficiis* 2.16.
39. The pavilion in Ptolemy II's Grand Procession, described by Athenaeus 5.2.6 (197), was spread with wool carpets with the pattern visible on both sides, embroidered rugs and ψιλαὶ Περσικαί, 'thin Persian things', which might be kilims.
40. See Bruce Healy, 'The Jaipur Garden Carpet', *Hali* 171, 69–71.
41. Tuplin 1996. See also the useful pages in Franks 2012, 80–83.
42. Sir William Temple, 'Upon the Gardens of Epicurus' (1685).
43. Genesis 2.8.
44. *The Garden of Cyrus* I.
45. Dalley 2013.
46. Leick 2001, 227ff. Other Mesopotamian kings who went in for gardening are Bel-Ibni, who came to the throne after his predecessor died of an overdose of porridge, and Beletanas, the successor of Semiramis, was a 'skilled plantsman and chief overseer of the palace gardens' (Agathias 2.25 = Alexander Polyhistor, *FGrH* 273 F 81): see further Drews 1974, 389ff.
47. Drews 1974, 389.
48. Dalley 2013, 162.
49. Dalley 2013, 163–65.
50. Dalley 2013, 100–03.
51. Müller, personal communication: see also Banaszkiewicz 1982 and Briant 2003b.
52. Prince of Wales 2007, 86.
53. Ecclesiastes 2.4–6, 11.
54. Sir Thomas Browne, 'Garden of Cyrus' (1658), I.
55. Xen. *Oec*. 4.20.
56. Kritovoulos; quoted in Wheatcroft 1993, 27.
57. Atasoy 2002, 268.
58. Esther 1.5; Briant 2002, 234.
59. Plut. *Artox*. 25.1.
60. Curt. 4.1.19–23; cf. Lane Fox 1973, 180.
61. Kriwaczek 2010, 174–75.
62. Tuplin 1996, sect. B.
63. Kuhrt II. 806–08.
64. Anab. 6.29.
65. Strabo 16.2.41.
66. Xen. *Oec*. 4.13.
67. Achilles Tatius, *Leucippe and Clitophon* I. 15.
68. R. A. Nicholson, *Selected Poems from the Divan-e Shams-e Tabrizi of Jalaluddin Rumi*. Bethesda, MD: Ibex 2001, 153.
69. Aelian *VH* 14.39.
70. Aelian *VH* 1.34.
71. Meiggs and Lewis 1969, 12. Translation from Briant 2002, 491.

72. Xen. *Cyrop.* 5.3.10ff.
73. Aelian *VH* 1.33 = Plut. *Artox.* 4.5.
74. Plut. *Alcib.* 24.5.
75. Athenaeus 12.531e–f.
76. Xen. *HG* 4.1.15; *Hell. Oxy.* 17.3
77. Strabo 12.8.10.
78. Xen. *Anab.* 1.4.10, 2.4.14.
79. Diod. Sic. 5.19.2.
80. Cf. Lincoln 2007, 84.
81. H. 7.31; Pliny *NH* 17.42.
82. Aelian *VH* 2.14.
83. Couperus 1930, 51–52.
84. Couperus 1930, 52–53.
85. Briant 2002, 235.
86. Lambert 1960, 161 and 157.
87. Strabo 16.1.14.
88. Emma Clark 2004, 142, quoting Atasoy 2002.
89. Phylarchus: Athen. XII, 539d: Briant 2002, 236.
90. The Seleucids continued the practice: Briant 2002, 315.
91. Athen. 13.608a: Briant 2002, 293.
92. Athen. 13. 608a with Briant 2002, 293; Heraclides *FGrH* 689 F2 = Athen. 4.145b.
93. Xen. *Cyrop.* 8.2.6.
94. Xen. *Cyrop.* 8.4.2–4.
95. Athen. 12.8–9; Clearchus F 49–52 Wehrli.
96. Lincoln 2007 shows how Achaemenid punishment performs a symbolic function.
97. Jacobs 2009 suspects all the stories involving women of being inventions, because they are found in Greek sources.
98. Kierkegaard 2007, 123.
99. Plut. *Artox.* 17.
100. Llewellyn-Jones 2013, 141.
101. Plut. *Artox.* 14.
102. H. 5.25.
103. Couperus 1930, 45.
104. Esther 9.13.
105. Jacobs 2009 explains in exhaustive clinical detail why you might expect to die if you had a sharpish wooden stake shoved up your anus.
106. Plut. *Artox.* 19.6.
107. Plut. *Artox.* 16.
108. Michel Foucault, *Discipline and Punish*. Harmondsworth: Penguin, 1991, 16 and 25.
109. Franz Kafka, 'In the Penal Settlement', from *Metamorphosis and Other Stories*. Harmondsworth: Penguin, 1962, 180 and 197.
110. Lincoln 2007, 101.
111. Lincoln 2007, 93.
112. See also Wiesehöfer 1996, 53.
113. Sancisi-Weerdenburg 1983, 29.
114. Wiesehöfer 1996, 53.

4 The Religion of Xerxes

1. The literature on Zoroastrianism is enormous. In this discussion I can do no more than touch the main bases. The standard treatments are Zaehner 1961, Boyce 1982, Koch 2002. Herzfeld 1947 is often hard to follow but full of brilliance.

2. Diogenes Laertius I. 8 lists the available sources in Greek, not all of which he had read: they include Aristotle, *On Philosophy*, Eudoxus' *Voyage around the World*, Theopompus' *Philippic History*, and, perhaps most regrettably lost, Hermippus' (315–240 BC) work on the Magi, which was in more than one book. Xanthus of Lydia surely also wrote about the Magi in his book, as did Heraclides Ponticus (F 68–70 Wehrli). See also Williams-Jackson 1899, 152–54, Kingsley 1990, West 2010, 8.
3. Boyce 1982.
4. Koch 2002.
5. Gnoli 1980, also De Jong 1997. On the linguistic argument see West 2010, 5.
6. Kriwaczek 2002, 206, rejects the traditional date, saying simply that it 'seems far too late'.
7. Ball 2010, 138–44.
8. Boyce 2001, 52.
9. Emp. F 117 DK; Mir Khwand 1832, 284–86. See in general West 1971. See also ch. 2.
10. *Les Prairies d'Or* 4.107.
11. Zaehner 1961, 33. The dating is also accepted by Gershevitch 1995, Koch 2002 and Soudavar 2012 (slightly modified to 618–541 BC).
12. Koch 2002, Henkelman 2008.
13. West translates as 'the Mindful Lord', echoing the Buddhist precept of mindfulness.
14. Herzfeld 1941, 30.
15. *Fravardin Yasht* 13.94–95. The *Yashts* are a set of twenty-one hymns collected in the Avesta, the sacred book of the Zoroastrians. All these texts were first written down in the ninth century AD, but many or all of them may be many centuries older.
16. Browne 1893 (1984), 395.
17. *Zend Avesta* part II (1883/1965), Darmesteter no. xxiv (328 ff).
18. The family of the hero Thraetona.
19. Darmesteter 1880/1965, II. 12.
20. *Yasna* 51.16–19, cf. 46.16.
21. West 2010, 161.
22. Briant 2002, 95–98. Some other gods are listed by Herzfeld 1941, xxviii–xxxiii, including Anahita, Apam Napat, and the stars Tistriya and Satavesa (Sirius and Canopus).
23. Cf. Kriwaczek 2002, 63.
24. Darmesteter 1880/1965, 128.
25. *Yasht* II. 22; II. 12; 189, XVIII.1 on priests who go through the forms but are not pure in soul.
26. Zaehner 1961, 45–50.
27. Foltz 2013, 137–52.
28. Diod. Sic. 1.94.2.
29. *Yasna* (Hymn) 33.3–6, quoted from West 2010, 79–81.
30. *Yasht* i. 1, cited from Darmesteter 1880/1965.
31. Trees are important to the religion too: Zoroaster II. 22 instructs Vishtaspa to 'go to the beautiful, high-growing holy trees, and to cut twigs and bind them according to the rites'.
32. Firdausi, tr. Warner and Warner 1905, V. 33–34. The episode of Zoroaster is provided only in summary in the otherwise more readable translation of Dick Davis.
33. Koch 2002, 16.
34. Al-Tabari 683; IV. 77 in Perlman's translation.
35. A Jewish prophet.
36. Mir Khwand of Bukhara, 1433/4–1498, who wrote his history at the request of Mir Alisher Nava'i, the author of a poem about Alexander the Great, *Alexander's Wall*. His name can also be transliterated Mirkhond.
37. Like Empedocles, F 117 DK.

38. The tradition is, however, dubious, and probably nothing was written down until the Sassanian period, when this legend was invented to explain the lack of pre-existing Zoroastrian books. See Ciancaglini 1997 and, briefly, Stoneman 2008, 42–43.
39. See Hägg and Utas 2003. *Vis o Ramin*, written ca. 1050–1055 by Fakhraddin Gorgani, also shows signs of Hellenistic influence on its Parthian Ur-text, as is argued by Dick Davis in the introduction to his translation (Penguin 2008).
40. See for example Irwin 1994 and Warner 2011.
41. Xerxes I, *Mor.* 173bc.
42. Amm. Marc. 23; translation by David Shea in Mir Khwand 1832. *CHI* 692 sees the role of the Magi as 'bringing the old gods into the Zoroastrian fold'.
43. Davis 1992–2006, 130.
44. *Yasht* 9.26, 15.35, 'Hutaosa of the many brothers'; she is also mentioned at 13.139, 17.45.
45. Tabari 688: IV 82 even gives the name of Esfandiyar's wife as Asturiya, i.e. Esther, to fit this identification with Xerxes. See Herzfeld 1941, 210.
46. Ferdowsi tr. Davis 2007, 1499ff.
47. F 9, p. 170, in the translation by Llewellyn-Jones and Robson 2010.
48. Herzfeld 1947, 48–66, in a complex and perhaps misguided argument deduces that Spitakes is Zoroaster, who thus becomes the elder half-brother of Cambyses, and a key player in the events following the death of Cambyses when Darius came to the throne in mysterious circumstances.
49. Lincoln 2007, 45.
50. Persian *baga-khvarnah*, 'glory of god'.
51. Herzfeld 1941, 208–09.
52. H. 3.67, DB 14.
53. Davis 1992–2006, 27–28. See also Foltz 2013, 153–63.
54. Razmjou 2004, 103–17, and 2005, 150–51.
55. De Jong 1997.
56. Briant 2002, 895.
57. Aristob. *FGrH* 139 F 42 = Strabo 15.1.62.
58. H. 1.140, Strabo 15.3.20. Cf. Brosius 1996, 98. Procopius 1.12.4 also refers to exposure of the dead, cf. 1.11.35.
59. Agathias, *History* 2.23.5.
60. Briant 2002, 94–95.
61. Herzfeld 1947, 747; but Jacobs 2005 is dubious because of the lack of evidence.
62. Boyce 1975. Ball 138–44 holds a contrary view, identifying a fire-temple at Nush-i-jan from as early as 800 BC (rejected by Boyce) and pushing back the origins of Zoroastrianism well before the Achaemenids, thus exercising an influence on Second Isaiah (sixth century BC) with the idea of the future Saviour.
63. Jacobs 1991. See also Polyaenus 7.12.15, Plut. *Artox.* 29.12, where the god is Apollo; also Xen. *Cyrop.* 8.3.12 and 24. At Xen. *Cyrop.* 5.57.2 Cyrus worships 'Zeus and Hestia', i.e. a sky-god and the hearth-fire, which would be a Greek's closest approximation to a god of fire.
64. Briant 2002, 244, with illustrations.
65. Curtis 2012.
66. Darmesteter 1880/1965, xci.
67. Diog. Laert. 1.9; Boyce 1982, 166.
68. H. 7.114.
69. Xen. *Cyrop.* 8.3.24.
70. *CHI* 688.
71. Bianchi 1977.
72. *Yasht* 10.21, cited from Darmesteter 1880/1965.
73. Article *haoma* in *EIr.*
74. Kreyenbroek 2005.

75. Soo too, for example, Zaehner 1961, 154–57.
76. Briant 2002, 96; De Jong 1997, passim. The standard view is well expressed by Xenophon, *Cyrop.* 8.1.23.
77. H. 1.131–32.
78. Aelian, *VH* 2.17, Diogenes Laertius i.7.
79. H. 9.42–43; Stoneman 2011, 51.
80. Zaehner 1961, 163.
81. Crawford 1885, 201–02.
82. Ctes. F 13.15–18; H. 3.70, DB 1–13; Briant 2002, 107–14.
83. Ball 2010, 143. The comparison with the Ayatollahs is inescapable.
84. H. 3.79.
85. Kuhrt's note, I. 170 n. 17, is somewhat despairing. It has been proposed that the term might simply be a Persian month-name, *bagayadiš*; Henning 1944 proved that the word existed in Sogdian, but the text in question attributed the slaughter to Alexander!
86. Zaehner 1961, 161.
87. Cf. Lincoln 2007, 45. See the discussion in ch. 1 above.
88. Koch 2002.
89. 1503ff; Ferdowsi, tr. Warner and Warner, V. 37.
90. Zaehner 1961, 154–75; Potts in Curtis and Stewart 2005; Ball 2010, 22.
91. Lest any conclusion be regarded as final, note that Wiesehöfer 1997, 100, reaches complete *aporia* regarding their precise role and nature.
92. The argument is that of Jamzadeh 1999.
93. *CHI* 688–92, C. Moore lii, Ball 2010, 22–24; Lincoln 2007, 43.
94. Lincoln 2007, 43.
95. Josephus, *AJ* 11.120.
96. Ch. 2, pp. 56–7 above.
97. Briant 2002, 491–92, but 494.
98. Harrison 2011, 82
99. XPh 4b, 35–41; Kuhrt I. 304.
100. Mir Khwand 1832, 312.
101. Firdausi V. 76 in the Warners' translation; quoted at the head of this chapter.
102. See also V. 81, and *Dinkard* 5.2.12 for the reference to Rum and Hind. Esfandiyar is presented as a champion of the faith also in the *Zaratosht-nama* of Bahman Pažbu: see *E. Iranica* s.v.
103. Dabashi 2007, 155–56.
104. H. I. 183. Vidal 1981, 602, supposes that he melted the statue down to make darics to pay for the Greek expedition.
105. Mülles 2011.
106. Scheer 2003.
107. See Briant 2002, 550–54, 965–67. Jamzadeh 2004 aligns this inscription with a passage in the *Shahnameh*, 347–48, in Davis 1992–2006, where Kai Khosrow (not Esfandiyar) sets out from Estakhr (Persepolis) to put down the daevas. He suggests that public recitation of the inscription led to its absorption into the oral tradition. It was, perhaps, the kind of statement that could be placed in the mouth of any suitable king.
108. See for example Herzfeld 1947, 409: Xerxes attacks the daevas and Artaxerxes restores them, as witness his coronation in a shrine of Anahita.
109. Bianchi 1977.
110. Sancisi-Weerdenburg 1980 and 1993.
111. Sancisi-Weerdenburg 1993, 157. Cf. Kuhrt and Sancisi-Weerdenburg 1987, 76ff.
112. XPh 35.
113. It is accepted by Briant 2002, 517 and 962–67, and Wiesehöfer 1996, 54.
114. Henkelman 2008, 9–10.

5 Invasion (I): The Cornerstone of Greek Freedom

1. Vidal 1981, 333; H. 7.8.
2. Davis 1992–2006, 140 etc. See also Introduction, p. 10.
3. H. 8.13.
4. H. 7.7.
5. Ruzicka 2012, 28.
6. Ezra 4.4–6.
7. I Esdras 5.70–73.
8. Grabbe 1992, 93–94.
9. Ctesias F 13 (26); Kuhrt I. 248. The evidence has been thoroughly examined by Rollinger 1998 and Waerzeggers 2003/04; the latter concludes that there was trouble, but that both the traditional view, entailing massive destruction in Babylon, and the revisionist view that nothing much happened at all, are untenable.
10. Jursa 2009.
11. Brosius 2000, no. 66.
12. Shayegan 2011, 259. Xerxes may have dropped his title of šar Bābili at this time, but other indications are that he retained it until at least his Year 20: Shayegan 2011, 259.
13. H. 3.153–58.
14. H. 3.159; Berossus *FGrH* 680 F 9a.
15. Ctesias F 13.26.
16. Διασκάψας; the word could also mean 'excavated'.
17. Οὔκ ἐστιν ἄμεινον. The phrase is typical of oracles, in answer to the question, 'will it be better if I x or y?' The answer here is 'it will not be better if you do not fill the sarcophagus . . .'.
18. Aelian *VH* 13.3, Ctesias F 13b. Loeb translation, adapted.
19. Strabo 16.1.5.
20. See Müller 2011, 124, and Wiesehöfer 1996, 53; the evidence, such as it is, is dismissed by Kuhrt and Sancisi-Weerdenburg 1987, but reasserted by George 2005. On Alexander and Xerxes see Henkelman et al. 2011, 452–57 and 465.
21. H. 1.178ff; Rollinger 1998.
22. Kriwaczek 2010, 256–57.
23. H. 7.8.
24. Cf. Lincoln 2007, 30.
25. Ctesias F 13.25.
26. H. 4.87.
27. Olmstead 1948, 230; Aesch. *Persians* 744–52. Froehlich 2013, 166, suggests that Herodotus was influenced by Aeschylus' portrayal of Xerxes, but to my mind Herodotus' is a much more subtle psychological exploration.
28. Couperus 1930, 71.
29. H. 7.5.
30. Diod. Sic. 11.1–2.
31. *FGrH* 690 F 12, from Athenaeus 14.652bc, making clear that they were dried figs.
32. Athen. 14.652f–3a; Holt 2012, 122.
33. He also only drank water from the River Choaspes: see ch. 1, p. 31. The story in Aelian *VH* 12.40 that Xerxes was dying of thirst on campaign until someone in his entourage found a drop of Choaspes water to bring him is probably designed as a counterpart to the famous story that Alexander refused water that was brought to him when the rest of his army was suffering from thirst.
34. H. 7.6.
35. H. 5.105; on Darius, see also H. 6.44.1, 94.1, and on Xerxes H. 5.97, 7.11.2.
36. Froehlich 2013, 142; Baragwanath 2008, 246.
37. Froehlich 2013, 143.
38. Cawkwell 2005, 87.
39. H. 7.9.

40. Aelian *VH* 12.62.
41. H. 7.9.
42. H. 7.10.
43. H. 7.10.
44. Xen. *Education of Cyrus* 8.7.2.
45. Oppenheim 1956, 249; see Stoneman 2011, 111. On the anomaly (not to mention the unlikelihood) of Greek epiphany dreams, see above all Harris 2009, ch. 1.
46. Cited in Shahbazi 1991, 81 n.20, an interesting note.
47. Stoneman 2011, 51.
48. H. 7.19.
49. Couperus 1930, 19.
50. Ralegh 1829, V. 132.
51. H. 7.101.
52. H. 7.239.
53. H. 5.51.
54. H. 5.118 ff.
55. H. 5.101.
56. H. 5.102.
57. Hanfmann 1975.
58. H. 5.52: see ch. 2, pp. 42–3.
59. Gawlikowski 1996.
60. H. 7.60ff.
61. N. G. Hammond in *CHI* IV, superscript 2, 518–91.
62. Moore 1971, xxi
63. S. West 2011 thinks the whole description too graphic for an official list.
64. Briant 2002, 353.
65. H. 7.73–74.
66. H. 7.88–99.
67. Keen 1998, 93–96, estimates there may have been 10,000 men.
68. Keen, ibid.
69. Pausanias 3.11.3.
70. H. 7.83.
71. H. 8.113.
72. Polyaenus 7.15.3. Xerxes' *matériel* is vividly evoked in Steven Pressfield's novel, *Gates of Fire* (Doubleday, 1999), 308: 'I saw weapons, brothers. Stands of arms by the tens of thousands. Grain and oil, bakers' tents the size of stadiums . . . Lead sling bullets stacked a foot high, covering an acre. The trough of oats for the King's horses was a mile long.'
73. H. 7.153ff.
74. H. 7.43.
75. Kritovoulos, quoted in Wood 1985, 38.
76. H. 7.43; other Greek rivers drunk dry: 58, 108, 109, 196.
77. Harrison 2002.
78. H. 7.43.2.
79. H. 8.54–55.
80. H. 7.191.
81. H. 7.189.
82. H. 8.35–39.
83. H. 8.65.
84. H. 8.129. The examples are assembled by Harrison 2002, 561.
85. H. 8.109.3.
86. H. 7.45–46.
87. William Lithgow, in his *Rare Adventures and Painefull Peregrinations* of 1632 (114) remarked 'Indeed it was a worthy saying, for such a heathenish monarch, who saw no further, than the present misery of this life.'

88. *Pythian* 3.61–62.
89. Compare, for example, Theognis 425–28; Sophocles OC 1225: 'Not to be born is best of all; but, once it has happened, second best is to return whence one came from as soon as possible.'
90. Ralegh 1676, I. iii. 6.2, 427.
91. Scipio's tears over Carthage, superficially similar, in fact have a quite different motivation: he weeps that it has already fallen, and foresees a similar fate one day befalling Rome – as he says to the historian Polybius, who is standing by: Polyb. 39.5.
92. Attar, *Conference of the Birds*, tr. Dick Davis (Penguin, 1984), 214.
93. Homayounpour 2012, 56.
94. Gruen 2010, 35–36.
95. Ralegh (1676) 1829, loc. cit.; a little below, the Persian fleet is again an 'armada'.
96. Hammond and Roseman 1996.
97. As described by Robert Byron in his classic work, *The Road to Oxiana* (1937/1981).
98. H. 7.35.
99. Boyce 1982, 166.
100. H. 7.56.1.
101. Aesch. *Persians* 65–72.
102. H. 7.37.
103. H. 7.50, 7.103, 7.105.
104. H. 7.29.
105. Kuhrt II. 646–47.
106. H. 7.114; Couperus 1930, 93–94.
107. Polyaenus 7.5.1–5. On the stay in Macedon see Müller and Heinrichs 2008, 287. An anonymous reader of this MS suggests that Xerxes may have been waiting for the Carneia and Olympic Games to begin so that the Greeks would be distracted.
108. H. 7.103, 7.105, 7.209–10.
109. Balcer 1995, 238–39.
110. H. 7.118–20.
111. H. 7.190 and 7.147.
112. H. 7.127.
113. H. 7.153ff.
114. H. 7.139, cf. 8.74.
115. H. 7.139.
116. *Fall of Princes* V, 2305–06.
117. Matthews 2006, 109, thinks he may have reached Thermopylae as early as 5–6 August, but this is surely too early. Why were there so few? Was it that the Peloponnesian allies did not want to go? Lazenby 1993, 136.
118. Cf. Matthews 2006, 102.
119. Cartledge 2006, 135.
120. H. 7.209.
121. Pressfield 1999, 368.
122. The difficulty of maintaining such tight order should not be underestimated, and it was perhaps not often achieved. Van Wees 2004, 189.
123. H. 7.226.
124. H. 7.211.
125. Pressfield 1999, 343.
126. H. 7.212.
127. Plut. *Mor.* 225D.
128. Cf. Thuc. 5.70–71 for the Spartan battle advance.
129. H. 7.223–24.
130. Balcer 1995, 252.
131. H. 7.228.

132. H. 7.235.
133. H. 7.188.
134. H. 7.190.
135. H. 7.189.
136. Balcer 1995, 253ff.
137. A sirocco – Bradford 1980, 130ff – or a second *meltemi*?
138. H. 8.4.
139. Lazenby 1993, 139–40.
140. H. 8.13.
141. H. 8.24.
142. Green 1970, 146.
143. Plut. *Them*. 8.
144. Pindar fragment 77.

6 Invasion (II): The Wooden Walls

1. H. 8.30.
2. H. 8.33.
3. John Lydgate, *Fall of Princes* III. 2409–15.
4. Diod. Sic. 11.14.5.
5. H. 8.41.
6. Plut. *Them*. 10.
7. Meiggs and Lewis 1969, 48–52.
8. Green 1970, 97–102.
9. Green 1970, 156–58.
10. D. Lieven, *Russia against Napoleon* (London: Penguin, 2009), 210: Kutuzow stated the dilemma, 'to lose the army or to lose Moscow'. All the civilians left on 13–14 September 1812; Napoleon entered the city on 15 September, and the fires continued to burn for six days.
11. Plut. *Them*. 9.4.
12. H. 8.52.
13. H. 8.53.
14. H. 8.54–55.
15. Moggi 1973 and Scheer 2003 for the arguments.
16. Cicero, *Republic* 3.14. Elsewhere (*Laws* 2.26) Cicero says that it was the Magi who put Xerxes up to it, but this would seem to be a misprision of Xerxes' relationship with that priestly caste.
17. Scheer 2003.
18. Cf. Klinkott 2007 and Müller and Heinrichs 2008, 208.
19. Pausanias 8.46.3 and 3.16.7; cf. H. 6.19.
20. Arrian 3.16.7–8.
21. Arrian 7.19.2.
22. Palagia 2008.
23. Hurwit 1999, 136.
24. Valavanis 2013, 49.
25. H. 7.140.
26. H. 8.140–41.
27. Stoneman 2011, 49–51, based on Parker 1985/2000.
28. H. 8.60.
29. Green 1970, 157. Lazenby 1993, 161, argues that defending the Isthmus was actually the better plan, and rejects the idea that the Persians could not take the Isthmus without the support of the fleet. I am not persuaded. Why did Xerxes bring a fleet here at all if it was unnecessary to his strategy?
30. H. 7.236–37.

31. The words are Walter Ralegh's, 114. Darius, too, had been advised to divide his army into several small ones, but declined to do so: N. Popper, *Walter Ralegh's History of the World and the Culture of the Late Renaissance* (Chicago, IL: Chicago University Press, 2012), 238.
32. H. 8.68.
33. Ralegh (1676) 1829, 121.
34. Green 1970, 146.
35. Green 1970, 172.
36. Green 1970, 176.
37. H. 7.89–95, Aesch *Pers.* 341–43; Shepherd 2010, 37.
38. Shepherd 2010, 39.
39. Plut. *Them.* 12.
40. Plut. *Them.* 13, *Pelop.* 21, *Arist.* 9.
41. Green 1970, 186; it is 'impossible to reconstruct'; cf. De Souza 2008, 103. Modern accounts include Hignett 1963, 230 ff.; Lazenby 1993, 165; Morrison, Coates and Rankov 2000, 55–61, a helpful summary; Shepherd 2010.
42. Aesch *Pers.* 388–401.
43. Aesch *Pers.* 386ff.
44. Morrison, Coates and Rankov 2000, 59–60.
45. Vidal 1981, 605, blames the Phoenicians for the defeat.
46. H. 8.89.
47. Lord Byron, 'The Isles of Greece'; but there is controversy over the location: Plut. *Them.* 13.
48. Ar. *Peace* 290.
49. Eustathius *prooemium ad Pindarum*, para 30 line 30, Drachmann.
50. Polyaenus 8.53.1–3. Lydgate goes off the rails here, calls Artemisia Themidora and has Xerxes mortally wounded in the fighting.
51. Aesch *Pers.* 418–28; see also Lysias 2.36.
52. Plut. *Them.* 15.
53. Aesch *Pers.* 407–71.
54. Balcer 1995, 269.
55. Thuc. 1.73.
56. H. 8.65. Another pretence by Themistocles? – Plut. *Them.* 16, Green 1970, 207. Cf. Lydgate 2488–92. But at H. 8.109 Themistocles informs Xerxes that the bridges are sound, no doubt in the hope of getting him quickly out of Greece as well as acquiring a reputation with the king for sound advice.
57. H. 8.97.
58. Green 1970, 172–74.
59. H. 8.98 and 8.54.
60. H. 8.102.
61. H. 8.100.
62. Plut. *Them.* 4.
63. H. 8.100–02.
64. H. 8.114.
65. H. 8.115.
66. Aesch *Pers.* 495–507.
67. Green 1970, 217: mid-December.
68. Couperus 1930, 225: 'In this there is no cruelty. The royal decree represents a logical deduction.'
69. H. 8.119.
70. Cf. Briant 2003, 551–52, on Darius III; John Lydgate, *Fall of Princes* III. 2497.
71. H. 8.102.
72. H. 9.115. For the details see ch. 8.
73. H. 8.140.

74. H. 9.13.
75. Green 1970, 241.
76. Giustina Monti 2012 argues that it is authentic and that the re-inscription of the decree was commissioned by Alexander the Great, in the wake of the revolt of Agis, to advertise the new-found 'unity' of the Greeks. The oath is cited in Diodorus, 11.29.3–4. See Tod GHI 2.204; Hignett 1963, 460–61.
77. Cartledge 2013a and 2013b.
78. H. 1.136.1: quantity is counted as strength.
79. H. 9.37 and 9.41.4.
80. Harrison 2002, 570.
81. Shepherd 2012, 34–37.
82. H. 9.61 and 9.63.
83. Cf. A. *Pers.* 147–49; Cawkwell 2005, 115.
84. H. 9.80.
85. Thuc. 1.129.
86. H. 9.78.
87. H. 9.90 ff.
88. H. 9.90.
89. Ctes. F 13.32.
90. Ctes. F 13.31, Kuhrt I. 294.
91. Dio Chr. 11.149 = Kuhrt I. 287. Even modern historians are not above the reinterpreting of the course of events: witness Jack Balcer's book, entitled *The Persian Conquest of the Greeks*. Cawkwell, too, has a chapter entitled 'The Persian Conquest of Greece'.
92. Referred to by Ctesias: see the edition of Lloyd-Jones and Robson, 63–64. See also Deinon F 9 = Athen. 14.633ce; Lenfant 2009, 131–45.
93. Lincoln 2007, 13.
94. Ar. *Wasps* 1078–90.
95. Hordern 2002, 122–24, is a useful summary.
96. *PMG* 536 and *PMG* 532–35.
97. Boedeker and Sider 2001.
98. Seaford 2012, 206–24.
99. Briant 2003, 551–52.
100. Seaford 2012, 221–22.
101. Diog. Laert. 8.2.57.
102. Trepanier 2004, 20–23. The palaeographic confusion is not obvious.
103. Sider 1982.
104. Huxley 1969.
105. These could be Jews or Pisidians.
106. H. 7.70 reports this of the Ethiopians.
107. Choerilus of Samos, FF 3, 5, 6.
108. Timotheus F 791.30–40.
109. Licymnius of Chios, *PMG* 772.
110. Grenet 2003; Stoneman 2012.
111. Another writer from Asia Minor, Musaeus of Ephesus, in the third century BC wrote an epic *Perseis* in ten books (*Supp. Hell.* 560), but we know nothing about it.
112. Couperus 1930, 207.
113. Vidal 1981, 141.

7 Persepolis

1. There is a good survey of later responses to the site in both Eastern and Western authors in Mousavi 2012.
2. Xen. *Cyrop.* 8.7.1, εἰς Πέρσας.

3. Diod. Sic. 17.71.3–8.
4. Shahbazi 2004, 22.
5. Diod. Sic. 17.70.1–3.
6. Plut. *Alex*. 37.5.
7. Alexander Romance II. 15
8. Sura 89.5–8.
9. Wiesehöfer 1998.
10. Crawford 1885, 189ff.
11. Compare DSf on Susa, which describes the import of cedar wood from Lebanon and yaka-wood from Gandhara, gold from Sardis and Bactria, lapis lazuli and carnelian from Sogdiana, turquoise from Chorasmia, silver and ebony from Egypt, and ivory from Ethiopia, Sind and Arachosia. Small fragments of gold gate-bands and lapis medallions have survived.
12. Herbert 1929, 86ff.
13. Curzon 1892, 153.
14. *Vers Ispahan* (1906).
15. Froehlich 2013, 135–40.
16. H. 2.158.
17. H. 3.134.3.
18. H. 1.184–87.
19. Dalley 2013, arguing that they were actually at Nineveh.
20. Brodersen 1996.
21. Kent 1950; to be supplemented by the more modern versions of many of the texts in Kuhrt 2007 and Brosius 2000.
22. See for what follows Koch 2006 (a translation of Koch 2001).
23. Sancisi-Weerdenburg 1997, 182. But Jacobs 2003/04 is sceptical.
24. Curzon 1892, 152ff.
25. Curtius Rufus 5.7.5.
26. His son Artabazus was soon to take over the satrapy of Dascyeion: Thuc. 1.129; Briant 560.
27. Vidal 1981, 615.
28. Sancisi-Weerdenburg 1989/2002; cf. Briant 2002, 567.
29. Mousavi 2012, 50.
30. Roaf 1983, 159.
31. Herzfeld 1941, 225.
32. XPe 11–17.
33. Mousavi 2012, 90.
34. DPh.
35. XPg, Koch 2001, 72 = Koch 2006, 23.
36. According to Koch; Shahbazi regards the north portico as the earlier.
37. Koch 2001, 130 = Koch 2006, 65–68.
38. Shahbazi 1976, 34; and also in *EIr*. See also Abdi 2005, who argues that this, and the *daeva* inscription, were moved by Artaxerxes because they depicted those he had murdered.
39. A1Pa 17–22.
40. Shahbazi *EIr* 14.
41. Esther 1.5.
42. Polyaenus 4.3.2; ch. 1.
43. John Dryden, 'Alexander's Feast', as set by G. F. Handel.
44. Koch 2001, plate 71.
45. Shahbazi 2004 143–44.
46. Koch 2001, 57 = Koch 2006, 109.
47. Wiesehöfer 1996, 67.
48. Diod. Sic. 17.71.1.

49. Momigliano 1979, 114.
50. Curtis 2012, 54.
51. Ball 2010, 25–26.
52. Boardman 2000, 126, 127.
53. Curzon 1892, II, 193–94.
54. Byron 1937/1950, 167–69.
55. So does Jacobs 2002. For Koch 1993, they are 'masterpieces'.
56. Boardman 2000, 224.
57. Jacobs 2002.
58. Kapuscinski 2007, 152–53.
59. Vidal 1981, 343.
60. If there was such a Peace, it was probably signed in 465 BC, or maybe in 450 or 449. See Badian 1987 and the discussion in ch. 10, 11ff.
61. Rilke, *Duino Elegies* II.
62. Stephen Spender, 'In Attica'.
63. Boardman 2000, 128–33. Miller 1997, 100ff, Brosius 2011.
64. Boardman 2000, 132–33.
65. DSf; Kent 1953, 144.
66. Momigliano 1975, 144.
67. Miller 1997, 100–01.
68. Diod. Sic. 1.46.4.
69. Diod. Sic. 17.69.
70. See also Kuhrt I. 304–05.
71. Shayegan 2011, 46 and 290; Shayegan 2012, 91–92.
72. Lane Fox 1973, 258.
73. Mousavi, 2012, 52.
74. Shahbazi 2004, 34.
75. Razmjou 2010.
76. Curzon 1892, 149.
77. XPc.
78. See Noble 1984.
79. Shahbazi 2004, 52.
80. Curzon 1892, 133.
81. Kriwaczek 2002, 243.
82. See e.g. Curzon 1892, 161.
83. Shahbazi, 2004, 103–04.
84. Barry 2004, 348.
85. Mousavi 2012, 89–90.
86. Ferdowsi 2007, 1499ff.
87. For example in Mas'udi: see *E. Ir(anica)* s.v. Jamshid.
88. Curzon 1892, 153.
89. Root 1979, 230, 278.
90. Lane Fox 1973, 258.
91. Curtius 5.6.12.
92. Hamilton 1969, 98.
93. Plut. *Alex*. 37.6.
94. Green 1974, 317. Balcer 1978 thinks Alexander did not bother with this Achaemenid festival, and 'conclusively disrupted' all the traditions of Achaemenid kingship.
95. Bosworth 1988, 92.
96. The quotations are from Green, ibid.

8 Family Romances

1. Vidal 1981, 615, cf. 621, Xerxes 'conducts his campaigns . . . in the houses of the harem'.
2. Vidal 1981, 406.
3. Hyperanthes, Abrocomes and Ariabignes.
4. Cibber, *Xerxes* Act II (p. 24).
5. Cibber, *Xerxes* Act II (pp. 24–25).
6. Cibber, *Xerxes* Act II (p. 61).
7. Aelian *NA* 1.14.
8. H. 7.61.
9. Aelian *VH* 12.1.
10. H. 9.107–13.
11. H. 9.108.
12. Llewellyn-Jones 2013, 64.
13. Like Pheretime of Cyrene, asking for a gift from the king of Cyprus. She wanted an army, and he gave her a golden distaff.
14. This was too much for Couperus, who has Atossa intervene with her whip, to compel Amestris to let the woman off.
15. Llewellyn-Jones 2013, 115. These are not from the families of the six co-conspirators, even though there are supposed to be only seven Persian noble families. See Wiesehöfer 1996, 37, on endogamy.
16. Llewellyn-Jones 2013, 16.
17. Llewellyn-Jones 2013, 139. See also Peirce 1993, 89, describing Hurrem's (Roxelana's) efforts to eliminate Mustafa and thus to protect her own son. Olympias protected Alexander III of Macedon in exactly the same way.
18. Diogenes Laertius 1.7. Mitchell 2012, and Mitchell 2013, 97–105, show that both polygamy and incest are relatively common among ruling families in Greece, notably in Sparta and Macedon, though not among ordinary people. See also Ogden 1999.
19. *Andromache* 174–75. Cf. *Dissoi Logoi* DK II. 408.
20. Agathias *Hist.* 2. 23–25.
21. *Book of the Laws of Countries* 29, in Eusebius *PE* 6.10.16–17; cf. 6.10.38.
22. *Recognitions* 9.20.4.
23. Broadbent 2012, 13.
24. Stoneman 2012.
25. Brosius 1996, 61.
26. Consider also the case of the Spartan Gorgo: Mitchell 2012.
27. H. 3.31.
28. Philo, *de specialibus legibus* 3.13.
29. Carney 2000, 101–05. Lynette Mitchell (in conversation) is dubious.
30. Strabo 15.3.17.
31. For the Ottoman situation, see the detailed analysis by Peirce 1993, 29–89.
32. H. 7.18.7.
33. Llewellyn-Jones 2013, 118, quoting Brosius 1996, 33.
34. Athenaeus 12.514b.
35. Briant 2002, 279.
36. Couperus 1930, 231.
37. Briant 2002, 280–83.
38. Diod. Sic. 17.77.7.
39. Xen. *Agesilaus* 3.3.
40. H. 5.18.
41. I Esdras 4.28–32.
42. Mathys 2010, 284–85.
43. Plut. 'Advice to Bride and Groom', *Mor.* 16, 140B; Mathys 2010, 258–60.
44. Briant 2002, 360.

45. Ctes. F 15 (55); Kuhrt II. 2007, 599ff.
46. Plut. *Them.* 26.
47. Plato *Alcib.* I. 123cd; H. 2.98.1.
48. Peirce 1993, 125.
49. Plato *Alcib.* I. 121.
50. X. *Anab.* 1.4.9, 2.4.27; Brosius 1996, 123.
51. Peirce 1993, 110, 258–60.
52. Brosius 1996, 181, Llewellyn-Jones 2013, 112ff.
53. Blow 2009, 173.
54. Couperus 1930, e.g. 35.
55. Brosius 1996, 199; Wiesehöfer 1996, 81.
56. Greeks, as usual, disapproved: Mitchell 2012, 11–12, referring also to Mania of Aeolis.
57. H. 3.119.2.
58. See also Sancisi-Weerdenburg 1983, 30.
59. H. 4.43.2; Brosius 1996, 117.
60. Diod. Sic. 57.1, Plut. *Them.* 13.
61. See ch. 9, p. 199.
62. Llewellyn-Jones 2013, 97.
63. Peirce 1993, 6. Montesquieu's *Lettres persanes* has a wonderful description of the harem at Esfahan.
64. Peirce 1993, 122.
65. Kuhrt I. 1995, 149 and 256; Briant 2002, 283; Sancisi-Weerdenburg 1987, 38 and 43: see Llewellyn-Jones 2013, 99. Brosius ignores the issue.
66. Olmstead 1948, 285.
67. Llewellyn-Jones, 2013, 106–07.
68. Bassano, 17 v, quoted in Peirce 1993, 62.
69. Peirce 1993, 138.
70. al-Tabari IV. 82; ch. 688; see also Mas'udi II. 127; Herzfeld 1947, 96.
71. Moore 1971, xli.
72. Athen. 12.9.
73. Moore 1977, 190–91 and 197; above, ch. 2.
74. See Moore 1971, 19; Mathys 2010, 243–65.
75. Moore 1971, l and 19.
76. Esther II. 16 and III. 7.
77. Moore 1971, xlvi and 24.
78. Dalley 2007.
79. Moore 1971, lviii.
80. Esther 9.20–28.

9 Assassination

1. Meiggs 1972, 81–83, argues for 466 BC.
2. He was the son of Pharnaces of the PFTs.
3. Diod. Sic. 11.54.
4. Diod. Sic. 11.56 versus Plut. *Them.* 26.
5. Diod. Sic. 11.56.6.
6. Letter 20.29–30; Doenges 1981.
7. Plut. *Them.* 27, following Phanias. If it was Artabanus, this implies that Xerxes was still alive, since he did not survive after Xerxes' murder. See also Doenges 1981, 72–73.
8. Thuc. I. 135–38.
9. Plut. *Them.* 27.
10. Keaveney 2003, 24–36; summary at 116. Frost 1980, 213–15, also accepts Thucydides against Plutarch. White 1964 does not even consider the alternative version of Plutarch.

11. See Appendix 1.
12. Plut. *Them.* 28.
13. Miltiades' son had received similar honours: H. 6.4.1.
14. Marr 1994 points out that this need be as barely literal as the claim that one of the Persian queen's estates had specifically to keep her in shoes.
15. As can be deduced from the Athenian Tribute Lists, 3, p. 111; Frost 1980, 97–98.
16. Doenges 1981: Letter 20.
17. Keaveney 2003, 75, following Marr 1994 and Meiggs 1972, 53–54. But the first recorded payments of these cities to the Delian League/Athenian Empire are not until 453 (Lampsacus) and 451 (Magnesia). Frost 1980, 220–22, suggests that it would be possible for cities that were tyrannies to be in the League, but it seems unlikely. Doenges 1981, 395, proposes that the cities were outside the Delian League until the 450s.
18. Plut. *Them.* 31.
19. Plato *Meno* 93e.
20. Plut. *Them.* 29.
21. Diod. Sic. 11.58.
22. Keaveney 2003, 96.
23. Marr 1995.
24. Plut. *Cimon* 10.
25. Mir Khwand 1832, 331.
26. The Marmares under attack from Alexander – Diod. Sic. 17.28.1–5; the Isaurians under attack from Perdiccas and Philip III – Diod. Sic. 18.22.1–8; the pirate Zenicetes – Strabo 14.5.7; the people of Xanthus under attack from Brutus – Appian *BC* IV. 77–80. Not to mention the Jews at Masada.
27. Diod. Sic. 11.60.5. We do not know who his mother was, except that she was not Amestris. Presumably she was one of the concubines.
28. Plut. *Cimon* 12.
29. Ruzicka 2012: in the 460s Xerxes turned to 'strictly maritime enterprises to counter Athens and her league allies'. There was no standing army: Cawkwell 2005, 132.
30. See note 1 above.
31. Plut. *Cimon* 12 and Diod. Sic. 11.60.
32. Diod. Sic. 11.60.4.
33. Plut. *Cimon* 13.
34. Briant 2002, 555–56, is a good account. Meiggs 1972, 129–51, favouring the existence of the Peace, puts it in about 450, more than a decade after Xerxes' death. So if Xerxes kept away from the sea, it was not because of any formal peace, and Plutarch's information may be overstated. The more usual view, of those who think there was a peace, is that it was agreed just before Xerxes' death, directly after the Battle of Eurymedon: Badian 1987 and article in *EIr*.
35. Justin 3.1.
36. Ctes. *FGrH* 688 F 14 (34); Diod. Sic. 11.69; Justin 3.1; conveniently assembled by Kuhrt I. 307–09.
37. Xen. *Cyrop.* 7.5.59.
38. Also the seven conspirators against Strattis of Chios (H. 8 end); and the seven counsellors of the Persian king: ch. 2, p. 61.
39. A puzzle is posed by Manetho *FGrH* 609 F 2/3a (p. 50, l. 20 in Jacoby), which states that Artabanus ruled as king for seven months. I do not know what to make of this.
40. Set by Leonardo Vinci and produced in 1730, as well as by Thomas Arne in 1762.
41. He features in Vinci's version but not in Arne's.
42. Plut. *Artox.* 15–16.
43. Arist. *Politics*, 1311 b 35ff.
44. See also Aelian, *VH* 13.3.
45. H. 7.10–18.

46. Couperus 1930, 298–99.
47. Mir Khwand 1832, 338.
48. *Meadows of Gold* II. 127; also Tabari 1987, 82; see Herzfeld 1947, 96.
49. Mir Khwand 1832, 343; the other Greek mentioned in this passage, Zimokrates, is an enigma.
50. Ferdowsi 2007, 414.
51. Ferdowsi 2007, 415.
52. A very Herodotean thought.
53. Ferdowsi 2007, 416.
54. Firdausi 1905, V. 252–53.
55. Couperus 1930, 298–99.
56. Diod. Sic. 17.114.4.
57. Sources collected by Briant 2002, 522–23.
58. Diod. Sic. 11.71.1–2.

Conclusion

1. H. 8.118.
2. Baragwanath 2008, 243–48.
3. Moore 1971, 14, 43, 74.
4. Ferdowsi 2007, 421.
5. H. 8.67–69, Baragwanath 2008, 250.
6. Branscome 2013, 96.
7. H. 3.134.3.
8. Baragwanath 2008, 257ff.
9. H. 7.133–7.
10. Baragwanath 2008, 271, 279.
11. H. 3.34–35; H. 9.108; H. 3.32; and H. 3.80.
12. H. 7.103.
13. Cf. Branscome 2013, 113 n.23, citing Donald Lateiner.
14. Firdausi 1905, V. 223 and 224.
15. H. 9.42–43; Stoneman 2011, 51 and n.42.
16. Edward Fitzgerald, *Rubaiyat of Omar Khayyam*, no. 19.
17. Fitzgerald, *Rubaiyat*, no. 110.
18. *Iliad* 6.145–49, trans. George Chapman.
19. *Iliad* 6.208–09, trans. George Chapman.
20. Esther 1.4.
21. Homayounpour 2012.
22. Ecclesiastes 2.4–11. The same passage is employed by the author of the early modern Greek *Tale of Alexander* to summarise his hero's achievement.

Appendix 1

1. Piemontese 1993.
2. Anquetil du Perron (1731–1805) developed a fascination with the Avesta and brought it back to Paris in 1762; it was translated into French in 1771.
3. See Loloi 2005.
4. B. Dobree, *English Literature in the Early Eighteenth Century, 1700–1740* (Oxford: Oxford University Press, 1959), 240. See Introduction.
5. Kirkpatrick 2009, 5.
6. Kirkpatrick 2009, 10, Markstrom 2007, 291.
7. Notes to the recording by Fabio Biondi and Europa Galante on Opus 111, p. 19.
8. It has no connection with an earlier opera of the same title, which is about Artaxerxes II: Markstrom 2007, 310.

9. On the recording by Diego Fasolis and Concerto Köln, EMI records 2012.
10. Markstrom 2007, 304–06.
11. There is a recording of Bach's version conducted by Christophe Rousset with Les Talens Lyriques, 2005. There is no complete recording of Pacini's version as far as I know.
12. M. Casari, *EI* s.v. Italy vii.
13. See Kimbell 2007.
14. Piemontese 1993, 23.

Appendix 2

1. Kuhrt 2003; Drews 1974. Like Moses he was exposed in a basket of rushes on the banks of the Euphrates, before being brought up by wild animals.
2. Stoneman 1992.
3. Another folk-tale motif: Stoneman 2012, 13.
4. Gaillard 2005, 93. Thence the story entered the Alexander legend in the *Shahnameh*, and its derivatives such as the Malay Alexander Legend: Broadbent 2012, 14–19.

Appendix 3

1. See Hignett 1963 for detailed discussion.
2. H. 7.183.
3. H. 7.188.
4. H. 7.206.1.
5. We cannot be sure which, because the timing of the Olympics depended on the Eleian calendar, which seems to have begun at the winter solstice. The Olympia took place in the eighth month (Hignett 1963, 449). If Eleian months began at the New Moon, then the closest one to the winter solstice was that of 19 December 479, and the one that began the month in which the Olympia were held is that of 3 August. Hammond in the *Cambridge Ancient History* follows the arguments of Kenneth Sacks 1976 in order to 'save' Herodotus' chronology. But Sacks' argument depends on placing the Olympia as late as September, while Carneius was probably equivalent to the Athenian month Metageitnion, which corresponds to August. Sacks (p. 247) dismisses this inconvenient piece of evidence with the remark that ancient calendars had frequent intercalations; though true, it is not legitimate to make this assumption without evidence. Sacks' chronology would give the following dates: Thermopylae 17–19 September; Phocis 22 September; Athens 27 September; Salamis 29 September.
6. Polyaenus 1.32.
7. See Taub 2003, 33ff. Typical examples are at Aratus 158, the evening rising of the Kids on 28 September foretells rough weather; cf. Pliny *NH* 2.106, who remarks enigmatically that the Kids are among the stars that 'move of themselves'. At Aratus 905, if the more northerly of the two stars in the Ass is bright, a north wind is coming. The rising of Arcturus is commonly said to bring rain, as is the rising of the Hyades ('rainy ones').
8. The name of Boreas survives in Turkish Poyraz, which is in fact a nor'easter, and the same could be true of Boreas.
9. H. 7.189.
10. 'the struggle [Artemisium] went on under a blazing August sun' – Green 1970, 145.
11. E. J. Bickerman, *Chronology of the Ancient World* (London: Thames and Hudson, 1968), 13–14.

Bibliography

Abdi, Kamyar 2005. 'The Passing of the Throne from Xerxes to Artaxerxes I' in Curtis and Simpson 2005, 275–86.

Al-Tabari 1987. *The History of Prophets and Kings*, vol. IV: *The Ancient Kingdoms*, trans. Moshe Perlman. New York: SUNY Press.

Anderson, Sonia 1989. *An English Consul in Turkey: Paul Rycaut at Smyrna, 1667–1678*. Oxford: Clarendon Press.

Atasoy, Nurhan 2002. *A Garden for the Sultan: Gardens and Flowers in the Ottoman Culture*. Istanbul: Aygaz.

Badian, E. 1987. 'The Peace of Callias', *JHS* 107, 1–39.

Bailey, H. W. 1943. *Ninth-Century Problems of the Zoroastrian Books*. Oxford: Oxford University Press.

Bakker, E. J., de Jong, I. and van Wees, H. (eds) 2002. *Brill's Companion to Herodotus*. Leiden: Brill.

Balcer, J. M. 1978. 'Alexander's Burning of Persepolis', *Iranica Antiqua* 13, 119–33.

Balcer, J. M. 1995. *The Persian Conquest of the Greeks 545–450 BC*. Constance: Universitätsverlag.

Ball, Warwick, 2010. *Towards One World: Ancient Persia and the West*. London: East and West Publishing.

Banaszkiewicz, Jacek 1982. 'Königliche Karrieren von Hirten, Gärtnern und Pflügern', *Saeculum* 33, 265–86.

Baragwanath, Emily 2008. *Motivation and Narrative in Herodotus*. Oxford: Oxford University Press.

Barry, Michael 2004. *Figurative Art in Medieval Islam and the Riddle of Hihzad of Heart (1465–1535)*. Paris: Flammarion.

Bataille, Georges 1973. *Oeuvres complètes*. Paris: Gallimard-Jeunesse.

Bianchi, Ugo 1977. 'L'inscription des daiva et le Zoroastrisme des Achéménides', *Revue de l'histoire des religions* 192, 3–30.

Binder, Carsten 2008. *Plutarchs Vita des Artaxerxes*. Berlin: de Gruyter.

Blow, David 2009. *Shah Abbas: The Ruthless King who Became an Iranian Legend*. London: I. B. Tauris.

Boardman, John 2000. *Persia and the West*. London: Thames and Hudson.

Boedeker, Deborah and Sider, David 2001. *The New Simonides: Contexts of Praise and Desire*. Oxford: Oxford University Press.

Bosworth, A. B. 1988. *Conquest and Empire: The Reign of Alexander the Great.* Cambridge: Cambridge University Press.

Boyce, Mary 1975. 'On the Zoroastrian Temple-Cult of Fire', *JAOS* 90, 454–65.

Boyce, Mary 1982. *A History of Zoroastrianism.* Leiden: Brill.

Bradford, Ernle 1980. *The Year of Thermopylae.* London: Macmillan.

Branscome, David 2013. *Textual Rivals: Self-Presentation in Herodotus' Histories.* Ann Arbor, MI: University of Michigan Press.

Briant, Pierre 2002. *From Cyrus to Alexander: A History of the Persian Empire.* Winona Lake, IN: Eisenbraun (original French edition Fayard 1996).

Briant, Pierre 2003a. *Darius dans l'ombre d'Alexandre.* Paris: Fayard.

Briant, Pierre 2003b. 'A propos du roi jardinier: remarques sur l'histoire d'un dossier documentaire', *Achaemenid History* 13, 33–49.

Briant, Pierre et al. 2008. *L'archive des fortifications de Persepolis* (Persika 12). Paris: Boccard.

Briant, Pierre et al. 2009. *L'organisation des pouvoirs et contacts culturels dans les pays de l'empire achéménide* (Persika 14). Paris: Boccard.

Bridges, Emma, Hall, Edith and Rhodes, P. J. 2007. *Cultural Responses to the Persian Wars: Antiquity to the Third Millennium.* Oxford: Oxford University Press.

Broadbent, Catherine 2012. *The Malay Alexander Legend.* Bloomington, IN: AuthorHouse.

Brodersen, Kai 1996. *Die sieben Weltwunder.* Munich: C. H. Beck.

Brosius, Maria 1996. *Women in Ancient Persia 559–331 BC.* Oxford: Clarendon Press.

Brosius, Maria 2000. *The Persian Empire from Cyrus II to Artaxerxes I.* London: LACTOR pamphlet 16.

Brosius, Maria 2006. *The Persians.* Abingdon: Routledge.

Brosius, Maria 2011. 'Greeks at the Persian Court' in Wiesehöfer, Rollinger and Lanfranchi (eds), 69–81.

Browne, Edward Granville 1893 (1984). *A Year amongst the Persians.* London: A&C Black (reprint Century 1984).

Bulliet, Richard 1972. *The Patricians of Nishapur.* Cambridge, MA: Harvard University Press.

Byron, Robert 1937/1981. *The Road to Oxiana.* London: Macmillan/Picador.

Cahill, Nicholas 1988. 'Taşkule: A Persian Period Tomb near Phokaia', *AJA* 92, 481–501.

Cameron, Averil and Kuhrt, Amélie (eds) 1983. *Images of Women in Antiquity.* Beckenham: Croom Helm.

Carney, Elizabeth 2000. *Women and Monarchy in Ancient Macedonia.* Norman, OK: University of Oklahoma Press.

Cartledge, Paul, 2006. *Thermopylae: The Battle that Changed the World.* London: Macmillan.

Cartledge, Paul 2013a. 'Taking the Oath', *Minerva* July/August, 20–23.

Cartledge, P.A. 2013b. *After Thermopylae: The Oath of Plataea and the End of the Graeco-Persian Wars.* Oxford: Oxford University Press.

Cawkwell, George 2005. *The Greek Wars: The Failure of Persia.* Oxford: Oxford University Press.

Christensen, A. 1936. *Les gestes des rois dans les traditions de l'Iran antique.* Paris: Librairie orientaliste Paul Geuthner.

Ciancaglini, Claudia 1997. 'Alessandro e l'incendio di Persepoli' in A. Valvo (ed.), *La diffusione dell' eredità classica nell' età tardoantica e medioevale: Forme e modi di transmissione.* Alessandria: Edizioni dell'Orso.

Clark, Emma 2004. *The Art of the Islamic Garden.* Marlborough: Crowood Press.

Clines, David 1984. *Esther Scroll.* Sheffield: Sheffield Academic Press.

Conybeare, F. C., Harris, J. R. and Lewis, A. S. 1913. *The Story of Ahikar: From the Aramaic, Syriac, Arabic, Armenian, Old Turkish, Greek and Slavonic Versions,* 2nd edn. Cambridge: Cambridge University Press.

Couperus, Louis 1930. *Arrogance: The Conquests of Xerxes.* New York: Farrar and Rinehart. Originally published as *Xerxes: of de hoogmoed* (Rotterdam, n.p., 1919).

Crawford, F. Marion 1885. *Zoroaster*. London: Macmillan.

Crébillon, Jolyot de. *Théâtre complet*. 4 vols. 1912. Paris: Garnier.

Curtis, John 2012. *The Oxus Treasure*. London: British Museum Press.

Curtis, John and Simpson, St John 2010. *The World of Achaemenid Persia*. London: I. B. Tauris.

Curtis, John and Tallis, Nigel 2005. *Forgotten Empire: The World of Ancient Persia*. London: British Museum.

Curtis, Vesta Sarkhosh and Stewart, Sarah 2005. *The Birth of an Empire: The Idea of Iran*, vol. 1. London: I. B. Tauris.

Curzon, George Nathaniel 1892. *Persia and the Persian Question*. London: Longman.

Dabashi, Hamid 2007. *Iran: A People Interrupted*. New York: New Press.

Dalby, Andrew 2003. *Food in the Ancient World*. London: Routledge.

Dalley, Stephanie 2007. *Esther's Revenge at Susa: From Sennacherib to Ahasuerus*. Oxford: Oxford University Press.

Dalley, Stephanie 2013. *The Mystery of the Hanging Garden of Babylon*. Oxford: Oxford University Press.

Darmesteter, James 1880/1965. *The Zend-Avesta*, vols 1–3. Oxford: Oxford University Press; reprint Delhi: M. Banarsidass.

Davis, Dick 1992–2006 [*sic*]. *Epic and Sedition: The Case of Ferdowsi's* Shahnameh. Washington DC: Mage.

De Jong, Albert 1997. *Traditions of the Magi: Zoroastrianism in Greek and Latin Literature*. Leiden: Brill.

Delemen, Inci et al. 2007. *The Achaemenid Impact on Local Populations and Cultures in Anatolia*. Istanbul: Turkish Institute of Archaeology.

Derow, Peter and Parker, Robert (eds) 2003. *Herodotus and his World*. Oxford: Oxford University Press.

De Souza, Philip (ed.) 2008. *The Greek World at War*. London: Thames and Hudson.

Dillery, John 2007. 'Greek Historians of the Near East' in J. Marincola (ed.), *A Companion to Greek and Roman Historiography*. Oxford: Blackwell, 221–30.

Doenges, Norman A. 1981. *The Letters of Themistokles*. New York: Arno Press.

Donzel, Emeri van and Schmidt, Andrea 2010. *Gog and Magog in Early Eastern Christian and Islamic Sources: Sallam's Quest for Alexander's Wall*. Leiden: Brill.

Drews, Robert 1974. 'Sargon, Cyrus and Mesopotamian Folk History', *JNES* 33, 387–93.

Dusinberre, Elspeth R. M. 2014. *Empire, Authority and Autonomy in Achaemenid Anatolia*. Cambridge: Cambridge University Press.

Estakhri tr. Sir William Ouseley 1880. *The Oriental Geography of Ibn Haukal [or rather Istakhri]*. London: Oriental Press.

Ferdowsi, Abulqasim, tr. Dick Davis 2007. *Shahnameh: The Persian Book of Kings*. Harmondsworth: Penguin (first published in Washington DC by Mage 2007).

Fields, Nic 2007. *Thermopylae 480 BC: Last stand of the 300*. Oxford: Osprey.

Firdausi, Abolqasem, tr. Arthur George Warner and Edmond Warner 1905. *The Shahnama*. London: Kegan Paul, Trench and Trubner, repr. Routledge 2000.

Foltz, Richard 2013. *Religions of Iran: From Prehistory to the Present*. London: Oneworld.

Franks, Hallie, 2012. *Hunters, Heroes, Kings. The Frieze of Tomb II at Vergina*. Princeton, NJ: American School of Classical Studies.

Froehlich, Susanne 2013. *Handlungsmotive bei Herodot*. Wiesbaden: F. Steiner.

Frost, F. 1980. *Plutarch, Themistocles: A Commentary*. Princeton, NJ: Princeton University Press.

Gaillard, Marina 2005. *Alexandre le Grand en Iran. Le* Darab Nameh *d'Abu Taher Tarsusi* (Persika 5). Paris: Boccard.

Gawlikowski, Michal 1996. 'Thapsacus and Zeugma: The Crossing of the Euphrates in Antiquity', *Iraq* 58, 123–33.

George, Andrew 2005. 'Xerxes and the Tower of Babel' in Curtis and Simpson 2005, 471–80.

Gershevitch, I. 1995. 'Approaches to Zoroaster's Gathas', *Iran* 33, 1–29.

Gnoli, Gherardo 1980. *Zoroaster's Time and Homeland*. Naples: Istituto universitario orientale.

Grabbe, L. L. 1992. *Judaism from Cyrus to Hadrian*. Minneapolis, MN: Fortress Press.

Graf, David F. 1994. 'The Persian Royal Road System', *Achaemenid History* 8, 167–89.

Green, Peter 1970. *The Year of Salamis*. London: Weidenfeld & Nicolson.

Green, Peter 1974. *Alexander of Macedon*, 2nd edn. Harmondsworth: Penguin.

Grenet, Frantz 2003. *La Geste d'Ardashir fils de Pâbag*. Die: Editions A. Die.

Gruen, Erich S. 2010. *Rethinking the Other in Antiquity*. Princeton, NJ: Princeton University Press.

Hägg, Tomas 2012. *The Art of Biography in Antiquity*. Cambridge: Cambridge University Press.

Hägg, Tomas and Utas, Bo 2003. *The Virgin and her Lover*. Leiden: Brill.

Halleux, Robert and Schamp, Jacques 2003. *Les Lapidaires grecs*. Paris: Les Belles Lettres.

Hallock, R. T. 1969. *Persepolis Fortification Tablets*. Chicago, IL: University of Chicago Press.

Hamilton, J. R. 1969. *Plutarch, Alexander: A Commentary*. Oxford: Oxford University Press.

Hammond, N. G. L. 1988. 'The Expedition of Xerxes', *Cambridge Ancient History*, vol. IV, 2nd edn, 518–91.

Hammond, N. G. L. and Roseman, L. J. 1996. 'The Construction of Xerxes' Bridge over the Hellespont', *JHS* 116, 88–107.

Hanfmann, George 1975. *From Croesus to Constantine*. Ann Arbor, MI: University of Michigan Press.

Harris, William V. 2009. *Dreams and Experience in Classical Antiquity*. Cambridge, MA: Harvard University Press.

Harrison, Thomas 2002. 'The Persian Invasion' in Bakker, de Jong and van Wees 2002, 551–78.

Harrison, Thomas 2011. *Writing Ancient Persia*. London: Bristol Classical Press.

Haubold, Johannes 2007. 'Xerxes' Homer' in Bridges, Hall and Rhodes (eds) 2007, 47–64.

Hawkins, F. W. 1888. *The French Stage in the Eighteenth Century*. London: Chapman and Hall.

Heltzer, Michael 1989. 'Persepolis Documents, the Lindos Chronicle, and Judith', *Parola del Passato* 44, 81–101.

Henkelman, Wouter 2008. *The Other Gods who Are*. Leiden: Brill.

Henkelman, Wouter, Kuhrt, Amélie, Rollinger, Robert and Wiesehöfer, Josef 2011. 'Herodotus and Babylon Reconsidered', in Rollinger et al. (eds) 2011, 449–70.

Henning, W. B. 1944. 'The Murder of the Magi', *JRAS* 2, 133–44.

Herbert, Sir Thomas 1929. *Travels in Persia 1627–1629*; abridged and edited by Sir William Foster. New York: Robert McBride.

Herzfeld, Ernst 1941. *Iran in the Ancient East*. Oxford: Oxford University Press.

Herzfeld, Ernst 1947. *Zoroaster and his World*. Princeton, NJ: Princeton University Press.

Hignett, C. 1963. *Xerxes' Invasion of Greece*. Oxford: Oxford University Press.

Hirsch, Steven W. 1985. *The Friendship of the Barbarians: Xenophon and the Persian Empire*. Hanover, NH: University Press of New England.

Holt, Frank L. 2012. *Lost World of the Golden King: In Search of Ancient Afghanistan*. Berkeley, CA: University of California Press.

Homayounpour, Gohar 2012. *Doing Psychoanalysis in Tehran*. Cambridge, MA: MIT Press.

Hordern, James 2002. *The Fragments of Timotheus*. Oxford: Oxford University Press.

Hornblower, Simon 2003. 'Panionios of Chios and Hermotimos of Pedasa' in Derow and Parker 2003, 37–57.

Huff, Dietrich 2010. 'Überlegungen zu Funktion, Genese und Nachfolge der Apadana' in Jacobs and Rollinger (eds) 2010, 311–76.

Hurwit, Jeffrey M. 1999. *The Athenian Acropolis: History, Mythology and Archaeology from the Neolithic Era to the Present*. Cambridge: Cambridge University Press.

Huxley, G. L. 1969. *Greek Epic Poetry: From Eumelos to Panyassis*. London: Faber & Faber.

Huxley, G. L. 1969. 'Choerilus of Samos', *GRBS* 10, 12–29.

Irwin, Robert 1994. *The Arabian Nights: A Companion*. London: Allen Lane.

Jacobs, Bruno 1991. 'Der Sonnengott im Pantheon der Achaemeniden' in J. Kellens (ed.) 1991, 49–69.

Jacobs, Bruno 1994. *Die Satrapienverwaltung im Perserreich zur Zeit Darius' III*. Basel: Universität Basel.

Jacobs, Bruno 2002. 'Achaimenidische Kunst', *AMIT* 34, 345–95.

Jacobs, Bruno 2003/04. Review of H. Koch, *Persepolis, AMIT* 35/6, 442–49.

Jacobs, Bruno 2005. 'From Gabled Hut to Rock-Cut Tomb: A Religious and Cultural Break between Cyrus and Darius?' in Curtis and Simpson 2005, 91–101.

Jacobs, Bruno 2009. 'Grausame Hinrichtungen – friedliche Bilder. Zum Verhältnis der politischen realität zu den Darstellungsszenarien der achämenidischen Kunst' in *Extreme Formen von Gewalt in Bild und Text des Altertums*, ed. Martin Zimmermann, Munich, 121–53.

Jacobs, Bruno and Rollinger, Robert (eds) 2010. *Der Achämenidenhof – The Achaemenid Court*. Wiesbaden: Harrassowitz.

Jamzadeh, P. 1999. 'Reflections of Darius' Propaganda and Aeschylus' Parody in Firdausi's Epic', *Acta Orientalia Belgica* 12, 253–58.

Jamzadeh, P. 2004. 'A Shahnama Passage in an Achaemenid Context', *Iranica Antiqua* 39, 383–88.

Jouanna, Jacques 1999. *Hippocrates*. Baltimore, MD: Johns Hopkins University Press.

Jursa, Michael 2009. 'On Aspects of Taxation in Achaemenid Babylonia: New Evidence from Borsippa' in Briant et al. 2009, 237–67.

Jursa, Michael 2011. 'Taxation' in Rollinger et al. 2011, 431–48.

Kaptan, Deniz 2002. *The Daskyleion Bullae: Seal Images from the Western Achaemenid Empire*. Leiden: Achaemenid History XII.

Kapuscinski, Ryszard 2007. *Travels with Herodotus*. Harmondsworth: Penguin.

Keaveney, Arthur 1996. 'Persian Behaviour and Misbehaviour: Some Herodotean Examples', *Athenaeum* 84, 23–48.

Keaveney, Arthur 2003. *The Life and Journey of Athenian Statesman Themistocles (524–460 BC?) as a Refugee in Persia*. Lewiston, NY: Edwin Mellen Press.

Keen, Antony G. 1998. *Dynastic Lycia: A Political History of the Lycians and their Relations with Foreign Powers, c. 545–362 BC*. Leiden: Brill.

Kellens, J. (ed.) 1991. *La religion iranienne à l'époque des Achéménides*, in *Iranica Antiqua Supplement 5*.

Kent, R. G. 1953. *Old Persian: Grammar, Texts, Lexicon*. New Haven, CT: American Oriental Society.

Kierkegaard, Søren 2007. *The Seducer's Diary*. Harmondsworth: Penguin.

Kimbell, David 2007. 'Operatic Variations on an Episode at the Hellespont' in Bridges, Hall and Rhodes (2007), 201–30.

Kingsley, Peter 1990. 'The Greek Origin of the Sixth-Century Dating of Zoroaster', *Bulletin of the School of Oriental and African Studies* 53, 245–65.

Kingsley, Peter 1995. *Ancient Philosophy, Mystery and Magic: Empedocles and Pythagorean Tradition*. Oxford: Oxford University Press.

Kirkpatrick, Adam 2009. *The Role of Metastasio's Libretti in the Eighteenth Century*. Saarbrücken: Verlag Dr Müller.

Klinkott, Hilmar 2005. *Der Satrap*. Frankfurt: Oikumene I.

Klinkott, Hilmar 2007. 'Xerxes in Ägypten' in S. Pfeiffer (ed.), *Ägypten unter fremden Herrschern zwischen persischer Satrapie und römischer Provinz*. Frankfurt: Verlag Antike, 34–53.

Koch, Heidemarie 1993. *Achämeniden-Studien*. Wiesbaden: Harrassowitz.

Koch, Heidemarie 2001. *Persepolis: Glänzende Hauptstadt des Perserreichs*. Mainz: Ph. Von Zabern.

Koch, Heidemarie 2002. 'Iranische Religion im achaemenidischen Zeitalter' in R. G. Koch, 2006. *Persepolis and its Surroundings*. Tehran: Yassakli.

Kratz R.G. (ed.) *Religion und Religionskontakte im Zeitalter der Achaemeniden*. Gütersloh: Kaiser, 11–26.

Kreyenbroek, Philip G. 2005. 'Zoroastrianism under the Achaemenids: A Non-Essentialist Approach' in Curtis and Simpson 2005, 103–9.

Kriwaczek, Paul 2002. *In Search of Zarathustra: The First Prophet and the Ideas that Changed the World*. London: Orion.

Kriwaczek, Paul 2010. *Babylon: Mesopotamia and the Birth of Civilization*. London: Atlantic Books.

Kuhrt, Amélie, 2003. 'Making History: Sargon of Akkad and Cyrus the Great of Persia', *Achaemenid History* 13, 347–61.

Kuhrt, Amélie 2007. *The Persian Empire: A Corpus of Sources from the Achaemenid Period*. Abingdon: Routledge.

Kuhrt, Amélie and Sancisi-Weerdenburg, Heleen 1987. 'Xerxes' Destruction of Babylonian Temples', *Achaemenid History* 2, 69–78.

Lambert, W. G. 1960. *Babylonian Wisdom Literature*. Oxford: Oxford University Press.

Lane Fox, Robin 1973. *Alexander the Great*. London: Allen Lane.

Lazenby, J. F. 1993. *The Defence of Greece 490–479 BC*. Warminster: Aris and Phillips.

Leick, Gwendolyn 2001. *Mesopotamia: The Invention of the City*. Harmondsworth: Penguin.

Lenfant, Dominique 1996. 'Ctésias et Hérodote – ou les rencontres de l'histoire dans la Perse achéménide', *REG* 109, 348–80.

Lenfant, Dominique 2004. *Ctésias de Cnide* (ed. and trans). Paris: Les Belles Lettres.

Lenfant, Dominique 2009. *Les histoires perses de Dinon et d'Héraclide* (Persika 13). Paris: Boccard.

Lewis, D. M. 1977. *Sparta and Persia*. Leiden: Brill.

Lewis, D. M. 1985. 'Persians in Herodotus' in *Greek Historians: Studies Presented to A. E. Raubitschek*. Stanford, CA: Stanford University Press. Reprinted in D. M. Lewis, *Selected Papers in Greek and Near Eastern History*. Cambridge: Cambridge University Press, 1997.

Lewis, D. M. 1987. 'The King's Dinner', *Achaemenid History* II, (1987), 79–87; reprinted in D. M. Lewis, *Selected Papers in Greek and Near Eastern History*. Cambridge: Cambridge University Press, 1997.

Lincoln, Bruce 2007. *Religion, Empire and Torture: The Case of Achaemenian Persia*. Chicago, IL: Chicago University Press.

Llewellyn-Jones, Lloyd 2013. *King and Court in Ancient Persia, 559–331 BCE*. Edinburgh: Edinburgh University Press.

Llewellyn-Jones, Lloyd and Robson, James 2010. *Ctesias' History of Persia: Tales of the Orient*. Abingdon: Routledge.

Loloi, Parvin 2005. 'Portraits of the Achaemenid Kings in Seventeenth- and Eighteenth-Century English Drama' in Curtis and Simpson 2005, 33–40.

Markstrom, Kurt Sven 2007. *The Operas of Leonardo Vinci, Napoletano*. Hillsdale, NY: Pendragon Press.

Marr, John 1994. 'Don't Take it Literally: Themistocles and the Case of the Inedible Victuals', *CQ* 536–39.

Marr, John 1995. 'The Death of Themistocles', *Greece and Rome* 42, 1995, 159–67.

Martin, Jacques 2003. *Les voyages d'Alix: Persepolis*. Paris: Casterman.

Mathys, Hans-Peter 2010. 'Der Achämenidenhof im Alten Testament' in Jacobs and Rollinger (eds) 2010, 231–307.

Matthews, Rupert 2006. *The Battle of Thermopylae: A Campaign in Context*. Stroud: Spellmount.

Meiggs, Russell 1972. *The Athenian Empire*. Oxford: Oxford University Press.

Meiggs, Russell and Lewis, David 1969. *A Selection of Greek Historical Inscriptions, to the End of the Fifth Century BC*. Oxford: Oxford University Press.

Mellink, M. J. 1971 and 1973. 'Excavations at Karataş – Semanyük and Elmalı, Lycia 1970', *AJA* 75 (plates 54–56) and 77 (plates 44–46).

Miller, Margaret 1997. *Athens and Persia in the Fifth Century BC: A Study in Cultural Receptivity*. Cambridge: Cambridge University Press.

Mir Khwand 1832. *History of the Early Kings of Persia*, trans. David Shea. London: R. Watts; reprinted Elibron 2005.

Mitchell, L. 2013. *Heroic Rulers of Archaic and Classical Greece*. London: Bloomsbury.

Mitchell, Lynette G. 2012. 'The Women of Ruling Families in Archaic and Classical Greece', *CQ* 62, 1–21.

Moggi, M. 1973. 'I furti di statue attribute a Serse e le relative restituzioni', *Annali della Scuola Normale Superiore di Pisa* 3, 1–42.

Momigliano, A. D. 1975. *Alien Wisdom: The Limits of Hellenization*. Cambridge: Cambridge University Press.

Momigliano, A. D. 1977. 'Eastern Elements in Post-Exilic Jewish, and Greek, Historiography' in *Essays in Ancient and Modern Historiography*. Oxford: Blackwell, 25–35.

Momigliano, A. D. 1979. 'Persian Empire and Greek Freedom', in A. Ryan (ed.), *The Idea of Freedom: Essays in Honour of Isaiah Berlin*. Oxford: Oxford University Press, 138–51.

Momigliano, A. D. 1993. *The Development of Greek Biography*. Cambridge, MA: Harvard University Press.

Monti, Giustina 2012. 'Alessandro e il giuramento di Platea', *Incideza dell'antico: dialoghi di storia greca* 10, 195–207.

Moore, Carey A. 1971. *Esther* (Anchor Bible 7B). New York: Doubleday.

Moore, Carey A. 1977. *Daniel, Esther and Jeremiah: The Additions* (Anchor Bible 44). New York: Doubleday.

Moore, Carey A. 1985. *Judith* (Anchor Bible 40). New York: Doubleday.

Morrison, J. S., Coates, J. F. and Rankov, N. B. 2000. *The Athenian Trireme*, 2nd edn. Cambridge: Cambridge University Press.

Mossman, Judith 2010. 'A Life Unparalleled: Artaxerxes' in N. Humble, *Plutarch's Lives: Parallelism and Purpose*. Swansea: Classical Press of Wales.

Mousavi, Ali 2012. *Persepolis: Discovery and Afterlife of a World Wonder*. Berlin: de Gruyter.

Müller, Sabine 2011. 'Die frühen Perserkönige im kulturellen Gedächtnis der Makedonen und in der Propaganda Alexanders des Gr.', *Gymnasium* 118, 105–33.

Müller, Sabine 2012. 'The Female Element of the Political Self-Fashioning of the Diadochi: Ptolemy, Seleucus, Lysimachus, and their Iranian Wives' in V. A. Troncoso and Edward M. Anson (eds), *After Alexander: The Time of the Diadochi (323–281 BC)*. Oxford: Oxbow, 199–214.

Müller, Sabine and Heinrichs, Johannes 2008. 'Ein persisches Statussymbol auf Münzen Alexanders I. von Makedonien', *ZPE* 167, 283–309.

Noble, David Grant (ed.) 1984. *New Light on Chaco Canyon*. Sante Fe, NM: SAR Press.

Nylander, C. 1970. *Ionians in Pasargadae*. Uppsala: Universitetet Uppsala.

Ogden, Daniel 1999. *Polygamy, Prostitutes and Death: The Hellenistic Dynasties*. Swansea: Classical Press of Wales.

Olmstead A. T. 1948. *History of the Persian Empire*. Chicago, IL: Chicago University Press.

Palagia, Olga 2008. 'The Marble of the Penelope from Persepolis and its Historical Implications' in S. M. R. Darbandi and A. Zournatzi (eds), *Ancient Greece and Ancient Iran: Cross-Cultural Encounters*. Athens: National Hellenic Research Foundation, 223–37.

Parker, R. C. T. 1985/2000. 'Greek States and Greek Oracles' in *CRUX* 298–326; also in R. Buxton (ed.), *Oxford Readings in Greek Religion*. Oxford: Oxford University Press, 2000.

Peirce, Leslie P. 1993. *The Imperial Harem: Women and Sovereignty in the Ottoman Empire*. Oxford: Oxford University Press.

Piemontese, Angelo Michele 1993. 'Persia e persiani nella drama per musica veneziano', *Opera e Libretto* II. Florence: Olschki, 1–34.

Pinault, J. R. 1992. *Hippocratic Lives and Legends*. Leiden: Brill.

Pirngruber, Reinhard 2011. 'Eunuchen am Königshof. Ktesias und die altorientalische Evidenz' in Wiesehöfer, Rollinger and Lanfranchi (eds) 2011, 279–312.

Ralegh, Sir Walter 1676. *History of the World*. London; also 1829, Edinburgh: Archibald Constable and Co.

Ratté, C. 1992. *Istanbuler Mitteilungen* 42, 135–61.

Razmjou, Shahrokh 2004. 'Lan Ceremony and Other Ritual Ceremonies in the Achaemenid Period: Persepolis Fortification Tablets', *Iran* 42, 103–17.

Razmjou, Shahrokh 2005. 'Religion and Burial Customs' in Curtis and Tallis 2005, 150–6.

Razmjou, Shahrokh 2010. 'Persepolis: A Reinterpretation of the Palaces and their Function' in John Curtis and St John Simpson (eds) *The World of Achaemenid Persia*. London: I. B. Tauris, 232–45.

Rhodes, P. J. 2003. 'Herodotean Chronology Revisited' in Derow and Parker (eds) 2003, 58–72.

Roaf, Michael 1983. *Sculpture and Sculptors at Persepolis (Iran*, 21).

Robert, Louis 1978. 'Arbinas', *Journal des Savants*, 3–34.

Rollinger, Robert 1998. 'Überlegungen zu Herodot, Xerxes und dessen angeblichen Zerstörung Babylons', *Altorientalische Forschungen* 25, 339–73.

Rollinger, Robert and Henkelman, Wouter 2009. 'New Observations on "Greeks" in the Achaemenid Empire' in Briant et al. 2009, 331–51.

Rollinger, Robert et al. (eds) 2011. *Herodot und das persische Weltreich – Herodotus and the Persian Empire* in *Classica et orientalia* 3, Wiesbaden: Harrassowitz.

Root, Margaret Cool 1979. *King and Kingship in Achaemenid Art*. Leiden: Brill; *Acta Iranica* ix.

Rose, Charles Brian 2007. 'The Tombs of the Granicus River Valley' in Delemen et al. 2007, 247–64.

Ruffing, Kai 2006. 'Salamis – die grösste Seeschlacht der alten Welt', *Grazer Beiträge* 25, 1–32.

Ruffing, Kai 2009. 'Die "Satrapienliste" des Dareios: Herodoteisches Konstrukt oder Realität?', *AMIT* 41, 323–40.

Ruffing, Kai 2011. 'Herodot und die Wirtschaft des Achaemeniden-Reichs' in Rollinger et al. (eds) 2011, 75–102.

Ruska, Julius 1912. *Das Steinbuch des Aristoteles*. Heidelberg: C. Winter.

Ruzicka, Steven 2012. *Trouble in the West*. Oxford: Oxford University Press.

Sacks, Kenneth 1976. 'Herodotus and the Dating of the Battle of Thermopylae'. CQ 26, 232–48.

Sancisi-Weerdenburg, Heleen 1980. 'Yauna en Persai'. Dissertation Leiden University.

Sancisi-Weerdenburg, Heleen 1983. 'Exit Atossa: Images of Women in Greek Historiography on Persia' in A. Cameron and A. Kuhrt (eds), *Images of Women in Antiquity*. London: Croom Helm, 20–33.

Sancisi-Weerdenburg, Heleen 1987. 'Decadence in the Empire or Decadence in the Sources? From Source to Synthesis: Ctesias', in H. Sancisi-Weerdenburg (ed.), *Sources, Structures and Synthesis* in *Achaemenid History* I. Leiden: Brill, 33–45.

Sancisi-Weerdenburg, Heleen 1988. 'A Typically Persian Gift', *Historia* 37, 372–74.

Sancisi-Weerdenburg, Heleen 1989. 'Gifts in the Persian Empire' in P. Briant and C. Herrenschmidt (eds), *Les tributes dans l'empire perse: Actes de la table ronde de Paris 12–13 dec 1986*. Paris: Travaux de l'institut d'études iraniennes – Sorbonne, 13; 129–46.

Sancisi-Weerdenburg, Heleen 1989/2002. 'The Personality of Xerxes, King of Kings' in L. de Meyer and E. Haerinck (eds), *Archaeologia Iranica et Orientalis, Miscellanea in Honorem Louis Vanden Berghe.* Gent: Peeters, 549–60. Reprinted in Bakker, de Jong and van Wees (eds) 2002.

Sancisi-Weerdenburg, Heleen 1993. Political Concepts in Old Persian Inscriptions' in K. Raaflaub (ed.), *Anfänge politischen Denkens.* Munich: Oldenbourg, 145–63, 379–81, 407, 423–24.

Sancisi-Weerdenburg, Heleen 1997. 'Alexander and Persepolis' in J. Coulsen (ed.), *Alexander the Great: Reality and Myth.* Rome (Analecta Romana Insituti Danici), 177–87.

Sancisi-Weerdenburg, Heleen 1998. 'Bājī', *Achaemenid History* XI, 23–34.

Schedl, Claus 1965. 'Nabuchodonosor, Arpakšad und Darius', *Zeitschrift der deutschen morgenländischen Gesellschaft* 115, 242–54.

Scheer, Tanja S. 2003. 'Die geraubte Artemis' in M. Witte and A. Alkier (eds), *Die Griechen und der Vordere Orient* (OBO 91). Freiburg: Universitätsverlag and Göttingen: Vandenhoeck & Ruprecht, 59–85.

Schmidt, E.F. 1953–70. *Persepolis* I–III. Chicago.

Schwinghammer, Gundula 2011. 'Die Smerdis-Story – Der Usurpator, Dareios und die Bestrafung der "Lügenkönige"', in Rollinger et al. (eds) 2011, 665–87.

Seaford, Richard 2004. *Money and the Early Greek Mind.* Cambridge: Cambridge University Press.

Seaford, Richard 2012. *Cosmology and the Polis.* Cambridge: Cambridge University Press.

Selden, Daniel 2012. 'Mapping the Alexander Romance' in Stoneman, Erickson and Netton (eds) 2012, 19–60.

Shahbazi, A. Shapur 1980. 'An Achaemenid Symbol II. Farnah "(God given) Fortune" Symbolised', *Arch. Mitteil. aus Iran* 13, 119–47.

Shahbazi, A. Shapur 1981. *Ferdowsi: A Critical Biography.* Costa Mesa, CA: Mazda.

Shahbazi, A. Shapur 1990. 'On the Xwaday-namag' in *Iranica Varia: Studies Presented to E. Yarshater.* Leiden: Brill, 208–29.

Shahbazi, A. Shapur 2004. *The Authoritative Guide to Persepolis.* Tehran: SAFIR.

Shayegan, M. Rahim 2011. *Arsacids and Sassanians: Political Ideology in Post-Hellenistic and Late Antique Persia.* Cambridge: Cambridge University Press.

Shayegan, M. Rahim 2012. *Aspects of History and Epic in Ancient Iran: From Gaumata to Wahnam.* Washington DC: Center for Hellenic Studies.

Shepherd, William 2010. *Salamis 480 BC: The Naval Campaign that Saved Greece.* Botley: Osprey.

Shepherd, William 2012. *Plataea 479 BC: The Most Glorious Victory Ever Seen.* Botley: Osprey.

Sider, David 1982. 'Empedocles' *Persica*', *Ancient Philosophy* 2, 76–78.

Soudavar, Abolala 2102. 'Astyages, Cyrus and Zoroaster: Solving a Historical Dilemma', *Iran* 50, 45–78.

Stoneman, Richard 1992. 'Oriental Motifs in the *Alexander Romance*', *Antichthon* 26, 95–113.

Stoneman, Richard 2008. *Alexander the Great: A Life in Legend.* London: Yale University Press.

Stoneman, Richard 2011. *The Ancient Oracles: Making the Gods Speak.* London: Yale University Press.

Stoneman, Richard 2012. 'Persian Aspects of the Romance Tradition' in Stoneman, Erickson and Netton (eds) 2012.

Stoneman, Richard, Erickson, Kyle and Netton, Ian (eds) 2012. *The Alexander Romance in Persia and the East.* Groningen: Barkhuis.

Stronach, David 1978. *Pasargadae.* Oxford: Clarendon Press.

Stronach, David and Mousavi, Ali (eds) 2009. *Irans Erbe in Flugbildern von Georg Gerster.* Mainz: Philipp von Zabern.

Tabari 1987. *The History of al-Tabari*, vol. 4: *The Ancient Kingdoms*, trans. Moshe Perlman. New York: SUNY Press.

Taub, Liba 2003. *Ancient Meteorology*. London: Routledge.

Tha'alibi 1900. *Histoire des rois de Perse. Texte arabe publié et traduit par,* H. Zotenberg. Paris: Imprimerie Nationale.

Trepanier, Simon 2004. *Empedocles: An Interpretation*. New York and London: Routledge.

Tuplin, Christopher 1991. 'Travellers', *Achaemenid History* 7, 37–57.

Tuplin, Christopher 1996. 'The Parks and Gardens of the Achaemenid Empire' in *Achaemenid Studies, Historia Einzelschriften* 99, 80–131.

Tuplin, Christopher 1998. 'Seasonal Migration of Achaemenid Kings', *Achaemenid History* XI, 63–114.

Tuplin, Christopher 2004. 'Doctoring the Persians: Ctesias of Cnidus, Physician and Historian', *Klio* 86, 305–47.

Tuplin, Christopher 2011a. 'Mapping the World: Herodotus on Achaemenid Imperial Organisation' in Rollinger et al. (eds) 2011, 39–63.

Tuplin, Christopher 2011b. 'The Oibaras Saga' in Wiesehöfer et al. (eds) 2011.

Turgenev, Ivan 1991. *Fathers and Sons*, trans. Richard Freeborn. Oxford World's Classics. Oxford: Oxford University Press.

Valavanis, Panos 2013. *The Acropolis through its Museum*. Athens: Kapon Editions.

Van Wees, Hans 2004. *Greek Warfare: Myths and Realities*. London: Duckworth.

Vidal, Gore 1981. *Creation*. New York: Random House.

Waerzeggers, Caroline 2003/04. 'The Babylonian Revolt against Xerxes and the "end of archives" ', *Archiv für Orientforschung* 50, 150–73.

Wales, HRH Prince of (with Stephanie Donaldson) 2007. *The Elements of Organic Gardening*. London: Weidenfeld & Nicolson.

Warner, Marina 2012. *Stranger Magic: Charmed States and the Arabian Nights*. London: Chatto & Windus.

Waterfield, Robin 1998. *Herodotus: The Histories*. Oxford World's Classics. Oxford: Oxford University Press.

Waterfield, Robin 2011. *Dividing the Spoils*. Oxford: Oxford University Press.

West, M. L. 1971. *Early Greek Philosophy and the Orient*. Oxford: Oxford University Press.

West, M. L. 2010. *The Hymns of Zoroaster: A New Translation of the Most Ancient Sacred Texts of Iran*. London: I. B. Tauris.

West, S. 2011. 'Herodotus' Sources' in Rollinger et al. (eds) 2011, 255–72.

Wheatcroft, Andrew 1993. *The Ottomans*. London: Viking.

White, Mary E. 1964. 'Some Agiad Dates: Pausanias and his Sons', *JHS* 84, 140–52.

Wiesehöfer, Josef 1996. *Ancient Persia: From 550 BC to 650 AD*. London: I. B. Tauris.

Wiesehöfer, Josef 1998. 'Johan Albrecht von Mandelslo in Pasargadai und Persepolis', *Achaemenid History* XI, 7–19.

Wiesehöfer, Josef, Rollinger, Robert and Lanfranchi, Giovanni (eds) 2011. *Ktesias' Welt = Ctesias' World*. Wiesbaden: Harrassowitz.

Wilamowitz-Moellendorff, Ulrich von 1881. *Antigonos von Karystos*. Berlin: Weidmann.

Williams-Jackson, A. V. *Zoroaster, the Prophet of Ancient Iran*. New York: Columbia University Press, 1899.

Wood, Michael 1985. *In Search of the Trojan War*. London: BBC Books.

Wright, Denis 1977. *The English amongst the Persians*. London: Heinemann.

Zaehner, R. C. 1961. *The Dawn and Twilight of Zoroastrianism*. London: Weidenfeld & Nicolson.

www.avesta.org

Encyclopaedia Iranica Online.

Index

Abbas, Shah of Persia 29, 65, 189
Abdalonymus, a gardener who became king 78
Abdera 133
Abydos 124, 126, 128, 149
Achaemenes, brother of Xerxes 110, 123, 136, 144
Achilles Tatius, Greek novelist 79–80
Aelian, author of miscellanies 52, 74, 81, 111–12, 182
Aeschines, Greek orator 140
Aeschylus 52
    Persians 2, 3, 20, 26, 113, 117, 124, 130, 146–48, 156, 157–59; setting of, 230–31
    Prometheus Bound 104–05
Aesop, Life of 51, 65
Agathias, Byzantine historian 100
Ahasuerus, Hebrew name of Xerxes 9, 56, 62, 77, 110, 187, 188, 194
Ahiqar, Tale of 25, 47, 51, 224
Ahriman 92, 99, 198, 207
Ahura Mazda 8, 17, 25, 28, 35, 38, 69, 88, 89–90, 92, 98–99, 103–04, 106–07, 157, 167, 171, 176, 177, 180
Alcibiades, rich Greek 81, 188–89
Alexander I, king of Macedon 132, 151
Alexander III (the Great) 2, 10, 12–13, 29, 33, 36, 42, 44, 47, 52, 67, 80, 83, 87, 90, 95, 104, 107, 112, 121, 124, 135, 142, 152, 155, 161, 162, 166, 169–70, 172, 175, 179, 214, 216–17, 222
    see also Iskandar

Alexander Romance 14, 40, 51, 60, 73, 116, 162, 186, 189, 193, 216, 231
Amesha Spentas 61, 92
Amestris, daughter of Otanes and wife of Xerxes 6, 23, 29–30, 58, 84, 87, 123, 184–85, 188–89, 193, 204–05, 207, 216
Ammianus Marcellinus, Roman historian 95–96
Amytis, mother of Cambyses 21, 84, 97
Amytis, daughter of Xerxes 61, 64–65, 84, 123, 132, 182, 203
Anacreon of Teos 52
Anahita, Persian goddess 31–32, 93, 96, 99
Anaxagoras of Clazomenae, Greek philosopher 54
Anaximander of Miletus, Greek philosopher 54, 90
Antigonus of Carystus 6
Apollo, god 105, 126, 133, 140–42, 153, 158
Apollonides, a lustful doctor 64–65, 84
Arabian Nights 187
Aramaic language 47, 50, 55
Architecture 49–50
Archives, Persian 51–52, 122, 167
Ardashir, Sasanian king 25, 168, 224
Ardashir, Book of the Deeds of 34, 159, 186, 224
Ardashir of the Long Arms (or Bahman) = Artaxerxes I (q.v.) 206
Arda Viraf Namag, account of hell 90
Ariabignes, brother of Xerxes 123, 147
Ariamenes, brother of Xerxes 95
Ariomandes son of Gobryas 201

Aristobulus, historian 100

Aristophanes, Greek comic poet 52, 63, 73, 156

Aristotle, Greek philosopher 29, 55, 66, 158, 213

'Aristotle' (pseudonymous) 44, 69, 87

Arne, Thomas, composer 221

Arphaxad, 'king of Media' 59

Arrian, Greek historian of Alexander 47–48, 78

Art, Achaemenid, compared with Greek 42, 172–76

Artabanus, uncle and adviser to Xerxes 5, 115–17, 126–28, 152, 203, 212

Artabanus son of Artasyras, conspirator against Xerxes 195, 197, 202–04, 206, 220

Artabazus, governor of Dascyleion 153, 196

Artaxerxes I 31, 42, 56–58, 64, 78, 84, 93, 95, 99, 105, 110, 166, 169, 171, 182–83, 187, 197, 199, 202–05, 208–09, 210, 220

Artaxerxes II 8, 29, 45, 62, 65, 67, 69, 121, 172, 186–87

Artaxerxes III 60, 63, 161, 172

Artayctes, governor of Sestos 155

Artaynte, daughter of Masistes 184–86

Artayntes, Persian general 154

Artemis 141–42

Artemisia, queen of Caria and general of Xerxes 55, 123, 144, 147–48, 150, 156, 190, 212

Artemision, Battle 64, 126, 129, 136–38, 144
    Date of 226–28

Artobarzanes (or Ariaramnes or Ariamenes) brother of Xerxes 23–25

Artystone/Irtashduna, wife of Darius I 23, 188

Ashurbanipal, Assyrian king 76, 116

Aspamitres, see Mithridates, conspirator

Aspasia, mistress of Cyrus the Younger 183

Assyrian Empire 41–42, 81, 173

Astyages, Median king 223–24

Athena 125

Athenaeus, Greek author 70, 83

Athens 55, 107, 112–14, 118, 140, 150, 151, 174, 195–96, 201, 226
    Acropolis 107, 125, 140–42, 143, 174
    Areopagus 141

Athos, Mt 5, 118

Atossa (Hutaosa), wife of Darius I and mother of Xerxes 9, 20, 21, 23–24, 25, 29, 64, 96, 103, 124, 165, 189

Attar, Farid ud-Din, Persian poet 127

Avesta, Zoroastrian sacred books 95, 106, 178

Axial Age 90

Babylon 10, 24, 31, 57, 58–59, 70, 80, 82, 89, 105, 106, 109–12, 115, 175–76, 180
    Hanging Gardens of 75–76, 165, 216

Bach, J. C., composer 216

Bactria 42, 43, 47, 95, 159, 185, 202, 205

Bagoas (various of that name) 60, 63

Bahman, son of Esfandiyar 186, 206

Bahram, legendary Persian hero 215, 218

Banks, John, playwright 219

Bardaisan of Edessa 186

Bardiya (Smerdis, Mardos) 18–19, 60

Bel, god of Babylon 105, 106, 111–12

'Belitanas', tomb of 111–12

Bel-šimanni, rebel king of Babylon 110–11

Beyzavi, Nizam al-Tawarikh 179

Bindusara, Indian king 114

Biography, Hellenistic 6–8, 211

Bisutun, inscription of Darius I 18, 22, 42, 60

Boccaccio, Giovanni 65

Boeotia 151

Boges, ruler of Eion 200

Boreas, the North Wind 129, 137, 156, 227

Boyce, Mary 32, 89, 98

Briant, Pierre 4, 15, 25, 187

British Empire 46

Browne, Edward Granville, writer on Persia 160

Browne, Sir Thomas, English author 75

Bukhara 46

Bull's blood as poison 21, 199

Byron, Robert, writer on architecture 46, 173

Byron, Lord 146

Callias, Peace of 174

Cambyses, king of Persia 18, 21, 23, 36, 55, 67, 85, 104, 175, 186, 213

Carneia/Karneia, Spartan festival of Apollo 133

Carpets 74, 168

Çatbaşı köyü 49

Cavalli, Francesco, composer 5, 222

Celaenae 47, 49, 130, 158

Chaco Canyon, New Mexico 177

Chardin, Jean 163
Chares, chamberlain of Alexander the
    Great 193
Charon of Lampsacus, historian 197
Chersiphron, architect 50
Chess 34
Choaspes, River 31, 57, 70
Choerilus of Samos, epic poet 158
Chosroes II (*Siroe*) 74
Chosrow Anushirvan 34
Chronicles, Book of 36
Cibber, Colley 5, 9, 139, 155, 182, 220
Cicero, M. Tullius 1, 2, 7, 142
Cilicia, Cilicians 50, 67, 74
Cimon, Athenian general 196, 199, 200–02
Cities, absence of in Persia 43
Clearchus, Greek philosopher 2, 83
Cleitarchus, historian 230
Coinage 45
Concubines 186–88
Contest of the Tamarisk and the Palm 82
Couperus, Louis, Dutch novelist 3, 9, 82,
    85, 113, 117, 159, 181, 187, 189,
    205–06, 208
Crawford, F. Marion, novelist 9, 103, 163
Crébillon, Jolyot de, playwright 220–21
Croesus, king of Lydia 35–36, 46, 50, 53,
    100, 121, 127, 158
Cruelty 84–87, 155, 211, 213
Ctesias, doctor and historian 3, 9, 11,
    20–21, 23, 39, 51, 52, 65, 95, 97,
    110–11, 148, 183, 188, 189, 202, 205
Curtius Rufus, Q., Roman historian 179,
    221
Curzon, George Nathaniel 164, 173,
    177–78
Cyrus the Great 21, 25, 30–31, 32, 35, 39,
    46, 48, 50, 53, 57, 62, 64, 67, 83, 90,
    91, 97, 98, 100, 102, 104–05, 115, 155,
    185, 222, 223–24
Cyrus the Younger 28–29, 45, 76–77, 84,
    85, 121, 183, 189

Daevas, false gods 91, 92, 106–08
Daeva-inscription 88, 106, 176, 214
Dara, legendary equivalent of Darius III
    207, 225
Darab, marries Homay 31, 207, 224–25
Dardanelles, *see* Hellespont
Darius I 3, 10, 18–23, 26, 49, 50, 60, 65,
    67, 95, 97–98, 103–04, 109–10, 111,
    112–13, 115, 123, 124 (ghost), 132,
    142, 161, 165, 168, 169, 170–71, 185,
    188, 190, 212

Darius II 187
Darius III 2, 15, 24, 42, 63, 115, 157, 189,
    207, 214
Darius, son of Xerxes 182, 184, 204–05,
    220
Dascyleion 44, 47, 49, 81, 118, 196
Datis, Persian general 146–47
Deinon of Colophon, historian 52, 114
Della Valle, Pietro, Italian traveller 163,
    222
Delphi 126, 140, 142, 153
Demaratus, exiled king of Sparta 23–24,
    67, 117–18, 124, 130, 134, 136, 144,
    199, 213
Democedes, doctor 62, 64, 73–74
Democritus, Greek philosopher 51, 54
Didyma 141–42
Dio Chrysostom, Greek orator 11, 52, 155
Diodorus Siculus, Greek historian 161–62,
    175, 177, 190, 196, 198–99, 201,
    202–03, 208, 221
Diogenes Laertius, Greek writer on
    philosophy 51, 100, 197
Doctors 62, 63–66
Dream divination 115–16
Dugh, a yoghurt drink 31, 70

Ecbatana (Hamadan), Persian summer
    capital 31, 35, 69, 70
Ecclesiastes, 'the Preacher' 76, 216–17
Egypt, Egyptians 18, 42, 55, 107, 109–10,
    173, 175, 202
Elam, Elamites 107, 122
Elmalı 49
Empedocles, philosopher 53–54, 90, 157
Ephedra, *see Haoma*
Ephesus 62
    Temple of Artemis 48, 50, 141, 174
Eranvezh 38–39
E-sagila, temple of Bel at Babylon 107,
    112, 180
Esdras, apocryphal book 52, 110, 188
Esfandiyar, legendary Persian hero 14–15,
    25, 57, 77, 88, 95–96, 98, 106, 109,
    178, 200, 206–08, 210, 212
Esther, Queen 13, 56–57, 59, 72–73, 85,
    169, 187, 190, 192–94
    Book of 9, 11, 38, 51–52, 56–57, 70, 73,
    77, 105, 116, 167, 169, 188, 192–94,
    206, 212–14, 216
Eunuchs 27, 61–63, 70, 84, 171, 183
Euphrates, River 121
Eurymedon, River, Battle of 196, 198, 199,
    201–2

'Evil Empire' 15, 218
Excarnation 30, 99–100, 208
Ezekiel, Hebrew prophet 57
Exposure of the dead, *see* Excarnation
Ezra, Hebrew law-giver 52, 58, 110

Farr (*khvarnah*) 32, 89
Fars (Persis) 39, 95
Ferdowsi (Firdausi) 4, 11–15, 17, 88–89,
    93–94, 98, 104–05, 106, 116, 206
    see also Shahnameh
Figs 70, 114
Fire worship, fire temples 30, 32, 89, 94,
    100, 102, 104, 178, 208
Fitzgerald, Edward 11, 210
Fortification tablets from Persepolis 44,
    50, 70, 107, 165, 172, 189
Foucault, Michel 85–86

Gadatas, Cyrus' chamberlain 62, 83
Gadatas, official at Sardis 67, 80–81
Gallipoli 135
Gardens 6, 29, 67, 70, 74–82, 114, 166, 215
Gathas, hymns of Zoroaster 89, 92, 99,
    107
Gaumata/Gomata the Magus 15, 18–19,
    21–23, 98, 104
Gift-giving 73–74, 130–32
Giraffes 40–41
Gobryas 20, 23, 113
Gods, Greek 125–26, 136–37, 140, 149
Golden plane tree 70, 82
Gorgo, wife of Leonidas 118
Gosans, Parthian story-tellers 95
Gower, John, English poet 67
Grand Designs 165, 212–13
Grand Vizier (*chiliarch, hazarapatiš*) 71
Green, Peter 140, 144–45, 179–80
Gushtasp, legendary Persian king (=
    Hystaspes); also known as Vishtasp
    12–13, 31, 90–91, 93–94, 95–96, 104,
    106, 110, 179, 206–07

Hafez, Persian poet 79, 215
Haggai, Hebrew prophet 58
Halys, River 121
Hamadani, Mahmud, *Book of Wonders*
    167
Haman, Susian villain 56, 72, 85, 193–94
Handel, George Frederic, composer 5, 9,
    29, 181, 216, 220–22
Haoma, sacred beverage 40, 91, 101
Harpagus, Persian general 223–24
Hasanlu 175

Hecataeus of Miletus, geographer 54
Hecatomnus, ruler of Caria 67
Hellespont 2, 100, 121, 125, 126, 149, 153
    Xerxes' bridge 114, 128–30, 148, 212
Heraclitus of Ephesus, Greek philosopher
    54, 90
Herbert, Thomas 65, 163–64, 179, 219
Hermotimus the eunuch 62
Herodotus 2, 5, 6, 8, 9, 10, 19, 23–24, 26,
    32, 38, 41, 42, 45, 51, 52, 54–55, 81,
    84, 87, 99–100, 102, 109, 112, 113–18,
    121–23, 125–27, 129, 130, 133, 135,
    141–43, 150, 151–53, 184, 189, 208,
    210–11, 213, 218, 223, 226–28
Herzfeld, Ernst 98, 100, 165, 172, 178
Himera, Battle of 124, 138
Hippocrates, doctor, author of *Airs
    Waters Places;* refused to work for
    Artaxerxes I 4, 64, 66, 207
Histiaeus, tyrant of Miletus 73
Holofernes, 'Assyrian general' 59
Homay, daughter of Bahman 186, 207, 224
Homayounpour, Gohar, psychoanalyst 10
    (quotation), 127, 181
Homer 215
Horse sacrifice 91, 99
Housman, A. E. 109
Human sacrifice 132, 145
Hunting 81
Hyacinthia, Spartan festival 151
Hybris 4, 10, 213
Hydarnes, commander of Immortals 123
Hyde, Thomas, historian of Persian
    religion 219
Hyperides, Greek orator 86
Hystaspes, father of Darius 22–23, 95–96,
    98
Hystaspes, son of Xerxes 95–96, 182,
    202–03, 205

Immortals 61, 82, 121, 123–24, 135
Incest 185–86, 211
India 91
Intaphernes, an accidental voyeur 190
Ion of Chios, tragedian and memoirist 55
Ionian Revolt 105, 118
Iram of the Columns 162–63
Irdabama, mother of Darius I 189
Isaiah, Hebrew Prophet 55, 57, 58, 89–90,
    92
Isfahan 46
Iskandar, Persian name for Alexander the
    Great 12, 31, 212, 225
Isocrates, Greek orator 52, 72

Isthmus of Corinth 124, 133, 144–45, 148, 151, 153

Jamshid, Persian culture-hero, in *Avesta* called Yima 32, 39, 96, 106, 179, 214–15
Jaxartes, River 36
Jerusalem 57–58, 67, 105
Jews 40, 47, 55–59, 89
Josephus, Jewish historian 57, 58, 105, 192
Judaea, Judah 50, 57, 67, 110
Judith, Hebrew heroine 59–60, 187, 192–93
Justin, Roman historian 19, 23–24, 202–03, 221

Kafka, Franz 86
Kai Kavus, legendary Persian king 4, 215
Kai Khosrow, legendary Persian king 12–13, 17, 89
Khayyam, Omar 11, 210, 214
Khoday-nameh (Book of Lords), lost medieval Persian chronicle 13
Kierkegaard, Søren 84
King's dinner 33–34, 70, 82–84
'King's Eye' 63
Korai 142, 174
Kotys, Thracian king 81

Lampon of Aegina 154
Lampsacus 198
Lane Fox, Robin 176–77, 179
Lear, Edward 1
Leonidas, Spartan commander 118, 124, 133–36, 137, 149, 227
Letoön trilingual inscription 55, 236 n. 77
Licymnius of Chios, Greek poet 158–59
Loti, Pierre 164
Lucian 52
Lycia 48, 202
Lydgate, John, fourteenth century poet 3, 109, 133, 140, 150, 249 n. 50
Lydia 49–50, 53, 118–21, 172, 175
Lysander, Spartan general 76–77
Lysias, Athenian orator 3

Maccabees 60
Magi 39, 53, 65–66, 92, 96, 100, 102–05, 117, 125, 130, 16, 198, 223–24
  Murder of 20, 103
  Revolt of 98
Magic 65–66
Magnesia on the Maeander 80, 197–99
Malachi, prophet 52, 58–59, 193
Mandane, daughter of Astyages 223

Mandrocles, architect 49, 50
Mani, Persian prophet 84, 92
Marathon, Battle of 18, 112–14, 155–56
Mardonius, Persian general 21, 23, 113–15, 122, 144, 148, 149–54, 201, 212
Masistes, brother of Xerxes 74, 84, 87, 123, 150, 154, 184–85, 211
Mas'udi, al-, Arab chronicler 162, 206
Mausolus 118, 123, 190
Maximus of Tyre 230
Medes 122
Megabyzus, husband of Amytis 61, 183
Megabyzus, satrap of Babylon 58–59, 111, 123, 155
Megabyzus, confidant of Artabanus son of Artasyras 64, 203
Mehmet the Conqueror 77, 125
Meltemi 136, 228
Mesambria (Bushire) 48
Metagenes, architect 50
Metastasio, Pietro, librettist 220–22
  Artaserse 203, 221
  Temistocle 9, 29, 198–99, 221–22
Meydancikkale 49
Miletus 36, 54, 118
Miltiades, tyrant on the Hellespont 66, 74
Mir Khwand, Persian historian 94, 106, 159, 206, 209
Mithra, god 91, 93
Mithradates, chamberlain of Xerxes 62
Mithridates I and II of Pontus 61
Mithridates, a conspirator against Xerxes 203–05
Mithridates, killer of Cyrus the Younger 85, 204
Moghul Empire 46
Momigliano, Arnaldo 7, 57, 172
Monstrous races 39, 53
Montaigne, Michel de 2
Montesquieu, Baron de 219
Moore, Thomas 160
Mordecai, father of Esther 56, 72, 116, 167, 193–94
Al-Mutawakkil, destroyer of Zoroaster's cypress tree 94
Mycale, Mt 150, 154
Myus 198

Napoleon 140, 248 n. 10
Naqsh-e-Rostam 48, 208
Nasturtiums 27–28
Nebuchadnezzar, the king of Assyria 59–60
Nebuchadnezzar of Babylon 35, 76, 112
Nectanebo II, Egyptian Pharaoh 64

Nehemiah, restorer of the walls of Jerusalem 52, 58–59
Nepos, Cornelius 8
Nineveh 76
Now Ruz, New Year Festival 32, 121, 177, 178–80, 186

Oedipus complex, reversed in Persia 10, 216
Olympia 153
Olympias 9
Olympic Games 226, 257 n. 5
Onomacritus, author of oracles 51, 114
Opera 6, 219–22
Oral tradition 11, 156
Osthanes, magus 55
Otanes, Persian noble, father of Amestris 20, 23
Ottoman Empire 46, 56, 62, 65, 73, 77, 82, 84, 171, 186–87, 188, 191–92, 219
Oxus, River 15, 46
    Treasure 41, 71, 74, 173

Pacini, Giovanni 221–22
Panyassis of Halicarnassus, poet 53
Paradise (*paridaida, paradeisos*) 75, 79
Parthian Empire 15, 100
Parysatis, mother of Artaxerxes II 62, 84, 85, 186, 189
Pasargadae 30, 32, 48, 78, 167–68, 176, 178
Pausanias, regent of Sparta 67, 124, 153–54, 196, 200
Pausanias, travel writer 142
Pax Persica 55, 107
Payava tomb 48
Penelope 142
Persepolis 1, 3, 10, 14, 17–18, 24, 30, 33, 44, 46–47, 50, 70, 90, 94, 95–96, 159, 160–80, 209, 212, 215 230–31
    Apadana 36, 165–66, 168, 173, 175
    Excavation of 165
    Gardens 78
    Gateway of All Lands 71, 167
    Hall of a Hundred Columns 169–70
    'Harem' 166, 171, 181–82, 190–92
    Imaginary temple of Ahura Mazda 163
    Tribute-bearers relief 40
    Palace of Darius (*tachara*) 166, 170–71, 177
    Palace of Xerxes (*hadish*) 166, 170, 171, 177
    'Qa'aba of Zoroaster' 32
    Stairway 167

Treasury 166, 168–69, 170, 172
Tripylon 171, 173
Persian Army 52, 121–24
Persian Empire 1, 15, 46–50, 60
    Court 36, 56, 60–63, 192–94
    economy 43–46
    extent of 35–43, 176, 193
Persian fleet 123–24, 133, 145–48, 201
Persian literature 52
Persian Royal Road 42–43, 121
'Persian version' 51
Phanias of Lesbos, historian 145
Pharnabazus, satrap 49, 187
Phaselis 201
Pherendates, nephew of Xerxes 201
Philo, Jewish philosopher 186
Phocis 139
Phratagyne, niece and wife of Darius 23, 186
Phrynichus, Greek tragedian 157
Phyllada tou Megalexandrou 217
Pindar, Greek poet 126, 138
Pirates 200
Pistachios 31, 234 n. 64
plane tree 81
Plataea, Battle of 2, 124, 150, 152–54, 156, 158, 176
    Oath of 152–53
Plato, Greek philosopher
    Alcibiades 26, 27, 62, 188–89
    Laws 3, 26, 27
Pliny the Elder, encyclopaedic author 50, 66
Plutarch, Greek philosopher, historian and essayist
    'Advice to bride and groom' 188
    'On the control of anger' 4–5
    On brotherly love 24–25
    Sayings of Kings and Commanders 8, 95
    Life of Alcibiades 47
    Life of Alexander 7, 180, 215
    Life of Artaxerxes 8, 29, 30, 62, 72, 85, 204, 210
    Life of Cimon 201–02
    Life of Themistocles 71–72, 99, 145, 147, 188, 191, 197
Polyaenus, Greek historian 33, 70, 82, 132, 147
Polybius 247 n. 91
    On Philopoemen 7
Polycrates, tyrant of Samos 47, 50, 52
Polygamy 185, 193
Probouloi, Greek delegates 124–25

Prostration or *proskynesis* 71–72
Ps-Clement 186
Pulvar, River 18, 30, 78
Pythagoras, philosopher 52
Pythius of Lydia 130–32, 213

Qazvini 14
Queen mothers 9

Ralegh, Sir Walter 3, 38, 45, 85, 117,
    127–28, 144, 249 n. 31
Rameau, Jean-Philippe, composer 222
Ramsay, Andrew Michael, novelist 219–20
Ratahshah, daughter of Xerxes 183
Razm o bazm, 'fighting and feasting' 34
Religion 10, 27, 53, 88–108, 141, 214
    Toleration 42, 105–06, 141
Rhoecus 50
Rhoesaces, Persian diplomat or double
    agent 200
Rilke, Rainer Maria 175, 217
Rivers, drunk dry 109, 125, 133
Rodogune, daughter of Xerxes 183
Root, Margaret Cool 172–73, 178–79
Rostam, legendary Persian hero 17, 207
Rumi, Persian poet 79
Ruth, Book of 193

Sa'adi, Persian poet 79
Salamis, Battle of 2, 123, 124, 126, 139,
    140, 142–48, 155–56
    Date of 146, 226–28
Samos 49, 52, 67, 74, 154
    Temple of Hera 50, 174
Sanchuniathon, Phoenician author 55
Sancisi-Weerdenburg, Heleen 107, 210–11
Sardanapalus, semi-legendary Assyrian
    king 11, 125, 230 n. 4
Sardis, capital of satrapy of Lydia 42, 44,
    46, 47, 62, 67, 81, 112, 118–21, 125,
    130, 141, 150, 154, 168, 175, 184, 190,
    199, 212
Sargon of Akkad 76, 223
Sasanian Empire 15, 42, 43, 84
Sataspes, explorer 38, 190
Satrap, satrapy 36, 38, 67, 123, 199
    Palaces 47, 71
Scarlatti, Alessandro, composer 220
Scylax, explorer 38–39, 46, 53
Scythes, tyrant of Zancle 67
Scythia, Scythians 18, 36, 40, 115, 158,
    168, 212
Seleucid Empire 14
Seleucus 190

Sennacherib, Assyrian king 60, 76, 112
Sestos 155, 196, 200
Seven, Council of 61
    Conspirators 20, 61, 113, 203, 206, 233
    n. 15
    Noble families 61
Shahbazi, A. Shapur 165, 169
Shahnameh 10, 15, 25, 95, 109–10,
    206–08, 214
Sheshbazzar, prince of Judah 57
Simonides, Greek poet 51, 136, 156–58
Simurgh 14, 207, 214
Slavery 61, 130
Smerdis 18–19, 61, *see also* Gaumata,
    Bardiya
Smilax, a nymph not to tangle with 80
Solomon 18, 179
Sparta (ns) 72, 124, 144, 149, 151, 188,
    195–97
Sphendadates 15, 21, 98
Spitama Zarathustra 89, 90, 93, 97–98
Stone lore 66
Strabo, Greek geographer 26–27, 44, 70,
    79, 82, 100, 112, 148
Stronach, David 32
Strymon, River 118, 132, 200
Substitute king ritual 78, 116
Susa, Persian winter capital 19, 24, 27, 42,
    44, 47, 57, 69, 70, 78, 82, 89, 98, 105,
    112–18, 121, 123, 141, 148, 150, 159,
    168, 175, 184, 190, 192, 197, 230–31

Tabari, Persian historian writing in Arabic
    13, 32, 74–75, 94, 159, 192
Tanyoxarces 21
Taoce 48
Taq-e-Bostan 81
Tarsusi, Abu Taher 212
Taşkule 49
Tehran Museum 168
Tempe, Vale of 125, 133
Temple, Sir William 75
Ten Thousand, the 45
Thales 54
Al-Tha'libi, *History of the Kings of Persia*
    14
Thapsacus, site of 121
Thebes 124
Themistocles, Athenian politician 67, 74,
    124, 126, 137, 140–41, 142–45, 148,
    190, 196–99, 200–01, 221–22
Themistocles, Letters of 197, 198
Theodorus, architect 50
Theomestor of Samos 154

Thermae 132, 136, 226
Thermopylae, Battle 122, 133–38, 140, 156
 date of 226–28
Thessaly 114, 124–25, 133, 140, 149
Thrace 118, 121
Thucydides 148
Tigris, River 121
Timotheus, lyric poet 158
Tissaphernes, satrap 45, 49, 81
Tithraustes, illegitimate son of Xerxes 201
Torture 84–87
Treasury Relief 71, 168, 209
Treasury tablets from Persepolis 48,
 165–66, 172, 175
Trees 5–6, 70, 75, 78, 81–82, 93–94, 95, 215
Tribute 41
Tritantaichmes, nephew of Darius 122
Trojan War 51, 53, 170
Troy, Xerxes at 51, 107, 125, 141
Turgenev, Ivan 10
'Turpentine-wood' 31

Udjahorresnet, Egyptian law giver 58, 64

Vamiq o 'Adhra 52, 85
Vashti, Ahasuerus' queen 56
Vedas 91
Vidal, Gore 8–9, 10, 15, 21, 22–23, 24,
 166–67, 174–75, 181–82, 215
Videvdad (Vendidad), Law against the
 Demons, Avestan text 38–39, 53
Vinci, Leonardo, composer 221
Vis o Ramin 186
Vishtaspa, see Gushtasp
Vivaldi, Antonio, composer 220
Voltaire, philosopher 219

Whittling 10, 21, 212, 216
Wiesehöfer, Josef 47
Windsor Castle, 'resembles Persepolis'
 164, 167
Writing 36–38
Women 30, 185–92

Xanthos, Lycia (city) 48
 Bilingual inscription 48, 55
Xanthus of Lydia (historian) 53–54, 55
Xenophanes of Colophon, philosopher
 53, 157

Xenophon 81
 Agesilaus 6
 Anabasis (Expedition of Cyrus) 6,
  28–29, 45, 76–77, 129
 Cyropaideia (Education of Cyrus) 25,
  26–28, 61, 64, 67, 72, 73, 83, 115, 161,
  178, 202, 219–20, 230
 History of Greece 4, 47, 72
 Memoirs of Socrates 6
 Oeconomicus 77 (quotation)
Xerxes, passim; also
 Accession 23–26
 Anger 4, 115
 Arrogance 3, 113, 115
 Brothers 122–23, 135, 206
 Buildings at Persepolis 50
 Character 2–5, 9–10, 210–16
 Death 111, 195, 202–09
 Education 26–28
 Ennui 9, 10, 34, 216
 Invasion of Greece 42, 109–59
 Laughter 113, 130, 134, 149, 213–14
 Love life 181–94
 Melancholy 126–28, 215
 Medieval Persian image, see Esfandiyar
 Reviews troops 126
 Sister 190
 Sons 182
 Tomb 208

Yahweh, the first gardener 75, 105
Yashts 90–91, 93, 96, 242 n. 15
Yasna 91, 92
Yima, Avestan name for Jamshid, q.v. 39

Zagros, mountains 17
Zahhak, demon king 104–05
Zariadres 52
Zechariah, prophet 57–58
Zendan-e-Suleiman 32
Zerubbabel, governor of Judaea 57–58,
 67, 110, 188
Zopyrus, governor of Babylon 111
Zoroaster 9, 13, 22, 38, 53, 66, 88, 89–95,
 96–98, 101, 102, 106–08, 219–20
 Cypress tree of 93–94, 96, 177
 Qa'aba of 32
Zoroastrianism 87, 89–95, 98–104, 106–08,
 132, 141, 170, 219, 222, 241 n. 1–2